IMAGES IN LAW

Images in Law

Edited by

ANNE WAGNER
Université du Littoral Côte d'Opale, France

and

WILLIAM PENCAK
Penn State University, USA

Routledge
Taylor & Francis Group
LONDON AND NEW YORK

First published 2006 by Ashgate Publishing

2 Park Square, Milton Park, Abingdon, Oxon OX14 4RN
711 Third Avenue, New York, NY 10017, USA

Routledge is an imprint of the Taylor & Francis Group, an informa business

First issued in paperback 2016

British Library Cataloguing in Publication Data
Images in law
1.Semiotics (Law) 2.Law - Language
I.Wagner, Anne II.Pencak, William
340.1'4

Library of Congress Cataloging-in-Publication Data
Images in law / edited by Anne Wagner and William Pencak.
p. cm.
Includes bibliographical references and index.
ISBN 0-7546-4720-X
1.Culture and law. I. Wagner, Anne II. Pencak, William

K487.C8I43 2006
340'.115--dc22

2006008608

ISBN 978-0-7546-4720-1 (hbk)
ISBN 978-1-138-26449-6 (pbk)

Contents

Biographical Notes

Sophie Cacciaguidi-Fahy is a Lecturer in Law (Legal French) with a research specialisation in Law, Language and Culture, Legal Discourse and Semiotics of Law. She has published extensively on the area of discourse and contemporary issues, Irish law and intercultural communication. Her current research focuses on the use of the language of diversity in human rights instruments.

Deborah Cao is a Senior Lecturer affiliated with the School of Languages and Linguistics and the Socio-Legal Research Centre of the Law School, Griffith University, Australia. She was educated in China and Australia in interpreting/translation, linguistics, and law. She has published in the areas of legal translation and philosophical and linguistic analysis of Chinese law and legal culture. Her books include *Chinese Law: A Language Perspective* (Ashgate, 2004) and *Translating Law* (forthcoming).

Neal Feigenson is Professor of Law at Quinnipiac University School of Law, where he teaches Torts, Evidence, Visual Persuasion in the Law, and Civil Procedure. Professor Feigenson's research interests include applications of social and cognitive psychology to legal decision making and the role of visual communication and rhetoric in law. He is the author of *Legal Blame: How Jurors Think and Talk about Accidents* (American Psychological Association Books, 2000).

Philip Gaines is Associate Professor of English and Director of University Studies at Montana State University, USA. His PhD is from the University of Washington. Professor Gaines's primary research interests lie in the area of legal language, specifically the discourse of attorneys. His publications include work on the O.J. Simpson and Menendez brothers trials as well as the US Senate hearings on the confirmation of Supreme Court Justice Clarence Thomas.

Shaeda Isani is full Professor at l'Université Stendhal, Grenoble 3 (France) where she teaches English for Specific Purposes (ESP) to graduate students in law and economy in the Department of Applied Linguistics. Her research work concerns language(s) and culture(s) of specialisation with a particular interest in law and the socio-professional areas of intercultural communication.

Nicola Langton LLB MA has designed and delivered client-specific courses in France and Hong Kong for the insurance, banking, legal and corporate sectors, as well as undergraduate/postgraduate Legal English courses at City University of Hong Kong (1994-2004). Her current post is to develop e-learning materials and strategies for the Law School, Cardiff University. Her research and various publications focus on acquisition and development of academic/professional legal competencies and general life-long independent learning skills.

Ronnie Lippens is Professor of Criminology at Keele University (UK). His research interests include, amongst others, images and imagery of law, peace and justice.

Annabelle Mooney is a Research Associate at the Centre for Language and Communication Research at Roehampton University. She has authored a number of papers and *The Rhetoric of Religious 'Cults': terms of use and abuse* (Palgrave, 2005).

William Pencak is Professor of History at Penn State University. He received his PhD degree from Columbia University in New York City in 1978. Although his major field is early United States history, he has written extensively on semiotics and served as President of the Semiotic Society of America in 2000-2001. His principal works in semiotics are the edited special issues on History and Semiotics (*Semiotica*, vol. 83, 3/4, 1991) and *The American Journal of Semiotics* (vol. 12, 1995 [98]), *History, Signing In: Studies in History and Semiotics* (Peter Lang, 1993), *The Conflict of Law and Justice in the Icelandic Sagas* (Rodopi, 1995), and *The Wit and Wisdom of Roberta Kevelson* (Peter Lang, 2001).

Paul Robertshaw has retired since producing his chapter after more than a quarter of a century at Cardiff University's School of Law. For the past 15 years his research was on empirical issues in a wide range of criminal justice topics. His active interest in language pragmatics in such contexts was fostered by Bernard Jackson at Liverpool and Katharina Sobota at Mainz, and led to a number of articles in journals such as the *International Journal for the Semiotics of Law*, and *Rhetorik*, as well as the book *Summary Justice – judges address juries*.

Phillip C. H. Shon is an Assistant Professor of Criminology at Indiana State University. He holds a bachelor's degree in philosophy, a master's degree in linguistics, and a PhD in criminal justice. His research examines the sociolinguistic organisation of police-citizen encounters. His works have appeared in journals such as *International Journal for the Semiotics of Law, International Journal of Law and Psychiatry, Critical Criminology, Discourse & Society, and Journal for the Psychoanalysis of Culture and Society.*

Christina Spiesel is a visual artist working in materials ranging from oil paint to digital photography and video; she is the author of *Law in the Age of Images: The Challenge of Visual Literacy* (with Neal Feigenson and Richard Sherwin) and numerous articles on visual semiotics and art history. She is a Senior Research Scholar at Yale Law School and an Adjunct Professor of Law teaching 'Visual Persuasion in the Law' at Quinnipiac University School of Law and New York Law School.

Anne Wagner is a Senior Lecturer in LSP affiliated with the Université du Littoral Côte d'Opale, France. She is the deputy Editor and the French Book Review Editor of the *International Journal for the Semiotics of Law* (Springer). Her main research interests include legal interpretation and discourse, law and culture and semiotics of law. She is the author of *La Langue de la Common Law* (Paris: L'Harmattan, 2002) as well as three books entitled *Contemporary Issues in the Semiotics of Law: Cultural and Symbolic Analyses in a Global Context* (Oxford and Portland Oregon: Hart, 2005), *Legal Language and the Search for Clarity: Practice and Tools* (Bern: Peter Lang, 2006) and *Interpretation, Law and the Construction of Meaning* (Dordrecht: Springer, forthcoming 2006).

Wouter Werner is professor of Public International Law at the Vrije Universiteit, Amsterdam. His main fields of interest are the theory of international law, international constitutionalism and the legal regime regulating the use of force. He is senior editor of the articles section of the *Leiden Journal of International Law*, with a special focus on international legal theory, and member of the Dutch Advisory Committee on Issues of Public International Law. Recent publications include: *Dealing with the Undesired: Responsibility, Risk and Precaution* (Netherlands Yearbook of International Law, 2005), 'The Never-Ending Closure: Constitutionalism and International Law' (in: N. Tsagourias (ed), *Transnational Constitutionalism: International and European Models*, Cambridge University Press, 2006) and Wagner A., Werner W.G, Cap D. (eds.), *Interpretation, Law and the Construction of Meaning* (Dordrecht: Springer, forthcoming 2006).

Robert A. Yelle is Postdoctoral Fellow in the Illinois Program for Research in the Humanities and Visiting Assistant Professor at the University of Illinois at Urbana-Champaign. He holds a JD from the University of California at Berkeley and a PhD in the History of Religions from the University of Chicago. He is the author of *Explaining Mantras* (Routledge, 2003) and a number of articles in scholarly journals, including most recently 'Bentham's Fictions: Canon and Idolatry in the Genealogy of Law', *Yale Journal of Law & the Humanities* 17 (2005): 151-79.

Introduction

William Pencak and Anne Wagner

Images in Law is part of an international interdisciplinary research project led by the *International Roundtable for the Semiotics of Law* whose main objective is to show the deep and close links between law, semiotics, visuality and visual persuasion.[1] It is fitting that in 2006 the *3rd International Roundtable for the Semiotics of Law* publishes a collection of essays on *Images in Law*.

Images in Law involves communicating with a number of people specialised in various research fields. This communication can lead to different meanings, various ways of seeing the world in which we are living. There is no legal constancy that requires a strict framework of seeing, imaging or imagining the world. As legal rules are never absolute and need to adapt to societal developments, so must people adapt to these changes. Viewing the images of law depends on how you tackle the whole issue and so deciphering the law allows for adaptations.

As our culture is increasingly based on signs – written, imaginative or imaginary – we need to write down some important insights in order to formulate and analyze an ongoing and increasing activity that is exacerbated by instability. Contrary to some ideas, legal language is not a language of fools, but an exceedingly well- and wisely organised product which evolves according to circumstances of time and space, and historical, political, socio-cultural and purely legal event.

Analyzing images in law 'can be seen from the point of view of a garden of forking paths. When we read any handbook on legal theory, we see that every theory leads to another, with some paths diverting in search of new destinies, in an endless discussion about the nature of the law'.[2] To put it another way:

> The nature or truth of an event is determined in part by the discourse into which it is put, and no event contains its own prescription for the correct discourse by which to know and communicate it. [...] So, the critical relationship is between the different discursive constructions of that event.[3]

The title *Images of Law* was used by Zenon Bankowski and Geoff Mungham in their 1976 critique of legal education and systems in modern capitalist society. They stressed that our image of law as objective and doing justice masks class and other

1 http://islandia.law.yale.edu/lawmediaproject/

2 Anne Wagner, Tracey Summerfield and F. Samir Benavides Vanegas (eds), *Contemporary Issues on the Semiotics of Law*, (Oxford: Hart Publishing, Oñati International Series in Law & Society, vol.12: 2005): 2.

3 John Fiske, *Admissible Postmodernity: Some Remarks on Rodney King, O.J. Simpson, and Contemporary Culture*, 30 *U.S.F.L. Rev*. 917, 918 (1996).

forms of bias. They insist that law's main function is legitimation and mystification of injustice through images conveyed by those who control legal institutions and their presentation to both legal professionals and the general public. By understanding how this works, Bankowski and Mungham argue, the poor and oppressed can begin to think about ways to overcome injustice both through exploiting inconsistencies in the legal system and through radical political action.[4]

A less politically controversial yet equally insightful approach to images in law appears in the works of Bernard S. Jackson – both his writings on modern law and legal semiotics and his historical work on ancient Judaic law.[5] Jackson argues that legal language and behavior – as in a courtroom – is addressed to different audiences for diverse purposes. Thus, a judge's charge may intimidate a jury but spur legal scholars to write articles questioning his wisdom, or begin a legislative process to confirm or cancel the opinion. The cycle of interpretation, however imperceptible to the semiotically untrained eye, is infinite. However, the images accompanying the 'narratives' put forth by various 'actors' do as much to shape the way communities interpret them as do the language of the law and the narratives themselves. For instance, the judge assumes by his tone and choice of words one stance of many he could have used to perform the same action.

Jackson's approach to images in law is close to that of the late Roberta Kevelson, founder of the Roundtable for Legal Semiotics which Jackson attended. Ten years ago, in 1996 in the Critic of Institutions series which she edited for Peter Lang Publishing, Kevelson edited a collection entitled *Spaces and Significations*[6] dealing with the images created by the 'spaces' of the law. Contributing to that collection was John Brigham, the first president of the International Roundtable which has evolved from the Round Table. In their 1996 essays, Kevelson and Brigham brought forth two of the themes of legal semiotics that the present volume now continues.

In her essay 'Law at the Border',[7] Kevelson noted that laws and legal systems which present themselves to the public as authoritative and coherent, as instantiations of 'truth, justice, and the [fill in any nationality] way' are not only riddled with holes, but that the holes are the essence of the system. These 'spaces', far from being empty or meaningless gaps which need to be filled in or explained away, are in fact the fertile points of contact where different notions of law, where legal inconsistencies and

4 Zenon Bankowski and Geoff Mungham, *Images of Law* (London: Routledge and Kegan Paul, 1976).

5 See the following works by Jackson: *Studies in the Semiotics of Biblical Law* (Sheffield: Sheffield Academic Press, 2000); *Making Sense in Law: Linguistic, Psychological and Semiotic Perspectives* (Liverpool: Deborah Charles, 1995); *Law, Fact, and Narrative Coherence* (Merseyside: Deborah Charles, 1988); *Semiotics and Legal Theory* (London: Routledge and Kegan Paul, 1985).

6 Roberta Kevelson (ed.), *Spaces and Significations* (New York: Peter Lang, 1996). Kevelson's first and major work of legal semiotics is *Law as a System of Signs* (New York: Plenum, 1988).

7 Roberta Kevelson, 'Law at the Border', in Roberta Kevelson (ed.), *Spaces and Significations* (New York: Peter Lang, 1996): 167-180.

paradoxes, meet in what she metaphorically termed 'border wars' that are the sources of new law, creativity, and human freedom. Unlike Bankowski and Mungham, who emphasised law as a confining force in modern society, Kevelson's world was filled with infinite opportunities for human agency. Mariana Net's essay in that collection, 'Representations of the Political Prison: Actual Spaces, Virtual Forms',[8] showed how Ceceascu's Romania, despite its totalitarian efforts, still afforded spaces – some as small as the palms of hands, where pieces of papers were smuggled to foreigners who were only permitted to view the rosy side of the regime – in which dissent could exist. While seemingly ineffective at the time, such dissent was the beginning of the end for a repressive regime.

Brigham's essay, 'Signs in the Attic: Courts in Material Life',[9] demonstrated how the architecture, appearances, and furnishings of courtrooms themselves – which are not mentioned in legal documents – create attitudes towards the law and those involved with it – defendants, prosecutors, witnesses, juries, police, and judges – that shape the application of law and public attitudes toward it. One of the paradoxes of modern democracy is that in societies which claim to be egalitarian and free, the courtroom is a rigid hierarchy in which speech is limited and ritualised. In keeping with Kevelson's own proclivity for paradox and refusing to limit enquiry herself, her own contrary essay stands besides Brigham's, leaving us to think for ourselves.

The chapters in Part 1 of *Images in Law* begin a fourth decade of inquiry into how the images of what people believe the law to be – or ought to be – convey meaning beneath and beyond the text. On the macro level these articles a) look at how many people – including the world's most powerful rulers and nations – view the world and see an image of legally abiding vs. lawless nations, assumptions blithely asserted rather than proven; b) examine how the shapes and configurations of words facilitate or deny possibilities for creative legal interpretation; c) explore how the appearance of figures in the legal systems shape the behavior of those systems; d) show how the presentation of courts on television affects and responds to public perception of the law; and e) consider how law attempts to deal with the gamut of behavior arising from racial prejudice, imaging people as 'other' than the norm.

Ronnie Lippens and *Wouter Werner* follow Kevelson by showing how nations that claim to stand for freedom are in fact foreclosing it by insisting that they and their institutions are the only way freedom can be achieved. Hence the United States in 2001, without any sense of irony, can impose a 'Patriot Act' that curtails concrete, demonstrable freedom in the name of an amorphous defense of freedom world-wide. *Lippens* notes that modern neo-liberal First World states such as Britain and the United States are simply assumed by their defenders to be the apex of human history and the defenders of moral and international law, while those states and

---

8 Mariana Net, 'Representations of the Political Prison: Actual Spaces, Virtual Forms', in Roberta Kevelson (ed.), *Spaces and Significations* (New York: Peter Lang, 1996): 135-150.

9 John Brigham, 'Signs in the Attic: Courts in Material Life', in Roberta Kevelson (ed.), *Spaces and Significations* (New York: Peter Lang, 1996): 151-164.

organisations which oppose the 'New World Order' are considered unnatural and metaphorically diseased, spaces where law does not exist and needs to be imposed – UN resolutions and World Court rulings to the contrary. Categories of lawful and 'outlaw' nations are constructed in accordance with the desires of nations claiming to stand for law without serious inquiry into who actually does what. (Here too, image rules, as civilian deaths from anti-terrorist measures are simply kept hidden by the perpetrators.) *Werner* continues this theme, and notes how First World nations have metaphorically taken over the entire globe by defining 'normalcy' as maintenance of their hegemony. Opposition to that hegemony anywhere on earth supposedly requires 'self-defense' even where First World nations are imposing 'order' thousands of miles from their borders. Security thus becomes impossible, as it denies historical change and becomes an indefinite yet potentially infinite and hence impossible quest.

Deborah Cao, on the contrary, shows how modern China, having undergone transitions from Empire to Republic to warring states to dictatorship to communism to neo-capitalism in the twentieth century, has adapted its legal language to suit these political changes. Chinese words are pictures facilitating the legal transitions, making legal actors aware of both continuity in the written characters that convey the thoughts of a civilisation thousands of years old while creating the opportunity for additions and variations; the very characters themselves convey an awareness that law and language, if not creatively reinterpreted over time, would mark a return to the insularity modern China has been trying to overcome.

As presented by *Shaeda Isani*, the robes and wigs worn by members of the English legal system – barristers, judges, and members of the House of Lords – are similar to the Chinese language Cao discusses. They are signs of both continuity and change in legal interpretation and social development. While the general public may regard these costumes as affectations or meaningless relics of an earlier age, actors in the judicial system themselves are very aware of the quality and length of wigs worn and color and quality of gowns. Modern prices for particular legal outfits and aesthetic standards thus (at the very least) subtly affect the outcome of cases and signal the relative prestige of legal actors. In the 1996 collection, Norma Procopiow, in 'Why Can't He: the Kente Case and Legal Discourse', discussed the legal ramifications of an African-American attorney who appeared in court wearing a dashiki. One is also reminded of the late United States Chief Justice William Rehnquist's insistence on wearing gold stripes on his robe to distinguish himself from the associate justices, and the ridicule it provoked (at least) in the liberal press.

As Bankowski and Mungham note, the real world of law 'takes place within the context of an epistemology that divorces man from the world'.[10] *Annabelle Mooney* considers how courts appear as spaces within a very different space – television – where popular attitudes toward law are shaped by the various shows in which trials are simulated. She singles out *Ally McBeal* – a show in which a pleasant but

10 Bankowski and Mungham, *Images of Law* (London: Routledge and Kegan Paul, 1976): 110.

odd young lady implausibly triumphs over more experienced and cunning counsels – which not only deflates the public image of courts as dignified sanctuaries of impartial justice but presents imaginative and unconventional plot twists where legal outcomes also satisfy our sense of moral legitimacy. Paradoxically, impossible courtroom scenarios become a subtle way of legitimating a legal system where such behavior would instantly result in contempt of court rulings.

In addition to a proliferation of laws, a proliferation of technology has characterised law in the recent world, leading to visual communication and visual persuasion as increasingly important elements of legal argument. Computers, like DNA evidence, are now routine. *Neal Feigenson* persuasively argues that judges, lawyers, and juries need to think not just about this sort of evidence, but about how the medium that is used can be manipulated to shape their opinion of the validity of that evidence. For instance, is dazzling virtuousity with computer 'language' a way of winning a weak case? He also optimistically notes that, in an increasingly computer literate society, people are in fact becoming semiotically aware of this very fact. (Clever attorneys, however, can build on this awareness and in turn attempt to manipulate that.) As he concludes, 'remediation, hypermediation, and interactivity are crucial attributes of the ways in which the world is represented in the digital age; to understand what truth looks like today, it is necessary to attend to them'.

Christina Spiesel builds on Feigenson's point: a talented lawyer can use photography, visual images, and the computer much like a film director to shape our sympathies or accent certain elements in a scene or case as 'important'. As an example, she points to how the painter Velasquez in *Las Meninas*, through the use of mirrors, exalted the dwarfs in the seventeenth century Spanish royal court while dwarfing the rulers. We can and should become aware, as Marshall McLuhan and his even more perceptive teacher Harold Innis, how these media affect the projected message.[11] The law, of course, can be seen as 'order backed by force', and the lawyer, in Anthony Kronman's interpretation, as the convener/builder of the social stage on which we enact our public lives.

The chapters in Part 2 of the collection examine legal language and how images of law emerge out of the conflict of laws between diverse legal systems and interpretations, which are becoming more frequent in light of an interactive global economy and the movement of peoples across borders. Here too there are 'spaces' that require interpretation and modification.

Nicola Langton examines the way that the legal codes of Hong Kong and China have interacted since the island became part of the larger nation. She shows that legal change in Hong Kong is an excellent way to teach students about the ambiguities of legal language – Hong Kong is able to adapt 'communist' law to one of the world's most flourishing capitalist cities. Langton points out that when conflicting laws apply to a situation, their interaction may lead to a convergence and thus legal creativity.

11 Harold Innis, *The Bias of Communications* (Toronto: University of Toronto Press, 1951).

Philip Gaines explains how conflicting legal discourses are in fact present every time a jury weighs evidence: a judge instructs a jury to consider 'facts' and 'evidence', but exactly what these are is a matter of theory as well as empirical enquiry: the attorneys' manner of presentation, for instance, shapes the way these are perceived even though it is not supposed to be considered. Jurors thus unknowingly become reconcilers of the conflict of ideal and real legal norms every time they render a decision.

Paul Robertshaw concretely explains how this happens: he examines two trials of a single defendant (the first resulting in a hung jury, the second in conviction) where the jury deliberations were taped for research purposes. He demonstrates how the jurors' discussions showed that the prosecution's altered presentation of the narrative of how the crime was committed became more coherent the second time around (in response to the failure to convict the first time), and was almost certainly the reason the verdict changed. Fact and evidence thus cannot be viewed apart from the narrative coherence and presentation that shape and provide them with coherence.

Phillip Shon moves from courtroom to police encounters. Here too, even the simplest interaction with the law as represented by the police requires a complex although almost instantaneous sifting of legal knowledge and cultural norms. For both the police and those who encounter them, a scripted narrative of sorts is either followed or disrupted. Police commands to citizens such as 'hands in the air' must share a mutual interpretive context – which Shon argues people learn in large part from television shows that portray such encounters – as to when, where, and how the hands are to be displayed. If such a shared community of interpretation did not exist, law enforcement would break down.

Moving from the jury room and street encounters to national legal systems, *Sophie Cacciaguidi-Fahy* looks at the problems of Irish law in recent times. Given the nation's conservative Roman Catholic heritage, law configures the Family as mother, father, and children, but as new living arrangements both within Ireland and through immigration from abroad develop, the law is inadequate to deal with the changes and courts must react creatively if not desperately. She urges that the image of the Family be enlarged to conform to the reality.

Dealing with the tremendous efforts which the government and human rights associations have made to eliminate racial discrimination and hate crimes in France, *Anne Wagner* notes that this very proliferation of law and great attention to the problem are themselves signs that the problem persists. Increasing attempts to eliminate racism lead as well to equally creative efforts by racists to get around the law, obliquely presenting visual and verbal images of foreigners through insinuation. As Philomena Essed and Teun Van Dijk have persuasively shown, while outright racist language is unacceptable to most educated Europeans and Americans, it is possible to criticise people's clothing, dialects, hygiene, and consumption patterns with decidedly racist undertones.[12]

Finally, *Robert Yelle* imaginatively considers why the use of 'images' in legal discourse and behavior is in fact a problem – or, to put it technically, he offers a meta-semiotic perspective on the entire collection. He attributes the power of images (as juxtaposed to 'text', 'reality' or 'the law' in this case) to patterns in western civilisation dating back to ancient times where images are perceived to be 'false' idols derailing access to God or the truth. This tension between the seductive power of images (from Baal to 'false' advertising) and the idealistic desire to achieve unadulterated certainty (or find the 'true God') is a cultural construction, not an inevitable way of looking at the world, as millennia of polytheism preceding its appearance demonstrates. Understanding this problem may help us to get over it, and realise that the image/reality problem, like the Cartesian dualism of mind and body, is a false dichotomy which semiotics has enabled us to overcome.[13]

12 Philomena Essed, *Everyday Racism: Reports from Women of Two Cultures* (Claremont, California: Hunter House, 1990); Teun van Dijk, *Racism and the Press* (London: Routledge, 1991); Teun van Dijk, *Elite Discourse and Racism* (Newbury Park, California: Sage, 1993).

13 John Deely, *Four Ages of Understanding* (Toronto: University of Toronto Press, 2001).

PART 1
Images of Law

Chapter 1

Deep Structures of Empire: A Note on Imperial Machines and Bodies

Ronnie Lippens

The 'Biological Culture' of Empire

In a recent paper, Nikolas Rose has aptly shown how a 'biological culture', over the past few decades, seems to have emerged and developed in the wake of neo-liberalism.[1] Indeed, Rose demonstrates, in an age when we are all constituted as individual actors who are constantly required to freely exploit opportunities and, while taking such initiative, to restrict ourselves from harmful excess, in short, to behave when necessary, then those who fail to combine both prescribed lines of action await a new form of regulation. Freely exploiting opportunities while self-restricting when necessary, in neo-liberalist ideology, should come *naturally*. Failing to do so constitutes *unnatural*, indeed unhealthy behaviour, and should therefore be dealt with accordingly. This line of reasoning, claims Rose, forms the backdrop or foundation of recent and current strategies of regulation and control 'that aim to identify, treat and control individuals predisposed to impulsive or aggressive conduct', and that should be implemented against 'those whose conduct seems to show *wanton* disregard for the moral *constraints* on the conduct of *free* individuals in a *liberal* society'.[2] Genetics, or medicine more generally, clearly has turned out to provide the logic with which unnaturally deficient individuals should be sanitized away from the allegedly natural, free flowing though orderly body of neo-liberal society. The latter, neo-liberal society, appears here – in this emerging 'biological culture' – as the natural, healthy state of humanity, that is a state that, as we have heard before, has moved beyond history after the fall of despotism and totalitarianism.[3]

Let us now have a closer look at a quotation. The contribution at hand shall attempt to delineate the quotation's 'narrative integration', as Barthes would have

---

1 Nikolas Rose, 'The Biology of Culpability: Pathological Identity and Crime Control in a Biological Culture', *Theoretical Criminology*, 4/1 (2000): 5-34.

2 Rose, 'The Biology of Culpability', p. 5.

3 Francis Fukuyama, 'The End of History', *The National Interest*, 16/Summer (1989): 3-16.

called it, referring to Greimas's notion of *isotopy*.[4] The quotation is in fact an extract from Prime Minister Tony Blair's congressional address on 17 July 2003, delivered shortly after the formal end of the Iraq War:

> We are bound together as never before. This coming together provides us with unprecedented opportunity but also makes us uniquely vulnerable. The threat comes, because, in another part of the globe, there is shadow and darkness where not all the world is free, where many millions suffer under brutal dictatorship; where a third of our planet lives in poverty beyond anything even the poorest in our societies can imagine; and where a fanatical strain of religious extremism has arisen, that is a mutation of the true and peaceful faith of Islam and because in the combination of these afflictions, a new and deadly virus has emerged. The virus is terrorism, whose intent to inflict destruction is unconstrained by human feeling.

Let us focus on just this extract, and on an emerging imaginary of Empire (an emerging new Law of Empire, that is) therein.[5] There is a way of reading this extract as another expression of a 'biological culture' in a neo-liberalist age, albeit on a bigger, global scale now. Blair's address seems to betray a particular imaginary. There is an image of a world – a world of 'technology, communication, trade and travel', Blair claims elsewhere in his speech – that is now truly connected, unified, full of opportunity, freedom, human feeling, and moral constraint. The state the world is in appears to be a natural state, albeit one that has emerged 'as never before'; it appears to be an accomplished state, not unlike the state of a natural body, a naturally healthy body. The global world of interconnected freedom, opportunity, and (self-) constraint, however, like any other body, is 'vulnerable'. Dangers lurk outside, in 'shadow and darkness'. The most lethal danger of all is of a medical, indeed epidemiological nature: it is viral. This virus, 'terrorism', is 'unconstrained', knows no boundaries, is wildly fanatical (rather than free and self-constrained), frequently crosses the skin of the healthy body, constantly threatens to unsettle its delicate, interconnected balance of freedom, opportunity, and order, and should therefore be dealt with *epidemiologically*. To deal with global terrorism is to adopt and to follow the logic of epidemiological emergencies and interventions. This is not the logic of a policeman, a diplomat, a magistrate, or a judge. It is the logic of a globalizing 'biological culture'.

In this short contribution, it will be argued that underneath this shift towards a biological, medical, and epidemiological culture of regulation and control, one could distinguish another one. This would be a shift from the imagination of Empire as highly effortful, ever-unaccomplished engineering, to the imagination of Empire as accomplished nature. It will be our contention here to argue that this change in the deep structures of the imperial imaginary is of the uttermost import for anyone who

---

4 Roland Barthes, *Image Music Text* (London: Fontana Press, 1977), p. 122ff.

5 For a more detailed discussion of this quotation and other textual materials, see: Ronnie Lippens, 'Viral Contagion and Anti-Terrorism. Notes on Medical Emergency, Legality, and Diplomacy', *International Journal for the Semiotics of Law*, 17/3 (2004): 125-39.

tries to come to grips with issues of contemporary regulation and control. 'Empire', in this contribution, stands not just for the (imaginary) logic of global or regional domination in matters of regulation and control, but for the imaginary of regulation and control as such.

Hobbes's *Leviathan*: Artificial Unity of Fragments

For a long time, Empire, or the location of regulation and control, tended to be imagined as unnatural, exhausting engineering, or, as the workings – ever-fallible workings at that – of a particular kind of machine, engine, or *machinerie* placed there, somewhere at the centre of authority, to bring stability, order, peace, or anything else that would lead to modernity.[6] Ever since Hobbes's *Leviathan* (1651), one might argue, Empire has, at least to some extent, been imagined as the painfully exhaustive and highly burdensome process of constructing, maintaining, and reaping the productive results of machines. *Leviathan* arguably lies at the heart of the modern imperial imagination. Let us be clear here: when writing *Leviathan*, Hobbes did not particularly have a global empire in mind (in fact, something like a British Empire did not yet exist fully-fledged). He merely tried to think through the need for a way of *modern* governance in a 'common wealth, ecclesisticall and civil' beyond, on the one hand, sheer anarchy and, on the other, utter tyranny. The images and imagery evoked and used by Hobbes, however, are telling. The engraving on the frontispiece of *Leviathan*, for example, has recently stirred some scholarly interest.[7] The well-known image – it has now indeed turned into an iconic image of modernity as such – shows a giant figure (the Sovereign) towering over a landscape dotted with towns and churches. The Sovereign thus towers over religious as well as public, or political life. Upon closer inspection, however, the body of this Sovereign (the *Body Politick*, *Civil Societie*, or the *State*, in Hobbes's view) appears to be not a physical, natural body, but a complex of countless minuscule little figures (the citizens) looking up to the Sovereign's head. Many of these little figures appear to be connected, as in a joint effort suggesting co-operation or collaboration. In order to avoid the sheer chaos (Hobbes wrote the book against the backdrop of the English Civil War) of utter, unconstrained, self-interested individuals, modern government should result from and should presuppose two moves.[8] The first move is the one whereby individuals become citizens in and through the agreement of a covenant (subsequent philosophers would call this a *social contract*), each thereby surrendering (some of) their personal sovereignty to an 'artificiall unitie', the State, or, in Hobbes's words, civil society. However, this artificial construction (indeed, it does not come naturally, it is a *feigned*

6 Ronnie Lippens, 'Imachinations of Peace', *Utopian Studies*, 13/1 (2002): 135-47.

7 Howard Caygill, *Art of Judgment* (Oxford: Oxford University Press, 1989), pp. 16-36; Noel Malcolm, 'The Titlepage of Leviathan, Seen in a Curious Perspective', *Seventeenth Century*, 2 (1998): 120-55.

8 Quentin Skinner, 'Hobbes and the Purely Artificial Person of the State', *The Journal of Political Philosophy*, 7/1 (1999): 1-29.

person[9]) can only come about, can only be a real unity, with a second move, that is if and when it can act as one person. *That* can only be the case if this artificial unity is represented by a Sovereign, that is a monarch or a committee (Hobbes himself was undecided on this issue), whose authority is based in the artificial covenant of civil society (and not in some divine right, for example), but whose own sovereign Being in turn is the only way in and through which this covenant, strangely and artificially so, can acquire a level of unity sufficient to prevent the chaos and the tyranny of an unchecked 'multitude' of self-interest. Hobbes here seems to read or to re-imagine the much older notion of the *Body Politick* as an artificial contraption (a *contract*-ion?), as a two-stroke engine, if you wish.

The imagination of governance and authority as that which goes on in the artificial and machine-like unity of covenants and sovereign representation should not have come as a big surprise in an age of trade and exploration that was obsessed with regularity, calculation, predictability, and so on, and that therefore also cultivated a serious penchant for machines, astrolabes and clockworks in particular. Nature itself, somewhere in the seventeenth century, turned into a machine, the predictabilities and regularities of which Isaac Newton was at pains to lay bare as the Great Machine-Maker's laws of physics. The sovereign machine of the impersonal State and its laws of the covenant were there to safeguard an orderly modernity from the whims of passion, unconstrained self-interest, and, Hobbes stresses, from anything that purports to be *natural* law. Hobbes was desperate to get beyond nature. His Leviathan may have appeared as a body; Hobbes meant for it to be an impersonal machine. A similar logic would one century later forcefully express itself in writings such as Cesare Beccaria's, which argued for the unpredictable, irregular, passionate, and subjective chaos of the *Ancien Régime* to be replaced with the simplicity and certainty of an objective, detached, smoothly running (like clockwork) system of tariffs. After the French revolution, this mechanics of governance would re-emerge, for example, in the idea that the judiciary can only be the impersonal and objective 'mouthpiece' of the law, as well as in bureaucratic *machinerie* that, as Zygmunt Bauman has claimed, all too often expressed and facilitated the typically modern logic of *adiaphorization*, that is detached, rule-centred, impersonal amorality.[10]

As Noel Malcolm has been able to establish,[11] Hobbes himself, when writing *Leviathan*, was heavily inspired by two particular forms of *machinerie* that were very much *en vogue* at the time. The first, a specially fabricated cylindrical lens that enabled 'catoptric anamorphosis', that is, a process whereby a viewer, looking through the lens, sees a coherent image emerging – artificially – out of a number – a multitude – of fragments drawn on a sheet of paper. And it is the lens, this 'curious perspective', a particular machine, an artificial engine, that in turn produces an artificial

9 David Runciman, 'What Kind of Person is Hobbes's State ? A Reply to Skinner', *The Journal of Political Philosophy*, 8/2 (2000): 268-78.

10 Zygmunt Bauman, *Modernity and the Holocaust* (Cambridge: Cambridge University Press, 1989).

11 Malcolm, 'The Titlepage of Leviathan, Seen in a Curious Perspective'.

unity. The second form of *machinerie* was the theatre, again an artificial world, a world of illusion and representation, a world of impersonal masks and roles.[12] Both machines, Hobbes noticed, had the desirable capacity to artificially transform the restless chaos of multitudes into an ordered, and therefore peaceful unity. However, the artificial unity and logic of the machine of the commonwealth is a work that is never finished. Like all machines, the commonwealth needs constant attention and maintenance. Empire here emerges as a never-ending process of creative production. Empire does not come naturally. It does not flow from natural rights or natural law. As Howard Caygill writes in his chapter on *Leviathan*, 'Hobbes identifies life with order, and order with a *continually* produced unity',[13] a commonwealth that 'is being *continually* re-created by the acknowledgement of the *imperium* of the sovereign and the ordering of the citizens as persons'.[14] It is this deep structure of Empire, this deeply rooted imaginary, that for centuries has framed the imperial imagination, not just with regards to the building of local commonwealths or nation-states, but also, and particularly so, during the age of colonization. Empire was something to be achieved, to be accomplished. It was a goal, and, as such, it was strived for. Empire was not just there, it was not given. Forces had to be marshalled, populations had to be subdued or mobilized or destroyed, crops had to be cultivated, peoples had to be disciplined and 'civilized', landscapes had to be changed, goods had to be transported, networks and dependencies had to be established, and ultimately, something like imperial integration or better, inclusion, had to be accomplished. Referring to Victorian writers such as Ruskin (who considered English architecture to be the imperial technology *par excellence*) and Lord Macaulay (who thought it was the English language itself), this is how Ian Baucom recently read the British Empire: 'a *factory* for the *production* of English identity'.[15] Out of a multitude of fragments, incoherence, and disunity, a unified Empire had to be artificially fashioned. So unnatural an enterprise, this Empire, in the words of Rudyard Kipling, the quintessential colonialist, was literally *the white man's burden*. The ideological machine that facilitated this *enterprise* was the twin-stroke engine of imperial representation and covenanted surrender.

New Leviathan: Organic Flux of Multitude

A new imaginary of Empire seems to be on its way to replacing the former one. The *Body Politick* of old now tends to be thought of as a body indeed, rather than as a machine. As the quotations at the beginning of this chapter seem to suggest, a notion of Empire as a full-fledged, interconnected, and organic whole has surfaced. In a

12 Skinner, 'Hobbes and the Purely Artificial Person of the State'.

13 Caygill, *Art of Judgment*, p. 22 (italics added, R.L.).

14 Ibid., p. 30 (first italics added, R.L.).

15 Ian Baucom, *'British to the Backbone*: On Imperial Subject Fashioning', in Ian Baucom, *Out of Place* (Durham: Duke University Press, 1999), pp. 75-100 (quotation from p. 79; italics added, R.L.).

thoroughly 'biological culture' this often tends to be expressed in 'biological', medical, or even epidemiological language, and this is not just the case when local regulation and control is concerned, as Rose argues, but also when it comes to international relations and geo-politics. Much of this language, for example, surfaced around the time of the first Gulf War,[16] and gained considerable momentum in the wake of the events of September 11th. One should of course add here that medical imagery as such, for example the use of words such as 'health' to describe the state of the nation, has origins that stretch beyond the nineteenth century. The use of epidemiological terminology in national or international governance has nineteenth century origins. Louis Pasteur's work in bacteriology, for example, made sure that already by the end of the nineteenth century, criminologies did tend to define crime in terms of bacterial 'infection'. The 'virus' metaphor too, so often used in the 'war on terrorism', does have a history in governance and international relations. In his 1947 statement before the House of Un-American Activities Committee, J. Edgar Hoover, FBI Director, spoke of the 'virus of communism'. However, this use of epidemiological imagery never managed to fully replace a *legal* logic of control and regulation. In Hoover's statement, for example, epidemiological destruction of communism still had a seriously legal tinge about it: 'I do favor unrelenting prosecution wherever they are found to be violating our country's laws. As Americans, our most effective defense is a workable democracy that guarantees and preserves our cherished freedoms'.[17] Only in very recent times, and particularly after September 11th, does medical and 'viral' imagery seem to gradually facilitate a 'biological culture' wherein governance and imperial intervention are conceived and practised as *medical* interventions, following an *epidemiological* logic.[18] This is the logic of New Empire.

Today's neo-liberal, post-Fukuyaman Empire is global, universal, and complete. Nothing needs to be included anymore. It may be, as Hardt and Negri recently argued, a 'multicentric' Empire, driven and fuelled by what they call the 'multitude' of desires and hopes.[19] It may not have a clear and obvious centre anymore. But it is, Hardt and Negri argue, global and complete, and it seems to have reached a point of no return. Indeed, prior to September 11th, it looked as if the global and globalizing 'multitude' and their 'multicentric' controls, that is Empire, in Hardt and Negri's view at least, were there, or here, to stay. Such an Empire does not need to be produced or maintained. It produces and maintains itself. It does not have to be made productive. Its productivity is determined by this multitude of desires and controls. There is no imperial centre that arranges for particular inclusions or that works towards integration. There is a multitude of interconnected desires and controls that

16 Francis A. Beer and Barry J. Balleck, 'Body, Mind, and Soul in the Gulf War Debate', 1993, at www.sobek.colorado.edu/~beer/PAPERS.

17 Taken from: http://edition.cnn.com/SPECIALS/cold.war/episodes/06/documents/hoover.

18 Lippens, 'Viral Contagion and Anti-Terrorism. Notes on Medical Emergency, Legality, and Diplomacy'.

19 Michael Hardt and Toni Negri, *Empire* (Cambridge: Harvard University Press, 2000).

interact with each other or resist each other. Indeed, as Prime Minister Blair claimed, elsewhere in his congressional address, 'freedom', 'democracy', and 'the rule of law' are 'not Western values', but 'the universal values of the human spirit and anywhere, and anytime, ordinary people are given the chance to choose'. If left on its own, the healthy body of Empire (of freedom-cum-rule of law) will emerge naturally and orderly. What therefore needs to be done is to make sure it *is* left on its own. According to Peter Fitzpatrick, for example, this 'new imperialism' assumes something like a 'complete givenness', something like the 'naturalism' or 'the implanted truth and the inevitability' of 'the neo-liberal order', while 'it assures itself that it has encompassed its own limit, achieved completeness, and marked the end of history'. Fitzpatrick also amply demonstrates how the 'new imperialism' of the 1990s tended to be imagined as that *particularly* Western but highly pretentious universalism that hides under words like 'human rights'. And this entailed massive exclusion, as, of course, 'those who do not behave in accordance with or aspire to human rights, must not be human'.[20] Empire seems to have lost much of its 'productive' and 'inclusive' connotations (however repressive at times such production and inclusion may have been). If anything, today's imagined Empire seems to be in need of exclusions. In the imaginary of President Bush Sr.'s new world order, for example, there was no room for 'rogue states'. Those should be kept at bay, or neutralized, or embargoed, or just contained. This imaginary Empire, that is, an almost naturally given of free-flowing forces and desires (free-flowing but orderly, new-world-orderly, that is), only needs to reproduce itself by excluding 'rogue states' (rogue-but-unfree, that is) and wiping out viral cultures (wild-but-fanatical), or at least by keeping them in check. Now this may be a strenuous job in itself, but, to use Michael Ignatieff's words, compared to the real and imagined *white man's burden* of yore, that most unnatural of tasks, today's Empire is an 'Empire Lite' that should come naturally.[21] Its natural health will manifest itself if, apart from keeping all kinds of *contagion* at bay, as little as possible is done.

This neo-liberalism of New Empire tends to operate within the bounds of a medical imaginary. As such it often surfaces, in the words of Nikolas Rose, as a 'biological culture'. Nothing needs to be constructed in such a culture. There are no huge projects to be mounted. There are no *machineries* to be built and maintained. There is no need for construction or reconstruction. There is no need to strive for Utopia, that 'place beyond all history'.[22] It is already here; we have, claims neo-liberalism, arrived beyond history. The only thing that needs to be done, in this imaginary, is to make sure the forces and flows of nature are allowed to run their natural course. The one thing that needs to be done, in other words, is to make sure

20 Peter Fitzpatrick, *Modernism and the Grounds of Law* (Cambridge: Cambridge University Press, 2001), pp. 208-16. See also Wouter Werner's contribution, this volume.

21 Michael Ignatieff, 'America's Empire is an Empire Lite', *New York Times*, 10 January (2003).

22 Fredric Jameson, 'The Politics of Utopia', *New Left Review*, 25, Jan Feb issue (2004): 35-54 (quotation from p. 36).

that the unnatural, that is those who are unable to combine natural freedom and natural order – indeed, disease and contagion – are either destroyed or contained, or, if possible, *pre-empted.* Imperial intervention, in this imaginary, is a matter of medical necessity. It should come naturally. Although some level of consultation and collaboration may be useful,[23] no particular *machinerie* – the UN and international law come to mind – is strictly necessary in the process. Today's 'common wealth' is not an 'artificiall' one. The *Body Politick* of today's Empire is just that: a body. Hobbes, and his *machinic* modernity of construction and maintenance, are memories of a distant past. The *naturally* ordered 'multitude' is back. We have, according to Blair, Bush, and Fukuyama, arrived beyond history, into sheer nature. Blair may have been describing today's global machine of networks, interconnections, and communications; he meant for it to be a natural organism, a body even, that has arrived beyond history.

Acknowledgements

The author wishes to thank Maria Markantonatou and the students in the MA course in Criminology (class of 2003-04) at Keele University (UK). Thanks also to the participants in the Roundtables for the Semiotics of Law seminar (July 2004, Lyon, France), in particular Lester Mazor, Richard Sherwin, Paul Robertshaw, Annabelle Mooney, and Neal Feigenson, for their supportive remarks. This contribution was first published in *Social Justice: A Journal of Crime, Conflict & World Order* (2005, issue 32/1). Thanks go to Gregory Shank and Global Options for allowing us to reprint the paper here.

---

23 On the dangers of the current relative absence of it, see Michael Cox, 'The Empire's Back in Town: On America's Imperial Temptation – Again', *Millennium: Journal of International Studies*, 32/1 (2003): 1-26.

Chapter 2

Intervention and The New Imagery of World Order

Wouter G. Werner

Introduction

Traditionally, international law is imaged as a decentralized legal order between sovereign states, based on state consent and a prohibition of intervention. International law, in other words, is imagined as a legal order between states-as-independent-persons. This imagery has affected the development of several legal doctrines and distinctions in the area of warfare, such as the rules on neutrality, the separation between criminals and public enemies or the distinction between domestic and foreign affairs. However, recent studies have suggested the existence of a new imagery of world order: world order or 'Empire' is imagined as a complete, global, self-sufficient, naturally evolving order, located at, or beyond, the end of history.[1] In his contribution to this volume, Lippens sets out how this imagery is embedded in a medicalized and biological discourse that gained momentum after the 9/11 attacks.[2] The medicalized discourse imagines (liberal) world order as a normal, healthy body that has to be defended against disturbing, unhealthy and unnatural elements. This imagery of world order has a profound impact on the way in which existing doctrines are interpreted, modified or sometimes simply set aside. In particular, this imagery challenges the idea of war as an armed struggle between *justa et aequalis hostes* and replaces it with notions such as 'enforcement operations on behalf of the international community' against 'law-breakers', 'criminals' or those that have put themselves at the verge or beyond the limits of international law.[3] From this perspective, interventions are conceptualized as exceptional measures, aimed at restoring a condition of normalcy. According to Hardt and Negri, imperial interventions take place in a permanent state of exception, in the form of operations

---

1 See, for a discussion of this imagery, R. Lippens, 'Viral Contagion and Anti-Terrorism: Notes on Medical Emergency, Legality and Diplomacy', *International Journal for the Semiotics of Law*, (2004), 125-139. Lippens argues that: 'Today, Empire is given. Nothing needs to be included anymore. Empire is global, universal, complete …' (129). See also: M. Hardt and A. Negri, *Empire* (Cambridge: Harvard University Press, 2000); P. Fitzpatrick, *Modernism and the Grounds of Law* (Cambridge: Cambridge University Press, 2001).

2 R. Lippens, 'Deep Structures of Empire: A Note on Imperial Machines and Bodies', Chapter 1.

3 For a more extensive analysis, see W.G. Werner, 'From Justus Hostis to Rogue State', *International Journal for the Semiotics of Law*, 17 (2) (2004), 155-168.

in between war and police measures, justified by the appeal to essential values of justice.[4]

This chapter examines in more detail the recent development of two forms of intervention: self-defence against terrorism and intervention for humanitarian purposes. It aims to set out how the imagery of world order as complete, global and self-sufficient has affected the interpretation and application of existing doctrines of international law and how it has contributed to a widening of exceptional, interventionist powers under international law.

Self-Defence

> We are acting in self-defence in the finest traditions that set our nation apart from most other nations.[5]

This quote nicely captures the interplay of normalcy and exception at work in the recent war on terrorism. It reaffirms the necessity of playing by the rules and upholding the international rule of law by referring to the generally recognized 'inherent right of individual or collective self-defense if an armed attack occurs…'.[6] At the same time, it sends a warning signal: it invokes the image of a dangerous world, where 'most other nations' (than the US) follow a different path. Self-defence thus becomes more than just the defence of the home land: it is an exceptional measure, necessary to uphold the rule of law and the international order against terrorists, who exploit failed states and who are supported by rogue states.

The coupling of self-defence and the fight against terrorism is not new to international law. From the 1960s on, the General Assembly has repeatedly indicated that subversion, indirect intervention or the sending of armed bands, groups or irregulars could qualify as a threat to international peace and security or even an armed attack against a state.[7] Moreover, since 1945 states have regularly relied on self-defence to justify armed measures against infiltrations by non-state groups or

4 Hardt and Negri (2000), 18.

5 U.S. Office of the Press Secretary, Press Briefing by Ari Fleischer, 31 October 2001. Quoted in F. Megret, 'War? Legal Semantics and the Move to Violence', *European Journal of International Law* 13 (2002), 361-401.

6 Article 51 UN charter. See also the recognition of the right to self-defence as a customary right in the *Nicaragua* case: Nicaragua v. United States of America, Merits, ICJ Rep. 1986.

7 See for example the following resolutions: Declaration on the Inadmissibility of Intervention in the Domestic Affairs of States and the Protection of Their Independence and Sovereignty, A/Res/213 (XX), 21 December 1965; Declaration on Principles of International Law Concerning Friendly Relations and Co-operation Among States in Accordance with the Charter of the United Nations; Resolution 2625 (xxv), 24 October 1970; Resolution 3314 (XXIX) on the Definition of Aggression, 14 December 1974.

against terrorist attacks on their territory or nationals.[8] These invocations of the right to self-defence have not always been successful. In some cases, the use of force by states was strongly condemned by other states and UN organs, while in other cases the use of force was accepted or condoned. International practice thus showed a willingness to accept that an armed response to terrorist attacks could in principle be lawful. However, it also showed that the legality of an individual action strongly depends on the concrete context. Or, as Franck summarizes the practice of the UN regarding armed reaction to state-sponsored terrorists and infiltrators: 'In each instance, UN organs seem to have eschewed narrowly dogmatic insistence on a traditional armed attack by a national army as the sole justification for an armed response in self-defence. Instead, they have focussed on relevant evidence, weighing the seriousness of each claim of necessity and the proportionality of each aggrieved party's countermeasures.'[9]

Against this background – and taking into account the factual circumstances – it is not surprising that the Security Council affirmed the right to self-defence immediately after the 9/11 attacks.[10] Although the Security Council only referred to the right to self-defence in general terms ('...*recognizing* the inherent right of individual or collective self-defense in accordance with the Charter...'), the symbolic meaning of this recognition immediately after the 9/11 attacks was clear and compelling. Equally clear was the support from the NATO member states, who for the first time in the history of the alliance invoked Article 5 of the NATO Charter (dealing with collective self-defence). On 12 September, NATO decided that, if it is determined that the attack against the United States was directed from abroad, it shall be regarded as an action covered by Article 5 of the NATO Charter. After the member states were convinced that the 9/11 attacks were conducted by Al-Qaida, they accepted the applicability of Article 5 of the NATO Charter.[11]

---

8 Some examples are: Israel-Egypt (1956), Israel-Uganda (1976), Israel-Lebanon (1982), Israel-Tunisia (1985), US-Libya (1986), Turkey-Iraq (1995), Tajiki-Afghanistan (1993), US-Sudan and Afghanistan (1998). For a more extensive analysis see Thomas M. Franck, *Recourse to Force, State Action Against Threats and Armed Attacks* (Cambridge: Cambridge University Press, 2002). For an extensive discussion of some of these examples (and others) see the discussion for the *European Journal* and *American Society of International Law*: www.ejil.org, www.asil.org.

9 Franck (2002), 67. As far as the UN practice regarding the invocation of self-defence to justify armed measures to protect nationals abroad is concerned, Franck offers two possible interpretations: 'Narrowly, recourse to force to protect nationals abroad may be said to have been condoned as legitimate in specific mitigating circumstances, even though that recourse is still recognized as technically illegal. Or, in a broader interpretation of practice, the system may be said to have adapted the concept of self-defence, under article 51, to include a right to use force in response to an attack against nationals, providing there is clear evidence of extreme necessity and the means chosen are proportionate.' Franck (2002), 96.

10 Resolution 1368 of 12 September 2001, S/Res/1368 (2001).

11 Note, however, that the US argued that such multilateral support for the war on terrorism was welcome, but not strictly necessary. Colin Powell made this position clear when

However, the effects of accepting such a right to self-defence in response to terrorist attacks are far-reaching. Self-defence now not only covers immediate responses to attacks by identifiable actors, but also open-ended operations against an amorphous enemy. A quick look at some recent codenames for anti-terrorist operations is telling in this respect.[12] In 1998, the US attacked targets in Afghanistan and Sudan under the codename 'Infinite Reach'. Following the 9/11 attacks, the US Department of Defense suggested 'Operation Infinite Justice' as codename for the planned military responses. After Muslim groups protested the name it was changed into 'Operation Enduring Freedom'.[13] While a codename like 'Desert Storm' invokes an image of a territorially and temporally bounded operation, terms like 'infinite' and 'enduring' suggest that something else is at stake. And indeed, the invocation of 'self-defence' in response to attacks by terrorist networks raises questions as to the boundaries of the right to self-defence in at least three respects: temporal, spatial and qua object.

The temporal limits of self-defence are put into question, because it can become unclear when the attack that triggered the right of self-defence took place. The right of self-defence against terrorist attacks can follow from 'a consistent pattern of violent terrorist action' against a state.[14] It is difficult to tell when such a consistent pattern exists and it is possible that a state can conclude that, in hindsight, it had already been at war with a terrorist organization for a considerable time.[15] Moreover, it is unclear when the war on terrorism will stop. The war on terrorism is, after all, not only a self-defence operation designed to do away with a specific attack, but an open-ended operation that will only end when 'every terrorist group of global reach has been found, stopped and defeated'. In this war, as Rumsfeld has argued, 'we should

---

he stated that: 'At the moment, notwithstanding all of the coalition building we have been doing, President Bush retains the authority to take whatever actions he believes are appropriate in accordance with the needs for self-defense of the United States and of the American people. We will be going to the UN for additional support ... but, at the moment, should the President decide that there are more actions he has to take, he will make a judgment as to whether he needs UN authority or whether he can just rely on the authority inherent in the right of self-defence.... '. Secretary Colin Powell, Remarks with His Excellency Brian Cowen, Minister of Foreign Affairs of Ireland, 26 September 2001. http://www.yale.edu/lawweb/avalon/sept_11/powell_brief19.htm.

12 See Megret (2002) for a discussion of the codenames in the war on terrorism.

13 http://www.globalsecurity.org/military/ops/infinite-justice.htm.

14 See also Cassese, A., 'The International Community's "Legal" Response to Terrorism', *International and Comparative Law Quarterly* (38), (1989), 558-596.

15 See Bob Woodward and Thomas E. Ricks, *Washington Post* staff writers, Wednesday, 3 October 2001, 'CIA Trained Pakistanis to Nab Terrorist But Military Coup Put an End to 1999 Plot', http://home.pacbell.net/reichar/operation.html: 'In the aftermath of last month's attacks on the United States, which the Bush administration has tied to bin Laden, Clinton officials said their decision not to take stronger and riskier action has taken on added relevance. 'I wish we'd recognized it then,' that the United States was at war with bin Laden, said a senior Defense official, 'and started the campaign then that we've started now. That's my main regret. In hindsight, we were at war.'

forget about exit strategies', because 'we are looking at sustained engagement that carries no deadlines'. This 'sustained engagement' knows no spatial limits either. After all, terrorists are spread out throughout the world and could – as the 9/11 and subsequent attacks have shown – even hide in the homeland. Yet, shortly after the 9/11 attacks, the US also attempted to reintroduce territoriality in the war on terrorism by emphasizing the need to deal with states harbouring terrorists. Any state or regime sponsoring or harbouring terrorist groups was equated with the terrorists themselves, while a neutral ground for third states was ruled out. The implications of this statement became clear in the war against Afghanistan. Here, a self-defence operation was used to realize a regime change and thus went beyond an operation aimed at repelling an armed attack. The operation rather aimed at incapacitating the enemy in very broad terms (to take away 'safe havens' for terrorists) and linked self-defence arguments to the struggle for a world without rogue regimes and failed states.

In international legal discourse such broadening of the right to self-defence still needs a link to some of the traditional categories of international law. Thus, the legal rationale was found in the link between Al-Qaida and the *de facto* regime in Afghanistan as well as in the refusal of this regime to take action against the terrorist network operating from its territory. Moreover, it has been argued that states can act in self-defence against terrorist organizations operating from states that are unable to undertake effective action to stop terrorist organizations.[16] In this way, traditional international law can be used to link the war on terrorism to the fight against rogue states and failed states – thus reinforcing questions regarding the relation between international law and hegemonic power.

In the US National Security Strategy, the US government made an attempt to further stretch the right to self-defence. Later in the chapter, we will examine in more detail how the Strategy uses the savage-victim-savior imagery to justify a world-wide fight against terrorism. For now, it suffices to point at the description of war against terrorism as 'of global reach' and 'of uncertain duration'.[17] In this war, the Strategy argues, the traditional limits of self-defence, and especially the legality of anticipatory attacks, should be re-evaluated.[18] Under the traditional criteria of international law, the legality of anticipatory self-defence is controversial.

16 See, for example, Y. Dinstein, 'Ius ad Bellum Aspects of the "War on Terrorism"' and T. Gill, 'The Eleventh of September and the Right of Self-Defense', in W. Heere, *Terrorism and the Military, International Legal Implications* (The Hague: Asser Press, 2003), at 13-23 and 23-39 respectively.

17 National Security Strategy, p. 1.

18 Similarly, Bush argued at the 2002 Graduation Exercise of the US Military Academy, West Point, New York, that anticipatory self-defence is necessary and legitimate in the war on terrorism, while Rumsfeld had argued before that: 'The best, and in some cases, the only defense is a good offense'. 'Secretary Rumsfeld speaks on "21st Century Transformation" of US Armed Forces', www. defenselink.mil/speeches/2002/s20020131-secdef.html. During the Cold War, Secretary of State Schultz had also repeatedly argued in favour of a doctrine of preventive self-defence, since the US should not become 'the Hamlet of Nations, worrying

Even those who argue that such a right exists, however, generally limit this right to a *pre-emptive* right to self-defence: a right to anticipate immanent and clearly identifiable armed attacks.[19] A more general right to *preventive* self-defence, meant to deal with potential threats, does not exist in international law. At first sight, the National Security Strategy seems to follow international law's distinction between pre-emptive and preventive strikes. The Strategy agues that 'legal scholars and international jurists often conditioned the legitimacy of pre-emption on the existence of an immanent threat – most often a visible mobilization of armies, navies, and air forces preparing to attack' (15). The Strategy continues, however, by redefining the concept of an 'immanent threat'. Under present day conditions, an immanent threat also covers 'acts of terror and, potentially, the use of weapons of mass destruction'. Against these new 'immanent threats', anticipatory self-defence should be allowed.

Preventive self-defence entails not only action against terrorists themselves, but also action against states that (could) harbour and support terrorists; the rogue regimes and failed states. ('It's a way of effectively closing down dangerous regimes before they become imminent threats.') In this way, self-defence is stretched from a limited reaction to an armed attack to the building of a new world order in which failed states are disciplined and rogue regimes destroyed. Here, the right of intervention as described by Negri and Hardt is clearly visible: an exceptional right, exercised in the name of universal values, in the form of a law-enforcing operation, aimed at perpetual peace, yet engaged in a struggle without spatial and temporal limits.

It remains to be seen whether the enthusiasm for preventive action in the form of regime change will survive the Iraq War. What will stay, however, is the combination of self-defence against terrorist attacks and the fight for universal values. The US government is not the only one which has defined terrorists as enemies of civilization, the free world or decent people. Self-defence thus becomes more than the defence of a state that is victim of an armed attack; it becomes the defence of states that embody universal values. As Bush explained, 'our Nation's cause has always been larger than our Nation's defense. We fight, *as we always fight*, for a just peace – a peace that favors liberty.'[20] The tendency of liberal democracies to universalise their own struggle for survival is not new. It is, as critics of liberalism like Schmitt and defenders of liberalism like Wellmer agree, inherent in the triad of liberalism, democracy and human rights: liberal democracies cannot fight for their own survival without, at the same time, fighting for the human rights of their enemies: '...Demokratien können nämlich für igenes Überleben als *Demokratien* nicht kämpfen, ohne zugleich für die Menschenrechte ihrer Feinde, letzlich die Mensenrechte aller, mitzukämpfen.'[21]

---

endlessly over whether and how to respond'; G.P. Schultz, *Turmoil and Triumph* (1993), pp. 645-653.

19 *Caroline* case, April 24, 1841, Mr Webster to Mr Fox (29 Brit & For St Papers).

20 President Bush, West Point, New York, 1 June, 2001. Quoted in the National Security Strategy, p. 1. Italics added.

21 A. Wellmer, *Revolution und Interpretation, Demokratie ohne Letztbegründung*, (Assen: Van Gorcum, 1998), 42.

This brings us to the second topic of this chapter: humanitarian intervention.

Humanitarian Intervention

The Rise of Exceptionalism: Political, Legal and Doctrinal Justifications

Since the 1990s, there has been an increasing enthusiasm for the use of international enforcement measures to protect human rights, sanction those who threaten international peace and security and restore normalcy. This enthusiasm is clearly visible in the reactivation of the UN Security Council after the demise of the Soviet Union. Formally, the Security Council is designed as a guardian of almost Schmittian proportions: it is empowered to determine the existence of threats to the international order and empowered to determine what needs to be done to counter these threats, including the adoption of extraordinary measures that set aside rules of international law that would apply in a situation of normalcy. Article 39 of the UN Charter gives the Security Council a broad discretion to determine the existence of any threat to the peace, breach of the peace, or act of aggression.[22] The Articles 40, 41 and 42 subsequently indicate the measures the Security Council can take in order to restore normalcy: the adoption of provisional measures (Article 40), the adoption of measures not involving the use of force (Article 41) and the adoption of measures necessary to restore or maintain international peace and security, including the use of force (Article 42).[23] The reactivation of the Security Council is symbolized in the 1992 declaration in which its members stated that: 'The absence of war and military conflict among states does not in itself ensure international peace and security. The non-military sources of instability in the economic, social humanitarian and ecological fields have become threats to peace and security. The United Nations membership as a whole, working through its appropriate bodies, needs to give the highest priority to the solution of these matters.'[24] The 1992 declaration effectively argued that any topic could be related to international peace and security and could trigger the use of exceptional powers by the Security Council. In line with this broad conception of peace and security, the number of Security Council resolutions rose from 15 per year in the period 1946-1989 to 64 per year in the 1990s, whereas the

---

22 The broad discretion of the Security Council was confirmed in the *Certain Expenses* Case, 1962, ICJ Reports 184-197, *Namibia* Case, ICJ Reports 1971, p. 16, Prosecutor v. Tadic, Interlocutory appeal Reprinted in I.L.M. (1996), 35.

23 Although the powers of the Security Council initially assumed the existence of standing agreements under Article 43 of the Charter, subsequent practice has confirmed that the absence of such agreement does not render the Security Council powerless to take action under the Articles 40, 41 or 42. As the International Court of Justice confirmed in the *Certain Expenses* case: 'It cannot be said that the Charter has left the Security Council impotent in the face of an emergency situation when agreements under Article 43 have not been concluded.' ICJ Rep., 1962, 151.

24 S/PV 3064, 143, 31 January 1992.

number of references to Chapter VII (dealing with threats to international peace and security and acts of aggression) was almost 35 times higher in the 1990s than during the Cold War.[25] Situations defined as a 'threat to peace' included internal armed conflicts, humanitarian disasters, human rights violations, the overthrow of democratically elected governments and terrorism. The Security Council did more than just determine a threat or breach of peace. It also proved willing to adopt far-reaching measures to restore or maintain international peace and security, like the establishment of criminal tribunals, the imposition of a war reparations procedure, the imposition of sanction regimes against more than ten states and against non-state forces, the authorization of peacekeeping and peace-enforcement forces and several enforcement operations involving the use of force. Moreover, especially after the 9/11 attacks, the Security Council assumed the role of 'legislator of the world community' by adopting resolutions in the sphere of counter terrorism, including the blacklisting of individuals and the imposition of far-reaching obligations for states.[26]

However, the increased enthusiasm for enforcement measures to protect human rights also led to disappointment about those instances in which the Security Council proved unable or unwilling to act. Especially in the contexts of the wars in the former Yugoslavia and the Rwanda genocide, the Security Council was criticized for failing to protect the victims of war, ethnic cleansing and genocide. In response to the inactivity of the Security Council, some states and/or regional organizations unilaterally assumed the role of enforcer of universal values. The most widely discussed example of this is the 1999 intervention of NATO in Yugoslavia. However, even more interesting examples can be found in Africa, where the Economic Community of West African States (ECOWAS) undertook large-scale interventions in Liberia (1990) and Sierra Leone (1997) without the prior approval of the Security Council. Although ECOWAS managed to obtain *ex post facto* authorization of the Security Council for its actions in Liberia and Sierra Leone,[27] it still claims a more general right to intervene, if necessary outside the framework of the UN.[28] A similar

25 S. Chesterman, *Just War or Just Peace, Humanitarian Intervention and International Law* (Oxford: Oxford University Press, 2001), p. 121.

26 See, *inter alia*, Resolutions 1267 (1999), S/Res/1267, Resolution 1333 (2000), S/Res/1333, Resolution 1373 (S/Res/1373, 28 September 2001) and Resolution 1540 (S.Res/1540, 28 April 2004). For a discussion, see P.C. Szasz, 'The Security Council Start Legislating', *American Journal of International Law*, 96, 4 (2002), 901-905.

27 S/22133, 22 January 1991. Resolution 788 (1992) explicitly welcomed the ECOWAS intervention. Resolution 1266 (1999) 'Commends ... the Military Observer Group of ECOWAS (ECOMOG) on the outstanding contribution which it has made to the restoration of security and stability in Sierra Leone, the protection of civilians and the promotion of a peaceful settlement of the conflict, and urges all States to continue to provide technical, logistical and financial support to ECOMOG to help it to maintain its critical presence and continue to perform its role in Sierra Leone...' S/Res/1260, 20 August 1999.

28 See the 'Protocol Relating to the Mechanism for Conflict Prevention, Management, Resolution, Peacekeeping and Security' adopted by the member states of ECOWAS on 10

right was subsequently claimed by the African Union. Following the example set by the ECOWAS Security Mechanism,[29] Article 4 (h) of the Constitutive Act of the African Union provides for 'a right of the Union to intervene in a Member State pursuant to a decision of the Assembly in respect of grave circumstances, namely: war crimes, genocide and crimes against humanity'.[30]

Such regional and unilateral enforcement measures are difficult to reconcile with positive international law. The UN Charter, after all, only allows for the use of force in self-defence or under authorization of the Security Council. In addition, Article 53 of the UN Charter states regional organizations can only undertake enforcement actions authorized by the Security Council.[31] Finally, the weight of scholarly opinion and the majority of states still deny the existence of a right to use force for humanitarian purposes without approval of the Security Council under positive international law.[32] In this context it is important to note that, after the 1999 Kosovo intervention, the 133 developing states of the G-77 (including many African states) twice adopted

---

December 1999.

29 Article 22 of the Mechanism charges ECOMOG with the task of, *inter alia*, 'humanitarian intervention in support of [*sic*] humanitarian disaster'. Unless we are to believe that ECOMOG is endowed with a rather macabre task, the most plausible interpretation of article 22 is that the term 'in support of' is the result of a mistake in the drafting and should be read as 'to prevent'. Article 25 states that the Mechanism is applied, not only in cases of aggression or international conflict, but also in cases of: (a) an internal conflict that threatens to trigger a humanitarian disaster or poses a serious threat to sub-regional peace and security; (b) serious and massive violations of human rights and the rule of law and (c) an overthrow of a democratically elected government or an attempt to do so. For a discussion of the Mechanism, see Ademola Abass, 'The New Collective Security Mechanism of ECOWAS: Innovations and Problems', *Journal of Conflict and Security Law* (2000), Vol. 5, No. 2, 211-229.

30 The Assembly is composed of the Heads of State and Government or their duly accredited representatives. Decision-making in the Assembly is by consensus or, failing that, by a two-thirds majority of the Member States eligible to vote (Art. 7). In 2003 the AU adopted an amendment to Article 4 (h) that broadens the right of intervention considerably. In its amended form, Article 4 (h) provides for a right of intervention also in case of 'a serious threat to legitimate order to restore peace and stability to the Member State of the Union …' Article 4 of the Protocol on Amendments to the Constitutive Act of the African Union, 3 February 2003. The intervention under the amended Article 4 (h) should be based upon recommendation of the Peace and Security Council, which is composed of 15 members of the AU. The position of the Peace and Security Council is set out in the Protocol Relating to the Establishment of the Peace and Security Council of the African Union, 9 July 2002.

31 Article 53 (1) of the UN Charter reads as follows: 'The Security Council shall, where appropriate, utilize such regional arrangements or agencies for enforcement action under its authority. But no enforcement action shall be taken under regional arrangements or by regional agencies without the authorization of the Security Council …'

32 For an overview of the current debate, see J.L. Holzgrefe and R.O. Keohane, *Humanitarian Intervention, ethical, legal and political dilemmas* (Cambridge: Cambridge University Press, 2003). See also: S. Chesterman, *Just War or Just Peace, Humanitarian Intervention and International Law* (Oxford: Oxford University Press, 2001).

declarations rejecting 'the so-called right of humanitarian intervention, which (has) no basis in the UN Charter or in international law'.[33]

It is, therefore, not surprising that states and regional organizations have attempted to justify their interventions in the language of exceptionalism, necessity and a turn to ethics. Thus, US Secretary of State Albright emphasized that Kosovo was a 'unique situation *sui generis* in the region of the Balkans' and warned that it would be dangerous 'to overdraw the various lessons that come out of it'.[34] Similarly, Germany warned that the Kosovo intervention should not set a precedent, while even the UK hesitated to embrace a full-fledged right to humanitarian intervention.[35] When confronted with the question whether the right of intervention claimed by ECOWAS is compatible with the UN collective security system, a representative declared that 'whilst the subregion appreciates the importance of its obligations under the United Nations Charter, its recent experience has shown that the cost of waiting for the United Nations authorisation could be very high in terms of life and recourses'.[36] Similarly, in the process of drawing up the Constitutive Act of the African Union 'questions … as to whether the Union could possibly have an inherent right to intervene other than through the Security Council … were dismissed out of hand. This decision reflected a sense of frustration … with instances in which the international community tended to focus attention on other parts of the world at the expense of Africa ... the leaders have shown themselves willing to push the frontiers of collective stability and security to the limit without any regard for legal niceties such as authorization of the Security Council.'[37]

The language of exceptionalism and humanitarian necessity has also been taken up in legal doctrine. Although, as mentioned above, the weight of scholarly opinion still comes down to a rejection of a right of unilateral or regional humanitarian

---

33 Ministerial declaration, 23rd Annual Meeting of the Ministers of Foreign Affairs of the Group of 77, 24 September 1999, http://www.g77.orgs/Docs/Decl1999.html. Declaration of the Group of 77 South Summit, Havana, Cuba, 10-14 April 2000, http://www.g77/Docs/declaration_G77Summit.htm.

34 US Secretary of State Press Conference with Russian Foreign Minister Igor Ivanov, Singapore, 26 July 1999. http://secretary.state.gov/www/statements/1999/ 990726b.html (5 March 2002). Quoted in M. Byers and S. Chesterman, in Holzgreve and Keohane (2003), p. 199.

35 For the German position, see Deutscher Bundestag, Plenarprotokol 13/248, 16 October 1998. For the UK position, which was more ambiguous, see Chesterman (2001), 216.

36 Statement by R. Laloupo, on behalf of ECOWAS, quoted in Abass (2000), p. 223, 224.

37 Ben Kioko, 'The Right of Intervention under the African Union's Constitutive Act: From non-interference to non-intervention', *RCIR* (2003) 85, pp.807-825, at 821. See also the arguments discussed by T. Mulawi, 'Reimagining African Unity: Some Preliminary Reflections on the Constitutive Act of the African Union', *African Yearbook of International Law*, Vol 9 (2001).

intervention under positive international law,[38] several discursive strategies have been developed to accommodate this position. Some authors, for example, have argued that humanitarian intervention is illegal, but that moral necessity and the factual situation in which a particular intervention takes place should be accepted as mitigating factors *in a concrete case*. In this way, the prohibition on the use of force is upheld and even strengthened, because the intervention is identified as a violation of this prohibition. At the same time, the focus shifts from the (il)legality of the intervention itself to the determination of the legal consequences of the intervention.[39] Others go beyond this purely circumstantial interpretation and consider the use of mitigating factors as part of a wider normative practice. Franck, for example, places pleas of mitigation in the context of an evolution in which international law increasingly becomes part of a liberal discourse, embodied in the UN as a 'continually dynamic, evolving institution imbued with a spirit of relevance, one in which the emphasis is on practical problem-solving rather than formal doctrinal exegesis'.[40] In this discourse, UN organs weigh the violation of the prohibition on the use of force against the expected outcomes of inaction. In several cases, UN organs – without accepting a right to humanitarian intervention as such – have acquiesced in the outcomes of interventions or at least refused to condemn these interventions as acts of aggression.[41] As the ongoing discussion on humanitarian intervention demonstrates, the positions taken by UN organs are understood as more than answers to a unique case only. They have, in Franck's words, 'an afterlife as … precedent'[42] and partly shape context for the evaluation of future humanitarian interventions.

Yet others turn to ethics to find a more coherent framework for humanitarian intervention or legal change. Such an approach may be found, *inter alia*, in the work

38 For dissenting voices, see: F.R. Tesón, 'The Kantian Theory of International Law', *Colombia Law Review* (1991), pp. 53-102; F.R. Tesón, *Humanitarian Intervention, An inquiry into law and morality* (New York: Transnational Publishers, 1997), p. 141, 142; W.M. Reisman, 'Unilateral Action and the Transformations of the World Constitutive Process: The Special Problem of Humanitarian Intervention', *European Journal of International Law* 11 (2000), 3-18.

39 See, for example, Chesterman (2001), at 230 and 227 respectively, who accepts the existence of contextual mitigating circumstances, but rejects desirability – or even the possibility – of developing *a priori* legal criteria for humanitarian intervention: '… all such criteria are doomed to redundancy. The very project assumes the possibility of an 'ideal' humanitarian intervention. That there has been no such ideal intervention is rarely taken into account. The impetus to develop some sort of normative regime is understandable but misplaced: the circumstances in which law may be violated are not themselves susceptible to legal regulation': and: 'certain acts are against the law, but … the decision of whether to condemn them is *outside* the law …'.

40 Franck, 'Interpretation and change in the law of humanitarian intervention', in Holzgreve and Keohane (2003), 204-231, at 205. See also Franck (2002), 135-192.

41 See Franck's discussion of the interventions in Bangladesh, Uganda, the Central African Republic, Liberia, Sierra Leone and Kosovo. Supra note 40.

42 Franck, in Holzgreve and Keohane (2003), at 207.

of Buchanan.[43] In case of a humanitarian intervention, Buchanan argues, the question is not simply whether the moral obligation to protect human rights trumps the legal obligation to abstain from the use of force. After all, states and scholars defending humanitarian intervention do not refer to values that are alien to international law. On the contrary: they rely on peremptory norms like the prohibition on genocide torture or grave violations of humanitarian law. The question, therefore, is not only whether a violation of international law (the use of force) is morally justified, but also whether the illegal use of force is required to prevent or stop violations of other core values of the international legal system. In this sense, Buchanan argues, the use of force might be 'lawful though illegal'.[44]

The Savage-Victim-Savior Imagery

The different justifications for humanitarian intervention discussed above all rely in some form on a humanitarian sensibility, combined with a sense of exceptionality and urgency. This sense and sensibility have been reinforced by the failure of the international community to effectively halt atrocities as took place in, among other places, Bosnia or Rwanda. Moreover, the sense of urgency and the sensibility of humanitarianism are often reinvoked by the way in which human rights violations are narrated. The narrative of human rights violations, as Mutua has argued, has a tendency to rely on 'a subtext that depicts an epochal contest pitting savages, on the one hand, against victims and saviors on the other'.[45] The first element of the savage-victim-savior metaphor invokes the image of acts of barbarism, carried out by 'an other' that lacks the discipline of human rights and civilization. The savage cannot exist without the second element: the victim. The victim is portrayed as a helpless and innocent individual or group, subjected to violations of their universal human rights. The victim, in its turn, is closely bound up with a third element: the need for help and a savior, who protects, civilizes and brings freedom. Needless to say that the savage-victim-savior metaphor nicely fits into the imagery of world order set out in the introduction – and thus, as we will see later on, affects the role of international law in international politics.

The way in which imageries of victimhood are related to the role of the savior is nicely captured in an article of Kennedy in which he analysed his identity as a human rights activist on a US delegation that visited Nicaraguan prisons in the 1980s.

---

43 A. Buchanan, 'From Nuremberg to Kosovo: The Morality of Illegal International Legal Reform', *Ethics* 111 (July 2001): 673-705; A. Buchanan, *Justice, Legitimacy and Self-Determination: Moral Foundations for International Law* (Oxford: Oxford University Press, 2003); A. Buchanan, 'Reforming the international law on humanitarian intervention', in Holzgreve and Keohane (2003), 130-173.

44 A. Buchanan, 'Reforming the international law on humanitarian intervention', in Holzgreve and Keohane (2003), 130-173, at 132.

45 M. Mutua, 'Savages, Victims and Saviors: The Metaphor of Human Rights', *Harvard International Law Journal*, Winter, 2001, 1 (accessible at: http://web.pdx.edu/~kinsella/ps448/mutua.html).

Kennedy argues that his identity depended on the images of victimhood that were invoked by the prisoners he met. When confronted with prisoners he could easily picture as passive victims of human rights abuses, Kennedy argues, he experienced a sense of purpose and the urge to act as savior. This sense of purpose and activism changed when he met with prisoners that pictured themselves as equals; as captured political activists, engaged in a greater struggle for human rights. Here, the sense of urgency and agency was replaced by solidarity:

> Ramon and Francisco seemed to carry themselves as temporarily defeated warriors in a greater political struggle, and that is how they seemed to view their own stories of capture, torture, and imprisonment. Imprisoned warriors like Ramon and Francisco seemed our equals; they needed no rescue. To them we were comrades, coparticipants in a political struggle. The connection we had felt when in their presence – achieved by contrast with our experiences at Punta Rieles – diminished my sense of purpose. Like Ana, Victor, the passive victim, awakens my indignation and motivates me to act. Suddenly, our meeting the next morning at the court might be more than a formal plea for pardon. We might be able to do something.[46]

In the context of humanitarian intervention, where states and international organizations use force in the name of humanity, the savage-victim-savior imagery takes a specific form. As Orford has set out,[47] narratives of humanitarian intervention often portray the international community as the bearer of progressive, universal values, that reflect a state of normalcy in international life. Violations of human rights are then viewed as a disruption of normalcy, carried out by locals who shock the 'consciousness of mankind' by brutalizing acts against powerless victims. Finally, (self-appointed) agents of the international community are portrayed as 'knights in white armour': determined, masculine agents that protect victims, calm international anxieties about powerlessness and restore and reaffirm normalcy.

The reconstruction of the savage-victim-savior metaphor is not meant to downplay the dilemmas posed by some large-scale violations of human rights and humanitarian law.[48] Neither should it be read as an *a priori* rejection of intervention

---

46 D. Kennedy, 'Spring Break', 63 *Texas Law Review* (1985), 1377. Kennedy's analysis is also taken up by A. Orford, 'Muscular Humanitarianism: Reading the Narratives of the New Interventionism', *European Journal of International Law* 10 (1999), 679-711. See also D. Kennedy, *The Dark Side of Virtue*: *Reassessing International Humanitarianism* (Princeton: Princeton University Press, 2004).

47 A. Orford, *Reading Humanitarian Intervention: Human Rights and the Use of Force in International Law* (Cambridge: Cambridge University Press, 2003).

48 The by-now almost classical formulation of one of the basic dilemmas was given by the UN Secretary-General in 1999: 'To those for whom the greatest threat to the future of international order is the use of force in the absence of a Security Council mandate, one might ask – not in the context of Kosovo – but in the context of Rwanda: If, in those dark days and hours leading up to the genocide, a coalition of states had been prepared to act in defence of the Tutsi population, but did not receive prompt Council authorization, should such a coalition have stood aside and allowed the horror to unfold? To those for whom the Kosovo

in all circumstances. Yet, such a reconstruction does highlight what often remains *unsaid* when the savage-victim-savior metaphor is used. The identification of the international community with progressive values and of those acting in its name as saviors, for example, makes it more difficult to examine the possible role of international actors in the emergence of a humanitarian crisis in the first place. Commentators have noted that: 'The representation of the intervention in Kosovo as the action of an international community interested in protecting human rights and humanitarian values serves to obscure the extent to which the international community has itself contributed to the humanitarian crisis that has emerged. In the former Yugoslavia as elsewhere, the project of economic restructuring and liberalization which remains central to the new world order contributed to creating the conditions in which such hatreds were inflamed.'[49]

The savage-victim-savior metaphor could also be easily used in justifications for the exercise of hegemonic power. An example of this can be found in the 2002 United States National Security Strategy.[50] One of the characteristic features of this Strategy is the justification of interventionism in terms of both humanitarianism and *Realpolitik*. The key concept linking these two is the concept of the rogue state. Not surprisingly, the National Security Strategy defines a rogue state as a state that rejects the universal values embodied as represented by the US (section V of the Strategy states that rogue states: 'reject basic human values and hate the United States and everything for which it stands'). However, for the purposes of this chapter it is more interesting to find that rogue states are predominantly defined as states that violate and reject some basic principles of contemporary international law: respect for human rights, respect for the sanctity of treaties (*pacta sunt servanda*), the prohibition of intervention and aggression, the non-proliferation of weapons of mass destruction and the obligation not to support terrorism in any form.[51]

---

action heralded a new era when states and groups of states can take military action outside the established mechanisms for enforcing international law, one might ask: Is there not a danger of such interventions undermining the imperfect, yet resilient, security system created after the Second World War, and of setting dangerous precedents for future interventions without a clear criterion to decide who might invoke these precedents and in what circumstances?'; Secretary-General's Annual Report to the General Assembly UN Press Release, 20 September 1999.

49 Orford (1999), 681/682. See also the more general critique that international law (and international lawyers) have the tendency to follow acute crises, to the detriment of more structural, less profiled, yet not less important problems such as world poverty. H. Charlesworth, 'International Law: A Discipline of Crisis', *Modern Law Review* 65 (2002), 450-462.

50 Available at: http://www.whitehouse.gov/nsc/nss.html.

51 Section V of the Strategy characterizes rogue states as follows: 'In the 1990s we witnessed the emergence of a small number of rogue states that, while different in important ways, share a number of attributes. These states:

> brutalize their own people and squander their national resources for the personal gain of the rulers;

Because rogue states are portrayed as rejecting basic human values and basic norms of international law, and because rogue states are presented as sponsors of global terrorism, the circle of their potential victims is virtually unlimited. If necessary, the fight against rogue states can thus be linked to a savage-victim-savior model writ large: an exceptional fight for normalcy by reasonable agents of humanity[52] against enemies of international law and civilization.

> display no regard for international law, threaten their neighbors, and callously violate international treaties to which they are party;
>
> are determined to acquire weapons of mass destruction, along with other advanced military technology, to be used as threats or offensively to achieve the aggressive designs of these regimes;
>
> sponsor terrorism around the globe; and
>
> reject basic human values and hate the United States and everything for which it stands.'

52 As section V reassures the possible victims and those who are worried about the exercise of US power: 'The reasons for our actions will be clear, the force measured, and the cause just.'

Chapter 3

Key Words in Chinese Law

Deborah Cao[1]

Introduction

The Chinese language is a major language system of the Tibetan-Mongolian language family, distinguished from the Indo-European language family. It is unique in its writing form consisting of scripts instead of alphabets and unique in its representation of the world seen through such a language. The Chinese language is part of the continuous Chinese cultural treasury and civilization, a constant and visible link between the past and the present, communicating and translating human experiences and wisdom. The Chinese characters are an art form as used in Chinese calligraphy and painting as well as a means of everyday communication. They are highly symbolic, visually and conceptually. They are extremely concrete as well as highly abstract. It is often said that a picture is worth a thousand words and in this case, the picture is the word, showing the paths to understand the word and the world it expresses. The Chinese language has always been a central part of Chinese culture, symbolic of Chinese cultural tradition and a carrier of its continuous civilization. By the same token, the Chinese language also occupies a central place in Chinese law, in particular for our understanding of this law.

The chapter examines the Chinese characters or words associated with law: *fa* (law), *xing* (punishment, criminal law), *lü* (statutes), and *quanli* (rights).[2] *Fa*, *xing* and *lü* were first used over 2,000 years ago when the Chinese conception of law and its dominant philosophical thoughts took shape. These Chinese characters are still used today, but they have undergone changes in modern and contemporary China. The study depicts and outlines the meanings of these words as used in classical Chinese texts and attempts a new interpretation of these linguistic signs from a semiotic perspective. It argues that the characters in Chinese are carriers and symbols of Chinese cultural beliefs and also represent powerful forces that create realities in modern Chinese society. The Chinese words are indexical, referential and evolutionary. Examining the images of the key Chinese legal concepts and tracing their evolutionary meanings can assist in our understanding of the developing conception and functioning of law in contemporary Chinese society. The layers of

---

1 I acknowledge the Griffith University Research Development Fund (2005) for its financial support.

2 The Chinese language consists of characters, not words. Despite the difference, for convenience, this article uses 'word' in most cases to describe the Chinese language.

meanings of these concepts can also reveal the knowledge as well as the image of law that they represent to the Chinese language user.

刑 *xíng*

In modern Chinese language, *xing* means 'criminal punishment', 'criminal law' and 'torture' or 'corporal punishment'. These meanings have ancient origins. *Xing* is believed to have been used in classical Chinese before the appearance of *fa* (law) and *lü* (code). It is believed that the character *xing* originated from early military practice: *xing shi yu bing* (*xing* started with the military, for punishing soldiers). Traces of corporal punishments have been found in archaeological finds of early Chinese human remains. Corporal punishment of soldiers in ancient China included decapitation, nose cutting, leg cutting and castration. This was before any written law was enacted. From these beginnings, in traditional Chinese usage *xing* first referred to decapitation. According to the authoritative classical Chinese dictionary, *Shuowen jiezi*, *xing jingye*, literally, '*xing* refers to the neck', that is, to decapitate.[3] Thus, *xing* was generally used to refer to 'corporal punishment' or 'punishment'. This meaning can be explained in the way the character was and is written. The modern form of the character comprises the ideograph for 'knife' (on the right) and balanced scale pans (on the left). The 'knife' radical symbolizes 'cutting' or 'using a knife'.

Another explanation is that the modern character *xing* is a variant of its original, archaic form which included *jing*, the radical meaning 'a well', instead of the present radical for 'scales'. The character for 'well' symbolizes nine plots of land farmed by eight families in ancient China. The ninth plot was farmed jointly to the benefit of the state. It was on this ninth plot that public functions (for example, executions) were held. Combined with the knife, this denotes punishment carried out by the state, usually decapitation. Thus, *xing* was used to refer to criminal or lawful punishments or punishments by the state. *Xing* later evolved to be a general term for laws that related to criminal punishment. Once written law came into existence, the meaning of *xing* was extended to include not only punishments but also any state prohibitions whose violation would result in punishments. In this usage, *xing* may be understood in the sense of penal law.[4]

---

3 *Shuowen jiezi (The Origin of Chinese Characters)* is the earliest and the most authoritative classical Chinese etymological dictionary. It is believed to have been written around 100AD by Xu Shen (*circa* 58AD- 147AD), a Han dynasty scholar. It uses the system of radicals to classify Chinese characters. Its main text contains 14 volumes, and lists 9,353 characters and a total of 133,441 entries. For discussion of the dictionary, see Burton Watson, *Early Chinese Literature* (New York/London: Columbia University Press, 1962/1971).

4 See Derk Bodde and Clarence Morris, *Law in Imperial China* (Philadelphia: University of Pennsylvania, 1973), p. 11. See also Liang Zhiping, 'Explicating "Law": A Comparative

One explanation for *xing* meaning 'criminal law' is offered in terms of its pronunciation. According to Schwartz, the graph is often used in ancient texts interchangeably with its homonym *xing* (form), suggesting that the two words are somehow closely associated in origin, so perhaps the punishments were thought of as means of re-forming men, and penal law as a kind of mould forcibly imposed from above to correct aberrant behaviour.[5] One example of the use of *xing* is found in the *Analects*:[6]

> The Master said, 'If the people be led by laws, and uniformity sought to be given them by punishments (*xing*), they will try to avoid the punishment, but have no sense of shame'. 'If they be led by virtue, and uniformity sought to be given them by the ruler of propriety, they will have the sense of shame, and moreover will become good'.[7]

An example of *xing* in classical Chinese is *xing bu* (Criminal Law Department). It refers to the legal or justice department in imperial China. This was changed to *fa bu* (Legal Department) in the early 1900s legal reform. Another example is *wu xing* (the five punishments) in traditional Chinese criminal law. The contents of *wu xing* varied in pre-imperial and imperial China. Originally they referred to the punishments of death, leg cutting, nose cutting, castration, and facial tattoo. From Tang to Qing dynasties, the five punishments stipulated in Article One of these codes were the punishments of beating with light or heavy bamboo, penal servitude, exile, and death.

In modern Chinese usage, the first and most common meaning of *xing* is criminal or criminal matters. For instance, *xingfa* means criminal law. The Criminal Law Code of China is named *Xingfa*. This meaning and usage is now dominant in the use of *xing*, but *xing* has also retained the earlier meaning of corporal punishment and torture. For instance, *yong xing* means 'to use corporal punishment or to torture'. Other examples of *xing* in the criminal law-related meanings include: *xingshi* (criminal matter), *xingshifan* (criminals), *xingshi susong* (criminal prosecution), *xingshi*

Perspective of Chinese and Western Legal Culture', *Journal of Chinese Law* 3/1(1989): 55-92, and Liang Zhiping, *Fayi yu renqing* (*Meaning of Law and Sentiment of People*) (Beijing: Zhongguo fazhi chubanshe, 2004).

5 Benjamin Schwartz, *The World of Thought in Ancient China* (Cambridge, London: The Belknap Press of Harvard University, 1985), p. 322.

6 *Lun Yu* or *The Analects of Confucius* (Confucius, *circa* 551BC-479BC) consists of 20 chapters, comprising a collection of sayings by Confucius including brief statements, short dialogues and anecdotes. It was believed to have been compiled by two successive generations of Confucius' disciples 75 years after his death, perhaps around 400BC. The original Chinese text and the English translation of the *Analects* quoted in this book are taken from the *Confucian Analects*, but with modifications including the use of *pinyin*. *Confucian Analects* was translated by James Legge, published in 1893 by Oxford University Press, and was reprinted by Hong Kong University Press: James Legge, *The Chinese Classics, Volume I: Confucian Analects, the Great Learning and the Doctrine of the Mean* (Hong Kong: Hong Kong University Press, 1970).

7 Legge, *The Chinese Classics*, pp. 263-264.

zeren (criminal responsibility), *xingchang* (execution ground), *xingfa* (penalty for criminal offence), *xingjing* (police dealing with criminal matters), *xingqi* (term of imprisonment), *xingxun* (interrogation by torture). It is noted that *xing* has lost its traditional usage as a generic term for law in modern Chinese, which is now *fa*, to be discussed next.

法 *fa*

In modern Chinese, *fa* is the generic word for 'the law', 'law' and 'laws'. The exact date when *fa* was first used is not known. Originally, in classical Chinese, according to *Shuowen jiezi*, *fa* had an ancient writing form:

灋

The character consists of a 'water' radical on the left, and this gives the word the meaning of 'being leveled or even as the surface of water'. On the bottom right of the word is the symbol *qu* (to go), which is said to symbolize that, if someone is not upright, then make the person go, that is, be removed. The ancient character *fa* also contains the symbol *zhi* on the top right. According to legend, *zhi* or *xiezhi* was a one-horned mythical beast, believed to be able to cure crooked things, giving rise to the meaning of making something or someone 'straight'. According to Bodde and Morris, this idea of a wild animal being a referee was reflected in the costume later worn by magistrates in China.[8] From Han dynasty (206BC-220AD) to the end of the imperial dynasty in the early twentieth century, Chinese legal officials wore the crests of *xiezhi* on their robes and hats, a practice that signified the function of expelling the crafty and the obsequious.[9] The modern character *fa* (see above) is a simplified version of its ancient form in which the symbol for *zhi* has been deleted on the top right, but it is unclear exactly when this simplified character was first used. Some Chinese scholars rely on *Shuowen jiezi*'s explanation to hold that etymologically the Chinese character *fa* contains both the meanings of fairness and justice, resembling the ancient meaning of law in other languages. However, Liang Zhiping has argued that this theory is wrong. Liang believes, citing the works of another scholar, Cai Shusheng, that the meaning of 'being leveled as even as water' in *Shuowen jiezi* was added by others in later generations and was unreliable. Cai had argued instead that the meaning of water is not symbolic but purely functional. It refers to placing a criminal on the water to drift away with the current – what is now

8 See Bodde and Morris, *Law in Imperial China*.

9 See Bodde and Morris, *Law in Imperial China*. See also Liang, 'Explicating "Law"'.

known as banishment.[10] In ancient China, this was a very harsh punishment, so one aspect of *fa* is to prohibit and another is to command based on the pronunciation of the ancient character.[11] Liang also pointed out that the word for the abstract sense of law in some Western languages, such as *il diritto* in Italian, *le droit* in French, *recht* in German, and *Jus* in Latin, contains the meaning of rights, uprightness and justice. This is in sharp contrast to the Chinese word *fa* where such meaning is not present.

For example, of the actual use and explanation of *fa* in ancient China, Han Fei, the well-known Legalist in pre-imperial China, said:[12]

> Though a skilled carpenter is capable of judging a straight line with his eye alone, he will always take his measurements with a rule; though a man of superior wisdom is capable of handling affairs by native wit alone, he will always look to the laws (*fa*) of the former kings for guidance. Stretch the plumb line, and crooked wood can be planed straight; apply the level, and bumps and hollows can be shaved away; balance the scales, and heavy and light can be adjusted; get out the measuring jars, and discrepancies of quantity can be corrected. In the same way one should use laws (*fa*) to govern the state (*yi fa zhi guo*) disposing of all matters on their basis alone.[13]

In short, *fa* is a very significant word in Chinese, in particular in modern China.

律 *lǜ*

In classical Chinese, the character *lü*, according to *Shuowen jiezi*, means *junbu*, a tool for adjusting a musical instrument. *Lü* carries the meaning of rhythm, standards or rules, some common pattern for people to follow or behaviour to be regulated. The original music-related meaning of *lü* is still used today in modern Chinese, for example, *xuanlü* (melody). *Lü* is a technical designation for the individual pitch-pipes, twelve in number and of graduated lengths, which were the basis for the Chinese twelve-tone scale.

The character *lü* appears rarely in a legal sense in the earliest Chinese texts. It was believed that it was during Shang Yang's law reform during the Warring States period (475BC-221BC) that *lü* started to be used frequently, when Shang Yang changed *fa* to *lü* in both linguistic usage and actual law. Since then and throughout imperial Chinese

10 Liang, 'Explicating "Law"'.

11 Liang, 'Explicating "Law"'.

12 Han Fei (*circa* 280BC-233BC), or Han Feizi, was a student of a Confucianist, Xun Zi (*circa* 313BC-238BC). Han Fei was a prince in the State of Han during the Warring States period. His works are mainly found in *Han Feizi*, a collection of essays. An English translation of selected passages of *Han Feizi* is found in *Han Feizi: Basic Writings*, translated by Burton Watson (New York: Columbia University Press, 2003).

13 Watson, *Han Feizi: Basic Writings*, p. 28.

history, *lü* was the technical designation for the major articles into which the imperial code was divided. As such *lü* may be translated into 'statute'. It also referred to the entire body of such statutes as a collective entity, in which case it may be rendered as 'code'. As Shang Yang reformed the legal and governmental system during the Qin State, the character *lü* became very important in the law codes of imperial times (221BC onwards to 1911). All the legal codes in the subsequent dynasties except the Song Code (*Xingtong*) and the Yuan Code (*Dianzhang*) were named *lü*, for example, *Qin Lü* (Qin Code), *Tang Lü* (Tang Code), *Daqing Lü* (The Great Qing Code).[14] The most important dynastic code was the *Tang Lü* (the Tang Code).[15] It was first enacted in 653AD and achieved its final form in 737AD. It was the oldest surviving Chinese code and was based largely on the now lost Sui Code of 581-583AD.

Due to the prominence of *lü* as the fundamental components of imperial Chinese law, in the study and interpretation of law, there was a branch called *lüxue* (study of statutes or legal codes). It essentially involved annotating and interpreting the imperial codes, usually carried out by classical scholars who wrote explanations as to the meanings of the statutory texts. As the successive imperial codes were all modeled after the Tang Code, the annotations together with the texts and amended texts became law in later codes. This has led to the claim that there was no theoretical or systematic study of law or jurisprudence in imperial China but only study of codes. In modern China, *lüxue* as a component of law or legal studies no longer exists, and the word is no longer used in the modern linguistic context either.

權利 *quánlì*

In the classical Chinese language and traditional Chinese law, there is no word or concept for the notion of 'rights'. The idea of rights was introduced to China from the West around the mid-nineteenth century with the introduction and translation of writings of Western social and political science. Rights, together with other ideas such as democracy, freedom and constitution, were brought to China from the West at a time of great social, political and cultural turmoil and transformation. W.A.P. Martin (1817-1916) was credited with being the person who created the word *quanli* for 'rights'. Martin first used the word in 1864 in *Wanguo gongfa*, the Chinese translation of Wheaton's *Elements of International Law*.[16]

---

14 English translation of *Da Qing Lü* is found in W. C. Jones, *The Great Qing Code* (Oxford: Oxford University Press, 1994).

15 The English translation is found in *The T'ang Code*, translated with an introduction by Wallace Johnson (Princeton: Princeton University Press, 1979).

16 Henry Wheaton, edited by A.C. Boyd, *Elements of International Law* (London: Stevens and Sons, 1836/1878). For discussion of Martin's translation of 'rights', see Stephen Angle,

The Chinese phrase *quanli*, prior to Martin's usage, had been used since ancient times but meant something totally different. *Quan* and *li* were mostly used separately, with *quan* meaning 'power' and *li* meaning 'profit', 'interest' or 'benefit'. *Quan* and *li* were only rarely used as a compound. Such use was occasionally found in philosophical texts. For instance, in a classical work from pre-imperial China, *Xunzi*, it says:

> For this reason, power and benefit (*quanli*) cannot subvert the exemplary person; neither can the common and ordinary people sway him. Nor can the world shake him.[17]

The various historical studies in recent years of Martin's works did not document or identify the sources or inspirations for his coinage of the term.[18] *Quanli* has been used as a semantic equivalent to 'rights' since.

When *quanli* was first used in this new legal sense of rights, Martin described how it was coined this way:[19]

> [International] law is a separate field of study and thus a specific vocabulary should be devised for this purpose. Therefore, when there are occasional passages in the original text which are difficult to render comprehensively in Chinese, then the translation may sometimes seem strained. Take for instance the character *quan*. In this book it carries not only the meaning of someone being in power but also the meaning of the share ordinary people ought to obtain (rights). Sometimes a character *li* is added to this meaning, such as in the passage 'the rights enjoyed by the common people' etc. Passages and terms like this

---

Human Rights and Chinese Thought: A Cross-Cultural Inquiry (Oxford: Oxford University Press, 2002); Lydia H. Liu (ed.), *Tokens of Exchange: the Problem of Translation in Global Circulations* (Durham and London: Duke University Press, 1999). See also Wang Gungwu, 'Power, Rights, and Duties in Chinese History', in Wang Gungwu, *The Chineseness of China: Selected Essays* (Hong Kong: Oxford University Press, 1991), pp.165-186. Svarverud believes that 'rights' was first translated into *quan* in *Haiguo tuzhi* in 1852: Rune Svarverud, 'The Notions of "Power" and "Rights" in Chinese Political Discourse', in Michael Lackner, Iwo Amelung and Joachim Kurtz (eds), *New Terms for New Ideas: Western Knowledge and Lexical Change in Late Imperial China* (Leiden: Brill, 2001), pp. 125-146.

17 From *Xunzi*. The characters *quan* and *li*, separately, are used extensively in *Xunzi*, to mean 'power' and 'to weigh' for *quan* and 'profit' and 'benefit' for *li*. *Quan* and *li* are also commonly found in other Chinese classics.

18 For discussions of Martin's translation, see also Angle, *Human Rights and Chinese Thought*; and Lydia H. Liu (ed.), *Tokens of Exchange: the Problem of Translation in Global Circulations*.

19 Liu, *supra* n.17, argues that *quanli* (rights) like *zhuquan* (sovereignty) and many other nineteenth century coinages no longer strike us as strange or un-Chinese, because they have been naturalized in the history of Chinese (and Japanese) political discourse and through 'repeated usage' for the past 135 years. Liu calls such neologism 'hypothetical equivalence' between English and Chinese. This is not true as much more than 'repeated usage' is involved, and such equivalences are far from being mere 'hypothetical'.

> may seem awkward at first but when one has encountered them several times one comes to realize that there is no other way than to use such an expression.[20]

Not only *quanli* seemed awkward linguistically at first; it has since been awkwardly ambiguous in Chinese culture and law, caused by both linguistic and cultural factors. The following discussion will only limit itself to the linguistic dimension.[21]

Quanli in Chinese is ambiguous linguistically and conceptually in several levels. Firstly, *quanli* has a homophone *quanli*, but this *quanli* means 'power' or 'authority'. The two *quanli* are indistinguishable in speaking in modern Chinese,[22] except by context. In writing, they are distinguishable by the second character *li.* The two *li* are written differently and carry different meanings. *Li* in *quanli* (power) means 'strength' and 'power' while *li* in *quanli* (rights) means 'benefits' or 'interests' or 'wealth'. In the actual use of these two words, there is often confusion even among educated Chinese. *Quanli* (rights) virtually disappeared from the Chinese vocabulary in Mao's China before its revival in recent years while *quanli* (power) has dominated in Chinese political discourse. The unfamiliarity with *quanli* (rights) among Chinese language users is the result of lack of practice, linguistic and mental, not helped by the linguistic similarity and ambiguity.

Furthermore, *quan* which has the basic and essential meaning of 'power' is a short form for both *quanli* (power) and *quanli* (rights). This linguistic ambiguity may indicate a perspective ambivalence in the Chinese thinking as the two terms may not be conceptually very different to the Chinese, and not as mutually incompatible as they are generally understood in Western languages.[23]

The conceptual ambiguity of *quanli*, first of all, arises from the meaning of *quan.* In classical Chinese, *quan* refers to a type of weight measuring instrument, thus, the phrase *quanheng* meaning 'to weigh', 'to deliberate' and 'to balance' in a political context. But the more common and the dominant meaning of *quan* is 'power', 'authority', and 'privilege', most often 'political power' to be exact.

In the more recent past and present China, the association and meaning of power and authority in *quan* remains. Firstly, *quan*, in the modern Chinese language, first and foremost, still means 'power' and 'authority'. For instance, in the Chinese

---

20 W.A.P. Martin et al., *Gongfa bianlan (A Practical Introduction to International Law)*, trans. (Beijing, 1878). The English translation is taken from Svarverud, 'The Notions of "Power" and "Rights" in Chinese Political Discourse', p. 134.

21 For discussions of the cultural impediments, for example, the traditional emphasis on duties and collectivism, to the meaning and practice of *quanli* (rights) in modern China, see D. Cao, *Chinese Law: A Language Perspective* (Aldershot: Ashgate, 2004).

22 The two *li* were distinguishable in ancient Chinese pronunciation: Edwin G. Pulleyblank, *Lexicon of Reconstructed Pronunciation in Early Middle Chinese, Late Middle Chinese, and Early Mandarin* (Vancouver: University of British Columbia Press, 1991), pp.188-189, cited in Svarverud, 'The Notions of "Power" and "Rights" in Chinese Political Discourse', p. 126.

23 See Svarverud, 'The Notions of "Power" and "Rights" in Chinese Political Discourse', p. 126.

Constitution, it states that 'All the power (*quanli*) of the People's Republic of China belongs to the people' (Art. 2), and 'The National People's Congress of the People's Republic of China is the highest organ of state power' (*quanli*) (Art. 57). Apart from *quanli* (power), other phrasal combinations with *quan* include *quanwei* (authority, authoritative), *quanxian* (limit of power, competence or jurisdiction), *quanneng* (power and function), *quanshu* (power games), *dangquan* or *zhangquan* (in power), *yuequan* (overstep one's authority), *shouquan* (to be authorized), *baquan* (hegemony), *quanyu* (lust for power), *quanzha* (political trickery, craftiness or political expediency), *quanmou* (political tactics, trickery). Other phrases with *quan* are *zhengquan* (political power), *tequan* (special power and privilege), *jiquan* (absolute power, dictatorial or totalitarian rule), *zhengduo quanli* (fight for power and privilege), *xingzheng quan* (executive power), *sifa quan* (judicial power), *lifa quan* (legislative power), *zhuquan* (sovereignty or sovereign power). All these phrases are in common use in modern Chinese political discourse, with *quan* a high-frequency word, widely used with strong political connotations associated with political power and authority. All the phrases in Chinese beginning with *quan*, with the sole exception of *quanli* (rights), carry the meaning of 'power'.

As for the sense of 'rights', *quanli* (rights) is the only Chinese word associated with such a meaning, with no synonyms. It is the only word that begins with *quan* but does not mean 'power'. *Quan* in this 'rights' sense is often used after other words to donate various rights, for instance, *gongmin quan* (citizen's rights), *xuanju quan* (the right to vote), *nannü pingdeng quan* (the right of gender equality), *shou jiaoyu quan* (the right to receive education). There are also *caichan quan* (property rights), *minquan* (civil rights), *fading quan* (legal rights) and others. In recent years, many more new words have appeared associated with rights, for instance, *xiaoxiang quan* (the right to use one's image), *shengyu quan* (the right to reproduction between husband and wife), *yinsi quan* (the right to privacy) and *chenmo quan* (the right to remain silent) which never existed before in China, and *shengcun quan* (right to survival or to life) now often used by the Chinese government.

Another usage of *quan* is *you quan*, 'to have the right or power to do something'. It is ambiguous, distinguishable only by context. For instance, *wo you quan jueding* can be either 'I have the power to decide' or 'I have the right to decide', depending on the context. Thus, *quan* is ambiguous when used referring to rights due to *quan*'s overwhelming connotation of power and authority.

In short, *quanli* (rights), since its introduction into the Chinese language and culture, has been fraught with complications. Its linguistic and conceptual ambiguity and multiplicity may reveal the ambivalence towards the notion and practice of rights in modern Chinese society. It may be symbolic of the struggle of the rights notion in contemporary society as a whole.

The Growth of Meaning and Culture

There are a number of implications arising from the foregoing description of the law-related Chinese words, in particular in terms of linguistic change and cultural evolution in relation to the conception of law, the changing meanings in Chinese society and culture, and in terms of legal studies in China.

Firstly, the Chinese language is unique in its writing form and linguistic structure and in the way it represents the world. It is part of the Chinese cultural treasury and civilization, a constant and visible link between the past and the present, communicating and translating meanings and experiences across time and space. The Chinese written language has always been central to Chinese culture, symbolizing and transmitting its civilization. By the same token, the Chinese language occupies a central place in Chinese law, particularly our understanding of this law. Law, whether in Chinese or other languages, depends on language for its representation.[24] Law is coded in language. It communicates and operates in and through language, and Chinese law operates in and through the Chinese language.

If we see language as a semiotic resource, more than just a means of communication, most of the ancient Chinese words and images live on. In linguistic continuity, many Chinese characters are still written in much the same way and retain the same essential meanings. None of these words, *xing*, *fa*, and *lü*, have disappeared or are dormant in modern Chinese. In fact, they are among the most frequently used words in today's Chinese vocabulary. Language has played a vital role in maintaining continuity and transmitting Chinese cultural values. These words, along with the ideas they represent, are passed on in formal eduction, through political and legal hierarchies and social interaction in cultural transmission.[25] The words, ideas and practices are passed on and inherited, and manifest themselves as part of the Chinese cultural entities. The Chinese written language has an unbroken history of around 3,000 years, and has been the single continuous linguistic carrier of Chinese culture for all this time. As pointed out, the Chinese written language has contributed significantly to the spread, cohesion and homogeneity of Chinese civilization, giving China a cultural continuity in time and unity in space.[26]

In terms of the Chinese conception of law, one cultural legacy is that the Chinese people throughout history, including today, often associate law with criminal sanction and punishment; thus, law is synonymous with criminal law. In traditional Chinese law, the imperial codes mostly consisted of criminal law. Even civil matters such as

---

24 See Brenda Danet, 'Language in the Legal Process', *Law and Society Review*, 14/3(1980): 447-563, and F. Schauer (ed.), *Law and Language* (Aldershot: Dartmouth, 1993), p. xii.

25 For different modes of cultural transmission, see L.L. Cavalli-Sforza and M.W. Feldman, *Cultural Transmission and Evolution: A Quantitative Approach* (Princeton: Princeton University Press, 1981).

26 Derk Bodde, *Chinese Thought, Society, and Science: The Intellectual and Social Background of Science and Technology in Pre-modern China* (Honolulu: University of Hawaii Press, 1991), p. 28.

marriage and inheritance were treated as part of criminal law. Some scholars in recent years question such a description, arguing that traditional Chinese law consisted of more than just criminal law. It is true that traditional Chinese law did contain civil law matters, but overwhelmingly, traditional Chinese law was criminal dominated and people's understanding and association with law were mostly criminal law-related.[27] Law, for most Chinese, until very recently, is first and foremost criminal law. Take for instance, from 1949 to 1976, the laws enacted in China were very limited in dealing with non-criminal matters. The major legislation during this period includes the Marriage Law (1950), the Trade Union Law (1950), the Land Reform Law (1952), the Constitution (1954), the Military Service Law (1955), and tax laws. But the laws, regulations and rules that were widely promoted and widely known were criminal law-related, such as the Rules on the Punishment of Counter-revolutionaries (1951), the Rules on the Punishment Concerning Corruption (1952), the Rules on Arrest and Detention (1954), The Organization Rules on the Public Security Bureau and Offices (1954), Rules on People's Police (1957), Rules on the Management and Punishment Concerning Law and Order (1957). One may say that the emphasis on and focus of criminal law in actual law in China during these three decades have reinforced the previous association law people had with criminal law in traditional China. The situation has changed in recent years due to the expansion of law and the increasing codification of law, in a wave of 'juridification', that increasingly pervades all aspects of Chinese life and society, in particular civil and economic areas. The modern criminal law association of *fa* (law) is a direct result of the meaning and long-standing practice of law in traditional China.

Similarly, due to the dominance of *lü* (codes) in traditional Chinese law, there has been a lack of philosophical study of law in China, in the past and today. Jurisprudence hardly existed in China, by which I mean the thinking and inquiry that ask the most fundamental questions about law, about the nature of law, about the authority and legitimacy of law, and the epistemological and ontological probing into law. *Faxue*, *falixue* or *fazhexue* (jurisprudence or legal philosophy) is not just a new word in Chinese, but also a new concept and new intellectual activity.[28] What imperial China had instead was *lüxue* (the study of imperial codes), the annotation of and commentary on the successive imperial codes, and there were scattered commentaries on some well-known cases. As Liang correctly pointed out, *lüxue* is not science or scientific study of law, and it is not the same as *faxue* (jurisprudence or legal science).[29] Self-reflexive questioning in the thinking of the nature and essence of law has been recessive in Chinese thought.

Secondly, language and culture are subject to continuity as well as to change. Chinese culture and language have been evolving and changing rapidly since the

---

27 See Liang (2004), *Fayi yu renqing* (*Meaning of Law and Sentiment of People*).

28 As studies have shown, the phrase *faxue* (jurisprudence) was coined by the Japanese and then borrowed into the Chinese language; see Liang, *Fayi yu renqing* (*Meaning of Law and Sentiment of People*).

29 Liang, *Fayi yu renqing* (*Meaning of Law and Sentiment of People*), p. 262.

mid-1800s, especially in the past two decades. The first cultural evolution took place in the late 1800s and the early 1900s. In that instance, profound changes took place in terms of Chinese culture and law with the introduction of Western law and legal thought along with a whole new legal vocabulary, to replace its ancient imperial law and the associated legal vocabulary in classical Chinese. This new vocabulary, sometimes expressed in newly coined words and sometimes in recycled Chinese classical words, was used to express a new meaning of an entirely foreign world of law. More importantly, the translation and introduction of Western laws and the creation of a new legal vocabulary were followed by the transplant of Western laws that have formed the basis of modern Chinese law. Such a process and practice continues today. The example here is the coinage of *quanli*, introducing a totally new concept of rights to the Chinese culture. However, the old meaning of *quanli* (power) did not just disappear overnight. Instead, *quanli* (rights) may have acquired a Chinese shade of meaning.

Like *quanli* (rights), many other introduced legal terms of foreign origin, such as *xianfa* (constitution), *faren* (legal person), *faguan* (judge), *fayuan* (court), and a host of others, have unfolded a life of their own in the Chinese legal context. The Chinese legal language and its terminology, far from serving as simple equivalents of imported ways of understanding, have often acquired new meanings that 'creatively alter, extend or even undermine established European conceptions'.[30] In our understanding of Chinese law, we may need to see and learn about 'the multilayered process of translation and appropriation from which these terms have emerged, not merely as deviations from the original Western meanings'.[31] As George Steiner observed, no language and no traditional symbolic set of cultural ensemble imports without risk of being transformed.[32] Meanings are grounded in the histories as well as in the external referents of language and expression of linguistic symbols. Language is a means of transmitting experience and beliefs from one language user to another, from one language community to another.

In terms of language and understanding, how the Chinese people understand, conceptualize and use the new vocabulary and how the new language relates to the world around them is a different proposition, which is connected with the indexical and referential nature of language if we refer to Peirce's theory. To put it in another way, in Habermas's language, when we use language to say something, we refer to something in the objective world, 'the' external world, and also to something in the shared social world, 'our' world, and in our own internal world, 'my' world.[33] These are the constitutive horizons of people's discourse. People's understanding, not just Chinese,

30 Joachim Kurtz, 'Coming to Terms with Logic: The Naturalization of an Occidental Notion in China', in Lackner, Amelung and Kurtz (eds), *New Terms for New Ideas*, p.10.

31 Kurtz, 'Coming to Terms with Logic', p. 10.

32 George Steiner, *After Babel: Aspects of Language and Translation* (Oxford: Oxford University Press, 1998), p. 415.

33 Jürgen Habermas, *On the Pragmatics of Communication* (Cambridge: MIT Press, 1998), pp. 89-92. See also Jürgen Habermas, 'Reconstruction and Interpretation in the Social Science', in Jürgen Habermas, *Moral Consciousness and Communicative Action* (Cambridge: MIT Press, 1996), pp. 21-42.

but everyone's, is not reconstruction but mediation or 'translation' of meaning. We all have our existing notions and pre-judgements which are indispensable in the act of understanding.[34] Such familiar horizons of one's world are the positive enabling conditions and the bases of our openness to the world in the transmission of meaning.[35] We understand, from within ourselves, the view of the world that is presented in another language.[36]

For our purpose, if we look at the understanding of Chinese law, as has been pointed out, we begin the study of Chinese law by projecting our preconceptions, which we derive from our own historical givens, either Chinese or non-Chinese.[37] Those preconceptions constitute only a provisional point of departure which we revise over time in order to project it again and again back on the world, with reasons each time, depending on the extent to which our prejudices in fact describe the world.[38] Furthermore, in the possible fusion of horizons in understanding, when we approach Chinese law, we also question our present, more familiar categories of law and of the world. Our interpretation of Chinese law and the interpretation of what constitutes law implicates us inevitably in the process of interpreting ourselves as well.[39] The understanding of Chinese law of the past undergoes a similar process, for Chinese and non-Chinese. Likewise, when Western law was first translated into Chinese, the Chinese interpreted the vastly different law written in both an alien and familiar language in translation. They interpreted it in their own ways, by projecting their existing familiar horizons tempered by the Chinese language and cultural traditions. In their understanding, one may say that a fusion of horizons, past and present, Chinese and non-Chinese, mediated in the transmission of meaning, creating new interpretive horizons. Despite the seemingly insurmountable conceptual and linguistic gulf, alleged and real, between the Chinese and Western laws and languages, the Chinese interpreters of the late 1800s and early 1900s, collectively and individually, interpreted and absorbed an otherwise unfamiliar law in translated Chinese. Such understanding could not possibly have been identical to an understanding from a Western perspective in a civil law or common law context, now or then, either as an individual or a culture as a whole. No exact equivalence or identity of understanding could be expected or was necessary. Meanings and interpretations are context-dependent and are necessarily diverse. In modern Chinese law, new knowledge and new realities were brought into existence through language.

Thus, it is only natural that the Chinese may understand the same notions or words in both similar and dissimilar ways. After the new legal vocabulary or new

34 Hans-Georg Gadamer, *Truth and Method* (New York: The Seabury Press, 1975), p. 240.

35 David E. Linge, 'Editor's Introduction', in Hans-Georg Gadamer, *Philosophical Hermeneutics* (Berkeley: University of California Press, 1976), p. xiv.

36 Gadamer, *Truth and Method*, p. 406.

37 Teemu Ruskola, 'Legal Orientalism', *Michigan Law Review*, 101/1(2002): 179-234, p. 232.

38 Ruskola, 'Legal Orientalism', p. 233.

39 Ibid.

legal language was created in modern Chinese, there is a more complex ongoing issue of cross-cultural understanding, communication, transfer and transmutation that cannot be mechanically superimposed. This involves interlingual translation – transferring Western legal language into Chinese, creating a new vocabulary. It also entails intralingual translation – interpreting by the Chinese linguistic community against the Chinese cultural and social background in understanding, conceptualizing and acting on this new language and law within its cultural and legal tradition. There is a parallel relationship between cultural and linguistic changes, and there may be convergence as well as dislocation. *Quanli* (rights) is a good example of a simple but key word that tells a complex story, revealing much about Chinese culture and society.

Lastly, the Chinese language and the formation of Chinese characters as illustrated by *xing*, *fa*, *lü* and *quanli*, are a good example of the Peircean sign in the iconic, indexical and symbolic representation and development. According to Peirce, there are three kinds of signs: firstly, there are *likenesses* or *icons* which serve to convey ideas of the things they represent simply by imitating them; secondly, there are *indications* or *indices*, which show something about things on account of their being physically connected with them; and thirdly, there are *symbols* or general *signs* which have become associated with their meanings by usage.[40] Such are most words and phrases, speeches, books and libraries.[41] In Peirce's description, words are symbols, 'applicable to whatever may be found to realize the idea connected with the word'.[42] Words do not in themselves identify those things. For instance, as Peirce described, the words such as 'bird', 'marriage', or 'to give', do not show us a 'bird', or enact before our eyes a 'giving' or a 'marriage', but 'suppose that we are able to imagine those things, and have associated the word with them'.[43] Furthermore and importantly, according to Peirce, there is no dynamic connection between the likeness and the object a word represents; 'it simply happens that its qualities resemble those of that object, and excite analogous sensation in the mind for which it is a likeness'.[44] In contrast, the index is 'physically connected with its object', but, according to Peirce, 'the interpreting mind has nothing to do with this connection' after it is established. Moreover, the symbol is 'connected with its object by virtue of the idea of the symbol-using mind, without which no such connection would exist'.[45] Furthermore, a symbol denotes a kind of thing, but cannot indicate any particular thing, and words as symbols 'live in the minds of those who use it'.[46] We think and reason in signs. Further to the nature of symbols, Peirce stated:

40 Charles Sanders Peirce, http://www.inpui.edu/~peirce/web/ep/ep2/ep2book/ch02/ch02.htm, p. 2.

41 Ibid.

42 Ibid, p. 5.

43 Ibid, p. 5.

44 Ibid, p. 5.

45 Ibid, p. 5.

46 Ibid, p. 5.

> Symbols grow. They come into being by development out of other signs, particularly for likenesses or from mixed signs partaking of the nature of likeness and symbols. … These mental signs are of mixed nature; the symbol-parts of them are called concepts. If a man makes a new symbol, it is by thoughts involving concepts. So it is only out of symbols that a new symbol can grow. *Omne symbolum de symbolo.* A symbol, once in being, spreads among the peoples. In use and in experience, its meaning grows. Such words as *force*, *law*, *wealth*, and *marriage*, bear for us very different meanings from those they bore to our barbarous ancestors.[47] (Italics in the original.)

If we think of the Chinese language in terms of Peirce's insight, a number of observations can be made.

Firstly, the Chinese written language undergoes the evolutionary process as other languages do. However, as Chinese is a pictographic language, one may say that the iconic, indexical and symbolic dimensions of linguistic evolutionary process as described by Peirce are readily seen in the Chinese language today. In particularly, the likenesses between the word and object in some of the basic Chinese characters have survived in or despite the evolutionary process. The directly imitative characters in Chinese where the words closely resemble the objects have come to stand for sounds, word roots, words, and ideas.[48] Chinese words or characters are symbols, but they have retained some of the early iconic traces of linguistic evolution. We can see this in the case of *xing* and *fa* illustrated above. The 'knife' in *xing* and the 'water' in *fa* are still vividly present before the language user's eyes. This is not to say that whenever a Chinese person uses these words, he or she immediately casts his or her mind back to two or three thousand years ago, seeing water running down or a brandishing knife in execution. However, today, when Chinese write these words, or when Chinese children learn to read and write, this is still the way in which the characters are described: *fa* starts with a water radical (literally, the water radical is called 'three drops of water' radical because the radical consists of two dots and a stroke), and *xing* has a knife radical on the right, and so forth. It is naïve to think that the layers of meanings and connotations these words have stored over the years have all disappeared given the vast changes between the early days of Chinese civilization and today.

We may use some of the examples Peirce used for further illustration. The word 'bird', in Chinese, still physically resembles the shape of a bird, with a stroke

47 Ibid, p. 6.

48 In the second century BC, Chinese lexicographers developed a classification system for Chinese characters in which the Chinese language was divided into six categories concerning the relation between form and meaning and between one graph and another, including pictogram (a character that is intended to resemble metonymically the shape of an object), ideogram (a word representing an idea or concept or quality that usually does not have a referent or an existence in itself), phonogram (the use of one graph as a morphographeme of another new graph to indicate the sound of the latter) and hypergram (a graph is used to superimpose on an existing graph, or a graph is loaned from an anterior graph). See Han-Liang Chang, 'Chinese Ideograms', *Encyclopedia of Semiotics*, Paul Bouissac (ed.), (Oxford: Oxford University Press, 1998), pp. 114-116.

resembling the crest and another the eye of a bird. There are many other basic Chinese characters such as *ri* (sun), *yue* (moon), *shan* (mountain/hill) that are pictographic. This is not limited to object nouns, but extends to abstract ideas. For another example from Peirce, 'wealth', in English, means what it means by convention because we assign such meaning to it. However, in Chinese, the character for wealth, *fu*, consists of three parts: a top radical depicting the roof of a house; under the roof, a mouth radical representing a person; under the person is the character for land. Even by today's standard, a person with a house and land is still considered quite wealthy, in China and elsewhere. For still another example of a word for an idea used in Peirce, 'marriage', or more precisely 'to marry', in Chinese has two equivalent words, *qü* (for a man to marry a woman), and *jia* (for a woman to marry a man). *Qü* is formed by the character *qü* (to get, to fetch), and *nü* (woman), that is, for a man to marry a woman, he simply goes and fetches a woman. But for a woman to get married, *jia* is formed by the character *jia* (home, family) and *nü* (woman), that is, a woman finally finds a home when she gets married. The character *jia* (home) consists of a roof and radical resembling the shape of a pig in the sense that a home is where there is a house and a pig (as food). The description of similar Chinese characters and their formation can go on and on. The Chinese language is not just a writing system but also an art form. Chinese calligraphy is known for both its symbolic abstractness and concreteness.

Thus, one may say that Chinese writing fully displays 'the whole range of semiological possibilities of writing'.[49] In Chinese, the physical likenesses and associations of meanings that motivated the original formation of the language are still present and current. But obviously, some such direct imitations get integrated or lost in the long historical evolution of the language. For most words in Chinese today, we assign and associate their meanings through convention or habits, as in the case of *quanli*, not through close physical likenesses. The original Chinese meaning *of quanli* is quite different from the new and introduced Western meaning of rights. It has evolved and changed its meanings over the years. So have *fa*, *xing* and *lü*. As Peirce stated, we as individuals, we as humanity, have some measure of control over our intellectual habits, and we have choice.[50] We can deliberately change our intellectual habits and change our minds and change how we think of a word as a sign. As Peirce said, symbols or words grow. So can knowledge and a culture, and in our case, the knowledge and culture regarding law in Chinese society.

49 Nina Catach, cited in Han-Liang Chang, 'Chinese Ideograms', p. 113.

50 Peirce, http://www.inpui.edu/~peirce/web/ep/ep2/ep2book/ch02/ch02.htm.

Chapter 4

Visual Semiotics of Court Dress in England and Wales: Failed or Successful Vector of Professional Identity?

Shaeda Isani

Aim and Scope of Study

The role played by visual semiotics in the creation and interpretation of professional identity is a rich field of study which has greatly contributed to understanding the dynamics of professionally revealing visual signs in such areas as proxemics (spatial rites and rituals related to professional locations, institutions and premises), graphics (logos, signs, letterheads, inscriptions, and so on), professional artefacts (gavels, scales of justice, blackboards and even laptops, briefcases and palm pilots), insignia (mottoes, crests, flags, pictures), colours and, finally, dress code which is the area this article proposes to explore with reference to legal professionals.

If the primary function of clothing is protection and modesty, the function of dress code is essentially taxonomic. French historian Michel Pastoureau, in his remarkable book on Western mediaeval symbolism, dates the legal codification and classificatory role of clothing to the Middle Ages:

> À la fin du XIIIe siècle, les interdictions et règlements ne portent plus seulement sur le costume des clercs. Toute la société laïque est désormais concernée, et le bas Moyen Age voit partout se développer la promulgation de textes normatifs et de lois somptuaires ou vestimentaires, spécialement en milieu urbain. Ces lois qui, sous des formes variées, perdureront parfois jusqu'au XVIIe ont une triple fonction. Tout d'abord une fonction économique: limiter dans toutes les classes et catégories sociales les dépenses concernant le vêtement et ses accessoires, car ce sont des investissements jugés improductifs. Ensuite, une fonction morale: maintenir une tradition chrétienne de modestie et de vertu; en ce sens, ces lois se rattachent au grand courant moralisateur qui traverse le Moyen Âge finissant et dont la Réforme protestante se fera l'héritière. Enfin, et surtout, une fonction sociale et idéologique: instaurer une ségrégation par le vêtement, chacun devant porter celui de son sexe, de son état et de son rang. Tout est réglementé selon les classes et les catégories socioprofessionnelles: le nombre de vêtements possédés, les pièces qui les composent, les

> étoffes dont ils sont faits, les couleurs dont ils sont teints, les fourrures, les bijoux et tous les accessoires de costume. (2004: 157)[1]

This study proposes to explore contemporary English legal court dress as a vector of professional identity – the representations sought and the perceptions generated – through an analysis of the triadic interactive dynamics involved between:

- the sign (legal court dress);
- the addressers or encoders (professionals who wear court dress);
- the addressees or decoders (the target public).

English Legal Dress Code

Singularity of English Legal Dress Code

While English legal dress code has always generated a degree of interest varying from amusement to scorn, it is, today, a subject of particular debate in the United Kingdom – and, by extension, in the 20-odd other countries where English legal dress code prevails[2] – due to the public interest generated by the Lord Chancellor's 2003 survey on public opinion concerning court dress in England and Wales.

The singularity of contemporary English court dress lies, of course, in the fact that it is the only seventeenth century professional dress code still in use today. Elise Brunet, curator of the Law Society Archives of Ontario, gives the following summary of its inception:

> Court dress as we know it, hails back to the late 17th century. As Edward I broke the hold of the church on the English legal profession in the 13th century, a new body of lay lawyers appeared. As representatives of the sovereign, they were expected to embody the dignity of the law and they adopted a style of dress similar to that of the nobles of the time. Legal garb followed the whims of fashion. By the end of the 1600s, the gown was

1 Loosely translated as: 'Towards the end of the 13th century, dress regulations are no longer restricted to religious communities but concern lay society as well. The late Middle Ages see the multiplication of normative texts regarding dress – particularly in urban areas – some of which will continue to prevail until the 17th century. These have a three-fold function: an *economic* function whereby they seek to limit expenses relative to dress and accessories, deemed unproductive investments; a *moral* function whereby they seek to maintain a Christian tradition of modesty and virtue, thus continuing the tradition of the great moralising laws which cross the late Middle Ages and which will subsequently be inherited by the Protestant Reform; and finally and most importantly, a *social and ideological* function whereby they seek to introduce segregation through dress, individuals being required to dress in accordance with sex, status and rank. As such, dress is carefully regulated according to class and socio-professional category: number of garments possessed, number of items per dress, type of fabric, dye, fur, jewellery and accessories.'

2 There having been considerable debate published on the subject in Australia and Scotland, this discussion will also be referring to data collected in these countries.

> being abandoned by the trendy crowds, but court officials, academics and clerics retained it as a symbol of their professions. As the robe became an emblem of legal expertise, a combination of regulation and convention crystallised the main characteristics of legal dress.[3]

Other professions also sport dress codes but, contrary to English court apparel, they are primarily defined and designed – and constantly updated – with a view to meeting the ergonomic needs of the profession. As such, professorial gown and mortar – as well as operating green scrubs, army combat fatigues and tennis wear – have all, over the years, forfeited tradition to functionality. The English legal professions remain the conspicuous exception.

It is important in this context, to underline that the debate over English court dress has less to do with the idea of professional dress code *per se* than with the idea of a twenty-first century dress code which has made very few concessions to change since its adoption in the seventeenth century.

All English courts, with the exception of Magistrates' Courts and Family Courts, require professionals and personnel, whether judges, barristers, solicitors, court clerks, recorders or ushers, to wear court dress. This discussion focuses on court dress required of English advocates and is part of an ongoing research project addressing the international and intercultural dimension of legal professional dress code through a comparative approach concerning France, the United Kingdom and the United States. In this comparative perspective, it is *lawyers* who present a more significant continuum on a scale of court dress which goes from the very elaborate (England), to a minimum (the Continent) and, finally, to the apparently nonexistent (the United States).

Another reason for this specific angle of approach is related to the fact that due to the more complex nature of lawyer-client relations, the English advocate, contrary to the judge, the court clerk and the usher, has, in fact, two dress codes: one for business conducted in Chambers and/or offices where interaction tends to be private, face to face and dyadic, and another for the courtroom, where communication is defined in terms of public and polyadic interaction. It is this latter which is the focus of this study.

Terminology: Court Dress

Since, as we have just seen, 'professional dress code' is a generic and therefore polysemous term which may cover differing apparel for different occasions within the same profession, the Lord Chancellor's office has been at pains to use and define the term 'court dress' in the foreword to the survey signed by Lord Irvine:

3 http://www.ontariocourts.on.ca/ojen/court&class/resources/articles/keepingtabs.html.

Terminology can be confusing when referring to 'court dress'. The standard meaning of court dress is the ceremonial clothing worn by officers of state and other dignitaries on royal and state occasions. This paper is not concerned with court dress in that sense.

The paper focuses on the working dress worn in higher *criminal* and *civil* courts in England and Wales by judges, barristers and other advocates, solicitors, court clerks and court ushers. It does not cover the magistrates' courts, where suits or similar are worn by all, nor ceremonial dress. – A Lord Chancellor's Department Consultation Paper, 'Court Working Dress in England and Wales, May 2003'.[4] (Author's italics)

As such, the apparel required of advocates during court appearances will henceforth be referred to as 'court dress' in this article.

Advocates' Court Dress in England and Wales

As this discussion concerns court dress specific to advocates in England and Wales – 'the world's oldest trademark', according to the *Daily Telegraph* (11 February 2001) – it will focus on the two main categories of professionals who plead in English courts: barristers (sub-divided into two categories, QCs and junior barristers) and solicitor-advocates who, since the 1990 Courts and Legal Services Act, have the right to plead in the higher courts.

The Lord Chancellor's paper on legal court dress provides the official description of required court dress for the three categories of advocates:

The requirements of Practice Direction (Court Dress) [1994] 1 W.L.R. 1056 of 19 July 1994 are therefore varied as follows: Queen's Counsel wear a short wig and silk (or stuff) gown over a court coat; junior counsel wear a short wig and stuff gown with bands; solicitors and other advocates authorised under the Courts and Legal Services Act 1990 wear a black stuff gown and bands, but no wig.[5]

In this document, destined for the lay public, we note the absence of any reference to the more 'exotic' details of advocates' court dress, such as colour (black, '*la couleur honnête*', according to Pastoureau [2004:156]), or variations in shape and size of wigs (the ornate full-bottomed barrister's wig required for more solemn occasions), or materials (the horsehair the wig is reputedly made of). The on-line source Lexonthenet provides a more detailed description of barristers' wig and gown which helps understand the taxonomic function of dress code based on the need to identify and classify:

Barristers are highly traditional in that they are required to wear a horsehair wig when they appear as advocates in court, with a black gown and a dark suit and a white shirt with strips of white cotton called 'bands' hanging before a wing collar.

QCs have always worn different gowns to junior barristers – traditionally a lace and tufted robe. The preferred dress for everyday court appearances became a silk gown –

4 http://www.dca.gov.uk.consult/courtdress/html.

5 http://www.dca.gov.uk.consult/courtdress/html.

hence the term 'silk' used to describe a QC – in keeping with their privileged connection with the royal court. This gown, still worn today, had a flap collar on the back and winged sleeves, a style common among men of dignity in Elizabethan and Jacobean times. A stuff gown continued to be worn during periods of mourning, however, and today, the stuff version is the robe of choice […] for everyday appearances in the crown court, Court of Appeal and High Court, while the silk gown must be worn in the House of Lords and Privy Council.

On ceremonial occasions, Queen's Counsel, judges, and members of the House of Lords wear floppy, shoulder-length, horsehair 'spaniel wigs' […]. The only time barristers wear these long wigs in real cases is when the Queen's Counsel, […] accompanied by their junior counsel, receive the speeches (judgements) of the Lords of Appeal in Ordinary at the bar of the House of Lords.[6]

Premise and Hypothesis

Multi-tiered Communication and Varying Degrees of Success

One of the first questions to arise concerns the identity of the *addressees* targeted by the visual communication of English court dress. The spontaneous answer to this question often tends to be, 'Why, the lay public of course'. However, closer analysis indicates that legal dress code, as a vector of professional identity, is a complex means of communication which functions concurrently at multiple levels and targets different sets of addressees. A basic three-tier level of communication may be identified:

- Extra-professional level: at this macro level, the first aim of all dress code is to distinguish between different corporations: doctors, lawyers, military, clerics, and so on.
- Inter-professional level: the function of dress code at this level is to distinguish between different branches of the same professional corporation, as, for instance, in the case of law, between judges, advocates, solicitors, notaries, recorders, and so on.
- Intra-professional level: at this level, the function of dress code may be defined as the visualisation of hierarchical identity within the same professional branch, such as, in the case of the legal professions, Queen's Counsel and junior barristers.

In view of these elements, it is possible to affirm that, as a vector of professional identity and according to the community of addressees targeted, English court dress functions in two Janus-headed directions: it is *exogenously* orientated when targeting a lay public of non-initiates and *endogenously* orientated when targeting a community of professional peers. That the two target communities do not enjoy the same status is self-evident and it would appear reasonable to assume that the *primary* and *overt*

6 http://www.lexonthenet.com.

level of communication targets the exogenous lay public while the endogenous and intra-professional level of communication targets peers and represents the *secondary* and *covert* level of communication.

The hypothesis put forward in this study centres on the paradox that court wear, as a means of visual communication and a vector of professional identity, is proving to be increasingly dysfunctional at the level of the primary and overt target community but enjoys considerable success at the level of the secondary and covert target community.

Court Dress as a Dysfunctional Means of Visual Communication: the Lay Public

Definition of the Lay Public

The foreword to the survey signed by the Lord Chancellor distinguishes between three categories of public concerned by the question of court wear:

> Let me make it clear that on the question of court working dress I shall, of course, have regard for the views of *the professionals* (the judiciary, lawyers and court staff) who operate the courts, but I am particularly keen to hear the views of *court users* and *the general public*.[7] (My italics)

The document goes on to specify that by the term 'court users' is meant:

> … those people for whom the courts are not a commonplace experience – the victims of crime, witnesses, jurors and defendants in the criminal courts, as well as claimants (formerly known as plaintiffs) and defendants in the civil courts.

It is, essentially, this community of 'court users' that we identify as the lay public and which, in the framework of this study concerning legal court dress as a vector of professional identity, represents the primary target community of addressees.

Divergent Representations and Perceptions

That court dress as a means of visual communication is generally assumed to be intended to target the lay public is evidenced by the Lord Chancellor's foreword to the survey which mentions six reasons commonly to justify the wearing of court dress; of these, four target the lay public, one targets both the lay public and professionals and only one specifically targets professionals:

7 http://www.dca.gov.uk.consult/courtdress/html.

Table 4.1 Lord Chancellor's Foreword (extract)

Perceived Representations of Court Wear	Principal Target Addressee
1. Symbolises the authority of the office holder	→ users
2. Helps instil a respect for the law	→ users
3. Reminds legal professionals that theirs is a solemn role	→ professionals
4. Emphasises the impersonal and disinterested approach of judges	→ users/professionals
5. Helps court users identify who's who	→ users
6. Wigs render wearers 'anonymous' to lay public thus providing security	→ users

The likelihood of addressers and addressees holding distinct and opposing views is also suggested in the text when Lord Irvine, distinguishing between the three types of public concerned by the issue of court wear, declares he is 'particularly keen to hear the views of court users and the general public' – as opposed, presumably, to those of the professionals.

This polarisation is confirmed by comparing the results of surveys carried out on the two different types of public, the lay public and professionals. The Lord Chancellor's 2003 in-street survey destined to poll the lay public with reference to the retention/abolition of legal court dress found that while 34 per cent of the respondents did indeed express a preference for retaining current court dress for barristers – an attitude summed up by one respondent's comment, 'I want to be represented by a proper barrister with a wig' – a clear majority of 61 per cent expressed the wish to see some changes rung in regarding barristers' court dress,[8] with a clear majority expressing a preference for 'business dress'.[9]

Concerning the views of professionals, on the other hand, a 2002 survey of 440 practising advocates in Scotland carried out by the Faculty of Advocates shows that 80 per cent of respondents wish to retain their distinctive courtroom dress.[10] For Roy Martin, Vice Dean of the Faculty of Advocates, the strict dress code provides advocates with a sense of identity:

8 In contrast, however, 68 per cent of respondents wished judges in criminal cases to retain wigs.

9 A previous survey carried out in England in 1992 showed massive support in favour of court dress. The findings of a survey carried out in the state of Victoria, Australia by the Law Institute of Victoria, in November 2003, also reported 54 per cent of respondents expressing themselves in favour of retaining both wigs and gowns.

10 These findings confirm a much earlier survey carried out in Australia (1975) by the Bar Council, in which a majority of the barristers consulted expressed themselves in favour of maintaining at least some aspects of current court dress: 60 per cent favoured retention of wigs, 78 per cent of gowns, 63 per cent of bar jackets, 51 per cent of wing collars, 61 per cent of bands. http:/www.lawlink.nsw.gov.au/lrc.nsf/pages/R31CHP10.

> Our members agree that dress code provides advocates with an obvious symbol of their professional identity in the mind of the public. It represents a positive link with the best traditions in the practice of the law by the independent bar in Scotland. Court dress is a long-established trademark, both within Scotland and internationally and it immediately identifies the wearer as an advocate. To dispense with something which is instantly recognisable would be of no benefit to the legal profession or the nation as a whole.[11]

That 80 per cent of the addressers should perceive court wear as a necessary and suitable vector of professional identity while 61 per cent of the addressees should wish to do away with it, confirms the existence of a hiatus between representations sought and perceptions generated by the representamen. It consequently implies a breakdown in the decoding process of recognition, identification and interpretation which can be attributed to the absence of a common code shared alike by addresser and addressee.

Antonymous Discourse

To scratch below the surface of the dry figures of 61 per cent and 80 per cent, discourse analysis of the language used to express these opinions was carried out through an analysis and classification of lexical items extracted from an on-line random sampling of opinions expressed in relation to lawyers' court dress by lawyers on the one hand, and by the general public[12] on the other. The corpus obtained was first analysed for broad matching by semantic affinity and then contrasted for semantic antonymy. This table reveals the distinctly antonymous pattern of the two discourses:

Table 4.2 Advocates' Court Wear: Antonymous Representations and Perceptions

Representations sought (addressers: professionals)	Perceptions generated (addressees: lay public)
authority; respect; solemnity; gravity; nobility; formality; importance; prestige; honour; sign of learning; emblem of legal expertise	wiggery; pageant; dressing gowns; drag; joke; tourist attraction; foppish; dandified; silly; preposterous; outlandish; absurd; ridiculous
historical; tradition; ceremonial	archaic; irrelevant; antiquated; fusty; out of touch; outmoded; outdated; old-fashioned; anachronistic; quaint; inappropriate; out of place; unnecessary
easily recognisable; identifiable	camouflage; disguise
uniformity	elitist; privilege
anonymity (protection, safety); mystique; impersonal	intimidating; frightening; alienating

11 http://news.bbc.co.uk/1/hi/scotland/232694.stem.

12 Professional and lay public respondents from England and Australia.

This antonymous and discordant discourse between addressers and addressees gains perspective when analysed in terms of Stuart Hall's (1980) notion of counter-hegemonic or oppositional reading by which the 'reader', whose social situation places him in a directly oppositional relation to the dominant code, understands the preferred reading but does not share the text's code, thus rejecting this reading and bringing to bear an alternative frame of reference.

Court Dress as a Vector of 'Professional Anonymity'

One argument frequently brought to bear in defence of legal dress is the claim that it provides a degree of professional '*anonymity*' for the wearer. Anonymity, however, as a vector of professional identity appears to be a somewhat oxymoronic construct and further analysis reveals it to be a highly complex notion which helps explain some of the dysfunctional aspects of court dress when used as a means of communication targeting the lay public.

Court Dress Anonymity as a Form of Protection

Wigs and gowns, it is often argued, provide the wearer with a degree of anonymity which is useful for the physical safety and protection of barristers (from the irate client whose case they lost), and judges (from victims of their sentencing).

This professional hazard, however, would appear to be more of a perceived risk than a real one. There are few reports of barristers being mugged by irate clients and the occasional report that does exist concerning judges describes aggressions carried out by defendants within the four walls of the courtroom. Furthermore, both judges and barristers, contrary to members of the lay jury, are identified by name in court and by the press. In addition, it may be noted that magistrates, who wear no specific court dress, also sentence but are, apparently, not deemed to be at risk. Could this frequently advanced argument be no more than a strategy to enhance the mystique and mystification of the profession?

Court Dress Anonymity as a Vector of 'Depersonalisation'

Another claim made with respect to anonymity is that court dress is destined to underline the principle of *peer parity amongst counsel* in that wigs and gowns, it is argued, conceal possibly discriminatory physical attributes, as confirmed by the 1982 New South Wales Law Reform Commission's Report:

> The Bar Association says that barristers 'should be required to wear the same dress so as to avoid distraction as a means of reducing the personal quality which one counsel may have to the prejudice of his opponent. A good looking advocate should not have, thereby,

an unconscious advantage. A wig serves to conceal what may be otherwise regarded as an unattractive or conversely, an overly attractive feature.'[13]

This perception appears to be shared by certain members of the lay public as well, as evidenced by the comments of one of the respondents to an on-line public survey carried out by the Law Institute of Victoria:

> It is important for judges and barristers to wear wigs and gowns as this ensures their being identified with the court and the legal profession rather than identifying them as individuals. This means that any decisions made by judges are attributed to the law and its institutions and not to individuals. Further it means that barristers are identified by their profession and hence juries and the public are less swayed by factors such as age, gender or race.[14]

The idea that wigs and gowns are endowed with the capacity to obliterate indications of age, gender and race is, at best, naive, as amply demonstrated by this insert[15] of four barristers: in spite of the professional accoutrement, the mature white male barrister, the young black male barrister, the young white male barrister and the young white female barrister are all easily identifiable.

Similar considerations arise concerning gender. If the Lord Chancellor's survey specifies that court dress for female barristers is 'skirt or trousers', the final arbiters regarding the acceptability of the court dress of advocates appearing in their courts are, *in fine*, the judges since they are empowered to exercise their right to refuse to 'see' a barrister they consider 'improperly' dressed by uttering the traditional

13 http://www.lawlink.nsw.gov.au/lrc.nsf.

14 http://www.liv.asn.au/news/media/20031105_wnwpcv.html.

15 Reproduced by kind permission of the UK Department for Constitutional Affairs (authorisation dated 18 November 2004).

formula, 'I cannot hear you'. In spite the fact that since 1995 female barristers are allowed to wear trousers in court, it is well documented that such professional, social and generational environments tend towards a certain degree of dress conservatism, often resulting in the view that trousers are not suitable formal attire for women. Female barristers, therefore, tend to favour skirts when pleading, a fact which reveals gender discriminatory elements that few gowns are long enough to conceal.

Court Dress Anonymity as a Vector of Collective Professional Identity

A more subtle argument based on the anonymity of wigs and gowns construct is that, like other forms of dress code, they are meant to forge a sense of identity within the profession and present a homogeneous and identifiable facade outside of the profession, 'to fit in and stand out at the same time', to quote Rankin (2003: 201), albeit somewhat *hors contexte*. As such, court dress is a powerful visual vector of the profession as a community, underlining the primacy of group identity over individual identity, a sartorial visualisation of the famous '*esprit de corps*'.

Is it, however, necessary to resort to eccentric head and neck apparel to do so? Apparently not, since other professions, like the armed forces, seem able to do without (even if they do display other eccentricities). The issue, therefore, seems to focus on the specific role played by wigs and gowns in the representations sought by the addressers. In this respect, one line of argument presented in favour of wigs and gowns is of particular interest. According to the professional culture of English barristers, the 'professional anonymity' construct goes beyond the notion of group identity primacy to extend to a virtual obliteration of any trace or hint of the *person* behind the professional, an analysis confirmed by Lurie with regard to the role of uniforms in general:

> The extreme form of conventional dress is the costume totally determined by others: the uniform. No matter what sort of uniform it is [...], to put on such livery is to give up one's right to act as an individual in terms of speech, to be partially or wholly censored. What one does, as well as what one wears, will be wholly determined by external authorities to a greater or lesser degree, depending on whether one is, for example, a Trappist monk or a boy scout. The uniform acts as a sign that we should not or need not treat someone as a human being, and that they need not and should not treat us as one. (1981: 17-18)

Consequently, the bewigged and gowned figure of the barrister must not be represented or perceived as a person or an individual but solely as a professional, embodying the famous professional 'detachment' of the calling. In an article entitled 'Why are Judges' Robes Black?', O'Neill writes:

> [...] robes became the eponymous distinction between 'Town and Gown'. This adornment in ancient regalia symbolically transformed the lawyer from a private individual to a 'law speaker' for the community. [...] Through the ages, this duty has been treated very seriously. Both judges and lawyers take oaths pledging to uphold the law regardless of their personal views. (2003: 5)

This line of thinking is not specific to Anglo-Saxon legal culture since French judge and analyst, Antoine Garapon, makes the same point about French – and by extrapolation, Continental – legal culture in his book on legal court wear:

> La robe est un vêtement institutionnel qui revêt celui qui le porte. L'homme ainsi revêtu marque la supériorité – temporaire – de l'institution sur l'homme. [...] La robe permet, pour celui qui la revêt, l'identification à son personnage. [...] Il est son vêtement: en enfilant leur robe, le juge, l'avocat et le procureur investissent leur rôle qui leur permet de ne pas « endosser » subjectivement la responsabilité de leurs actes. [...] Le juge, l'avocat et le procureur se cachent derrière leur robe qui les dépersonnalise: elle s'apparente à un masque. (2001: 84)[16]

This line of reasoning appears, however, to be losing ground today in light of recent claims to ethnic identity and subsequent special dispensations granted to barristers from minority communities in England, authorising the substitution of the wig for traditional ethnic head coverings. Such is the case for barristers of Sikh origin, for example, who are entitled to wear Sikh turbans in court instead of a traditional English barrister's wig.

And we note a subsequent readjustment on the scale of exoticism – in the midst of a bevy of bewigged barristers, the barrister's wig suddenly finds itself rendered banal alongside headgear which, by refusing to conform to the norms of the established professional dress code, appears outstanding, as evidenced by this extract from the *Daily Telegraph* dated 13 May 2004:

> Of the three counsel at the High Court this week representing Iraqis whose families allege they were unlawfully shot by British troops, only Michael Fordham was wearing a barrister's wig. Rabinder Singh, QC, sported his usual white turban, while Shaheed Fatima modestly covered her hair with a striking black silk scarf.[17]

In terms of group identity and individual anonymity, it is clear that the substitution of the wig for an exotic turban – or *yarmulke* or *hijab* – clearly focuses on all those personal, private and individual aspects which the black gown of the professional is meant to conceal. Lurie analyses the phenomenon of dress 'ethnicisation' in her classic work on the language of clothes:

> The appearance of foreign garments in an otherwise indigenous costume is similar in function to the use of foreign words or phrases in standard English speech. [...] It can be a deliberate sign of national origin in someone who, otherwise, sartorially or linguistically speaking, has no accent. Often this message is expressed through headgear. The Japanese-

16 Loosely translated as: 'Court apparel is an institutional form of dress which costumes the person wearing it, thus marking the (temporary) superiority of the institution over the man. It allows the person so attired to identify with his personage: he becomes his dress. Because of court dress, judges, advocates and prosecutors are able to assume their roles without having to bear any 'personal' responsibility for their acts. Like a mask, court wear conceals and depersonalises judges, lawyers and prosecutors.'

17 http:/www.telegraph.co.uk/news2004/05/13/nlaw113.xml.

> American lady in Western dress but with an elaborate Oriental hairdo, or the Oxford-educated Arab who tops his Savile Row suit with a turban, are telling us graphically that they have not been psychologically assimilated; that their ideas and opinions remain those of an Asian. (1981: 17)

Such cross-cultural sartorial markers are deployed as a key symbol of otherness, pointing to the latent cultural differences behind the professional façade of homogeneity and leading to the establishment of specific identity sub-categorisations as 'the Sikh barrister' or 'the Muslim barrister', and so on – an evolution which clearly undermines the principle that barristers' wigs and gowns are meant 'to provide anonymity, not in the sense of providing a disguise or camouflage, but a distancing from personal involvement' (Lexonthenet).

In view of these arguments, it would appear that the justification of barristers' court dress as a safeguard against individualisation and personalisation of counsel can no longer be considered as valid, and that we are today witnessing a trend away from a common and uniform dress code as a vector of collective professional identity towards a growing affirmation of distinct cultural professional otherness – if not otherisation – through the deployment of highly visual signs and symbols to indicate a different cultural belonging. This trend merges into a wider perspective relative to the growing mediatisation of the legal professions and the ensuing focus on personal traits, a phenomenon which Gies (2003: 261) has called 'a politics of the person'.

One of the reasons behind this move away from a common and uniform professional identity towards the affirmation of distinct cultural professional otherness is undoubtedly linked to the need for barristers to promote their reputation as specialists. In certain areas of law such as racial discrimination, immigration, political asylum, and so on, belonging to the same community of origin as the potential client base concerned by such litigation is an asset which deserves highlighting. As such, altering standard professional dress code to incorporate visually identifiable signs of minority cultural belonging conveys a subtle but nevertheless significant personal added-value with regard to the professional identity of a particular barrister, however incompatible that may be with the original rationale behind the use of court dress. The head scarf, the turban and the skirt itself on certain occasions thus become so many badges, signs and symbols which successfully 'speak' to the lay public, thus fulfilling their role as effective representamen – something which official court dress often fails to do.

Court Wear as a Successful Means of Visual Communication: Professional Peers

The paradox that is beginning to emerge is that if signs of individual cultural appurtenance added to professional court wear are successfully identified and interpreted – *visible et lisible*[18] – by the lay addressees targeted, the same cannot

18 *visible et lisible*: visible and legible.

be said for the finer details of professional court dress. The distinguishing signs of visual professional identity are, at this level, so highly codified that they become either confusing or opaque for the lay public, as illustrated by the sheer complexity of the directives on judicial court dress issued by the Lord Chief Justice in 1992:

> When sitting in the Court of Appeal, (Criminal Division), High Court Judges, like other members of the Court of Appeal, wear a black silk gown and a short wig, as they do in Divisional Court. When dealing with criminal business at first instance in the winter, a High Court judge wears the scarlet robe of the ceremonial dress but without the scarlet cloth and fur mantle. When dealing with criminal business in the summer, the judge wears a similar scarlet robe, but with silk rather than fur facings. A Queen's Bench judge trying civil cases in winter wears a black robe faced with fur, a black scarf and girdle and a scarlet tippet: in summer, a violet robe faced with silk, with the black scarf and girdle and scarlet tippet. On red letter days (which include the Sovereign's birthday and certain saint's days) all judges wear the scarlet robe for the appropriate season.[19]

Even though advocates' dress code may not be quite so highly codified, it is quite clear that only initiates possess the degree of knowledge required to interpret the taxonomic code encrypted in the intricacies of their court dress – as Lurie confirms (1981: 17): 'These costumes only look like uniforms to outsiders; peers will be aware of significant differences.'

We thus observe a significant shift in focus with regard to the community of addressees targeted. This complex level of encoding, largely lost on the lay public, is for the community of professional peers, the focus of constant and active decoding and interpretation. As a vector of identity, court dress here becomes a *meaningful* means of visual communication, fully understood and interpreted by the target community, a situation which may be likened to Hall's construct of dominant or hegemonic reading where the reader fully shares the text's code and accepts and reproduces the preferred reading.

Contrary to lay perceptions, for the community of professional peers, court wear is not a dead symbol but relates to intense and constant preoccupations in that it is the visual representation of rank and status. As such, it becomes the visible arena of the otherwise invisible power struggle *inter pares* – professional identity and status are inter-hierarchical tectonic plates whose fault lines are expressed in terms of visual semiotics which proclaim loud and clear what censorship, modesty, discretion or humility forbid to do in words.

Considering counsel in general, it is possible to identify five major areas of friction regarding professional identity and court wear:

19 http://www.sixthform.info.law/01_modules/mod2/11_3_legal_profession/4_ barristers_ wigs.html.

1. solicitor / solicitor-advocate;
2. solicitor-advocate / solicitor silk;
3. solicitor-advocate / barrister;
4. Queen's Counsel / junior counsel;
5. Queen's Counsel / judge.

The wearing of the wig appears to be the focal point of this struggle for visual identification and recognition of status, with entitled wig-wearers determined to cling to exclusivity and those excluded clamouring for entitlement.

Wigs as a Symbol of Internecine Power Struggle

The wig controversy cuts across all professional ranks, from solicitor at one end of the scale, to judge at the other, as this brief analysis hopes to demonstrate.

a) The Solicitor-advocate

Solicitors do not, in principle, wear wigs when attending court to instruct barristers. However, since the 1990 reform giving solicitor-advocates 'rights of audience', they are entitled to speak directly on behalf of clients in court. Various visual semiotics, however, are carefully engineered to highlight their inferior rank as regards the 'proper' advocates, barristers. If they are indeed entitled to some form of court dress (black stuff gown with white bands), it is distinct from that of the barrister in that their gown must be shorter. And, perhaps more significantly, they are not entitled to a wig. Proxemics also contribute to reinforcing the 'lower' status of the solicitor-advocate by requiring him to be seated behind the barrister during court appearances. As might be expected, solicitor-advocates feel this 'pain of unbelonging' and perceive these visual distinctions as a professional rebuff which is demeaning, discriminatory and damaging to their client, a point illustrated by a recent English lawyer joke: 'The reason a barrister needs a wig is so the jury will know which side should win.'

Solicitor-advocates view the ban on wigs as a contradiction of Britain's new Human Rights Act and calls for parity between solicitor-advocates and barristers in court have been officially made by the Law Society, as reported by this extract from the 9 May 2003 issue of *The Times*:

> Carolyn Kirby, the President of the Law Society said there should be parity between solicitor-advocates and barristers. 'At the moment, only barristers wear wigs, solicitors do not. QCs appear on the front bench and other advocates in the row behind. This should not be the case. It creates a perception among victims and defendants that the other side's advocate has an advantage.'

If the distinction in court dress underlines the difference of status between solicitors and barristers and risks being perceived to the solicitor's detriment by members of the lay public, jurors and clients alike, a large body of solicitor-advocates also feels it generates dangerous perceptions with the rank- and status-conscious Bench itself, a view endorsed by the 1982 New South Wales Law Reform Commission Report:

> A number of solicitors and court officials also expressed the view that some judges are less favourably disposed to solicitor advocates than barristers. The likelihood of such unfair discrimination occurring is increased by the present distinctions in court dress, indeed, if those distinctions were removed, it might become common for judges to be unaware whether an advocate appearing before them is a barrister or a solicitor.
>
> In our [the Commission's] view, the present distinction between solicitors and barristers in relation to court dress is inappropriate and unfair. It is an undue deterrent to solicitors who are competent and willing to act as advocates in appropriate cases, and it increases the possibility of some judges, jurors and others being less favourably disposed towards solicitor advocates than towards barristers. These consequences can have adverse effects for clients as well as for their solicitors. And whether or not unfairness actually results, many people whose advocates are solicitors, not clad in special dress, cannot but feel that they are disadvantaged if their opponents are represented by barristers who are clad in special dress, particularly when the judge is in similar attire.[20]

In view of these arguments, it is easy to understand the logic that drives solicitor-advocates to swim against the current by demanding the right to wigs at a time when public opinion prefers to abolish them. As long as solicitor-advocates plead alongside and against bewigged barristers, in the world of visual semiotics, representations and perceptions, their enforced bare-headedness can only be interpreted as a sign of inferior professional status – and its corollary, an inferior degree of competence and skill.

b) The Solicitor Silk

The creation of the solicitor silk in 1998 led to the addition of yet another rung in the solicitor hierarchy. While the solicitor-advocate must still go wigless, by some quirk of hierarchical logic, the solicitor silk is entitled to wear a wig, as Reeves (1998) explains:

> When solicitors were permitted to appear in the higher courts, attempts to abolish the traditional wig of the barrister failed. Confusion reigned when some solicitor advocates wore a wig and others appeared bare-headed. [...] Eventually, by edict of the Lord Chancellor and Lord Chief Justice, solicitor advocates were forbidden to wear a wig in any court.
>
> That was not the end of the story. With solicitor silk created for the first time [1998], the rule was modified. At the appointment ceremony, it would no doubt have spoiled the display if some of the main participants did not follow tradition. For the sake of uniformity, solicitor silk were permitted to wear the customary bellbottomed wig. Also, when in court,

20 http://www.lawlink.nsw.gov.au/lrc.nsf/pages/R31CHP10.

> they must, on the Lord Chancellor's instructions, wear a wig. Other solicitor advocates continue to appear without one.[21]

In view of the careful visual flagging of identity within the solicitor hierarchy, it is worth noting that, on the whole, the general public tends not to be aware of the existence of the solicitor silk or his functions. Consequently, in their eyes, that he should be wigged or not is a relatively moot point.

c) The Barrister

Of all the legal professions, it is undoubtedly barristers who project an image of prestige and nobility, representing, as Reeves (1998) puts it, 'the legal knighthood'. As such, they are the jealous guardians of the sartorial privileges of their rank, aware that these constitute a powerful means of visual communication. Concerning the lay public, barristers wish to be perceived as an elite group, highly trained in the art of advocacy and therefore naturally defend their traditional sartorial privileges as a means of visualising and broadcasting their superior status:

> A recent chairman of the Bar Council of England, Roy Amlot, QC [...] believes the distinction is important. He has argued that dress code reflects the difference in education between barristers, who are 'specialists', and solicitor-advocates, who 'do not have the same level of training and experience in advocacy.'[22]

Concerning intra-professional target addressees, wigs in particular are carefully orchestrated to highlight these differences of rank *inter pares,* as illustrated by the QC's right to silk and a full-bottomed formal ceremonial wig, a privilege denied to junior barristers.

Wigs may also express other, more subtle, nuances of intra-professional identity and status and in this context, one of the most revealing is colour. It has often been pointed out that barristers' wigs tend to look dingy and yellow. The lay public has been led to assume that, given the cost of a wig reputedly made from the tail hairs of a white Arab stallion, wigs are not replaced for reasons of economy – a somewhat naive consideration in view of the fees barristers command. A more plausible explanation concerns the perceptions of experience, learning and knowledge generated by a tatty, yellowed wig – 'the prized badges of seniority' according to *The Times* (9 May 2003) – as compared to those generated by a pristine white wig, 'the virginal wig', connotative of youth and inexperience, a recurrent theme in Mortimer's *Rumpole* series:

> '[...] Albert tells me you're always before some Court of Petty Sessions. They must be keeping you pretty busy and you're not such a white wig after all. Although, come to think

21 http://www.adamsmith.org/policy/publications/pdf-files/silk-cut.pdf.

22 http:/www.legalaffairs.org/issues/May-June-002/scene_rangappa_mayjune2. html.

> about it, you don't wear wigs in those inferior courts, do you? So your wig's probably as white as ever.'
>
> I resolved to get hold of my wig and kick it around the dusty floor of the chambers' cellar until all its whiteness had gone for ever. (2004: 19)

Finally, the message conveyed by these different wigs is to be correlated with the ultimate reference in the matter, the wig worn by the judge himself, described by the *New York Times* (15 May 2003) as 'the $2,500 Rolls-Royce of perrukes'. Subsequently, it is therefore possible to have, in the same court room, at the same time and at the same hearing, six different messages relayed by the wearing of a wig, or not, in the persons of the judge and the different categories of counsel (QC, junior counsel, solicitor, solicitor-advocate, solicitor silk), as illustrated by the hearings in the case of *Birmingham City v. H (a minor)* (1994) 1 AER 12 where five Queen's Counsel, each with a junior, were engaged to protect the child's interests, while separate solicitors and senior and junior counsel appeared for each of the mother, the father and the guardian *ad litem*.

It is clear that if the lay public sees these variations on wigs as meaningless hieroglyphs – *visible mais illisible*[23] – for the professionals themselves, they represent meaningfully encoded, intelligent signs.

Conclusion: Court Dress as a 'Discursive Genre'

If the failure of English legal court dress as a vector of professional identity with regard to its primary and overt target community of addressees and, inversely, its success with regard to its secondary and covert target community of addressees remains paradoxical when conceptualised in terms of visual semiotics, the phenomenon finds a degree of coherence if the disciplinary locus is shifted to discourse analysis and the phenomenon analysed in the light of concepts borrowed from the field of *genre studies*, notably such key concepts as *speech community*, *genre* and *discourse community*.

The concept of 'speech community' is broadly defined as referring to a sociolinguistic speech community based on shared linguistic forms, regulative rules and cultural concepts whose members inherit membership by birth, accident or adoption. In terms of the fabric of society, it tends to be *centripetal* in that it absorbs people into that general fabric. 'Discourse communities', on the other hand, are socio-rhetorical networks that form in order to work towards common goals. The concept of discourse community is in turn closely linked to the concept of '*genre*', which may be apprehended as classes of communicative events which generally possess features of stability and recognition. In our case, the concept of genre would be extrapolated to that of court wear as a communicative event. In this respect, it is worth noting that one of the characteristics that defines the members of a discourse

23 *visible mais illisible*: visible but illegible.

community is possession of and familiarity with the genres that are used in the communicative furtherance of common goals.

For Swales (1990), one of the architects of genre theory, genres are the specific properties of discourse communities, as opposed to individuals, other kinds of groupings or other wider speech communities. Contrary to the notion of 'birthright' which is closely identified with speech communities, a discourse community recruits its members by persuasion, training or relevant qualification and is *centrifugal* in nature in that it tends to separate people into occupational or speciality-interest groups.

With reference to this discussion, if it may legitimately be supposed that the English lay public and English legal professionals do indeed belong to the broad concept of the speech community of the English-speaking world, the genre in question, court dress, does not represent the common *shared speech variety* but a form of *discourse* which remains restricted to the established members of a closed discourse community, that is, English legal professionals. Viewed in this perspective, the visual semiotics of court dress as a means of communication is comparable to a specialised genre, possessing a specific 'jargon', meaningfully encoded and decoded by members of the discourse community with reference to matters of interest specific to the community. As such, it represents an endogenous code of communication and is therefore, *ipso facto*, hermetic to outsiders. Far from being restricted or isolated phenomena, such communicative situations are common to all forms of specialised discourse, whether professional or not, and as Swales reminds us:

> It is hard to conceive [...] of well-established members of a discourse community communicating amongst themselves on topics relevant to the goal of the community and not using lexical items puzzling to outsiders. (1990: 26)

The 'lexical items' in the context of our discussion are quite simply barristers' gowns, bands and wigs declined according to the visual grammar of legal court dress as defined by and for members of the profession for communication *inter pares*.

Chapter 5

The Drama of the Courtroom

Annabelle Mooney

Introduction

Ally McBeal is arguably one of the most original television dramas of recent years.[1] While it takes what is for television the familiar setting of the law, it defamiliarises it in a number of ways. Traditionally, legal dramas deal with justice and power in a more or less realistic way. As an audience we are asked to be spectators on a legal process that is bureaucratic, constrained by technicalities and fraught with power relations (whether these be related to gender, race or socio-economic status). Often, these dramas are coded so as to make clear (or indeed to centrally problematise, especially in the case of power) the difficult issue of accessing or procuring justice in society; the perennial conflict between 'man made law' and 'true justice' for example (Rafter, 2001). There are certainly exceptions to this simple taxonomy. *LA Law*, for example, invited us to participate in the lives of the lawyers as well. Some 'legal dramas' are essentially detective thrillers. Thus the well known Perry Mason series of films shows an advocate moonlighting as detective along the lines of a Miss Marple or Poirot. However, in *Ally McBeal*, as Denvir notes: 'Love takes precedence over narrow legal conceptions of Justice' ('Legal Tender'). At the same time, justice itself is problematised in that it is dealt with in more than just a legal context.

While *Ally McBeal* is concerned with justice, I will argue that it is concerned with a very different type to the institutional and brutal social justice normally considered in legal dramas. Marek notes: '*Ally McBeal*'s style is unique and the characters are unusual. It is difficult to evaluate because it is not the typical lawyer show. It is, instead, a comedy' (1999: 81). However, to type it as a comedy, while an important aspect of the series, and a central consideration in this analysis, risks relegating *Ally McBeal* to the *merely* comedic. *Ally McBeal* questions the very reality on which justice is based, and indeed the reality of reality (as great comedy does). It does this, in part, by using a number of semiotic resources: music, animation, interiority and imagination. In *Ally McBeal* there is not one reality, but *layers* of reality. Different parts of Ally's world are framed in different ways; the legal framing is just one of these. At the same time, the various 'realities' of the law (context, circumstance and the like) also frame the world in various ways. Indeed, *Ally McBeal* can be understood as taking the reality of the practice of law to its logical (though ludic) conclusion.

1 It was introduced to American television in 1997.

This is especially powerful because of the way in which the drama itself questions divisions between fantasy and reality, the inner world and the outside world.

In this chapter, I first ask why *Ally McBeal* is relevant to the law, and more specifically, to images of law. I then turn to work that has already been conducted on *Ally McBeal*, and then to the issue of how it can be read as inviting the audience to transform reality by examining a particular episode. By creating a series of hypothetical spaces, *Ally McBeal* asks us to imagine the law, ethics and the world differently. The visual and aural medium of television is essential in creating this hypothetical space. A number of semiotic resources contribute to the realisation of this alternate world, among them music, visible hallucinations and audible thoughts contribute to creating a 'reality' which is multi-faceted and self-reflexive. While such examples cannot be reproduced here, they will be discussed in conjunction with transcripts of scenes.

Images of Law

It is important to remember that visual representations are images in at least two ways. Firstly, they are images in the sense that they are visual. But every representation (whether visual or otherwise) makes choices about what to represent. These choices contribute to a worldview and, more broadly, to a framing ideology. The text of *Ally McBeal* is an image in both senses.

Ally McBeal is not a realistic portrayal of the law (as critiques outlined in the following section make clear). That is not to say that it is not relevant to the semiotics of law. Given that research shows that the vast majority of people gain their knowledge of the real world of law from the media (Hans, 1990; Robbennolt and Studebaker, 2003), *Ally McBeal* presents an image of the law which challenges the reality in potentially productive ways. If one considers that lawyers and others involved in the real world drama of the law may watch and engage with the series, it is possible that the show represents a space for transformation.

In the tradition of scholarship around the semiotics of law (proper) this resonates with the seminal work of Bankowski and Mungham (1976). In this work, attention is drawn to the implicit political values and power structures in the law, especially in relation to lawyers and the court room trial.

Bankowski and Mungham note that 'the formation of informal groups among [lawyers] is relevant in two ways'; first, in respect of how they conduct themselves as lawyers, especially with clients; and second, the pressure to conform to 'appropriate professional behaviour' (1976: 84). It will become clear that the lawyers in *Ally McBeal* do no such thing. This is exactly where critique of the series for not being 'realistic' is rooted. The real world of law 'takes place within the context of an epistemology that divorces man from the world' (Bankowski and Mungham, 1976: 110). This is not the world of Ally McBeal (person and series).

Images of Law also argues for a new kind of trial, one 'made possible by the refusal of radicals to accept traditional courtroom roles, rules and rituals' (1976:

116). As will be discussed, the lawyers in *Ally McBeal*, the witnesses and indeed the jury do reject, or at least contest, the usual roles they are supposed to inhabit. Moreover, 'the audience, usually passive, is brought into the drama' (1976: 116) or at least invited in through the creative exploitation of contemporary moral, personal and political issues.

Previous Work

Before taking up the questions of reality and justice, it is worth considering how *Ally McBeal* has been written about up until now as it helps to introduce the question of reality and mimesis. There are three clear currents of writing about the show. The first relates to the feminism/post-feminism debate. The second, a legal point of view, appears to occupy less room, and centres on arguments that are essentially about mimesis. That is, it asks whether *Ally McBeal* is an authentic representation of what the legal world is like, particularly with respect to working as an attorney. This, in common with some work around feminism, asks whether Ally is a good role model. The third current addresses the comedic nature of *Ally McBeal*, particularly as a transformative queer space. This current is slender. However, it is distinctive (and important) enough to separate out from other concerns. This comedic nature of *Ally McBeal* makes it possible to talk about a different kind of mimesis.

Current One – Feminism

The first current of existing work is concerned mostly with feminism and post-feminism and whether or not Ally is a good role model, and what the series implicitly says about feminist objectives (Newman, 2000; Dow, 2002; Dubrofsky, 2002; Ouellette, 2002; Moseley and Read, 2002). It is perhaps testament to the responsiveness of the series that exactly the question of role models and feminism is addressed in one episode. Ally says to her room-mate Renee:

> I dreamt I was on the cover of *Time* as the symbol of post-feminism (McKenna, 2002: 298).

Indeed, Calista Flockhart (the actress who plays Ally), invoking her television alter-ego, *was* on the cover of *Time* magazine together with Gloria Steinem, Betty Friedan, and Susan B. Anthony. For the character Ally, however, being told that she had been selected as a role model is not a dream but a nightmare. In direct response to this dream/nightmare, Ally says: 'I do want to change the world, I just want to get married first.' The woman who greets Ally with the news that she has been selected as role model insists she has to fatten up, change her attitude, the way she dresses and so on. She tells Ally: 'you have to be what we tell you to be'. In response, Ally bites off her nose and spits it out. While Moseley and Read note: 'fantasy and the real are made indistinct in *Ally McBeal*' (2002: 244), here fantasy within the fantasy of television, a liminal space within a liminal space, is a way of directly addressing the 'real'; that is, the media commentary.

At the same time, David E. Kelley, the writer and executive producer of the series, has been criticised in the press for directly countering the criticisms made by the press in this way. I find the interaction between the commentary and consumption arm of the mass media pertinent, poignant and, dare I say it, funny. Indeed, given the way in which television is often derided for being a passive medium, such interaction should be welcome.

While the feminist/post-feminist arguments are engaging, this is not a paper about feminism. I do feel it necessary to say, however, that I am a feminist; not 'a feminist but ...'. It is clear, particularly in some of the topics raised in *Ally McBeal*, that women do not have it all. Further, while the situation of young women is certainly an improvement on that of their mothers, that is not to say that all is well. Thus feminism still has a role to play. Those who understand post-feminism as an era in which feminism is finished confound me.

This post-feminist reality is taken up by some of the feminist critique of *Ally McBeal*.

> Only because of the changes that feminism made can a character like Ally exist at all, and only because of the raised awareness created by feminism, can the storylines on the show address issues like sexual harassment and gender discrimination in an informed, albeit often amusing, fashion. Indeed, there are senses in which we should all be delighted that finding a man is Ally's biggest problem (Dow, 2002: 263).

McKenna puts it succinctly: 'The legal drama of *Ally McBeal* speaks to the contradictions of postfeminism' (2002: 290). However, some interpret the post-feminist stance as the position that 'there is no longer any need for feminism because woman have made it' (Dubrofsky, 2002: 269). If this is the case (and it seems that this is a vast simplification of work in post-feminism or at least of the post-feminism 'era') then Ally McBeal embodies these contradictions. While Ally does have a good job because of a good university education, her preoccupation with finding a relationship means that her professional skills are sometimes taken less seriously (in theory if not in practice). Indeed, her professional achievements are somewhat taken for granted by Ally herself. She is often shown, for example, sleeping in her Harvard Law School t-shirt; suggesting that this achievement in her life does not need to be explicitly signalled outside of the house.

Dubrofsky, however, argues that *Ally McBeal* is not political at all, rather, that it is regressive, that it 'actually encourages political stasis and reinforces and re-inscribes the present political structures ... by diverting our attention away from these back to the personal' (2002: 279). It seems to me that the personal is the political; something I actually understood as fundamental to feminism. I do find it difficult to see how a television series about individuals can do anything but deal with the personal (in the most banal sense). The series has, as its setting, working in a firm of attorneys. Such work by its very nature deals with the personal and particular, though in direct contact with the legal and general. Narratives are always personal in so far as they are particular. That does not mean that they do not have something to say about the political. Further, I would argue that focusing attention 'back to the personal' is a valid and indeed powerful way of understanding the effects of and critiquing the power of the political.

Moseley and Read conclude: 'It [*Ally McBeal*] sees the choice between personal life and professional life for women today as unrealistic, and articulates the tensions of living in the world where most of us do in fact reside, where they are mutually pervasive and impossible to separate' (2002: 247). In part they are right; the part that claims we live in a world where personal and professional lives should be distinct. In *contrast* to this, all the characters in *Ally McBeal* have connected personal and professional lives and seem to be better (though the more confused) for it. These people live their inner worlds on the outside; quite literally. The live lives at work. This is not to say that work is life; rather the two mix. One of the founding partners of the law firm, Richard Fish, claims that he set the firm up so he could make money and 'have fun'; the former surely aligning with the predominantly capitalist values of professional lawyers (see Bankowski and Mungham, 1976: 120).

As mentioned, the series is often held to account for not critiquing systemic institutional barriers to women. Ally's 'equation of female agency with the freedom to wear a mini skirt stopped short of addressing the social construction of gender and the gendered politics of looking relations' (Ouellette, 2002: 324). Ouellette argues that: 'Sexual objectification is recognized, accepted, and controlled by a conventionally attractive, Ivy League-educated, professionally employed, White woman' (2002: 325). The speech that Nelle Porter (an attorney in Ally's firm) makes to the court on exactly this issue (on Ally's behalf) may not transform social order, but it does point to the inherent contradictions in the objectification of women. Nelle argues that women are placed in a no-win situation. To be taken seriously professionally, they have to be attractive; but they cannot be too attractive (that is, sexy) as then they are objectified and placed outside 'professional' lines. Cohen and Ribak, taking a different perspective to Ouellette, point out that 'Ally McBeal's discourse constructs gender politics as an ongoing, day-by-day routine' (2002). This strikes me as particularly realistic, powerful and to the point.

Baum points out that most who criticise the programme 'seem, to take [it] too literally' (2002: 6). She argues that 'self-reflexivity, uncertainty and irresolution are at the core of the series' (2002: 12). She sees the unisex toilet,[2] for example, as a 'liminal space of desire' (2002: 13). She concludes:

> The series puts the character and the audience in play, by holding out the lure, or the enticement of there being a space and a time where all conflicts may be resolved, a beyond that is analogous to the romanticized, hypothetical space described in the song 'Over the Rainbow' – where Being may be recuperated … One would hope, at least, that perhaps by becoming aware of the relative and arbitrary nature of its normative values, and by creatively manipulating the 'screen' of the gaze, we may begin to realize a society based

---

2 The offices of Cage and Fish have a single toilet room for both men and women. It is often where personal issues are discussed in the office.

> on more equitable values. Then, perhaps … we may come to share a sense of community despite our individual idiosyncrasies, our behavioural and physical peculiarities, beyond the mirrors of our individual identities, in a reality circumscribed by heterogeneity, where relations with the other are grounded in reciprocity rather than reductive subordination (2002: 26).

While this place might not be realised in a 'real' way, it is presented as being worth pursuing nonetheless.

For the purposes of this chapter, I will maintain that a reception theory analysis of the programme overcomes many of the feminist objections (see Cohen, 2002; Brown, 2001: 301). This is an analytic stance which has already been rehearsed in the literature in relation to sexuality (McKenna, 2002). It is true that *Ally McBeal* shows only hints and traces of transformation of the gender political landscape; but the questions it raises gestures towards the possibility of active and 'real' transformation, even though this is not realised in the series.

Current Two – Legal Models

The second current of academic research focuses on whether Ally is a good role model for lawyers and indeed for public understanding of what legal institutions are like, as research shows that most people's knowledge about the law is derived from drama series as opposed to direct contact with any legal or law enforcement institutions (Marek, 1999; Osborn, 2001: 169). This I will be brief about as it has been mentioned above. While one commentary from a female attorney (Friedman, L) rails against being personally identified with *Ally McBeal*, others point out (for example, Sharp, 2001, 2002) the value of representing lawyers as people with lives, feelings and heart. Questions have also been raised as to whether this is realistic or viable in a professional sense. To this I would say two things: (1) lawyers are people and (2) *Ally McBeal* is not a training video. Further, the imperative, not only in the law but in many professions, to take self out of work, to sideline personal ethics, emotions and histories seems to me both unrealistic and undesirable for us as individuals and for us as a society (particularly from a feminist perspective). Whether or not the image of the law presented is a 'true' one (or even whether it is a good one) is asking the wrong question. As I argue later, I do think that this kind of legal process is good; but it is certainly not a true representation of the 'real' world. It never pretends to be. Indeed, that is the point.

Firstly, the cases that Cage and Fish (and later McBeal) take up and are approached with are, to put it mildly, bizarre. As Marek notes, the show is 'not meant to illustrate a real court of law' (1999: 82). Examples include a man wanting to annul his marriage on the basis of sexual addiction; Ling[3] suing a radio programme for causing a hostile working environment in her factory; and a French restaurant being sued for serving horse meat. Likewise the depiction of one judge (Happy Boyle) as making decisions

---

3 A friend of Nelle Porter's (attorney at Cage and Fish) who is also a lawyer and has a relationship with Richard Fish.

on the basis of dental hygiene is equally 'unrealistic'. However, this bizarreness, this 'queerness' does allow for discussion of the very real issues the parodies derive from. While these are not real cases, the lawyers in Cage and Fish make clear in their arguments that they are *analogous* to real law and real cases. Common law operates by precedent, similarity and analogy. *Ally McBeal* may leap rather than creep in these analogies but the functioning of the law in *Ally McBeal* is at least sometimes comparable to actual legal principle. It is also, like the law, intertextual. Characters from other television series (most notably *The Practice*) are often guests for particular story lines.

Current Three – Comedy

This queer comedy is a third strand of work around the series (Cooper and Pease, 2002). Cooper and Pease argue that *Ally McBeal* can be understood as creating a queer space, that is, one which 'challenge[s] and confuse[s] our understanding and uses of sexual and gender categories (Doty, 1993, xvii)'. The senior partner, Richard Fish, is a major player in the creation of this queer space, especially his 'Fishisms' (essentially post-modern maxims or personal proverbs)[4] and his oft repeated argument that gender discrimination laws are in place to protect women because they are weaker.[5] Cooper and Pease argue specifically about homosexuality with respect to the 'Boy to the World'[6] episode. In series two, an episode with a case that deals with wrongful termination on the basis of colour (the plaintiff is orange) makes a similar case. 'Kelley's narratives make it easier to question other, more brutal bigotries' (Cooper and Pease, 2002) by pushing them to extremes.

Cooper and Pease argue for the value of comedy and the queer space for serious discussion (2002). They note that 'hegemonic ideals can be safely questioned by lampooning them because the humour context allows audience members to participate in the mockery without feeling threatened or alienated'. Speech play is important in the transmission of what would otherwise be threatening messages. Judge Happy Boyle is another part of reminding us that judges are also people with lives and

4 For example, 'Helping other people is never so rewarding as when its in your own self-interest.'

5 For example, 'On sex and sexual harassment, women don't see straight. Women as a rule hate other pretty women. Women as a rule also sympathize with other women victims because they are women. Women want other women to be destroyed, but as women they don't want to be the destroyer themselves.'

6 This episode has a dual story-line, each commenting on the other. The 'comic' plot deals with partner Richard Fish's uncle who has died. The uncle did not like short people. Fish eventually decides to take the church (where the funeral will be held) to court to allow Fish to talk about his uncle's bigotry in the eulogy. This is eventually allowed by the judge. At the service, the choir sing 'Don't Want No Short People' at the end. Meanwhile, Ally is defending a prostitute, Stephanie, who turns out to be a male-to-female transsexual (Stephen). Ally wants to keep Stephanie/Stephen out of prison. In this she is successful. However, a client, apparently horrified that Stephanie is Stephen, murders her.

histories and preferences; one of his normal courtroom questions to counsel is for them to show their teeth, to make sure they are clean (this seems to be transformation of having to come to the court with 'clean hands'). The law is not a straightforward application of well-established logical rules. If this were the case, computers would by now have replaced judges. The most notable computers in *Ally McBeal* are those which supply animation (to provide objective correlatives for what is in characters' minds).[7]

Ally Itself and Herself

Ally McBeal speaks to cultural moments. Claims that society (especially in the US) is inherently litigious are now mundane and indeed incorporated into many areas of professional life in an (arguably) unprecedented way. Comments on the litigiousness of Ling (a character who eventually becomes a lawyer in the practice) are common place in the series. Indeed Fish (one of the senior partners) sees Ling's proclivity to sue as a way of her expressing personal pain. Thus the personal is made public in an institutional setting in order for it to be recognised and ratified (or even dismissed, but at least engaged with). When threat of litigation is the major reason for conduct in (especially professional) ways of life, ethics and morals become luxurious. *Ally McBeal* is an attempt to restore the system not whole scale, but case by case.

I suggest that *Ally McBeal* extends an invitation to personalise the law and to discuss issues raised in moral, personal and queer ways. Sharp writes that the programme 'uses legal issues and the public's familiarity with "the trial" to merely backdrop the real concerns and interest of the show: dysfunctional relationships' (2001). The courtroom is both a backdrop and a standard. Action takes place with respect to legal rules, but often flouts them for effect. Further, I would argue that the range of ideas extends beyond 'dysfunctional relationships'. In fact, the series can be read as questioning the very conventions that underpin categorisation of anything (though perhaps especially relationships) as 'dysfunctional'.

Cooper and Pease write that 'the incongruity [in the show] makes a new perspective possible' (2002). It asks us not only to question the law, but also social rules. In fact, the use of the legal backdrop is not accidental. What we 'know' about the law is that it is about rules. The rules that *Ally McBeal* deals with are not just legal but social, and often particularly related to love and personal relationships. McKee (2004) sees Kelley (the writer and creator of the series) as a popular philosopher, concerned particularly with the difficult issue of 'happiness'. This is justice writ large (and small and personal).

Ally McBeal makes a new perspective possible, and indeed I think appealing, using some of the techniques already mentioned. The lawyers are unapologetically people, as are the judges, as is everyone involved in the legal drama (see Sharp, 2001). While having stated that the show attempts to personalise the law, in fact I

7 For example, Ally imagines herself licking the face of a particularly attractive man; we see this.

want to suggest that it seeks to use the frame of the courtroom to debate issues which are germane to our cultural moment (though perhaps some issues are more enduring than others). Discrimination, gender politics and love are the fodder of these cases. Not withstanding the possibility of bringing legal actions for 'emotional pain and suffering', it would be something close to a miracle if any cases actually resembling those presented in *Ally McBeal* ever made it to trial. Indeed, many of their cases do not, even in the context of the series; 'settling' is often the outcome, sometimes they even lose. This is a pragmatic solution within a difficult legal system; a system not as sensitive as it might be to context and circumstance. A sympathetic reading may see this as a form of ADR and indeed there are cases of this in the series. This is an obvious and already institutionalised alternative to litigation. However, note that Ally herself never *settles*, especially when it comes to her relationships.

Legal Dramas

Because of legal dramas, we are all familiar with the structure and features of the 'drama of the courtroom'. We know that there is a judge appropriately costumed, we know that there is a lawyer for each side and that there are rules about who speaks when and what they can say; for example, whether a 'yes or no answer' is required and when it can be compelled. Such details and power implications of the court are the routine concerns for scholars of legal discourse. These conventions are exploited in that the characters exploit and ignore them. The rules of the court in *Ally McBeal* provide a stable set of rules of conduct which are courted with jouissance. However, in *Ally McBeal* questions about the 'fairness' of life are debated. More than this, the cases brought to the firm inevitably have (or shortly will have) some immediate relevance to the characters that we follow. This is not legal positivism; the characters struggle with justice and morality at a personal level. The law court becomes a forum for discussing the personal and enduring injustices we face. This is not far from reality in the view of Bankowski and Mungham who argue that in the real courtroom 'any "drama" exists only in the sense of "theatre", rather than as "confrontation" or "struggle"' (1976: 100). In *Ally McBeal* there is confrontation and struggle, but in an introspective and existential mode.

John Cage is perhaps the best at these performances. Brown notes that his character 'simply carries his performance role to absurd extremes' (2001: 287). It is, for example, 'fairly clear that by asking the jury to repeat, chorus-like, certain things he has said he is breaking down their sense of distance, urging them to become complicit with his version of events and making it easier for them to remember' (2001: 287). And yet as the rhetorical questions are real (in as much as they are answered), the 'performance' is also real in that it is the only way of encoding that which needs to be communicated. It is not the normal 'logos' of the courtroom; pathos and ethos are invoked. His own body sometimes provides the 'sound track' in the court, reminding us 'just how unmusical real life is by comparison with cinematic and televisual life' (Brown, 2001: 291). It is not accidental that Cage shares his name with an avant-garde composer. This is an example of self-reflexivity at an ontological level.

Public Law and 'The Real World'

The law is traditionally public, at least the tradition stemming from Attic Greece. The public were expected to decide on cases. Early Greek drama also commented on the law and legal cases. Indeed, the voting on drama festivals was closely bound to social standing and power, and this was also active in the court. Machura and Ulbrich note the particular similarity of American courts to Greek drama (2001: 125).

> The 'scene', where the action in Greek tragedy takes place, is similar to the space in front of the bench where opposing counsel act, plead, and question witnesses. The 'orchestra', where the chorus sings and dances, has its functional equivalent in the jury box (2001: 125).

While attorneys in the series do not wear wigs and the like, the characters do have signature styles (Ally wears short skirts, Renee wears low cut tops). John Cage often brings props with which to argue his case. He is routinely accused of attempting to disrupt or dishonour court proceedings with these and with strange personal accoutrements (he has, for example, a remote control for flushing the toilet in the office – he 'likes a clean bowl').

Law is drama; that much is clear. In *Ally McBeal*, the law is used as a stage to articulate problems of personal justice. As one of the criticisms that is levelled at *Ally McBeal* is that it is not mimetic, it makes sense to address this. The argument is that practising the law in the real world does not resemble the law practised in *Ally McBeal*. If we broaden the argument, one might say that the real world is not like the world in *Ally McBeal*. Seeing dancing babies, hearing theme songs and the whole office transforming into a musical is not normal. *Ally McBeal* does not pretend it is. Rather, I suggest, it asks that the world *could* be like this, or at least asks us to consider the possibilities such a transformation might bring. In being reflexive about how the 'reality' of *Ally McBeal* is constructed, it asks us to do the same.

That what is shown in the series is not real (and being aware of this in some way) is made explicitly and repeatedly. In an exchange between Ally and her current therapist (Tracy), Ally protests that she is not receiving 'normal therapy'. Tracy responses that Ally is 'not a normal person', rather Ally is 'a cracker'.

To show the questioning of reality and the invitation to make the world otherwise, I now use some short extracts from a single episode, the first of the second series, 'The Real World'. As the title suggests, it questions the separation of reality and fantasy, legal rules and natural justice.[8]

8 Brown's work on the soundtrack of Ally McBeal points to the importance of music in the show. Each show will include at least one scene in the bar, an improbable space in many

The episode opens with Ally having a dream about touching fingertips with a man she cannot see. When Ally's room-mate Renee comes in to Ally's room, Ally tells her about a dream that was so vivid 'it felt like it was more than make believe'. It was so much more than fantasy that it felt 'real it wasn't only just a dream; it was more'.[9] At the same time, there is music being played and sung during the opening dream sequence; this episode's theme tune, 'In Dreams'. Vonda Shepard is the resident jazz musician in the bar beneath the law offices. She also provides themed music for each episode. McKee notes that music is used 'as a form of citation, drawing on previous texts to make and support arguments' so that they need not be restated (2004: 398). This particular song includes lyrics such as: 'in dreams we do so many things we set aside the rules we know' and 'If only we could always live in dreams'. This refers directly, at the start of the episode, to the issues which will be covered.

The dream that Ally has becomes relevant to the case that she will be working on. It happens that the main witness for the prosecution, Jason Tression, had the same dream as Ally (except that he was the man she could not see). It should also be noted that Renee (Ally's room-mate and District Attorney) comes into Ally's room as she 'hears' Ally dreaming. This tells us that the dream state (and visual and aural hallucinations) are not just 'real' for the characters experiencing them; they are also accessed by those close to them.

The legal case in this episode deals with the matter of statutory rape. Ms Jewel, a 39-year-old woman, is brought before the court on charges of having sexual relations with a then 16-year-old, Jason Tression. Now, Jason is 18. He makes clear to Ally and John (who are defending Jewel) that he did not want the case to come to trial.

When Ally cross-examines Jason, she asks him about when he had first noticed and spoken to the defendant. Jason comments that he asked Jewel why 'she always seemed so sad'. Ally asks Jason whether he interpreted 'this sadness as as ah – loneliness?' Jason answers that it 'seemed a little worse'. Quite viciously, Ally demands to know 'what could be worse than being alone', then composes herself and rephrases to ask how it seemed worse. Jason observes that lonely people have 'a look'. Ally asks 'What kind of look?' Jason implies that lonely people still have hope and that Jewel was 'just sad', 'like she knew too much'. Of course, Ally has to find out what this knowledge is. Jason replies with another observation, or perhaps even personal philosophy, that 'Some people find love permanent' while 'some are just meant to be alone'. Jewel, Jason guesses, 'knew what she was'. Ally is so caught up in Jason's testimony that the judge has to call on her by name a couple of times before she emerges from her thoughts.

The shots of various people in the court during this exchange make it clear that Jason is speaking to them; or rather they are listening. In Ally's case, it is clear that

---

ways, just below the law offices, where Vonda Shepard sings with her band. In this episode, the theme song is about dreams and reality ('In the Real World').

9 (.) indicates pauses. ? indicate rising intonation. Bolding indicates emphasis. Breaking a word into syllables indicates slowing of speech with emphasis (that is, every syllable stressed).

she is personally interested in what Jason *knows* about loneliness and hope and love. Her questions, 'what kind of look?' and 'what did she know?' are asked as much (if not more) as an individual than as an attorney. Ally wants to see what Jason saw and, more importantly, to know how she would be seen (see Lacan, 1977).

In this episode, the relation of the case to Ally's life and thoughts is made explicit as she eventually goes out on a date with Jason. Before this, however, she is already personally involved in the story. Cases in *Ally McBeal* routinely have a connection to the lives of those working at Cage and Fish. This suggests that the courtroom is a place for the characters to work as well as to work on their own 'issues'. The lawyers also bring their personal experiences to the cases they argue, as we will see in John Cage's closing argument. Ally, as central character, is often directly involved. After this day in court (this apparently not being therapy enough), Ally runs to her therapist to recount the events.[10] By way of explaining the situation in the courtroom, Ally says 'it's as if he was talking about me'. She then confesses to having 'unpure thoughts' and when this is queried by Tracy, she emphasises 'unpure sexual thoughts'. With typical aplomb, Tracy responds: 'Oh as opposed to philosophical impurities, gee thanks for clearing that up'.

The presence of a therapist in the show is a constant. Who the therapist is, and their techniques, change. Tracy, played by Tracey Ullman, engages directly with Ally's worlds, usually by demeaning them. Tracy also manages to normalise (though perhaps not soothe) Ally's anxieties, as we see presently. In this episode, it is not just the relation between dreams and reality that is questioned, but also the connection between institutional and social laws. Tracy is instrumental in making this explicit; as is the closing argument in court, to be examined shortly. In response to Ally's assertion that having sexual feelings for an 18-year-old is unnatural, Tracy responds that: 'If it were against **nature** then they wouldn't have to pass the **laws** would they?' The vocal emphasis here (indicated in bold) captures exactly the distinction at issue; just to make it even clearer for Ally.

In a later therapy session in the same episode, Tracy again questions these social rules. She asks Ally why she cannot date this boy; an idea that Ally finds disturbing and somehow disgusting. Tracy concludes: 'It can't last forever – of course not – but who made up the rule that the best loves do.' Indeed, if a therapist is supposed to be a reality check, Tracy is a rude one. The therapy space is one where the ludic is made logical. In trying to come to terms with Ally's feelings for Jason, Tracy connects it to her losing of Billy's love as a young woman (Billy being her first love, now married to someone else and working in the same firm). Tracy explains that Ally is worried that she has already experienced her big love affair. She then advises Ally not to give herself a hard time for having these thoughts, as Ally 'could be one hundred percent right'.

We see in the following section that the laws of love are crucial here. So too are love myths and the discourse of romantic love in particular. Further, romantic love as

---

10 Indeed, she seems to have open access to her therapists. Another example of the unreal representation in this series.

depicted in films (as fated, consuming, physical and soulful) is the particular model being worked with.

Law and Law

Legal discourse will always transform representations. The way I might describe how my car was stolen will not be the manner in which a legal professional would describe it for a court. In this case, we also see a transformation. While using legal terminology, Ally and John Cage transform the legal account (of statutory rape) into an emotional episode (of romantic love). Central to this transformation is the use of words that are available in two frames of reference at once; in particular, 'insanity' and 'boy'. In defending Laura Jewel, John Cage makes use of the distinction between sanity and insanity in the context of love and intimacy. This is only possible because of the legal defence of 'insanity'. Drawing on his own experiences of a film as a young man, he asks the jury to consider more than the letter of the law; he asks them to consider the 'logic' of love.

In describing her relationship with Jason to Cage, Laura Jewel makes it clear that it was mutual. When cross-examined by Renee (Ally's room-mate and the District Attorney), the romanticism is held up to question by the standards of the law. In Jewel's testimony under cross-examination, on which I focus here, she makes explicit the distinction between terms of law and terms of real life. It is perhaps worth noting that a prosecution lawyer would not allow a hostile witness to make speeches as occurs here; they would certainly not provide the conversational structure to do so – here when Renee asks 'Such as?' In this sense, Jewel is a defendant acting 'without fear and uncertainty' (Bankowski and Mungham, 1976: 101). Further, in contrast to 'real' courts of law, Jewel (as defendant) does have 'a history, voice, [and] individual identity' (see Bankowski and Mungham, 1976: 92).

In cross-examination of Jewel, Renee queries the testimony Jewel has already given. Renee puts it to Jewel that her narrative sounds romantic and rational, even though she has entered a plea of insanity. Jewel then makes the first of many distinctions, first stating: 'My lawyers plead insanity. They say the term has a legal distinction for medical insanity.' Renee leaves this line of questioning and starts on the law. 'You had sex with a boy,' she says, in what is a statement rather than a question. Jewel responds that 'there was nothing gratuitous' and Renee simply repeats her statement, with added emphasis on both 'sex' and 'boy'.

Jewel then introduces the distinction between legal and lay definitions, linking this to her answers about the insanity plea. Renee asks whether Jason was a 'boy' to Jewel. She agrees that he was and indeed confesses that she may have been attracted to him "because he was a boy". Not surprisingly, Renee queries this, in another quasi-statement, '**Because** he was a boy'. Jewel explains that while sexually Jason was a man, she also 'felt his willingness to just surrender … to love to the moment', adding that 'a young man's moment can last a while'. When asked to elaborate on this preference for boys (in a similar vein to Ally's probing of Jason earlier), Jewel argues that as men 'get older they lose the essence of the very thing a woman most wants' which is'"simple intimacy'. She then describes the feelings she experienced with Jason and concludes: 'There are things in him that I'm sure will go dead as he grows older. Perhaps I was celebrating the boy inside him, I was celebrating the boy inside me.'

The defence of 'insanity' is particularly pertinent, having a legal meaning and a lay one. While it invokes psychological science, it is not actually part of that discourse. Different discourses, especially professional discourses, model the world in different ways. The pertinent detail about models is that they always leave something out while prioritising what is considered salient; in short, they are representations. Laura Jewel is given an unrealistic (in terms of real court rooms) opportunity in being able to spell out what 'boy' means to her. The speech attempts to make salient his emotional maturity as opposed to his chronological age.

The distinction between the law and nature is also made explicit in the closing arguments. Indeed this is not only a two-part, but a three-part distinction. First, we have the law which states unequivocally that age is age and '16 is 16' as the District Attorney repeats several times. Renee reminds the jury that if the gender roles were reversed, the jury would have no trouble returning a guilty verdict. We also have a questioning of the rigidity of the law. John Cage, as defence attorney, also makes distinctions. Specifically, in his closing he argues that 'if Jason Tression had picked up a gun and shot a few classmates (.) we'd have no trouble seeing him as an adult'. However, when it comes to falling in love with an older woman, 'he must be a child'. Indeed, '[t]o be able to reach out on a lazy afternoon and sexually gratify this woman over and over and over …' is as far as Cage gets before the judge interrupts him.

This undermines the first claim, that the law-is-the-law. Even 'the law' (though lexically often giving the impression of being monolithic) draws distinctions based on context (for different kinds of crimes, for example). Here, Cage contrasts violent crimes with love. The formulation, 'over and over and over' attempts to mirror action in syntax. This kind of representation steps over the lines of representational propriety in the court; hence Cage is stopped by the judge.

The final strand is the questioning of the distinction between adult and child; between man and boy. This is made clear in Laura Jewel's testimony cited above. What a woman needs (emotionally) is a boy. But this is not only a legal distinction, it is a social and even personal one. It brings into question what is 'natural' and this is unmistakably an appeal to natural justice and social norms. Ally sees this contradiction; between what she needs and what she thinks is possible and socially acceptable. She says to Billy, though as much to herself in an attempt to 'know' who she is: 'Maybe I'm meant for a boy and that's why of course meant to be alone.'

The structure of Ally's conclusion is to the point. While she is only 'maybe' meant for a boy, 'of course' she is meant to be alone. Logically this does not follow. Ally, it seems here, has already decided 'which one' she is; that she is meant to be alone. Thus her quest becomes to find out why this is the case; the distinction between man and boy, and the unavailability of the latter, provides her with a possible answer.

Billy counters Ally's 'logic' with what is a tempering of the social order, in the same way that John Cage has pointed out the tempering of the legal order. Billy argues for 'another possibility'. He suggests to Ally that she's 'meant for this boy'. Essentially Billy suggests it is a question of personal context. Not that Ally is meant for *boys*, but that she is meant for this boy; he moves the impossible general statement into a possible particular. The problem is mitigated somewhat in that Jason, now 18, is no longer legally a boy. (This allows a space for Ally to explore Billy's hypothesis by going on a date with Jason.)

John Cage also re-appropriates both legal and social rules into the context of this story when he sums up for the jury. He starts by telling the jury about a film he saw as a teenager – *Summer of 42* starring Jennifer O'Neil as an 'older woman' who 'seduces' a younger man. John explains that at the end of the film, the couple came together and it was the ending the audience wanted. He explains that this is the 'logic', the 'sanity' of love. He appeals not only to narrative cohesion and his own personal experience, but also to social conceptions of emotional justice. Cage admits that Jewel 'fell victim to her love' in a way that exceeded the law. Cage then expresses a personal wish to 'know that kind of passion', indeed to act insanely. He argues for the sanity of falling in love and feeling its consequences.

Cage explicitly questions the 'sanity' of having laws about love at all and invites the jury to be complicit with him. While the invitation is rhetorical, it is actually taken up. It is taken up, one assumes, because Cage and Ally have, during the course of the trial, represented the personal reality of Jewel and Jason in such a way that the jury can also enter into this world. Because they have been able to imaginatively inhabit the world of the witnesses, they have essentially experienced 'that particular reality' and thus can engage with it on its own terms (see Bankowski and Mungham, 1976: 121). John Cage merges this reality with the law. He points out to the jury that Renee will 'beat that drum the law is the law is the law' as this is her job. However, he asks the jury, 'when it comes to love there really is no law is there?' This is a real question in the sense that the jury answer, in the negative, with one voice. For this, they are rebuked by the judge.

In rejecting the view that there are rules in love, the jury also reject the rules of the courtroom and have to be chastised by the judge (see Bankowski and Mungham, 1976: 116). John Cage is right. The District Attorney does 'beat the drum' about 16 being 16; this is the 'real' face of the law. But in a series which is intensely musical, and dare one say, melodic, a drum will not be enough. In her closing, Renee reminds the jury that 'if this were an adult male and a 16-year-old girl you wouldn't even hesitate' to convict. She characterises the gender stereotypes Cage is exploiting as based on a distinction between sex and love, between the physical and the emotional: 'when a man cheats he's a bum (.) a woman cheats (.) she's just bridging her Madison County'.[11] She argues that this is both 'crass' and a 'form of gender discrimination'. Her final comment is her constant refrain: '**And 16 is 16**'.

---

11 Reference to *Bridges of Madison County*, a romantic novel then film starring Meryl Streep and Robert Redford.

Renee attempts to bring the debate back to absolutes; this is her role as representative of the (monolithic, certain) law. In response to her argument we might say, 'but 16 *isn't* always 16' and indeed, this is **not** a case of an adult male and a young girl. What is clear is that despite the jury returning a verdict of not guilty, by reason of insanity (because for a 39-year-old woman to seek emotional solace with a boy she must be 'insane', as Cage has argued) the rules are not clear; even if they can be represented as such. We are presented with questions, not with answers.

Indeed, when the jury returns its verdict very quickly, Ms Jewel asks John Cage to interpret the significance of this. She asks: 'What does this mean them coming back quickly?' to which Cage nonchalantly responds: 'They have weekend plans.' This is pragmatism pure and simple. The law is the law, but it is also pragmatic, flexible and contextual. This does not always mean it is just; just that it is not fixed and absolute. Juries consider cases but they are also people with weekend plans.

It should be noted that in this case, the jury act as legislators, as interpreters of the law. They take on the role of the judge, as described by Kevelson in the following:

> ... the judge not only must consider himself as an 'ideal legislator' and act as a legislator might if confronted with actual, changing circumstances, but it is the social and cultural values which are hypothesized, and which function as the leading premise in free judicial decision. In other words, it is not the statute which is antecedent ... but it is the *consequence of a legal decision* – the custom and value of a society – which is taken hypothetically as the primary assumption in the process of judicial interpretation, definition and decision-making (1982: 243).

The consequence of the jury finding Jewel guilty would be a rejection of the narrative ideals of romantic love. It would be the wrong end to the story. It is not surprising that they find Jewel not guilty. It is not so much a legal innocence (as Renee makes clear, 16 is 16) but a moral innocence. There was nothing the jury could find in the details of this case that made Jewel morally culpable.

In this, the decisions of juries (and judges) are fundamentally different from legislation. It is hardly imaginable that exclusion clauses could be drafted into legislation to cope with situations like this (as Kevelson suggests). Legislation has to be general and specific enough to be useful. But the 'custom and value of a society' are often best implemented by a jury of peers who share those customs and values. In this way, *Ally McBeal* is an implicit argument for the retention of the jury.

After the trial, Ally finds herself alone in an elevator with Jason. He confesses that he dreamt about her. It is the same dream she had about him; about fingers nearly touching but not quite. On the basis of this synchronicity they go out on a date. Despite the fact that he wants to see her again, Ally declines. The conclusion to this exchange is Ally remarking to Jason that she 'might be too young' for him.

The episode does not even come close to suggesting that sexual relations with children are acceptable. But in the case of a 16-year-old boy, as indeed with a 16-year-old girl, we are in a grey area. While the law is the law, even the law has space for discretion and distinction.

Conclusion

Burke reminds us that:

> The Greek word for justice *(dike)* was in its beginnings as thoroughly an 'act' word as *tao, yoga, and hodos.* Originally it meant *custom, usage, manner, fashion.* It also meant *right.* The connection between these two orders of meaning is revealed in our expression, 'That sort of thing just isn't done,' and in the fact that our word, 'morality' comes from a Latin word for 'custom.' Liddell and Scott's lexicon notes that in *the Odyssey* the word is used of mortals, gods, kings, and suitors, referring to their *custom, way of acting, law of being.* After the homogeneous tribal pattern of Greek life (with its one 'way' or 'justice' shared by all) had dissolved into a political state, with its typical conflicts of property interests, *dike* became a word of the law courts ('A Grammar of Motives', Bizzell and Herzberg, 2001: 1309).

In 'The Real World' we see the difficulty of negotiating the various laws (social, legal, moral) in a setting which is at once general and institutional and at the same time personal. The hypothetical space has always been one of transformation and redemption, at least potentially. *Ally McBeal* provides this space, but also furnishes it with the characters and conventions so that the space is useful. Questions can be asked in particular contexts and answers thus given.

Bankowski and Mungham, following Kaupen (1971), note the public have too '"idealistic" an image of the courts and the court structure and that coming in contact with the reality of the courts tended to shatter that image' (Bankowski and Mungham, 1976: 23). The 'obvious' answer is to 'make the courts in the "image" of the people' (Bankowski and Mungham, 1976: 22). It seems to me that *Ally McBeal* presents these images and raises questions for us to consider rather than providing determinate answers. They are questions familiar to us. They are certainly close to the characters in the show. The cast thus provides a safe and particular vantage point for the audience to consider the principles in context. The legal forum is used as a way of articulating, in a pre-determined legally dramatic way, the various arguments.

Arguments from pathos figure greatly in the series; Moseley and Read note that Ally usually wins her cases:

> Significantly, she does this most often through applying the logic of her personal life to her professional role. Cases are often won by asking the jury to empathise, to apply their own experience to the case under consideration. Similarly, she solves problems in her personal life through using and making connections with her professional life (2002: 245).

Lives are not divided in Ally's world; man (or woman) is not divorced from the world (Bankowski and Mungham, 1976: 110). In this sense, Ally's lives are dialogic and interdependent. It hardly needs pointing out that arguments in a courtroom are constructed dialogically; lawyers construct their arguments using the testimony of witnesses, evidence (texts and other artefacts) and interaction with other legal professionals. This resulting narrative is usually an exercise of the will of those in power (see Jackson, 1990). This case, in particular, asks us to consider what the 'law' would look like if this dialogue and the resulting narratives were real.

The show questions the rules, legal and social, that we live by. Denvir writes: '"Ally" puts in question not so much the morality of the law as it is practiced in the United States, but rather its sanity. The show challenges us to ask whether sane people would choose to live this way' ('Legal Tender'). It also offers us the chance, if only momentarily, to see (quite literally) other possibilities.

In *Ally McBeal*, the personal invokes the ethical and is thus potentially political (if we take up the invitation made). The series seeks again and again to question the legal and social rules that we live by. We are invited to question these in a contextual, personal and ethical way. It is not the answers to the questions that matter, it is the fact that they are posed at all. It seems to me that *Ally McBeal* (and the eponymous heroine) is predominantly concerned with hope. By its very nature, hope is hypothetical. It is, to quote Aristotle, a waking dream.[12] Bankowski and Mungham write:

> What is important is not just to break the orderly consensus [of the dominant ideology] to show that there is a fight, but also to show a vision of the world that, by corresponding with men's [and women's] real interests as free and creative beings, will establish a world that will free them instead of dominating and enslaving them (1976: 131).

Hope, the image and the hypothetical, are transformative. While the lawyers in *Ally McBeal* may 'quarrel in print' and in court and sometimes 'by the book', in the words of Touchstone, 'Your If is the only peacemaker; much virtue in it'.[13] David E. Kelley states: 'In my naive dream … I wish that the world could be like this.'[14] Much virtue in that too.

12 Quoted in Lives Diogenes Laertius (1925), book V, sec. 18.

13 Shakespeare, *As You Like It*, V, iv.

14 Quoted in Braxton (1999).

Chapter 6

Digital Visual and Multimedia Software and the Reshaping of Legal Knowledge

Neal Feigenson

Introduction

More and more lawyers are using digital technologies, including PowerPoint, computer animations, trial presentation software such as Sanction II and Trial Director, and digital video, to create and display evidence and arguments. They are writing books[1] and conducting seminars to teach each other the virtues of these new devices. They proclaim that digital visual displays enhance their effectiveness as advocates because the displays increase audiences' attention to and retention of trial information; they recognize that these technologies allow them to simplify complex issues, streamline case presentation, and adapt their displays on the fly to conform to trial testimony.[2] Lawyers know that the new technologies can help them do better what they already do well: marshal their evidence and tell persuasive stories that further their theories of the case.[3]

That is the practitioners' perspective, and they know what they are talking about. But there is much more to this digital practice than those who are engaged in it have expressed. Even given the homeostatic tendencies of Anglo-American legal systems, the increasing use of digital visual and multimedia technologies will change, indeed is already changing, not only how legal decision makers decide what to believe in particular cases – what information they process and how they do it – but also the very notion of what legal knowledge and legal meaning consist of.

Let me try to be as clear as possible about this. In one sense, 'legal knowledge' refers to what third-party decision makers (prototypically jurors and judges), in

---

1 For example, Michael Arkfield, *The Digital Practice of Law* (Phoenix: Law Partner Publishers, 2001); Deanne Siemer and Frank Rothschild, *PowerPoint for Litigators* (Notre Dame, IN: National Institute for Trial Advocacy, 2002).

2 For example, Arkfield, *The Digital Practice of Law*; Stanley Sandstrom and Adam Bloomberg, 'An Ancient Art Jazzed by High Tech', *The National Law Journal* (5 November 2001): B14-15; Shelley Watts, 'Technology Creates Winning Visual Evidence', *Trial* (September 2000): 68-70.

3 For example, Brian Carney and Neal Feigenson, 'Visual Persuasion in the Michael Skakel Trial: Enhancing Advocacy Through Interactive Media Presentations', *Criminal Justice*, 19 (2004): 22-35.

the course of reaching judgments about the matters under dispute and based on the evidence and arguments presented at hearings and trials, believe to be true about the world relevant to their judgments – the who, what, where, when, and why of a case.[4] In a second sense, 'legal knowledge' refers to what reflective observers of the legal system (among them decision makers and other participants in the legal system, as well as the public generally) think about how those first-order beliefs emerge from the information presented at trials – the truth-status of those beliefs and their relationships to that information. Legal knowledge in this second sense is partly an epistemological question (how do decision makers come to know what they know about the case-relevant world?), but it is also a question of how decision makers (and publics) extract meanings from what is said, shown, and done at trial, and thus is inherently semiological as well.

I would like to argue that digital multimedia are reshaping legal knowledge in both senses. Consider an analogy: the increased use and technical refinement of forensic DNA technology has affected judges' and jurors' decisions in particular cases.[5] It has also led to the 'CSI effect,' whereby jurors in criminal trials have come to expect prosecutors to produce such evidence (and have held the lack of such evidence against the state) because the popular television show about forensic investigation has taught them that that is what legal proof and legal truth ought to look like.[6] Similarly, digital multimedia technologies are changing what legal decision makers believe in particular cases; they are also changing what decision makers and others believe about what legal truth in general looks like.

That digital visual and multimedia technologies are affecting first-order legal knowledge, what decision makers believe about the matters before them, may be easier to explain.[7] Some of the mechanisms by which such effects are produced

4 For present purposes it does not matter whether judges and/or jurors actually articulate these beliefs, for example, as findings of fact, statements to fellow jurors during deliberations, or even silently within their minds, or whether those beliefs remain as inchoate components of more explicit judgments. Nor does the analysis depend on a simple positivist conception of knowing: of course legal decision makers' beliefs about the world are bound up with their inherently normative ultimate judgments (some of which may also be legally relevant judgments, for example, in a negligence case, whether the defendant behaved reasonably under the circumstances) and are guided by normatively framed evidence and arguments; I assume, for instance, that stories (and other mental frameworks, intuitive or explicit) and facts make each other up (to paraphrase Richard Shweder, *Thinking Through Cultures* (Chicago: University of Chicago Press, 1991), p. 2). One can nevertheless properly speak, as judges, jurors, lawyers, and the public do, of the factual component or aspect of beliefs about the world.

5 For example, Barry Scheck, Peter Neufeld and Jim Dwyer, *Actual Innocence* (New York: Doubleday, 2000).

6 Richard Willing, '"CSI Effect" Has Juries Wanting the Evidence', *USA Today* (5 August 2004), http://www.usatoday.com/news/nation/2004-08-05/csi-effect_x.htm.

7 There is as yet a paucity of experimental findings proving such effects, but more is likely to emerge soon (see Neal Feigenson and Meghan Dunn, 'New Visual Technologies in Court: Directions for Research', *Law & Human Behavior*, 27 (2003): 109-126.

(for example, vividness, associative logic, and so on) can be traced to the influence of visual representations generally on belief and judgment. The aspects of digital multimedia on which I will focus in this chapter, however, are those that are either unique to digital presentations or that digitization facilitates and/or makes more salient. These include (but are certainly not limited to): remediation,[8] or the 'repurposing' of (and hence borrowing of credibility from) features of older media in digital media (and vice versa); hypermediation,[9] the use of (and audiences' investment of greater credibility in) less transparent, more highly mediated representations; heightened interactivity between user and interface; and the digital evocation of popular cultural narrative conventions as implicit frames for audiences' uptake of trial information.

I will discuss how these overlapping, intersecting features of digitization are at work in five examples of digital displays used in law today: (1) a medicolegal slide show/animation; (2) a 'virtual reality view'; (3) a multimedia compilation of deposition excerpts and relevant documents using Sanction II software; (4) an excerpt from the 'DigiStrip,' a system for presenting a fetal heartbeat monitoring tape; and (5) a custom-designed multimedia presentation system used in closing argument in a high-profile criminal case. These displays illustrate different levels of technological and rhetorical complexity, different styles of remediation and hypermediation, and different degrees of interactivity. My inquiry moves simultaneously inward toward the details of practice – the particular technologies used and the legal purposes for which they are deployed – and outward toward the culture at large, where these displays resonate with audiences' digital experiences in everyday life.

The proliferation of digital multimedia technologies also has the potential to change second-order legal knowledge: the extent to which reflective participants in and observers of the legal system think that true beliefs about the world can be derived from what is said, shown, and done at trials in general. (I assume, but will not attempt to argue here, that accurate fact-finding is an important goal of Anglo-American legal processes, although it is certainly not the only or necessarily even the most important goal.[10]) Here is the argument in a nutshell. In the philosophy of science,[11] the philosophy of language,[12] linguistics,[13] and many other fields, it is now generally understood that meaning depends on context and that truth depends on the

---

8 Jay David Bolter and Richard Grusin, *Remediation* (Cambridge, MA: MIT Press, 1999).

9 Ibid.

10 For an illuminating discussion of factors affecting what a legal culture deems to be optimal fact-finding processes, see Mirjan Damaška, 'Epistemology and Legal Regulation of Proof', *Law, Probability & Risk* (2003): 117-130.

11 For example, Bruno Latour, *Pandora's Hope* (Cambridge, MA: Harvard University Press, 1999).

12 For example, J.L. Austin, *How To Do Things With Words* (Cambridge, MA: Harvard University Press, 1962); Ludwig Wittgenstein, *Philosophical Investigations* (G.E.M. Anscombe, trans.) (New York: Macmillan, 3rd ed. 1958).

13 For example, Eve Sweetser, *From Etymology to Pragmatics* (Cambridge, UK: Cambridge University Press, 1990).

ways in which it is represented. Objectivism may no longer be viable, but its demise does not entail relativism;[14] rather, across many disciplines, scholars have sought to explain how knowledge is locally constructed through culturally embedded practices[15] and through techniques of investigation and representation.[16]

So too in Anglo-American legal studies, many have recognized that legal meaning is produced by the ways law is practiced,[17] and that rhetoric in its many guises is constitutive of, not opposed to, truth.[18] Yet many participants in the legal system and much of the public seem to hold tenaciously to the belief that the two aspects of the trial, the search for truth and the adversarial battle, are mutually exclusive – that to accept the semioticians'[19] wisdom that 'it's all signs' would threaten the faith that trials (sometimes, often) yield provable truths about the world out there.[20] An unbridgeable gap between what legal decision makers believe they need to know and what, on reflection, it seems that they can know, their confinement to a universe of representations that seems to turn their urge for real world knowledge back upon itself, is for many a cause for real anxiety.

The problem, then, is how to impress upon legal decision makers and the interested public what is already recognized in many other fields: that representations can thoroughly mediate knowledge (in the case-specific sense) without seeming to dissolve that knowledge into mere adversarial contentions – that legal truth can be obtained through, not obscured by, the complex mediations that advocates create for and at trials. I would like to argue that the proliferation of digital visual and multimedia displays has a good chance of bringing about this understanding, for at least two reasons.

First, the features of (many) digital displays – their informativeness, clarity, and vividness, but also (and perhaps especially) the distinctive features on which I will focus in this chapter – are likely to lead judges, jurors, and the public to rely

14 For example, Richard Bernstein, *Beyond Objectivism and Relativism* (Philadelphia: University of Pennsylvania Press, 1985).

15 Clifford Geertz, *Local Knowledge* (New York: Basic Books, 1983); Richard Shweder, *Thinking Through Cultures*.

16 Peter Galison, *Image and Logic* (Cambridge, MA: Harvard University Press, 1997); Ian Hacking, *Representing and Intervening* (Cambridge, UK: Cambridge University Press, 1983).

17 For example, Karl Llewellyn, *The Common Law Tradition* (Boston: Little Brown, 1960).

18 For example, Richard Sherwin, 'Dialects and Dominance: A Study of Rhetorical Fields in the Law of Confessions', *University of Pennsylvania Law Review*, 136 (1988): 729-849; Richard Sherwin, 'Law Frames: Historical Truth and Narrative Necessity in a Criminal Case', *Stanford Law Review*, 47 (1994): 39-83.

19 Thomas Sebeok, *Signs* (Toronto: University of Toronto Press, 1994).

20 See, for example, the 'Received View' of trials in Robert Burns, *A Theory of the Trial* (Princeton: Princeton University Press, 1999); see also Charles Nesson, 'The Evidence or the Event? On Judicial Proof and the Acceptability of Verdicts', *Harvard Law Review*, 98 (1985): 1357-1392.

on them as providing effective and convincing representations of the real, making possible that sense of comprehension of disputed matters that decision makers need to resolve difficult cases. That decision makers and observers believe that they have arrived at the truth of the matter does not, of course, imply that they actually have; digital multimedia (like any other representational medium, including spoken or written language) may mislead as well as enlighten.[21] I will return to this issue at the conclusion of the chapter. The claim at this point (which the examples below will, I hope, support) is simply that the more that legal decision makers and observers are exposed to digital multimedia in court, the likelier they are to believe that trials can yield (good enough) knowledge of case-relevant matters.

Second, by making their mediating presence known, digital multimedia displays promise to lead legal decision makers and observers to recognize the essential role of technologies of representation in the creation of legal meaning and the doing of justice. In particular, increasingly hypermediated digital displays should enhance people's awareness of the crucially constructive role of the interface; so too will interactive digital environments, which provide users with the experience of knowledge not as a simple 'read-off' from objective reality but as the result of the knower's active intervention in the world.[22] The perceived value of and need for digitally represented reality, the recognition that there is no choice but to work within a universe of mediated truth, may bring about a legal culture in which the pervasiveness of digital mediations is viewed not as a cause for cynicism but as an opportunity and a challenge to become as critically informed as possible about how digital multimedia help construct legal reality.

---

21 This seemingly uncontroversial assertion, of course, presumes some sufficiently reliable method for determining the fact of the matter that is extrinsic to the trial itself and thus can be used to gauge the accuracy of the first-order legal knowledge that the trial produces (that is, to distinguish reliably between mistaken and true beliefs). In the vast majority of cases litigated as far as trial, no such method exists, of course; one of the main rationales for conducting trials in the first place is precisely to get at the truth where it is hotly disputed. I will, nevertheless, indulge in the presumption for the present purpose, and revisit it briefly in the conclusion.

22 Shulamit Almog and Ely Aharonson, 'Law as Film: Representing Justice in the Age of Moving Images', *Canadian Journal of Law and Technology*, 3(1) (2004): 1-18, argue that the legal system maintains legitimacy only by fobbing off represented, rhetoricized reality as 'like the real thing.' Whatever its other merits, this argument underestimates the public's sophistication in appreciating how their beliefs are shaped by mediations and (relatedly) diverts attention from the specific ways in which particular courtroom mediations affect belief. In this chapter, to the contrary, I contend that legitimacy is likely to be enhanced by *increasing* recognition of the law's digital rhetorics.

How Digital Displays Create Legal Knowledge: Five Examples

Medico-legal Slide Show/Animation

In a medical malpractice case, expert testimony is ordinarily required to explain what the defendant physician did, how (according to the plaintiff) that contrasts with reasonable medical care, and what the consequences were. Traditionally, expert witnesses illustrated their testimony by diagramming the defendant's methods and standard procedure on a blackboard and/or by pointing to drawings or diagnostic images (for example, x-ray, MRI) prepared before trial. Some experts today choose to augment their testimony regarding the diagnostic images with an animated digital slide show, such as one created by Vitae Publications.[23] The slide show displays schematic and vivid color illustrations of the site of trauma (in this case, a patellar fracture), the recommended procedure (tension band wiring), the procedure the defendant physician used, and the adverse consequences. Each image is briefly captioned and the important details are clearly labeled. In the courtroom, the images are displayed on a large screen or monitor, as the expert (or the lawyer whose witness the expert is) clicks through the slide show in synchrony with the testimony.

These instantly intelligible images appear to provide reliable information about the matters in dispute. Although intended to be iconic, they are not at all photorealistic, nor do they stand in an indexical relation to extralegal reality; indeed, they are at many removes from direct access to that reality. The creators of the display almost certainly did not see the knee or the medical procedure at issue.[24] So what makes this display credible and effective? Among other things, once the expert has warranted that it fairly and accurately depicts what it purports to depict (the authentication of visual evidence minimally required by Federal Rule of Evidence 901[25]), viewers can focus on the essential features of the procedure (that is, the display simplifies; the representation is highly legible); viewers are not distracted (or repulsed) as they might be by a photograph or video of the actual operation, and they are not puzzled as they might be by an x-ray or MRI (even one accompanied by expert interpretation).

In these respects, though, simple drawings or still diagrams on poster board would do just as well. What does digitization add? First, there are several heuristic cues to persuasiveness shared by many digital displays: the advocate's use of (what is generally perceived to be) cutting-edge technology bespeaks expertise, preparation, and command of the case, hence reliability and credibility; and the interactive software allows the advocate to cue the visuals to the testimony as desired, a further

23 Vitae Publications, 2003 (CD-ROM).

24 Indeed, they may never have seen a patellar fracture or tension band wiring. They may have started from medical illustrations in standard texts (or perhaps on-line) and then, in collaboration with the plaintiff's lawyer and possibly after looking at images of the procedure produced by or in consultation with a medical expert (whether radiological films or sketches, we do not know), used specialized software to depict the standard procedure, the alleged surgical error here, and the consequences.

25 Federal Rule of Evidence 901 (2005).

indicator of competence and command. Second, the animated sequence converts a synchronic contrast between the standard procedure and the defendant's error into a simple, vivid story, clearly depicting both the defendant's deviation from professional norms and the cause-and-effect relation between that deviation and the bad outcome.[26]

Third and most importantly, specific visual features of this slide show borrow credibility from other media. The symmetrically composed visual frames and hierarchical verbal/visual order of the entire (white-bordered portion of the) screen, as well as the overlays and animations of the illustrations, evoke the pages and transparencies of traditional anatomy textbooks, thus appealing to analog sensibilities and gaining authority by implicit reference to that standard information source.[27] The shallow visual space of the slide frames also suggests traditional medical dioramas and models (as in, for example, the La Specola museum in Florence). This is an instance of remediation,[28] the 'repurposing' of one medium through its representation in another. Thus, this medicolegal slide show/animation is likely to be taken up as a highly credible depiction of what it purports to represent because it presents expert information in the way that a modern audience expects it to be presented (an interactive screen), but also because it appeals to viewer expectations drawn from earlier media (for example, medical textbooks and reference works) that are themselves associated with reliable knowledge of the world.

'Virtual Reality View'

Photographs have been used at trials since the late nineteenth century to illustrate eyewitness testimony, letting jurors and judges see how things were and (sometimes) what really happened. Indeed, the legal category of demonstrative evidence was created in response to these early proffers of photographic and other visual evidence. Mnookin[29] explains that the category reflected an attempt to negotiate the tension between, on the one hand, photographs' exceptionally powerful iconic and indexical authority, their seeming ability to transcribe nature directly, and on the other, their status as human artifact and hence their capacity to manipulate and mislead. (The doctrinal settlement, according to Mnookin, was eventually to admit photographic evidence but to domesticate it by analogizing it to other, older visual evidence, such as maps and drawings, as 'merely illustrative' of verbal testimony rather than as

---

26 See Neal Feigenson, *Legal Blame* (Washington, DC: American Psychological Association, 2000). From the advocate's point of view, however, a possible downside of this or any other slide sequence (or animation or video) is that once the lawyer or expert clicks on the next slide, the preceding image is gone; it is therefore much less likely to remain a focus of attention.

27 This is the kind of reference work that would typically be admitted into evidence as a 'learned treatise,' see Federal Rule of Evidence 803(18) (2005).

28 Bolter and Grusin, *Remediation.*

29 Jennifer Mnookin, 'The Image of Truth: Photographic Evidence and the Power of Analogy', *Yale Journal of Law & the Humanities*, 10 (1998): 1-74.

'substantive' evidence in itself.) Videos, of course, are now also routinely used: surveillance videos contemporaneous with the events in question, crime scene 'walk throughs,' or videos of an accident or crime location made months later.

Digital photography and video is now commonplace, but digitization is also making possible interactive, three-dimensional visual representations. The 'virtual reality view' from WIN Interactive, Inc. is the digital successor to earlier forms of photorealistic evidence.[30] It can be offered to illustrate eyewitness testimony (just as a properly authenticated photograph or video might be) or to substitute for a traditional jury view of the location at which the litigated events occurred. The virtual reality view offers a 360-degree view of any scene; users can adjust at will their field of vision laterally or (within limits) vertically; they can zoom in on details as if physically moving toward particular features of the scene, and then zoom out to take in a wider field. In Ireland's Bloody Sunday Tribunal, for example, witnesses have been able to interact with computer-generated views of various locations in Derry and thus virtually revisit scenes, observing them from any angle and drawing arrows on the screen to describe the events and movements they recall. In some instances the virtual reality system has enabled the Tribunal to confirm that it was physically possible for witnesses to have seen what they remembered seeing, given the layout of the city and the witnesses' locations at the time.[31] Although the virtual reality view is currently designed to be displayed on a screen, the technology for more thoroughly realized, more immersive three-dimensional virtual environments already exists, and some courtrooms may in the not too distant future be outfitted with the devices needed to accommodate them.[32]

The virtual reality view aims for verisimilitude. Like traditional photographic or video evidence, it purports to provide access to the real through immediacy and transparency,[33] and thus appeals to naïve realism in its purest form: there is a real

---

30 WIN Interactive, 2003 (CD-ROM).

31 See 'The Bloody Sunday Inquiry', http://www.bloody-sunday-inquiry.org.uk/; Darius Whelan, private communication with author (2005).

32 The fabrications involved in any relatively new and unfamiliar technology are bound to raise evidentiary concerns. For instance, does the composition of the seemingly synchronous visual space of the virtual reality view out of many photographic or video images that were necessarily taken over time undermine its reliability? What about the likelihood that no real eyewitness could have perceived everything depicted in this interactive display? The response to these concerns may be that, just as 'ordinary' photographs are introduced as illustrative aids, to set the scene the witness orally describes, and not as substantive proof, so the virtual reality view ought to be admissible for the same purpose so long as a competent witness testifies that the view fairly and accurately represents what the witness saw (Brian Carney, private correspondence with author (2005)). (After all, no eyewitness could possibly have perceived everything depicted in an ordinary photograph, either.) To the best of my knowledge, although virtual reality views have been used at several trials, only the individual photographs comprising the views, and not the files containing the interactive operations, have been admitted into evidence (ibid.).

33 Bolter and Grusin, *Remediation.*

world out there, knowable to anyone who can see it. But digitization goes beyond traditional forms of photorealistic displays by allowing the viewer (or user) to interact with the represented environment, and thus experience a more compelling sense of presence, of 'being there.'[34] It is presence that has led some to treat more fully immersive virtual environments (of which the two-dimensional virtual reality view is but a precursor) as the culmination of millennia of effort to produce the 'essential copy' of reality.[35] Accordingly, one reason the virtual reality view would be both credible and convincing evidence of 'how things were' is that it so seems to resemble an unmediated experience of reality that it should be especially powerful in eliciting from users the kinds of cognitive and emotional responses users would have to the corresponding real-life phenomena.[36]

This same interactivity, however, also reflects a conception of what learning and knowing is about that is quite different from naïve realism, because audiences are likely to take up on the virtual reality view's implicit reference to a very different kind of reality – namely, video/computer gaming. The virtual reality view, like the typical 'first-person shooter' computer game or many more complex and sociable virtual worlds, places the user/participant in a seemingly unbounded environment. The field of vision changes as the participant interacts with the environment by manipulating the interface to redirect his or her attention. What the participant discovers in the virtual reality view, as in other virtual worlds, he or she finds out as a result of these interactions.[37]

The implicit model of knowledge as interaction which computer gaming visualizes has been propounded often in the last 20 years in cognitive linguistics, cognitive neuroscience, and philosophy,[38] but the virtual reality view evokes the

34 Jonathan Steuer, 'Defining Virtual Reality: Dimensions Determining Telepresence', in Frank Biocca and Mark Levy (eds), *Communication in the Age of Virtual Reality* (Hillsdale, NJ: Lawrence Erlbaum Associates, 1995), pp. 33-56.

35 Frank Biocca, Taeyong Kim and Mark Levy, 'The Vision of Virtual Reality', in Frank Biocca and Mark Levy (eds), *Communication in the Age of Virtual Reality* (Hillsdale, NJ: Lawrence Erlbaum Associates, 1995), pp. 3-14.

36 See Feigenson and Dunn, 'New Visual Technologies in Court'.

37 I have, of course, touched on only a few, basic (and even superficial) features of virtual worlds in order to identify an important similarity between the new virtual demonstrative evidence and those virtual worlds. Things get more complicated when we recognize, for instance, that many computer games also *remediate* standard Hollywood film conventions regarding character and action, thus normalizing players' virtual experiences (see Lev Manovich, *The Language of New Media* (Cambridge, MA: MIT Press, 2001); thus, virtual demonstrative evidence may evoke both computer gaming and, through that medium, the medium of popular movies (see discussion of multimedia closing argument below).

38 For example, Patricia Churchland, *Brain-Wise* (Cambridge, MA and London: Bradford Book, MIT Press, 2002); George Lakoff and Mark Johnson, *Metaphors We Live By* (Chicago: University of Chicago Press, 1980); George Lakoff and Mark Johnson, *Philosophy in the Flesh* (New York: Basic Books, 1999); Alva Noë, *Action in Perception* (Cambridge, MA: MIT Press, 2004).

experience (and not just the declarative knowledge) of this notion.[39] It is therefore especially likely to appeal to the increasing number of jurors who bring from their own experiences in virtual worlds this same intuitive sense that only their active intervention makes the perceived world 'real.'[40]

There is yet another sense in which the virtual reality view may encourage decision makers to understand legal knowledge as pragmatically constructed rather than simply discovered. For people whose virtual experiences include complex virtual worlds, the virtual reality view may also evoke models of community and social interaction that may encourage them to understand their fact finding task as part of a collaborative decision making endeavor – a negotiation with represented reality.[41]

Thus the virtual reality view, which at first may seem to be 'ultrarealistic,' upon reflection tells us something about how digital visuals may problematize naïve realism in law. Understood as the 'essential copy' of reality, virtual reality evidence forces courts to consider, as they did when photographic evidence was first offered, whether visual displays may be too persuasive as representations of reality for the legal process to contain. Yet understood as images of the real that would not exist but for intensive and arcane technological interventions, virtual reality evidence may help viewers/users appreciate to what extent our (credible and accurate) impressions of the way the world is are due not to unmediated access to the world, but to manipulations of it, to the artful deployment of technologies to capture and reconfigure the world and make it intelligible to us. The virtual reality view, because of its novelty (for the time being at least), also makes highly salient the extent to which legal audiences'

---

39 As used thus far in American trials and the Irish Tribunal, the virtual reality view is operated by the witness, not the judge or jurors, so the sense of participant interaction is to this extent vicarious. In at least one case in Great Britain, the *Soham* kidnapping and murder trial, jurors were allowed to play the prosecution's random-access evidentiary CD-ROM in the jury room. It is conceivable that in the (near?) future, more decision makers themselves may be given access to the controls.

40 In different virtual reality experiences this may variously be true from percepts – consider, for example, the relatively low-speed, screen-based virtual worlds in which there is a discernable lag between the user's turning of direction or attention and the filling out of the visual field – to the contents (including avatars) that the user himself/herself chooses to create (see, for example, Cory Ondrejka, 'Escaping the Gilded Cage: User Created Content and Building the Metaverse', *New York Law School Law Review*, 49 (2004): 81-101). For an introduction to virtual reality and its legal significances, see generally Beth Noveck, 'Introduction: The State of Play', *New York Law School Law Review*, 49 (2004): 1-18.

41 On on-line dispute resolution, see Louise Teitz, 'Providing Legal Services for the Middle Class in Cyberspace: The Promise and Challenge of On-Line Dispute Resolution', *Fordham Law Review*, 70 (2001): 985-1016; on on-line resolution of both real world and virtual world disputes, see Ethan Katsh, 'Bringing Online Dispute Resolution to Virtual Worlds', *New York Law School Law Review*, 49 (2004): 271-291. (Note that actual on-line 'cyberjuries' do not yet typically feature deliberations; see Nancy Marder, 'Cyberjuries: A Model of Deliberative Democracy?', in Peter Shane (ed.), *Democracy Online* (New York: Routledge, 2004), pp. 35-46.)

uptake of visual media will depend on their extralegal experiences with those media. In contrast to the epistemology of naïve realism, in which accurate knowledge is passively read off (visually or otherwise) from objective reality, the perceived credibility of the virtual reality view – the extent to which it accurately represents a real world and thus helps build useful, case-relevant knowledge – may depend in part on what viewers/users are accustomed to doing in virtual worlds in everyday life.

Sanction II Deposition Video and Document Compilation

In a breach of contract case, the exact terms of the agreement are of course critical. Advocates can draw on several sources to satisfy their burdens of proof on this issue, including testimonial and documentary evidence. Digitization now allows advocates to combine and present traditional evidence in new and powerful ways. Using Sanction II, a digital trial presentation system created by Verdict Systems LLC,[42] a lawyer can (for instance) capture an excerpt from an opposing party's videotaped deposition; digitize the letter containing the contract terms, signed by the opposing party, and highlight the crucial portions of the letter; and then juxtapose on a single screen the portions of the deposition and the letter that prove the advocate's point (for instance, to show during cross-examination of the opposing party that his trial testimony is inconsistent with his prior deposition testimony and the terms of the letter).[43]

Compared to the methods a lawyer without digital technology would use to accomplish the same goal, namely, having the witness read from the deposition transcript and introducing the document into evidence and circulating it to the jury, the Sanction II digital presentation is likely to be taken up by the judge and jurors as a highly credible and effective representation of the truth of the matter. To some extent this is due to the increased vividness[44] and speed of the presentation. The videotaped deposition can be much more compelling evidence of the prior statement than are mere words in a transcript: the audience can watch the witness saying the words and can contrast his demeanor at the prior time with what he looks like at trial, and the highlighted projection of the digitized document focuses attention on its most important aspects (relevant content of letter, witness's signature). In addition, digitization makes it possible for advocates to 'smooth out the edges' of older demonstrative evidence, such as old photos or documents, and present that evidence accurately and with the same degree of clarity and 'finish' as more recent evidence.[45]

---

42 Verdict Systems LLC (2002) (CD-ROM).

43 The same video/document compilation could also be used, as video depositions often are, to preserve the testimony of a witness who may be unavailable for trial, to be used as a substitute for direct examination of the witness. And it could be used (again) during closing argument if the facts involved were sufficiently important to bear repeating.

44 Cf. Brad Bell and Elizabeth Loftus, 'Vivid Persuasion in the Courtroom', *Journal of Personality Assessment*, 49 (1985): 659-664.

45 Carney and Feigenson, 'Visual Persuasion in the Michael Skakel Trial'.

However, I would like to call attention to two other features of this multimedia display that suggest a dramatically new kind of information framing, and hence a new mode of making legal meaning.

First, digitization facilitates the juxtaposition of disparate evidence within a single frame. Consider the history of these images. From thousands of paper and computerized records relating to the interactions of the corporate parties and their employees, a two-page letter typed and signed in April 1992 has been culled. Three and a half years later, the author of that letter is deposed and the deposition is recorded on video (a firm hired by the deposing lawyers does this) as well as by stenography. Some four years after the deposition is taken, the letter has been scanned, logged into the trial presentation software program, and annotated (partially zoomed in and highlighted); the video of the deposition is searched, an excerpt is identified, edited, and logged into the program, and then the excerpt is montaged with the modified images of the letter. All of this converges on a single point of fact, made visible and audible on a screen in court: the inconsistency between the witness's trial testimony and certain facts established by the documentary (and prior testimonial) evidence.

This culling and eventual bringing together of different pieces of evidence makes manifest how digitization allows information to be mobilized to an unprecedented degree to further the advocate's aims.[46] Once converted to electrical signals, information can be replicated instantaneously and inexpensively (at nearly zero marginal cost); it can be converted from one modality to another (for example, from sounds to text, and vice versa); it can be immediately transported to any location the signals can reach; and it can be recombined with other digitized data from almost any origin whatsoever (software compatibility issues aside). Digitization allows vast amounts of information from sources widely dispersed in both time and space to be brought together and juxtaposed within a single frame or sequence of frames, revealing relationships that might otherwise remain obscure.[47]

---

46 See Bruno Latour, 'Drawing Things Together', in Michael Lynch and Steve Woolgar (eds), *Representation in Scientific Practice* (Cambridge, MA: MIT Press, 1988), pp. 19-68.

47 As such, digitization greatly advances the transformation of cognition by inscription technologies (techniques for creating *immutable mobiles*, representations that can be transported and widely disseminated without losing their essential significations) that took such a great leap forward in early modern Europe, making possible that era's scientific revolution (Latour, 'Drawing Things Together').

The juxtaposition of digitized data on the screen is not without epistemological, evidentiary, and rhetorical risks. The placement and composition of material within a frame (the edges of the screen or borders depicted within it), including resulting distortions in relative size among visual elements, may create the illusion as opposed to the reality of meaningful relationships among the elements. The conversion of multiple images from analog to digital media may also make either more or less salient correspondences or differences between the images, possibly affecting case-relevant judgments (see *Connecticut v. Swinton*, 268 Conn. 781 (2004), in which the Connecticut Supreme Court ruled on the prerequisites for authenticating and thus admitting into evidence a Photoshop overlay of (1) a digitally enhanced (originally analog) forensic photograph of teeth marks on a homicide victim's body and (2) a digitized

Second, viewers of Sanction II evidentiary compositions see the truth of the matters in dispute through hypermediation. In contrast to the virtual reality view and the medicolegal slide show, which appear to represent what could be seen (at least in principle) by ordinary, unmediated vision, the Sanction II assemblage does not even purport to simulate or represent something that could be experienced without mediation. It is knowledge via simultaneous access to multiple media.[48]

And hypermediation is likely to be an especially credible mode of representing reality precisely because it has become ubiquitous in most people's everyday lives. While hypermediated visual informational environments can be found, for instance, in medieval European art and early modern 'cabinets of wonders'[49] and in early twentieth century files of newspaper clippings,[50] hypermedia are far more pervasive in people's lives today. Most people are now accustomed to getting their news of the world from television with multiple screens, icons, and as many as three crawling texts; split-screen movies have migrated from the artistic periphery (such as Andy Warhol's *Chelsea Girls* in the 1960s) to mainstream Hollywood (for example, *Time Code*)[51]; and perhaps most important of all, people spend more and more of their time working with and playing on computers interfaces with multiple windows. Hypermediated courtroom displays appeal to (and help train) a different sense of what it is to acquire knowledge.

'DigiStrip' Fetal Heart Monitor Presentation System

An even more striking illustration of legal hypermediation is the 'DigiStrip,' a digital system created by High Impact Graphics for presenting a fetal heart monitor strip in a case involving catastrophic injury allegedly resulting from negligence in obstetrical

---

image of a pencil drawing of the defendant's teeth which an odontology expert had made by taking a wax mold of the teeth, placing the mold on a photocopy machine and printing out the image, and then tracing it). Finally, the 'flattening' of all digitized data, whatever its origin, into a uniform, two-dimensional, non-tactile screen format may sacrifice some of the persuasive impact of what the law refers to as 'real' evidence – the thing itself (although the point may be extended to actual documents as opposed to their screen displays) – namely, the sense of presence, of contiguity with wrinkled, lumpy, three-dimensional reality.

48 Nor does the meaning of the display (or its rhetorical force) derive from its *iconicity* in a Peircean sense: because there is no necessary correspondence between the particular spatial arrangement of the elements in the screen and their referent, the display is not a *diagram* (and it is certainly not an *image*); see Sebeok, *Signs*.

49 Bolter and Grusin, *Remediation*; Barbara Stafford, *Good Looking* (Cambridge, MA and London: MIT Press, 1996).

50 Anke te Heesen, 'News, Paper, Scissors: Clippings in the Sciences and Arts around 1920', in Lorraine Daston (ed.), *Things That Talk* (New York: Zone Books, 2004), pp. 297-327.

51 Caryn James, 'Splitting. Screens. For Minds. Divided', *The New York Times* (9 January 2004): E1.

or gynecological care.[52] The fetal heart monitor, invented in 1957,[53] continuously records the fetal heartbeat, providing early warning of possible fetal distress and thus allowing appropriate and timely interventions to be undertaken. It is one of a long line of technologies including EKGs, EEGs, and the like, going back to the late nineteenth century, by which physiological functions not readily or at all observable by unaided vision could be made visible, recorded, and perhaps most importantly, made amenable to quantitative description and analysis.[54] In all of these respects, the inscriptions produced on paper by the fetal heart monitor – the product of a highly complex set of medicotechnological interventions involved in the giving of prenatal care in hospitals – unquestionably increase available knowledge about fetal development and the course of prenatal care in any given situation.

The DigiStrip converts that paper record, which can be dozens of yards long, into digital form, allowing the data to be displayed more clearly and efficiently. The advocate can scroll back and forth along the strip at any speed. Digitization also allows portions of the strip to be excerpted, highlighted, annotated, and juxtaposed and/or overlaid with any other kind of information in any audiovisual form whatsoever. For instance, pausing at a critical moment in the strip, the advocate can select from pull-down menus definitions of key medical terms or excerpts from authoritative texts that elucidate the data; the advocate can also show excerpts from the videotaped deposition testimony of the attending nurses or physicians to explain what was happening at the hospital during the time represented in the heart monitor data.

I want to call attention to three aspects of the DigiStrip that distinguish it from the other digitized displays already discussed. First, the digitization and visual enhancement of the fetal monitor strip bring quantitative scientific representation into the courtroom in clear and intelligible form. Measurement and quantification are often thought to be hallmarks of scientific knowledge,[55] and so are common cultural markers for scientific authority, and hence, reliable access to reality. In other contexts, such as the formerly prevalent use of autoradiographs to show a DNA 'match,' courtroom visualizations of quantitative information can be obscure or even unintelligible.[56] By contrast, the digitized strip signifies the most precise

---

52 High Impact Graphics (2004) (CD-ROM).

53 'Dr. Orvan Hess, Who Helped Develop Fetal Heart Monitor, Dies at 96', *Yale Bulletin and Calendar*, 31(12) (22 November 2002), http://www.yale.edu/opa/v31.n12/story13. html.

54 Robert Brain, 'Standards and Semiotics', in Timothy Lenoir (ed.), *Inscribing Science* (Stanford, CA: Stanford University Press, 1998), pp. 249-284 (describing the work of Etienne-Jules Marey).

55 In the famous words of Lord Kelvin: '[W]hen you can measure what you are speaking about, you know something about it; when you cannot measure it . . . your knowledge is of a meager and unsatisfactory kind.' Lord Kelvin, *Popular Lectures and Addresses* (1891-94), http://zapatopi.net/kelvin/quotes.html.

56 Visual obscurity, though, can have its own rhetorical payoffs, for example, allowing the expert witness to demonstrate his expertise to a grateful jury (Charles Goodwin, 'Professional Vision', *American Anthropologist*, 96 (1994): 606-633) and triggering other connotations that

possible information both indexically (authenticating testimony verifies the accuracy of the fetal heart monitor in general and links the strip in this case to the device that measured this particular fetus's heart rate) and, of course, iconically (once highlights, annotations, and other augmentations of the display help viewers to read it properly).

Second, the DigiStrip extends the visual logic of juxtaposition, seen in the Sanction II software, to represent diverse diachronic information iconically. Changes in fetal heart rate can be shown in continuous (albeit usually speeded-up) time, and selected portions of the moving strip can be visually and thus temporally matched to relevant representations of other evidence (for example, physicians' and nurses' notes and/or deposition clips describing the events, analogous to Sanction II's juxtaposition of deposition testimony and documentary evidence regarding the same event). They can also be contrasted with representations of 'normal' sequences of fetal heart rate and relevant medicolegal standards of care (this is analogous to the illustration of proper tension band wiring in the patellar fracture surgery slide show). Thus, viewers see (and hear) even more information simultaneously yet clearly, allowing the advocate to mobilize even more support for his or her version of the facts and making it that much harder for the opponent to counter effectively.[57] The hypermediation of multiple screens, images, and texts that Sanction II makes possible is carried even further.

In the sense of Barthes' early semiological theory,[58] this kind of hypermediation signifies 'better access to important information.' Just as the display ad for the Italian food company Panzani which Barthes famously analyzes[59] conveys 'coded iconic messages' of Italianicity, freshness, and domestic preparation, so the ordered proliferation of audiovisual messages within the DigiStrip screen conveys the warrant, 'Here is the information you need, because this is what knowledge looks like today.'

A third and final feature of the DigiStrip display underscores this point. Surrounding this multiplicity of audiovisual information is the interactive interface itself – the VCR controls, toggles, pop-ups, and so on. In the medicolegal slide show and the virtual reality view, the interactive interfaces are also visible – for example, in the former, viewers can see the cursor moving to the index label and calling up the desired image – but they are minimized, and on one side only of the

may help the proponent's argument (Neal Feigenson, 'Visual Rhetorics of Science and Law', paper presented at Law and Society Association annual meeting, Budapest, 2001).

57 See Françoise Bastide, 'The Iconography of Scientific Texts: Principles of Analysis', in Lynch and Woolgar, *Representation in Scientific Practice*, pp. 187-229; Latour, 'Drawing Things Together'.

58 Roland Barthes, 'Myth Today', in *Mythologies* (Annette Lavers, trans.) (New York: Hill and Wang, 1972), pp. 109-159; see also Bernard Jackson, *Semiotics and Legal Theory* (London: Routledge and Kegan Paul, 1985), pp. 12-13 (discussing 'secondary semiotic system'); pp. 22-23 (discussing Barthes and connotation).

59 Roland Barthes, *Image Music Text* (Stephen Heath, trans.) (New York: Hill and Wang, 1977).

focal image. In the DigiStrip, the visual design flaunts the means of interaction. The interface literally frames the information presented, and so conceptually frames the audience's uptake of that information. By representing an interactive device (or, to be more precise, a hybrid of two such devices: the VCR (a visual 'repurposing' of a familiar technology) and the personal computer (for example, the drop-down menus and multiple windows)), the mediation implicitly encourages the audience to interpret the audiovisual content as a database of diverse material to be surveyed and constructively connected by the audience's own cognitive efforts – just as audiences click and toggle their way through DVD and computer interfaces to get news and entertainment and to communicate with one another in their everyday lives. The assimilation of the cognitive habits associated with personal computer use into the trial process could hardly be more complete.

Interactive Multimedia Closing Argument

In 2002 Michael Skakel, a cousin of the Kennedy family, went on trial for the 1975 murder of his Greenwich neighbor Martha Moxley (when both were teenagers). The prosecution had no eyewitnesses to the crime and no DNA evidence linking the defendant to it. It had only circumstantial evidence of the defendant's guilt, including a telephone interview which Michael Skakel had given to an author in 1997 in which he said, among other things, that he experienced a 'feeling of panic' when Martha's mother asked him the morning after Martha was killed if he knew where Martha was. The defense theory was that Skakel felt this panic because he thought that he had been seen masturbating in the trees outside the Moxley home the night before. The prosecution theory was that Skakel felt panic because he knew that he had killed Martha.

The prosecution did, however, have a custom-made, interactive, multimedia presentation system designed by WIN Interactive, Inc., which it used throughout the trial to display demonstrative evidence, including photographs of the neighborhood and diagrams of the locations at which real evidence had been found by the police. During the prosecution's closing argument, by means of this same digital system, jurors heard excerpts from Skakel's audiotaped phone interview and simultaneously followed a transcript of the audiotape projected onto a large courtroom screen. And when Skakel mentioned his 'feeling of panic,' jurors saw why, according to the prosecution, he felt that way: crime scene photos of Martha Moxley's body flashed on the screen next to the transcript.[60]

Like the Sanction II and DigiStrip excerpts discussed above, the prosecution's multimedia closing draws together disparate elements (recorded testimony, transcript, photo) created at different times and for different purposes. But the goal is not simply to juxtapose pieces of evidence to make a point. The discrete elements are left identifiable (to make clear that each was already admitted into evidence, and

60 For a detailed description and analysis, see Carney and Feigenson, 'Visual Persuasion in the Michael Skakel Trial'.

to counter any possible charge of manipulating the evidence and/or misleading the audience), but the aim is to integrate the elements into a self-contained audiovisual narrative.

Of course, many lawyers try to relate their cases as persuasive stories, because that is the way people tend to make sense of things in everyday life;[61] accordingly, it is the way that jurors tend to think through the information presented at trial.[62] And for the last century, movies and television programs have offered some of the most well-known and hence rhetorically powerful stories for lawyers to evoke.[63] Digital technology, however, allowed the prosecution in the Skakel case not just to allude to, but to exemplify, the desired cultural model – to present (part of) its case in an audiovisual medium similar to that of the model. And by so doing, the prosecution was better able to trigger the habits of thinking and feeling that the audience is accustomed to using when responding to film and video narratives outside of court.

Which movies? Perhaps jurors would be inclined to respond to the prosecution's argument as they do to standard expository documentaries,[64] in which the rhetor assembles elements from different sources to make an explicit claim and does not put his own role in the assembly process 'on screen,' but rather presents the material as objective truths about the world.[65] But jurors are also susceptible to the viewing habits they have developed in watching murder dramas on television and in the movies: the emotion-wrenching close-ups of the victim; the killer's confession (here, to a third party rather than a Perry Mason-like breakdown on the witness stand); and the audience's confidence that the state can put the circumstantial pieces together and establish guilt beyond a reasonable doubt, so that justice can be done at the end of the show.[66] This is (part of) what the truth about these matters looks and sounds like to audiences of popular murder mysteries today, because those popular dramas frame audiences' understandings of 'the way things happen' and hence their

61 For example, Jerome Bruner, *Acts of Meaning* (Cambridge, MA: Harvard University Press, 1990).

62 For example, Nancy Pennington and Reid Hastie, 'The Story Model for Juror Decision Making', in Reid Hastie (ed.), *Inside the Juror* (Cambridge, UK: Cambridge University Press, 1993), pp. 192-221.

63 Consider, for example, the personal injury victim's lawyer who implicitly portrays his client as the underdog hero in *Rocky*; see Neal Feigenson, 'The Rhetoric of Torts: How Advocates Help Jurors Think About Causation, Reasonableness, and Responsibility', *Hastings Law Journal*, 47 (1995): 61-165.

64 Bill Nichols, *Representing Reality* (Bloomington, IN: University of Indiana Press, 1991).

65 In the *Skakel* case, in contrast to the prototypical expository documentary, the prosecutor (rather than a visible narrator or visually absent 'voice of God') provided the voiceover (in between segments of audiovisual material) that helps to unify and explain the displayed images and sounds.

66 See Sherwin, 'Law Frames'.

expectations about what the prosecution's case should look like.[67] By triggering and then satisfying those expectations, the prosecution enhanced the perceived credibility of their version of reality.[68]

Michael Skakel has appealed his conviction for the murder of Martha Moxley.[69] In their arguments to the Connecticut Supreme Court,[70] both the prosecution and defense lawyers have approached the prosecution's use of digital technology at trial in a largely predictable, if somewhat unsatisfactory, way. Skakel's lawyers have claimed that the closing argument audiovisuals created 'deceptive visual connections' designed to inflame the jury's passions, and even 'conveyed false . . . subliminal messages to the jury.'[71] Tellingly, they describe the prosecution's multimedia argument as a 'movie' (which, they claim, distorted and misused the evidence). That is, the new technology is not to be trusted; rather than allowing the jury to see the truth plainly, it deceives and conveys falsehoods. The multimedia display framed the case as a movie, and movies are fictions. The prosecution's response, in effect, is that it simply used digital multimedia to marshal previously admitted evidence to reconstruct the story of what happened, which is its legal duty. Surely the prosecution could have done this by telling jurors what it believed the defendant was thinking and holding up a picture of the victim, so there is nothing wrong with doing the same thing digitally, on a screen.[72] Thus, the prosecution has downplayed the novelty of its use of digital technology, arguing that it should be assimilated to existing methods of representing the truth.

These arguments replicate the nineteenth-century debate over the admissibility of photographic evidence.[73] Opponents pointed to the then relatively new visual technology's capacity to distort and falsify; proponents emphasized its ability to

---

67 See Michael Shapiro and T. Makana Chock, 'Psychological Processes in Perceiving Reality', paper presented to the Association for Education in Journalism and Mass Communication, Baltimore, MD, 1998.

68 The prosecution's use of multimedia in the closing argument may also well have gained credibility from its use of the same CD-ROM during the evidentiary phase of trial, in which the technology was understood as (merely) illustrating testimony vividly and truthfully (for example, 'here's what the Moxley house looked like'). And in contrast to the *more* interactive use of the technology during witness examination (the lawyers, for example, would click and zoom in and out on photographs to fit the testimony), in the midst of a *more* complex live performance (prosecuting attorney interviewing witness, interrupted by objections from Skakel's attorney), the use of the multimedia in closing argument (in which the prosecutor, speaking largely without interruption, simply started and stopped as desired a separate file on the CD-ROM specially prepared for closing argument) may have seemed relatively linear and familiar.

69 The case was argued before the Connecticut Supreme Court on 14 January 2005. As of this writing, no decision has been rendered.

70 The parties briefed the issues presented by the prosecution's use of the CD-ROM but did not have time to reach these issues during oral argument.

71 *Connecticut v. Skakel*, S.C. No. 16844, Brief of Defendant-Appellant, pp. 59, 61.

72 See Carney and Feigenson, 'Visual Persuasion in the Michael Skakel Trial'.

73 Mnookin, 'The Image of Truth'.

document truthfully and directly. The law of demonstrative evidence, in admitting photographs only as illustrations of verbal testimony (like drawings and maps), ostensibly confirmed their artifactuality but at the same time allowed them to be seen by jurors who (as courts and commentators recognized) were likely to consider them as much more persuasive proof of reality than drawings or maps. In *Skakel*, the defense lawyers have contended that the new technological mediation takes decision makers further from the truth. The prosecution has responded as the courts did to photography: the new technological mediation is not really new, and does not threaten to distort or mislead any more than the customary mediation of words and photos does. Both sides, that is, are arguing within the conceptual framework of naïve realism: reality is best known directly, immediately, through the least, or at least the least salient, manipulation.

Both sides are partly right but are mistaken at a more fundamental level. The prosecution is correct that the technology it used in closing argument is not wholly novel. Simpler, off-the-shelf software such as PowerPoint, which has become widely used and accepted in court,[74] has some of the same capabilities (for example, to array audio and/or video clips, text, and images, albeit in a preset, mostly noninteractive sequence) as the custom-made system Skakel's prosecutors used. But the larger issue is that neither the simpler nor the more sophisticated digital presentations are 'just like' a lawyer's spoken words augmented by an enlarged photograph. Digitization makes possible representations of reality that are very different from what has come before. In the *Skakel* case, random-access audio, synchronous transcript, and photographic images that could be resized and relocated to suit the advocate's purposes gave the jurors a representation of reality that could not exist in the analog world. Explaining away the distinctive features of the digital mediation of reality, as the prosecution has done in its (well-advised) attempt to legitimize its position within the framework of existing legal doctrine and practice, only prevents us from even inquiring into how such uses of digital technology affect what the jurors believe and how they think.

On the other side, Skakel's lawyers' attempt to demonize the digital display as tricky and false, even if it succeeds in this case, reflects a benighted approach that is doomed to failure in the not-very-long run. Any medium of communication (including words, of course) may be used to deceive, but there is nothing inherently deceptive about digital visual technology, any more than there is about photographs, X-rays, or any other medium created in the last two centuries to record and display information.[75] And yet the defense's characterization of the multimedia closing argument as a 'movie' captures something profound about this use of digital technology. As I have asserted, the digital argument did implicitly invoke for its audience the visual cultural model of movies. The meanings that jurors take away from courtroom screens when used as they were in the *Skakel* case are likely to be

74 Federal Judicial Center/National Institute for Trial Advocacy, *Effective Use of Courtroom Technology* (Washington, DC, 2001).

75 Carney and Feigenson, 'Visual Persuasion in the Michael Skakel Trial'.

shaped by jurors' screen experiences in their everyday lives, including their uptake of the meanings of standard cinematic conventions regarding camera angle, distance, and montage.[76] The defense lawyers are right about that.

But they are wrong simply to equate movies with fiction (and to oppose fictional portrayals to truth). The matter is much more complicated. Certainly it can be argued that when the world is represented in film and video, viewers may be led to reconstruct legally relevant reality erroneously. For instance, people attend carefully to the substance of incoming messages only if they are both willing and able to do so;[77] moving images tend to occupy more of audiences' sensory and other on-line cognitive capacities than do speeches (even augmented by still visual displays), impairing audiences' ability to attend to message content, and to the extent that film and video are more entertaining than talk-plus-still-pictures, they may reduce audiences' inclination to process critically as well. Moreover, people are in general not very good at distinguishing between the fictional and factual sources of their beliefs,[78] and may actually be readier to incorporate into their beliefs about the world information presented in a fictional context, because they are disinclined to treat fictions as critically as they do information framed as factual.[79] Thus, by using the media in which audiences are accustomed to imbibing cinematic fictions, legal advocates may induce in their audiences uncritical acceptance of their propositions. On the other hand, consider how much of people's (more or less truthful) knowledge of the world derives from film and video documentaries and television news.[80] Consider also how even cinematic fictions, like literary ones, can provide deep understandings about matters of human emotion and intentionality that are often essential to doing justice[81] – perhaps especially where, as in *Skakel*, the facts of the matter are so uncertain and so highly charged.[82]

---

76 See Christina Spiesel, Richard Sherwin and Neal Feigenson, 'Law in the Age of Images: The Challenge of Visual Literacy', in Anne Wagner et al. (eds), *Contemporary Issues of the Semiotics of Law* (Oxford: Hart Publishing, 2005), pp. 231-255.

77 See, for example, Richard Petty and John Cacioppo, 'The Elaboration Likelihood Model of Persuasion', in Leonard Berkowitz (ed.), *Advances in Experimental Social Psychology*, 19 (Orlando, FL: Academic Press, 1986), pp. 123-205.

78 See the literature on *reality monitoring*, for example, Marcia Johnson and Carol Raye, 'Reality Monitoring', *Psychological Review*, 88 (1981): 67-85.

79 Deborah Prentice and Richard Gerrig, 'Exploring the Boundary Between Fiction and Reality', in Shelley Chaiken and Yaacov Trope (eds), *Dual-Process Theories in Social Psychology* (New York: Guilford Press, 1999), pp. 529-546.

80 The extent to which news, documentaries, or other ostensibly nonfictional genres actually do offer truthful knowledge of the world is, of course, an extremely rich and complicated topic of its own, spanning several academic disciplines; I do not intend to tackle it here.

81 For example, Martha Nussbaum, *Love's Knowledge* (New York: Oxford University Press, 1990); Martha Nussbaum, *Poetic Justice* (Boston: Beacon Press, 1995).

82 To infer from circumstantial evidence whether (for example) a party *intended* to commit a given act, a decision maker must draw on the culture's storehouse of understandings about how and why people behave as they do, a storehouse which includes (along with the

Advocates who implicate movies as the cognitive and emotional frame of response to legal argument do not necessarily lead legal decision makers closer to or further from the truth. What they do is to change the way legal decision makers take up case information and form their beliefs and judgments. And technologies like the one used in the *Skakel* trial do something else as well: they make their mediating presence known, and thereby make clear what many legal scholars have previously tended to ignore: the essential role of the technologies of representation in the creation of legal meaning and the doing of justice.

Legal Knowledge in the Age of Digital Multimedia

My broader argument is that the increasing use of digital multimedia technologies throughout Anglo-American legal proceedings is significant for legal theory because it promises to change how members of the legal culture think about legal knowledge in general. I will conclude by restating and expanding this argument.

Legal theory includes descriptive jurisprudence, which concerns itself with how legal decisions are made and justified. Legal decisions combine factual, legal, and moral judgments. Factual (as well as legal and moral) judgments depend in part on how the world is represented to the decision makers. And digital multimedia represent the world, and therefore likely affect factual (as well as legal and moral) beliefs about the world, in new ways. So any systematic changes that digital multimedia may make to what I have called first-order legal knowledge are a proper concern of legal theory. Some of these changes are being produced by features that digital multimedia share with older, analog visual media.[83] Some, however, are due to features that digitization in particular heightens or makes possible. Remediation, hypermediation, and interactivity are crucial attributes of the ways in which the world is represented in the digital age; to understand what truth looks like today, it is necessary to attend to them.

What does this have to do with what I have called second-order legal knowledge – what legal decision makers and other participants in the legal system (as well as the public generally) think about the truth-status of first-order beliefs and how they emerge from the information presented at trials? The problem is the current unease, or even schizophrenia, if you will, concerning the status of those factual judgments which, interwoven with judgments of law and morality, make up legal decisions. On the one hand there is the positivism and objectivism seemingly

decision maker's reconstructions of personal experience from memory) dramatic fictions distilled and absorbed into the decision maker's 'common sense.'

83 See, for example, Richard Sherwin, 'Law in Popular Culture', in Austin Sarat (ed.), *The Blackwell Companion to Law and Society* (London: Blackwell, 2004), pp. 95-112. I and my colleagues discuss these and related subjects in a forthcoming paper. Richard Sherwin, Neal Feigenson and Christina Spiesel, 'Law in the Digital Age: How Visual Technologies are Transforming the Practice, Theory, and Teaching of Law' (manuscript on file with author).

inherent in the stereotypical 'Received View'[84] of trials: that the 'Rule of Law' requires that substantive law be applied to facts ascertained in a value-free manner, within evidentiary rules that generally privilege direct perception of reality over mediated access to reality. On the other there is the relativism seemingly inherent in the conception of trials as adversarial contests in which decision makers have access to extralegal reality exclusively through advocates' representations. Each view of law's factual judgments – as truths on a par (ceteris paribus) with those of history or the other human (and sometimes biological and/or physical) sciences, or as mere upshots of whatever rhetorical ploys happen to be more persuasive – seems perfectly sensible. Yet in legal culture as a whole, they are treated as if they were in tension, if not irreconcilable. There seems to be a widespread difficulty in grasping how truths can be represented through rhetoric yet still be sufficiently truthful to support people's confidence that legal decisions have 'got things right'; how facts can be shaped and indeed constituted by the narratives in which they are located[85] while still being sufficiently grounded in 'the real.' Underlying this difficulty seems to be something like the naïvely realist belief that truth is what is not fabricated,[86] so that the evident role of mediations in the production of legal facts is taken to undermine their reliability and truthfulness. And if the only alternative to unmediated truth is 'mere' fabrication, then the only alternative to naïve realism seems to be the cynical view that trials produce not legal knowledge, but only the consequences of stronger or weaker advocacy.

I want to argue that with greater exposure to digital multimedia displays in court, participants in and observers of the law will be better able to overcome this frustrating opposition between lawyers' representations and 'real' knowledge; that it will be clearer than ever before how legal knowledge can be mediated through and through and still be the most reliable kind of knowledge we can practicably expect[87] – indeed, that the methods of mediation help explain why the resulting factual judgments warrant belief.[88] The argument is based on three claims.

---

84 Burns, *A Theory of the Trial.*

85 For example, Anthony Amsterdam and Jerome Bruner, *Minding the Law* (Cambridge, MA: Harvard University Press, 2000).

86 For a brilliant exposition and various critiques (anthropological, sociological, historical, philosophical) of this aspect of naïve realism, see Latour, *Pandora's Hope*, especially the chapter 'Circulating Reference'.

87 By 'practicably' I mean to refer to (and defer any detailed discussion of) the specific limitations of various Anglo-American adversarial legal processes as practices for finding things out about the extralegal world. Of course there are many ways in which legal rules and practices regarding pre-trial discovery, admission and exclusion of evidence, and jury conduct could be (and, in some instances, are being) modified to enhance the reliability of resulting factual judgments; see, for example, G. Thomas Munstermann et al. (eds), *Jury Trial Innovation* (Williamsburg, VA: National Center for State Courts, 1997). For some of the epistemological problematics of such reforms, see Damaška, 'Epistemology and Legal Regulation of Proof'.

88 Cf. Latour, *Pandora's Hope.*

First, as the medicolegal slides, the Sanction II assemblage, and the DigiStrip (if not also the other examples) show, digital visual and multimedia displays can offer clearer and more informative presentations of extralegal reality than are possible with analog technologies (or without demonstrative evidence at all). Decision makers who see and hear such (well-crafted and well-timed) mediations may be likelier to believe that they understand what happened and why, that they have 'gotten things right,' than those who do not have the opportunity to see them – and observers of the process may agree. Individual cases will vary, but on the whole, decision makers and observers are likelier to be more confident in the legal knowledge yielded by digital multimedia.

Can I go beyond the claim that decision makers and observers will tend to believe that digital multimedia offer them more reliable first-order knowledge of the world, to assert that these new technologies actually will do so, on the whole? To ask the question is to shift from a semiological and/or anthropological mode of discourse, in which the topic is how a changing legal culture makes meanings and forms beliefs, to another, more traditionally epistemological one, in which one constructed truth is held up as the measure of another. On the latter terms, the proposition that digital multimedia will generally enhance first-order legal knowledge is in principle probably undecidable: the proportion of cases in which it is just not possible to say whether the decision makers' beliefs as to the important facts are accurate, because no more reliable extrinsic metric for determining such accuracy exists, is too large.[89] And the courtroom uses of digital multimedia vary so greatly from one case to the next – some are used to present evidence, some argument; some are used to illustrate eyewitness testimony, some to make visible an expert's analysis; and of course, multimedia displays differ in the software and hardware employed, the technical and aesthetic skills of their creators, and the importance of the display to and its fit with the advocate's theory of the case – that it may not be worthwhile to pursue the issue at such a high level of generality anyway.

Nevertheless, concerns that the increasing use of digital multimedia in court may undermine rather than improve reasoned and accurate judgment are sufficiently widespread that it seems advisable to respond (albeit speculatively) to and not simply to appear to dodge the question. Particular digital displays can mislead as well as inform. Kassin and Dunn's seminal research, for instance, showed that computer animated simulations can facilitate judgment (by making it easier for jurors to decide in accordance with the (undisputed) verbal evidence) or prejudice it (by leading jurors to decide contrary to that verbal evidence).[90] And while any other medium of communication, including the spoken word, presents the same possibilities, it seems that if digital multimedia can be more persuasive and therefore likelier to lead legal decision makers to correct understandings (as I have suggested), they necessarily also pose greater risks of leading them astray. Assuming that hypermediation, interactivity,

89 See supra note 21.

90 Saul Kassin and Meghan Dunn, 'Computer-Animated Displays and the Jury: Facilitative and Prejudicial Effects', *Law & Human Behavior*, 21 (1997): 269-281.

and other features of digital multimedia are increasingly what the truth looks like to jurors, there is no reason why those features have to mediate any particular content; they may be just as readily deployed by the party whose facts and story are 'really' less true (again, assuming that there is some way of knowing that). [91]

Yet there are grounds for believing that the increasing use of digital multimedia at trials will not only change the ways in which first-order legal knowledge is constructed but may also, on the whole, enhance the accuracy of legal judgments. One source of support is research on multimedia learning, including, for example, studies showing that people who watch animations of complex processes and simultaneously hear explanations of the process understand those processes better than people who do not see the animations or do not hear the explanations.[92] Another is that the more confident people are that they know something, the more likely it is that they really do.[93] People do consistently overestimate their abilities to get it right across a wide range of perceptual and cognitive judgments,[94] and their degrees of confidence that

91 In addition, how could digital multimedia yield a net benefit to judgmental accuracy when it will become increasingly common for *both* adversaries to use these more persuasive technologies, yet presumably both cannot be offering accurate versions of the facts? One response may be that even in those cases in which the parties' versions of the facts differ clearly enough so that it can be said that both cannot be true (as opposed to the many cases in which the real dispute is about the categorization of the facts – for example, was the defendant negligent? – or the evaluation of the facts – for example, how much compensation is needed to make this accident victim whole?), as long as the decision maker would not have reached the correct decision (once again, assuming that this could be reliably determined) without *some* multimedia presentation (not necessarily by the party who 'should' win; it could be that the adversary's digital display makes it clearer than it otherwise would have been that that party deserves to lose), then digital multimedia may still improve the accuracy of judgments.

92 Richard Mayer and Richard Anderson, 'The Instructive Animation: Helping Students Build Connections Between Words and Pictures in Multimedia Learning', *Journal of Educational Psychology*, 84 (1992): 444-452; Richard Mayer and Valerie Sims, 'For Whom Is a Picture Worth a Thousand Words? Extensions of a Dual-Coding Theory of Multimedia Learning', *Journal of Educational Psychology*, 86 (1994): 389-401; but see Richard Lowe, 'Extracting Information from an Animation During Complex Visual Learning', 14 *European Journal of Psychology of Education*, 14 (1999): 225-244 (in some circumstances, animations may be instructionally inferior to static diagrams because animations make greater demands on viewers' processing capacities).

93 Dale Griffin and Amos Tversky, 'The Weighting of Evidence and the Determinants of Confidence', in Thomas Gilovich et al. (eds), *Heuristics and Biases: The Psychology of Intuitive Judgment* (Cambridge, UK: Cambridge University Press, 2002), pp. 230-249.

94 For instance, people overestimate their ability to detect changes in the visual field (Brian Scholl, Daniel Simons and Daniel Levin, '"Change Blindness" Blindness: An Implicit Measure of a Metacognitive Error', in Daniel Levin (ed.), *Thinking and Seeing* (Cambridge, MA: MIT Press, 2004), pp. 145-163); to have predicted past events (Baruch Fischhoff, 'Hindsight ≠ Foresight: The Effect of Outcome Knowledge on Judgment Under Uncertainty', *Journal of Experimental Social Psychology: Human Perception & Performance*, 1 (1975): 288-299); to determine whether an eyewitness is telling the truth (Saul Kassin and Christina Fong, '"I'm Innocent!": Effects of Training on Judgments of Truth and Deception in the

they have got it right may be imperfectly calibrated with whether they actually have done so (people sometimes underestimate and often overestimate their accuracy); but by and large, their confidence in the correctness of their judgments is positively correlated with the probability that those judgments are indeed correct.[95] So if judges and jurors who are exposed to digital multimedia displays will feel more confident about their knowledge of the matters before them than they otherwise would (as I have argued), then they probably will know those matters better (even if not so much better as they might believe).

At the same time, fears that the new visual and multimedia technologies will mislead legal decision makers (especially jurors) may be exaggerated. Even though digital multimedia may be persuasive in court partly for the same reasons that they are persuasive in the culture at large – and even because they are meaningful and persuasive in the wider culture – the decision making context in court is likely to mitigate some of the aspects of multimedia that might otherwise be most inimical to reasoned judgment. When jurors watch digital displays in court, unlike their typical experience watching advertisements (for example) in everyday life, they know that they are doing so as part of their important obligation as citizens to participate in the justice system; they are carefully instructed on the substantive and procedural rules that are supposed to guide their judgment; they know that their decisions will have serious consequences for real people; and they must deliberate before reaching those decisions. The felt importance of the task and the sense of accountability,[96] among other things, tend to attenuate jurors' unreflective (and largely subconscious) reliance on the kinds of judgmental shortcuts which many advertisements seek to elicit and which, left unexamined and unchallenged, could indeed undermine reasoned decision making. The greater interactivity of some digital displays (especially if jurors are given the freedom to interact with the depicted information themselves[97]) may encourage jurors to examine both the displays and the rest of the trial evidence more actively and critically than they otherwise would, again departing from the largely passive viewing habits inculcated by television and movie viewing. Indeed, by thinking about and discussing with each other their responses to advocates' digital visual representations, jurors may be able to bring to consciousness aspects of their reactions to the case that might otherwise have remained hidden,[98] enriching deliberations and judgment.

Interrogation Room', *Law & Human Behavior*, 23 (1999): 499-516); and to explain things in depth (Frank Keil, Leonid Rozenblit and Candice Mills, 'What Lies Beneath: Understanding the Limits of Understanding', in Levin, *Thinking and Seeing*, pp. 227-249).

95 Griffin and Tversky, 'The Weighting of Evidence and the Determinants of Confidence'. (Once again, the assertion presumes that there is some reliable extrinsic measure of judgmental accuracy.)

96 For example, Jennifer Lerner and Philip Tetlock, 'Accounting for the Effects of Accountability', *Psychological Bulletin*, 125 (1999): 255-275.

97 See supra note 39 (*Soham* case).

98 See Gerald Zaltman, *How Customers Think* (Boston, MA: Harvard Business School Press, 2003).

Moreover, digital displays in court, unlike advertisements, movies, or television programs, generally must first be approved by (more or less) vigilant trial judges applying (more or less) rigorous authentication requirements that are intended to ensure both relevance to the matters at hand and sufficient tethering to other known facts about the world.[99] Trial judges will also exclude displays that they deem to be unfairly prejudicial or too confusing or that pose too great a risk of misleading the jury,[100] or may demand that the displays be modified or contextualized to minimize these dangers.[101] Finally, courtroom displays are subject to objections and counterarguments by opposing counsel,[102] further reducing the likelihood that those displays will persuade without imparting reliable and relevant knowledge. It must be emphasized, however, that the success of these constraints on unreliable or even deceptive displays, and thus the prospects for maximizing the net benefit of facilitative over prejudicial effects of digital multimedia, depends on the willingness and ability of all participants in the legal system – judges, advocates, and jurors – to develop enough digital visual literacy to appreciate how particular features of digital multimedia (including those analyzed above) may affect the meanings that can be extracted from them.[103]

My second claim in support of the argument that digital visual and multimedia displays will transform second-order legal knowledge is that the very conspicuousness of digital representations promises to make the mediated basis of (reliable) legal knowledge clear to an unprecedented degree. When lawyers use digital technologies to represent reality visually, the fact of mediation, of fabrication, is just too plain to be ignored. Unlike a witness's or lawyer's words, which do not seem to require a techne at all and thus, if believed, are intuitively taken up as windows onto reality, hypermediated displays such as the Sanction II screens, the DigiStrip, and the multimedia closing argument in *Skakel* seem to locate the production of legal

99 Authentication (Federal Rule of Evidence 901-902 (2005)) requires the proponent of evidence to satisfy the court that the item sought to be introduced is what it purports to be, thus assuring the court both of its genuineness and its relevance to the case, although relevance is also separately required (Federal Rule of Evidence 401 (2005)).

100 Federal Rule of Evidence 403 (2005).

101 For example, Federal Rule of Evidence 106 (2005).

102 To whom, ideally, the display will have been disclosed (where consistent with the protection of the confidentiality of the proponent's 'work product'; see Federal Rule of Civil Procedure 26(b)(3) (2005)) sufficiently in advance of its courtroom use to allow for intelligent objections and counterarguments where appropriate.

103 See Sherwin, Feigenson and Spiesel, 'Law in the Digital Age: How Visual Technologies are Transforming the Practice, Theory, and Teaching of Law'.

knowledge in the mediating technology itself.[104] Legal knowledge will increasingly be perceived to be reliable because it is mediated.[105]

And third, this will be so precisely because people are spending more and more of their everyday lives in mediated realities. Jurors and judges who increasingly rely on hypermediated screen images for the information they need and use at work, for their news about the world, and for their private entertainment should be quite comfortable with the notion that digital hypermediations can provide sufficiently reliable grounds for the factual judgments they need to make to resolve difficult disputes. As a result, ever more mediated common sense will enter into legal decision making – the habits of thinking and feeling inculcated by decision makers' screen-based experiences in their everyday lives, habits that are themselves changing as people become increasingly sophisticated in the uptake and uses of digital visuals.[106]

All of this is only to pose (more clearly, I hope), not to resolve, the issue of legal knowledge in the digital age. Appreciating how digital displays mediate reality will help decision makers and participants in the legal system to do a progressively better job of understanding the potentially misleading as well as the probative effects of any given display. The more sophisticated that decision makers become in the ways of digital representation, the more insightful and reliable their factual judgments will be – the more likely that advocates' displays will facilitate rather than prejudice decision making. In any event, it is becoming increasingly clear that digitally

---

104 Hypermediation plainly makes the mediation of reality more salient. The effects of remediation are more equivocal. On the one hand, by assimilating the experience of new media to that of older media, remediation tends to diminish awareness of the fact of mediation. On the other, increasingly media-savvy audiences are likely to become more aware of the remediation itself, and hence of the multiply mediated nature of their experiences; moreover, the cumulative effect of various and pervasive remediations throughout the culture at large will be to make audiences more aware of their immersion in a nearly all-encompassing multimedia soup.

105 This generalization elides distinctions between different representational technologies and over time. Specifically, as judges and jurors become increasingly familiar with a given technology, they may habituate to it, to the point of failing to notice its mediating status and instead 'seeing through it' as a 'window onto reality,' as naïve audiences have tended to do, for example, with photographs and television. See Neal Feigenson, 'Too Real? The Future of Visual Reality Evidence', *Law and Policy* (forthcoming).

106 For instance, it is possible that as digital visual technologies become ever more capable of simulating unmediated experience, people's faith in verisimilitudinous representations as accurate depictions of reality will *decline* because people will realize that any representation can be manipulated or even faked. (I thank medical and scientific animator David Bolinsky for making this point, which is in tension with some of the observations above regarding the virtual reality view.) But since legal decision makers must continue to decide somehow, and presumably will want to continue to believe that their decisions map onto or are at least consistent with external reality, the consequence may be that other forms of legal visual rhetoric besides the verisimilitudinous will ascend in credibility and importance – perhaps the diagrammatic, or the hypermediated, or other combinations of words and images that I cannot yet envision.

mediated reality is here to stay in law as it is in the culture at large. It will no longer be an option for advocates or legal decision makers to retreat to an epistemological ideal of naïve realism. The implication for legal theory is that anyone interested in the production of legal knowledge today – how beliefs are formed and judgments made in individual cases and in general – ought to study techniques of digital multimedia representation.

Chapter 7

A *Las Meninas* for the Law

Christina Spiesel[1]

'At present this semiotic instrument, like that life, is doomed to repetition, because of failure of theory, because of abstracting, a-historical discourse, because of a language with little responsibility towards the real.'[2]

Figure 7.1 Dagnan-Bouveret, Pascal-Adolphe-Jean, *Wedding at the Photographer's*, 1872-1875, in the collection of Musée des Beaux-Arts, Lyon, France
We gratefully acknowledge their permission to reproduce this work.

1 The author wishes to thank Sydney Spiesel and Neal Feigenson for their thoughtful reading and responses in the preparation of this text, and Anne Higonnet for her generous collegiality in matters of art history.

2 Marshall Blonsky, Introduction to *On Signs* (Baltimore, Maryland: The Johns Hopkins University Press, 1985) p. xv.

Prologue

Juxtaposed above are two epigraphs, one verbal and one visual. They both invoke 'the real' in the service of a larger communicative enterprise: the one, a critique of semiotics in the academy; the other, a black and white reproduction of a realist painting, a genre scene, that depicts the recording of 'the real' by a photographer painted in oils by a French artist in the latter part of the nineteenth century. What do either of these epigraphs have to do with the law? Like the painting that inspired its title, this paper is a reflection (pun intended) on the situation of law's discourses in this new millennium, refracted, like King Philip IV and his family in Velásquez' famous painting, through a conceptual prism and not just through a mirror.

In 1656 when Diego Velásquez painted his masterpiece, *Las Meninas*,[3] it was a revolutionary leap to make a self-referencing meta-image about the act of representation. It is a painting that now comes with an enormous bibliography; it is a node for discussions of power and authority, the role of the artist and the act of representation itself, and the modernist fracturing of point of view, among other things.

This chapter will attempt to use these two paintings as analytical tools for understanding a cultural shift that is occurring now, and the metaphor of painting in general for bringing diverse phenomena into conversation about how these changes may affect the law.[4]

---

3 Diego Velásquez, *Las Meninas* 1656, Prado Museum, Madrid. Readers can view a large color reproduction of this painting at Mark Harden's Artchive: http://www.artchive.com/ftp_site.htm. Accessed 28 August 2005.

4 Semiotics has trouble dealing with the totality of a picture because its elements are not language in the sense that words are. To write about pictures is to translate them from the simultaneity of spatial arrangements to the time-based syntactical unfolding of words. Efforts to construct a critical semiotic language for discussing pictures, such as Theo van Leeuwen and Carey Jewitt's *Handbook of Visual Analysis* (London: Sage Publications, 2001) which contains many useful analytical tools, can only suggest a prismatic variety of many approaches, and the book does not address well the contribution to semiotic meaning of the expressive nature of the materiality of visual texts. The same can be said of David Crow's *Visible Signs* (Switzerland: AVA Publishing SA, 2003). He writes, 'the marks made by a paintbrush or the sounds used in music could be described as paradigms which use codes with no clear distinction between the choices' (p.43). Semiotics needs to be able to account for the shifting contexts of the visual reading, including the play of visual ambiguities – with the meanings generated not just by elements of denotation and connotation but also by the touch of the stroke, the fantasies engendered by texture, and so on. 'The awareness that artificially produced patterns are, by definition, made or crafted experiences should not doom them to the non-reflective realm of simplistic sensation. Good design gives value [I add cognition and meaning] to visually encoded information.' (Barbara Stafford, *Good Looking* (Cambridge, Massachusetts: MIT Press, 1996) p.125.) The materiality of the visual text is important, whether it is in oil paints or pixels, and it is not encompassed by essentially narrative thinking. (See Bernard Jackson, *Making Sense in Law* (Liverpool: Deborah Charles Publications, 1995), chapter five.) I have emphasized the materiality of the manufacture, and issues of design,

First Riff

Las Meninas now lives on a wall in the Prado Museum in Madrid. I am neither the first nor will I be the last person to notice how radical the painting must have been when it was first made and how it continues to puzzle us. Just as perspective encodes the placement of the *dramatis personae* inside the painting, so it configures the position of the viewer looking at the scene from the outside. The viewer assumes a position between the painter and the King and Queen who are reflected in the mirror on the back wall of the cavernous studio room.[5] In the hierarchical world of seventeenth century Spain, putting the viewer next to the King is every bit as radical as placing the dog prominently in front of the Prince and both of them in focus while the King is a dim image in the background.[6]

---

because it is often in the non-denotative and non-connotative elements of the visual text that significant, indirect meaning is contributed to the picture as a whole, perhaps a kind of visual enthymeme at the level of perception. See Kevelson, *The Law as a System of Signs* (New York: Plenum Press, 1988) p. 5 on the Peircean conception of the enthymeme.

While we may say that the law is a semiotic system (see Kevelson and Jackson) and my topic is about what it means to bring picturing into the discourse of law, what I am discussing does not fit into the analytical frame of legal semiotics. It does, however, fit into Peircian phenomenology that begins 'with the carving out of the phenomenal experience a general "quality" to be investigated methodologically' (Kevelson, p. 9). I am attempting to use my ekphrasis to catch something about the law between two visual signs. This gives me the opportunity to explore an essentially spatial construction – elements sitting in a frame – rather than a hierarchical, linear, analysis.

5 See Michael Atlee, 'LAS MENINAS: The World's Best Painting,' 2003, http://www.artchive.com/ftp_site.htm (accessed 23 March 2005) and Michel Foucault, '*Las Meninas*' in *The Order of Things, An Archeology of the Human Sciences* (New York: Pantheon Books, Random House, 1970).

6 There is much debate about the position of the viewer in the literature: see Foucault, *The Order of Things*, pp. 3-16; Jonathan Miller, *On Reflection* (London: Yale University Press, 1998), pp. 77-79. See also John R. Searle, '*Las Meninas* and the Paradoxes of Pictorial Representation', *Critical Inquiry*, Spring 1980, Vol. 6, Number 3, pp. 477-488, and Svetlana Alpers, 'Interpretation without Representation, or, The Viewing of *Las Meninas*', *Representations*, February 1983, Vol. 1, Number 1, 1983, pp. 31-42. All agree that there are paradoxes in the painting and assume, quite properly, that the paradoxes were not naïve but part of the intentional coding of the work by Velásquez. They differ in how they make meaning out of these puzzles. Looking at *Las Meninas* as a treatise on pictorial meaning-making, we can find Velásquez alluding to Peirce's categories – firstness, secondness, and thirdness – with its snapshot catching of a moment in action for all the 'players', our further perception of them in their various identifications through position, dress, abd so on, their secondness, and in a room full of paintings and themselves subjects of a painting – thirdness. (Definitions can be found at: http://www.helsinki.fi/science/commens/terms/firstness.html; last accessed 1 September 2005) This is the process of perception and representation in full motion and circulation. Reading Velásquez in this way, there is no need to resolve paradoxes because the disparity between the inward self and the existence of the outer world, the constructedness

What/who is the ostensible subject of the painting – its back to us, the viewers – that the painted painter in *Las Meninas* is working on? The King and Queen? The Infanta with her servants? Is it the painter himself, looking into a mirror behind us? The viewer – us? Are we the subject, standing beside the royals? Are Velásquez's spectators the King and Queen reflected in the mirror across the room? If so, then every viewer steps into the shoes of the King and Queen or stands beside them, making royals and viewers equals.

That this is a subtle political statement seems obvious – painting's version of Mozart's *The Marriage of Figaro* in foreshadowing the rise of democracy. The power of the artist is juxtaposed to the power of the king.

Second Riff

A little more than 200 years later, a talented provincial French academic realist painter, Pascal-Adolphe-Jean Dagnan-Bouveret (1852-1929),[7] displayed the height of his ambition in a painting variously called *The Photographer's Atelier*, *Wedding at the Photographer's*, and *Night at the Photographer's*. This painting, committed to 'straight depiction of the real,' gives an account of the various ways in which we see what we look at, only this time we are viewing a photographer under his black hood arranging a formal wedding portrait while all around him, outside his viewfinder, the painter catalogs the responses of the photographic subjects, the assistant, the onlookers.

When first I saw this painting in the Musée des Beaux-Arts in Lyon, France, in the summer of 2004, its connection to *Las Meninas* was the most immediately striking thing to me about it, that which drew my attention and caused me to puzzle over it.[8] Who would make such a painting? Who else but a young, ambitious, French provincial painter staking a realist claim against the tide of Impressionism, a young painter pitting the skills of his hand against the camera he himself used for making his own photographs. How do we compare an overarching masterpiece considered by some the 'world's greatest painting' and the solid painting efforts of a minor artist?

The relationship between the two may be an index of painterly aspiration by a younger man towards an Old Master; imitation is a standard pedagogical practice in all art education and would have been part of Dagnan-Bouveret's tool kit.

I begin with the presence of an artist – but who is the artist here? The photographer or the painter? If it is the painter, then the painter is taking the role of the implied

---

of our conceptions of both, is the 'true' subject and this semiotic process is not capable of reduction. The painting is playful in the deepest sense of that term.

7 Readers can find a color reproduction at http://www.atelier-rc.com/Atelier.RC/b-dayCalendar/01.07-PAJDagBouvt-NtAtPhotg.jpg. Accessed 28 February 2005.

8 In conversation, March 2005, art historian Anne Higonnet told me that this painting has been discussed in the literature for the presence of the photographer, not for its ambitions as a painting.

spectator in Velásquez. Dagnan-Bouveret offers us an ostensible subject for the representational task – the bridal couple – and puts a representer, the photographer, in the center of the picture. Who then sees the scene if not the painter, absent from the painting itself but present in the act of framing? We are standing where the painter would have stood to make the projection he made; perspective places us in the role of the artist and there is no confusion or ambiguity about this. Is this a democratizing role or another version of elitism in a dialogue between painting and photography at a time of great change in image making technology? Is it an assertion of the trained hand against mechanical reproduction?[9]

Light enters *Las Meninas* through a door at the back, and raking across the scene from a window on the right – we only see its left edge. The space is cavernous; there are barely perceptible frames of many paintings hanging in the gallery (or studio?) where the artist is at work. Assembled are members of the royal household (whose names are known)[10] – at the rear door, two young maids with the Infanta, a nun, and older woman servant, a dwarf (presumably for amusement), a dog being prodded by the foot of the young Prince. In *Wedding at the Photographer's*, on a dais at the back, the bridal couple poses formally in front of what we can see is a choice of backdrop – there are others behind. We are cued to understand that the photographer is constructing a picture from among possibilities. The bride and groom tilt their heads up, their eyes on the distance ahead and not what is happening in the room around them; this is a photograph being taken to mark the event 'forever.' The gown of the bride is being adjusted by a kneeling seamstress or older relative who looks up at them from the right side of the painting. Her view is narrowed by close proximity. To the left of the groom are two gentlemen (we see their top hats and cloaks on a chair and table in the left foreground) in conversation – one is looking upward, as if reflecting on what the other has just said to him with a slight tilt of the head. We do not know whether they are discussing the scene or something else altogether. Similarly, we see three young women on the left. Two seem to be engaged in an interaction; the third is looking past them towards the bridal couple. Just below her, a little to the right, a gentleman in a top hat is sitting on a low chair looking up at the couple with what we assume from his relaxed back to be admiration; he is holding a bouquet of flowers in his arms. In the center of the composition, a little to the right, is the photographer, hard at work under his hood, framing up the shot. His concentration is into the camera – he is closing out all the other stimuli, his back to us. Behind the photographer, leaning against a door frame, is a little girl who gazes steadily, thoughtfully, not at him but at us. Her hands are behind her waist, her elbows raised leaving her torso open and unguarded; she has a look of inquiry on her face as if there is something more to be seen that she is just beginning to apprehend.

---

9 See Walter Benjamin, *The Work of Art in the Age of Mechanical Reproduction*, 1936 at: http://www.marxists.org/reference/subject/philosophy/works/ge/benjamin.htm. Accessed 23 March 2005.

10 See Jonathan Brown, *Images and Ideas in Seventeenth-Century Spanish Painting* (Princeton, New Jersey: Princeton University Press, 1978).

Finally, in the lower right, closest to us, is a young man – father or uncle? – who is blowing smoke into the eyes of a little boy who has been restrained by the smoker's hand around his neck as if he has just been making trouble – like the impatient Prince nudging the dog with his foot in *Las Meninas*. The little boy's eyes are closed and he only looks inward. The atelier is less cavernous than the palace; light comes in from a window on the left and a ceiling skylight. The mirror on the left wall seems to reflect a couple who are not otherwise represented – perhaps figures about to come through the open door. (A prefiguring of the transition into marriage – what Americans might identify as stepping over the threshold?)

So we have a catalog of spectatorship: lookers looking in frank admiration, others discussing something with each other (both male and female pairs), perhaps inspired by the scene, perhaps not. The older woman adjusting the bridal skirt is looking at details while the photographer is selecting a picture out of a larger scene, ignoring the others. The boy looks inward and the father, too, is closed off in his own world. In contrast the girl looks outward directly engaging the viewer. The room is well lit and there are 'empty frames' – covered opaque panes of glass maybe signaling the presence of a darkroom in addition to being signs for unknown pictures? The door girl leans on leads inward but we cannot tell where it would take us, unlike the castle in Spain where a rear well-lit doorway and stairs going up suggest a way to the private apartments, a door guarded by a courtier who holds a curtain back. Are we on the main floor of the castle in the public space of a monarch? The skylight in the atelier suggests we are probably in the attic, and if not, then in a single story building which would not have been in a fashionable neighborhood in a late nineteenth century French city. We must be in a neighborhood looking at the rituals of a middle class wedding, a stop at the photographers' between the ceremony and the party. These wedding photographs are images commissioned by people with modest budgets. One of the gifts of photography was to make portraiture available to anyone with modest income; they were no longer the domain of just royals and oligarchs.[11] Where Velásquez used the occasion of an informal moment in the royal household to unpack representation itself, Dagnan-Bouveret's interest seems to lie more completely in technological change as it moves into his studio, and he seems to assure us that he is up to the challenge.

Development

The law, of course, can be seen as 'order backed by force,'[12] and the lawyer, in Anthony Kronman's interpretation, as the builder of the social stage on which we enact our public lives.[13] Both views evoke the metaphorical artist who has near-

11 See Beaumont Newhall, *The History of Photography* (New York: The Museum of Modern Art, 1982), chapter five.

12 See H. L. A. Hart, *The Concept of Law* (Oxford: Clarendon Press, 1963).

13 Anthony Kronman, 'Rhetoric', 67 *University of Cincinnati Law Review* (1999), pp. 677-709.

absolute power over the domain of the painting and, inside it, convenes the stage whereon all the elements play out their stories within the image.

In *Wedding at the Photographer's*, we are witness to the beginning of a legal event, a marriage, and the bridal couple is staring into the future like an abstract construction of rule or principle; they are enacting a prescribed social role. Others, both men and women, are present and commenting; they might stand for the proliferation of legal meaning as it is refracted through the social lenses of legal actors and the legal academy. The detail-oriented older woman may be like those legal professionals who are most interested in rules and procedures rather than larger issues of jurisprudence.

The deliberate obscuring of vision in the puff of smoke reminds us that sometimes things are too painful to see or that our eyes are closed by the self-interest of others or that not everything is, in fact, cognizable in terms of the law. Perhaps, in this little allegory, the photographer will give us the evidence even as we will be denied the direct experience, but it is his evidence and he will have composed it. We will have to believe in his methods and the reliability of his picture but we know that in clicking the shutter, his view is limited to what appears before the camera's lens under those specific conditions of lighting and atmosphere. The painter, however, is looking at and composing a larger scene of all the players, including those the photographer cannot see.

And the little girl? She is looking outward, eye to eye with the viewer, and by breaking the aura of the picture as a seamlessly contained account that we are able to enjoy voyeuristically, she both implicates us and suggests that there is a view outside that which either the artist or the photographer – or the law – provides. Her look is too knowing to be attributed to innocence but her youth means that she is not yet part of the system of adult socially validated meanings. She opens the possibility of doubt in the painting.

So what is Dagnan-Bouveret asserting about painting and photography with this image? Certainly the painting contains more points of view harmonized in the single frame than the picture about to be taken by the photographer. Unlike the camera's 'eye,' which will compose everything that appears before it, the painter's eye can obscure some facts and choose to remain silent on some details while emphasizing others. The painter can allude to grime on the covered inner windows but does not have to give us the gritty surface. These acts of selection, as well as execution, are the acts of a professional. The lawyer too has to craft his or her case, must choose what is relevant, must bring it into conversation with standards of 'representation' contained in professional practices.[14]

Technological change is now sweeping into the practice of law. If we use painting as a metaphor, what do we find if we substitute the lawyer for the painter in Dagnan-Bouveret; what do we see about the law? A professional stands and surveys the

14 Robert P. Burns, *A Theory of the Trial* (Princeton: Princeton University Press, 1999), pp. 36-52.

scene – his[15] power is greater than any of the single views; it is his role to bring them together into a single picture, just as the lawyer brings together his theory of the case with the facts and legal rules and precedents that govern them.

The lawyer is the rhetorician, closer to an artist than a judge because it is through rhetoric that feeling, color, enters the legal conversation, and the lawyer has to persuade – whatever the arena of legal activity.[16] The judge is like the artist because the judge is the architect of the proceeding and its final arbiter; the judge exercises rhetoric in written opinions, but differently, for the judge speaks for the law where the lawyer speaks for the person. We can certainly see legal subjectivity divided between the two professional positions and then any account must also include the jury and the public.

Third Riff

So why isn't *Wedding at the Photographer's* a painting great enough to challenge *Las Meninas*? Setting aside the usual response to such questions – it is in the eye of the beholder – I submit that Dagnan-Bouveret's reflections on the meaning of his painting remain confined within a conventional frame.

Dagnan-Bouveret studied with Gérôme and Corot; the one known especially for his meticulously realistic paintings of exotic subjects, particularly from the Middle East, and the other as a painter of dreamy Romantic landscapes. Both were successful painters on the Parisian scene. Dagnan-Bouveret would have felt that he was carrying on a tradition, not deviating from one as he painted provincial genre scenes. His social position, as evidenced by his work, is that of a comfortably integrated member of the bourgeoisie. He may import references to *Las Meninas* to cue his viewers that he is painting about representation, but unlike Velásquez, he does not make viewers experience the semiotic puzzle but rather illustrates a catalog of ways of seeing. The absent, ambiguous figure is the painter himself. If we, the

15 In the nineteenth century, the law was overwhelmingly a male profession; the first woman lawyer to pass the bar in the United States was Belle Babb Mansfield in 1869. I use the masculine pronoun because I am drawing parallels between represented male figures in the paintings to the legal profession at the time. See http://campus. northpark.edu/history/WebChron/USA/WomanLawyer.CP.html.

16 This formulation is not intended to further entrench the old view that rhetoric is mere ornamentation relative to reasoned legal truth and that therefore rhetoric is opposed to a substantive construction of meaning. Current cognitive science shows that emotion enters judgment at the level of perception before its elaboration by the cortex. See Antonio Damasio, *Descartes' Error* (New York: Avon Books, 1994); Patricia Smith Churchland, *Brain-Wise, Studies in Neurophilosophy* (Cambridge: MIT Press, 2002.) Within art history as a discipline, there has also been a long tradition of tension around color as opposed to black and white in pictures. Drawing, still mostly expressed as line with or without development of tonal contrast, is seen as having a special relation to truth over color. See the first chapters in John Gage, *Color and Culture* (Boston: Bullfinch Press Book, Little, Brown and Company , 1993) and Martin Jay, *Downcast Eyes* (Berkeley: University of California Press, 1994).

viewer, step into his shoes, we may be aspiring to the power of the painter but that power has no epic proportions. We take the place of a professional but not the king. The painter is sharing space with another representational medium, making some claims for painting but not rejecting those of photography.

Dagnan-Bouveret accepts the machinery of the realist (as opposed to the optical) enterprise and, perhaps, posits the socially more elite role of the hand painted image. That he is moved to do so points to the already changed relationship between painting and its culture.

> But it does seem clear that another shift in what philosophers talk about is happening … I want to call this shift 'the pictorial turn.' In Anglo-American philosophy, variations on this turn could be traced early on in Charles [Sanders] Peirce's semiotics … [which] explore the conventions and codes that underlie non-linguistic symbol systems and (more important) do not begin with the assumption that language is paradigmatic for meaning.[17]

Peirce was writing at the same time as Dagnan-Bouveret was painting, and they were both working when photography was becoming transportable and ubiquitous. The conceptual development of semiotics, which opened questions of meaning that undermined the surface of traditional verities, and the technical development of photography (which made it possible for many people, and not just elite artists, to make their own pictures) opened what must have seemed a similar chasm arising from the shifting of cultural tectonic plates.

In like manner, the world of the older visual media saw a collision of sorts between painting and printmaking (the 'traditional' means of reproduction), on the one hand, and photography, on the other, so carefully explicated by Stephen Bann.[18] (Painters had come to rely on engravers for the dissemination of their work and reputations[19] and both were subsequently challenged by the invention of photography; engraved reproductions of works of art, which were very time-consuming to make by hand, could themselves be photographed and made ready for publication very quickly.)

A machine for picture making relieved the hands of their labor. With the power of the Salon waning, there was bound to be uncertainty about picturing itself, as gatekeeping functions could no longer be closely controlled by ruling elites.[20] Both speed and reproducibility are, of course, analogs to industrial production, and it is not hard to read the anxiety around picturing as a reflection of larger disquiets.

---

17 W.J.T. Mitchell, 'The Pictorial Turn', in *Picture Theory* (Chicago: University of Chicago Press, 1994), p. 11.

18 Bann, Stephen, *Parallel Lines: Printmakers, Painters and Photographers in Nineteenth-Century France* (New Haven: Yale University Press, 2001).

19 Bann, p. 3.

20 For two different analyses of gatekeeping, oblique associations, to be sure, see Walter Kendrick's *The Secret Museum* (New York: Viking, 1987) and Diana Crane's *The Transformation of the Avant-Garde, The New York Art World, 1940-1985* (Chicago: University of Chicago Press, 1985).

The democratization predicted by *Las Meninas* was happening on a grand scale in the industrialized world where a mass audience developed for cultural products. So *Wedding at the Photographer's* allies itself with realism, the attitude of both brush and the 'pencil of nature,'[21] both confirming a social consensus about what things look like.[22] This is a conservative position; it ties the representational act to a form of perception that can control the subject and not draw attention to itself as a representation. It has a kind of inevitability about it that many would have found comforting amidst proliferating change. The law, too, has its own conservatism (and not just because it reproduces hierarchies)[23] in the way current problems are systemically embedded in the history of legal decision making through processes of analogizing and distinguishing cases.

By the time this artist put the talents of his hands up against the mechanism of the camera, photography was fairly routinely a part of courtroom practice. Where the painting accepts that photographs are made by people (we see no image in the camera, just the photographer's rear end pointed at us – an acerbic joke or expression of ambivalence?), in the courts, the view that photographs are constructed pictures competed with what I will call the naïve realist view that the photograph was especially truthful because a dispassionate machine, not a human, made it.[24] The tension between these two positions continues even today.

New technology was invading the courtroom through lawyers' practice at the same time that the profession was undergoing profound changes as well. In American law during the same period, the numbers of lawyers increased about two and a half times going from almost 41,000 practitioners in 1870 to almost 115,000 in 1900.[25] At the same time, formal legal education largely supplanted apprenticeship as the preferred means of training lawyers, legal education became institutionalized, and C.C. Langdell and C.W. Eliot of Harvard with Theodore Dwight of Columbia,

> the heroes of the revival of legal education, argued for the *practical* superiority of their teaching to apprenticeship training because of its basis in scientific principles.[26]

> [Its] presumed virtues were being touted during exactly that period in which the business of the upper bracket of the bar was undergoing a shift in emphasis from advocacy to office practice.[27]

---

21 Henry Fox Talbot, *The Pencil of Nature* (London: Longmans, England, 1844-45).

22 Of course there is the alternative photographic tradition of using the camera to extend our vision, to show us things we cannot see with the naked eye.

23 See Duncan Kennedy, *Legal Education and the Reproduction of Hierarchy, A Polemic Against the System* (New York: New York University Press, 2004).

24 Jennifer, Mnookin, 'The Image of Truth: Photographic Evidence and the Power of Analogy', 10 Yale Journal of Law & Humanities, Winter 1998.

25 United States Census, 'Occupations' Volume 13.

26 Gordon, Robert W., 'Legal Thought and Legal Practice', in Gerald Geison (ed.), *Professionals and Professional Ideologies in America* (Chapel Hill: University of North Carolina Press, 1983), pp. 72-73.

27 Gordon, 'Legal Thought and Legal Practice'.

So we have, in the latter part of the nineteenth century, a conjunction of rising mass media (made possible by literacy and the technologies of mass image production) and new professional identities for lawyers. This change was accompanied by a great expansion in the ranks of lawyers. This enabled the media and the law to begin their long dance together. But back then, the law was striving for formally understood relationships, something like scientific principles, a sense of itself as occupying a disciplinary ground, striving for professional identity and the respect that comes with that.[28]

Rhetoric did not fit into that schema very well. The emphasis on appellate advocacy instituted at the top echelon of law schools could not but underscore law's self-definition as a profession based in a professional language and literature. To the degree that the law was conceived as an abstract system derived from the data of case decisions, it also acquired an aura of impersonal inevitability that would be challenged in the future by the legal realists. The 'pencil of nature' in legal rules could join industrial production, metaphorically speaking. New technology could fit right into this regime.

Lawyers are trained to be good with words, not pictures. As long as they could be convinced that the picture was just an illustration of the words, there was not a large problem. We are once again in a time of dramatic change, still working out the pictorial turn, but this time with significantly different technologies of picture production and distribution. I submit that this time the pictorial turn will affect not just the content of the law (new kinds of cases, new problems in decision making) but also in fundamental assumptions about how the activity of constructing legal meaning ought to be carried out, what needs to be documented and archived, what texts will be available in future legal archives.

> Law's force depends partly on the inscription on the soul of a regime of images. Religion and law have a long history of policing images, coupled with an economy of permitted images or icons, an iconomy, and a criminology of dangerous fallen and graven images, an idolatry. This peculiar and shifting combination of iconoclasm and iconophilia ... is still a central part of the operations of law ... organized around the regulation of the relationships between object, image, and text.[29]

The iconomy has changed. The digital revolution poses a semiotic challenge to older ways of legal thinking because it makes more complex the relations of object, image, and text; the proliferation of meaning has in important ways slipped out of the boundaries of reliable social control. While we still need to account for ways of seeing, as did Dagnan-Bouveret, the digital revolution has engendered an intertextual meta-culture that has spread world-wide. Stories appear in one medium,

---

28 Richard L. Abel, *American Lawyers* (Oxford: Oxford University Press, 1989), p. 4.

29 Costas Dzouinas and Linda Nead, *Law and the Image, The Authority of Art and the Aesthetics of Law* (Chicago: University of Chicago Press, 1999), p. 9.

are taken up and developed in another, and may be resolved in still another.[30] (This can be seen as a development out of the more traditional medium of television which has long given viewers serial experience of characters and stories over the time of a season with a complexity not matched by the self-contained drama in a theater that may last two or three hours.)

What is called the blogosphere,[31] the realm of public comment made by anyone who chooses to engage in it on the World Wide Web, now competes with regular news sources to release stories. Increasingly the stories are visual; we are truly writing with pictures as well as words.[32]

The common culture represented by the World Wide Web is both hierarchical (some servers are gatekeepers, some information technology personnel have a great deal of power over the system) and decentralized, organized around nodes that represent spheres of influence. Individuals can access the World Wide Web using digital tools from any location that supports them; one way or another, they can publish without gatekeepers. While some may consider this the Wild West of free expression and seek to bring it under a regime of control, the digital tools – hardware, operating systems, applications software, programming skills – have been so widely dispersed, and the behaviors involved in their use so deeply entrenched, that it is hard to imagine that the genii will be put back into the lamp. The democratic revolution

---

30 A case in point is the recent controversy around the removal of the feeding tube sustaining Terry Schiavo's persistent vegetative state. The family lobbied against its removal by posting short homemade videos on the Web; regular news coverage re-circulated these and added medical pictures shown by experts trying to explain her condition to the public. Eventually there was a special act of Congress, a number of judicial decisions, and segments on late night television, including *South Park*, 'Best Friends Forever' (Comedy Channel, 28 March 2005) and *The Daily Show with Jon Stewart* (Comedy Channel, 2005, which can be seen at: http://newclips. crooksandliars. com/The_Daily_Show_Frist_Wingers.mov; last accessed 29 September 2005). To track the social meanings being generated, one would have to dip into all these media. It is no longer possible to have any idea of what the public is being told without recourse to a broad spectrum of texts that count on the audience's knowledge of the others.

31 See, for example, Eric Boehlert, 'Citizen journalists? Try partisan hacks. Right-wing bloggers shrieked that the GOP Schiavo memo was a "liberal media" fraud. Now that they've been proven wrong, are they apologizing? Why, no!', at http://www.salon.com/news/feature/2005/04/08/schiavo_memo/index.html, accessed 8 April 2005. See also, '"Measuring the Blogosphere": Earlier this week, Technorati, a Web site that indexes blogs, released its semiannual "State of the Blogosphere" report. It records a steady, and astonishing, growth. Nearly 80,000 new blogs are created every day, and there are some 14.2 million in existence already, 55 percent of which remain active. Some 900,000 new blog postings are added every day – a steady increase marked by extraordinary spikes in new postings after incidents like the London bombing. The blogosphere – that is, the virtual realm of blogdom as a whole – doubles in size every five and a half months.' *The New York Times*, 5 August 2005 Friday, Late Edition – Final, Section A; Column 1; Editorial Desk; pg. 14.

32 Lawrence Lessig, Free Culture, How Big Media Uses Technology and the Law to Lock Down Culture and Control Creativity (New York: The Penguin Press, 2004), p.36.

predicted in Velásquez' painting, insofar as it has to do with access to information and cultural production, has occurred on a scale unimaginable in the past.

There are the many important issues for the law emerging with this new space, and they will have to be left out of this discussion. In the remainder of this chapter, I will focus on the fundamental changes that this revolution is bringing to legal practice and challenges for the legal academy.

A New *Las Meninas:* This Time for the Law

The painter paints on a canvas, a support of definable dimensions that frames the picture by limiting its boundaries. The elements inside the frame are in conversation with one another through proximity even before they are related by other qualities of consonance, contrast, iconography, and so on. The relations of the parts to each other are uncertain – that is, definitive, closed readings are not possible when we discuss meaning because our reading is conditioned by what we are looking for, the task with which we approach the picture. Rarely do we read long enough to come to a complete account of all its elements.[33] The absence of definitive syntax that determines the reading order of elements in pictures makes logic in the traditional meaning of the term irrelevant – the logics are figurative, associational, not propositional. The painter, who has to build the image through steps, cannot reveal the whole until it is done. When it is complete, the reader, the receiver, sees the whole and then will enter the frame and begin where it makes sense to begin in that moment of starting under those starting conditions.[34] The artist's picture of the law contains both thoughts and sensations: some thoughts are expressed as pictures (they are ordered sensations because designed but appeal directly to the senses) and other thoughts as chains of words. In this metaphor, both kinds of text sit as equals within the frame of legal knowledge. We have a highly developed legal consciousness in words; the same cannot be said for pictures.[35]

My focus here is on picture texts and what the law faces as it tries to assimilate them into legal frameworks. Not that such texts have not been there since the nineteenth

33 A study by A. Yarbus (1967), quoted in Patricia Smith Churchland's *Brain-Wise, Studies in Neurophilosophy* (Cambridge, Massachusetts and London: The MIT Press, 2002), p.51, demonstrated that eye movements were affected by task. The data was differentiated by both saccadic and resting movements.

34 Symbolic logic is excepted from this formulation as are some other kinds of graphic expression that are directly propositional by demanding that elements be read like symbolic logic.

35 Both the iconic picture as sign and the word as sign can, perhaps, be considered as combining 'two sorts of elements of consciousness' which Peirce explains through the metaphor of music – the tones stand for sensations, the melody for their orderly sequence, and 'thought is a thread of melody running through the succession of our sensations.' Charles S. Peirce, 'How to Make Our Ideas Clear', *Popular Science Monthly* 12 (January 1878) available at http://peirce.org/writings/pll9.html accessed 24 March 2005.

century, but the mass media and the digital revolution have combined to loosen the control (or the illusion of control) that words once used to have over them. There are many more kinds of picturing in play: charts, graphs, maps, diagrams, photographs, the traditional stuff of demonstrative evidence, have been joined by digital still and motion photography, computer animations, videos, film, machine readouts of all kinds from scientific testing, virtual reality environments, and multi-media displays. But instead of sitting within the box of the courtroom or the files of the law office, these pictures are circulated in a broader public context of mass media that surrounds and interpenetrates them.[36] Some statistics may be helpful in understanding what has happened in the media world. In 1950, 8.8 per cent of American households owned a television.[37] By 2005, 98 per cent of households do.[38] This can seem like an orderly progression when it is compared to similar statistics for the World Wide Web. Before the Web was a public space, in 1969, there were about eight hosting servers; by 2005 we are approaching one billion servers[39] and one hundred million web sites. The Internet, a prior creation that enables the existence of the World Wide Web, experienced a doubling in its use every one hundred *days* between 1994 and 1997. Some comparisons: it took 38 years for radio to reach 50 million listeners; television took 13 years, and the Internet only four.[40] No wonder the law has some serious catching up to do. While the law has been quick to adopt technologies for its own uses all along, it has been slow to understand them; principally, I think, because the culture of written text was so firm and strong that it was hard to see that words might not tame the picture into being a 'mere illustration.' The three big changes that the digital revolution has brought about that concern me here are: 1) there are changes in how we read text; 2) we can include all our means of representation in a single frame; 3) we are all now practitioners.

Reading

When we read verbal text, we read one word after another, or, if we are fast readers, we read groups of words followed by groups of words, and when we skim we grab bits of data and fill in the blanks; in short, reading is linear and therefore time-based. When it became possible for anyone, including a child just beginning to write, to

---

36 For an extensive discussion of this, see Richard K. Sherwin, *When Law Goes Pop* (Chicago: University of Chicago Press, 2000).

37 These numbers were based on a variety of sources including Neilson and the United States Census Bureau and are quoted by Susan Ashworth in 'TV Facts Then & Now' in *Digital World*, February 2005, at http://www.pcworld.com/news/article/0,aid, 118945,00.asp, accessed on-line 26 March 2005.

38 Ashworth.

39 Robert H. Zakon, 'Hobbes' Internet Timeline', 2005 'Hosts', http://ww.zakon. org/ Robert/internet/timeline, accessed 26 March 2005.

40 http://www.unc.edu/depts/jomc/academics/dri/011/growth.html, titled 'The Exponential Growth of the Internet' and based on statistics from the United States Department of Commerce.

type text that looked published and to easily alter that text, to make it better through changes, the vision of published text as a single stable object disappeared. Text is fluid and anything written in Times New Roman can seem to have authority because it looks published regardless of whether it represents authoritative thinking or not. And people, too, can acquire authority on the World Wide Web outside the usual channels. Michael Lewis in his account of the digital revolution, *Next*,[41] tells us about the most popular on-line lawyer, Marcus Arnold, who happened to be 15 in 2001 when Lewis was working on the book, and who kept his status even after his age was made public.

But there is more to this picture of the revolution than people believing either in their own judgments of authority or believing (alas, naively) that some kind of gatekeeping is going on. The additional piece of the picture comes from a profound and widely held skepticism over whether anything is true. The public is treated to so much spin and disinformation by speakers with social authority that a television show which advertises itself as purveying 'fake news,' *The Daily News with Jon Stewart*, is regarded as having as much or more authority than regular news outlets even while it deconstructs the spin of the 'real' newsmakers.[42] The question of belief in communications, why and how we believe what we do, has come to the foreground.[43]

In addition to the problems of belief, the fluidity of electronic text and its publication on-line have given us new habits of reading. While all of us might skip ahead to read the conclusion of an exciting book, or dive into the middle and then go forward or back, reading on the Web we have to decide whether to exercise the options given us to follow links. Not only does this interrupt the sequence developed by the author over time, it can also lead us away from the text, never to return. With linking, we have a wholly new unit of speech that is poorly understood at that: *the link*. The Second Circuit Court of Appeals chose in *Universal v. Reimerdes*[44] to assume that a link was neutral – without meaning in itself. Reimerdes, a 'zine publisher, had provided the means, by directing readers to another web site, for individuals to download code that allowed them to circumvent the security controls on DVDs and thus engage in criminal acts as defined by the Digital Millennium Copyright Act. (The Act distinguishes between access to technologically protected work and copying it. Copying is permitted as a fair use, but not using hardware or software devices to circumvent protective measures.)

---

41 Michael Lewis, *Next, The Future Just Happened* (New York: W.W. Norton, 2002), chapter 3.

42 *The New York Times*, 27 August 2004 Friday, Late Edition – Final, Section B; Column 3; Metropolitan Desk; 'Public Lives', p. 2.

43 Neal Feigenson, 'New Visual Technologies in Court: Directions for Research' (with Meghan Dunn), *Law and Human Behavior*, 27 (2003), pp. 109-126.

44 See *Universal v. Reimerdes*, at http://www.eff.org/IP/Video/MPAA_DVD_cases/20011128_ny_appeal_decision.html, accessed 10 May 2005.

The language in the US Copyright Office's summary is in the endnote.[45] (Had the justices understood the link as speech, they might not have upheld the conviction on appeal.) Links do create relationships but their meaning requires decoding just like all other speech acts. All of our browsing through the Web is link-based. Any web pages we make require us to make links ourselves and our choices can be as semiotically rich as we are capable of being. As legal filings become part of case webs, a structure of visible relationships will become part of the official records and lawyers will have to scrutinize carefully these other kinds of text for their accuracy and probative value because links will add meaning.

Now that visuals are so routinely a part of case presentation, we will have to move toward including them in case files. When, in the course of a file, are we readers going to be asked to move to the pictures and what effects will that have on the reading of the written text that follows? Or if the pictures precede the written material, how will they affect our reading? This will change the parameters of legal databases, published cases in hard copy, and so on. (And it will surely raise copyright questions.)

Linking to pictures in a case web will expand meaning still further. What standards will apply to quality and quantity of visual materials? Will there have to be documentation of their presentation? These are first questions.

Reading in a Frame

Many texts today are produced not on a ruled yellow pad or white sheet of paper, but on the representation of a white sheet of paper on our computer screens. Increasingly, we are also reading texts written by others on the same screen.

We can, in fact, place our writing (or our digital picturing) beside the works of those we admire, window to window. Even though a page is a frame for the words inscribed on it, words on a screen that changes – that evokes the picturing of film and television – are more visibly what they have been all along: pictures of a particular

---

45 Section 1201 divides technological measures into two categories: measures that prevent unauthorized *access* to a copyrighted work and measures that prevent copying. *The Digital Millennium Copyright Act of 1998.* 'Copying' is used in this context as a short-hand for the exercise of any of the exclusive rights of an author under section 106 of the Copyright Act. Consequently, a technological measure that prevents unauthorized distribution or public performance of a work would fall in this second category. *Copyright Office Summary December 1998*, p. 4.

… Since copying of a work may be a fair use under appropriate circumstances, section 1201 does not prohibit the act of circumventing a technological measure that prevents copying. By contrast, since the fair use doctrine is not a defense to the act of gaining unauthorized access to a work, the act of circumventing a technological measure in order to gain access is prohibited. From: *The Digital Millennium Copyright Act of 1998*. U.S. Copyright Office Summary December 1998, available at: http://www.copyright.gov/legislation/dmca.pdf, accessed 9 May 2005.

kind.[46] We are instantly reminded of the abstraction of words compared to image material like a photograph. The computer screen makes it possible for us to fluidly juxtapose words with still or moving pictures (with or without sound files) within a single frame, so we have a text that combines time-based word-after-word reading with the all-over reading of the visual field called for by pictures, so we are reading in two modalities simultaneously: the meaning of words emerging as a property of flow; the meaning of pictures as a property of spatial display.

The picture maker may try to control through design the order in which information unfolds, but it is only a statistical chance that any one person will in fact read the image in the order designed because we each go to the picture with different tasks in mind. Formal logical reasoning, because it depends upon sequential ordering, does not flourish in this environment, although graphic expressions of some kinds of propositions are very powerful. Whether containing pictures or words, the frame defines the space in which the visual interactions will take place; it reminds us that we are in the realm of representation.

The digital revolution has put the frame of the monitor as central to our participation in this new culture. Unlike the movie screen where we can watch pictures larger than ourselves, or the television screen, where we mostly watch pictures smaller than ourselves, the computer screen is 'our size.' Peer to peer defines not only software interactions, it is a good descriptor for our relationship to our computer screens.[47] We make things happen on it and with it. 'Interaction is a process that dictates communication. It can also be a communication that dictates process. It provides options, necessitates a change in pace, and changes as you change it.'[48] In this semiotic situation, the new experience of reading in a multi-media context, the reader can quite literally grab information and move it around and in so doing alter all the relationships in the 'structure' of the information space; that information may be expressed in sound, still pictures, or moving picture clips.[49] This is no longer the interactivity of the highlighter or marginalia we make with pen or pencil as we read. We may not be just moving information around, we may be characters in complex gaming scenarios that involve both our puzzle-solving abilities and deep levels of our fantasy lives. This too becomes part of our associations to the tool and part of our background expectations.

What will happen to legal process when both legal practitioners and the public expect to interact with all texts as a result of the ubiquity of the interactive Web in their lives – whether they play interactive video games or not? Will the stability of the legal text, the bedrock of legal reasoning, remain?

46 Richard Benson, *Notes on Pictures*, Devane Lecture, Yale University, New Haven, 2001.

47 And we think of our screens as people. See Byron Reeves and Clifford Nass, *The Media Equation* (New York: Cambridge University Press, 1996).

48 Mark Stephen Meadows, *Pause and Effect, The Art of Interactive Narrative* (Indianapolis: New Riders, 2003), p. 37.

49 I am describing Thinkmap technology. An example is *The Visual Thesaurus* at http://www.thinkmap.com/visualthesaurus.jsp.

The frame is a metaphor for point of view, frame of reference, the set of its contents. It is a metaphor for boundary as well – what is inside is a human construction; what is outside is, well, outside. Inside, relationships are intensified, because the act of framing selects elements for our attention and focuses their visual relations along many axes: position in space, light, color, symmetries, form, consonance and dissonance of elements in relation both to each other and to the ground. Many of the pictures we are casually exposed to are photographs. An estimated 25 billion photographs are made in America each year.[50] Scholars talk about the indexical power of photography to give us an illusion of the surface of the world. Equally important to its effect is what Richard Benson has called its capacity to bring the diversity of the world into a harmonized image.[51] I would add that the resolution of the photographic surface (whether granular or smoothly analog) may allude to things of the world but it transforms the illusion of the real; in the photograph, everything is made of the same stuff. This might well have been a necessary conceptual precursor to making tools that actually make/represent everything in digital code just as the cards for the Jacquard loom can be seen as a precursor 'pattern' for the discontinuous representation of pixels.

So the digital revolution allows us to bring into the frame of our computer monitors multiple windows that may deliver us sight and sound, still images and moving ones simultaneously with windows where we are acting upon digital files that may be about anything at all.

We Are All Makers

Finally, technology has made it easy for anyone to accomplish representational tasks formerly available only to those who could spend years developing their talents – you should hear the anguish of older photographers over what the youth can now do with a click of the mouse – and, almost at the same time, that technology has come down in price for consumers in general. With the creation of the Internet and the World Wide Web, we can combine our making with seemingly infinite cultural resources. The result is a contemporary American culture where digital experience is invading 'real life' and real life is increasingly occupied with semiotic battling as we contest representation – who gets to do it and under what circumstances as well as who uses what images to what purpose, not to mention the problem of what the image actually purports to be. The result of all three of these things – changes in reading, interactivity, broadly disseminated means of image production – is a complex ecology of image exchange in which codes in one medium are referred to in another.

For instance, WABC was credited with a photograph published on the front page of the 24 July 2003 edition of *The New York Times*. It was a video still taken the

---

50 Anne Higonnet, *Pictures of Innocence, History and Crisis of Ideal Childhood* (London: Thames and Hudson, 1998), p. 87.

51 Richard Benson, conversation in Newport, Rhode Island, June 2003.

day a city councilman was shot in City Hall. It is a grainy image taken from above, probably from the vantage point of a news helicopter. Why did *The New York Times* choose this photo when, in all likelihood, there would have been print photographers covering whatever was happening that day at City Hall? Was a grainy black and white photograph, more like surveillance footage, more apt for this news? Or was it more 'credible' because of the visual reference to fixed cameras that record whatever looms in front of them even though it was a news crew that might well have been shooting with a handheld camera – a new version of the old view of the photograph as involving little if any human intervention?[52]

On 10 July 2002, with the corporate scandals of Enron and WorldCom much in the news, *The New York Times* published a front page, above the fold, picture of President George W. Bush addressing the topic of corporate responsibility.[53] We know that because behind him is 'wallpaper' with those words on it as if from the glossy pages of a corporate annual report. It is a screen shot of a television screen or monitor – we can dimly see the reflections off the glass surface (the same method of verification of the mirror used by Velásquez 350 years earlier). We know it is television because we see the CNBC logos and the informational tickers running along the bottom. The stock quotes are in their usual places along the right side. That day there were little red arrows pointing down as stocks lost their value. Where was the President? The broadcaster, using blue screen editing, could insert any desired background; he could have been anywhere. The question for the reader of the picture is whether the picture editor, or the editorial board, wanted to offer a quiet signal of disapproval with those little red arrows? It must have been assumed that the audience would not be thrown by the composite image – that it would, in fact, have immediately recognized its parts.

To represent their clients' interests, lawyers need to track their cases in the media to gain information about how the public is thinking so that they may be able to craft their arguments persuasively. How many would have recognized the story being told, again on the front pages of *The New York Times*, about Howard Dean's campaign for the presidency? On 15 December 2003 Dean is shown at the podium, his arms open, bent at the elbows in a wide gesture. Behind him is a solemn Al Gore. Dean looks like a winner. He also, because of the camera angle and generous gesture, looks taller than he actually is.[54] On 13 January 2004, *The New York Times* published a photograph, this time below the fold on the left, of Mrs Dean in jeans and athletic shoes sitting on a child's chair in a classroom.[55] Her image in the picture ran counter to all the First Ladies. The woman in the picture was not dressed as a public figure but was shown on a visit to a school dressed in what conservatives would think of as an outfit for yard work on a Saturday. Without addressing the complex issue of

52 Surveillance matters are outside the scope of this essay. Citizens are using cameras and cellular phones to protect themselves from harm at the hands of authorities.

53 CNBC photo, *The New York Times,* front page, 10 July 2002.

54 James Estrin, *The New York Times*, front page, 15 December 2003.

55 Ruth Fremson, *The New York Times*, front page, 13 January 2004.

how women are portrayed and how they can look powerful, this picture seemed to throw down the gauntlet – 'Do you want this kind of woman to represent the nation in the White House? Is this our image?' Ten days later, on 23 January 2004, Dean was shown above the fold being congratulated by Kerry and Edwards and Al Sharpton.[56] John Kerry, John Edwards, and then Howard Dean form a long diagonal in the picture, from a tall Kerry to a short Dean, so while he is the focus of the picture, and the mood is congratulatory, Kerry's raised hand, and Edwards' hand on Dean's arm echoing Kerry's, shows him being metaphorically shoved out of the picture. Six days later, on 29 January 2004, we see Dean in a studio rehearsing the speech that ended his campaign.[57] The candidate is in focus in the background, seated at a table with a sheaf of papers in his hand. In the left foreground of the photograph, we see Dean's head on a monitor looking very large, so close to us that the picture is cropped, and out of sharp focus. He is looking down, seemingly about to say something. In many ways the media image is more 'real' than the guy at the table. What did the editors intend with the publication of this picture? Did they just think it was 'interesting' or were they showing off – 'We did it!'[58] Or were they making some kind of judgment like: 'This guy just doesn't know how to handle us yet'? What if this was not Howard Dean but a client in a big case? How would the lawyer handle the public conversation? Increasingly, litigation public relations is part of the practice of the law.

In August of 2003, *The New York Times* carried a story about a Coney Island entrepreneur who set up a live game in an alley called 'Shoot the Freak.'[59] He figured that there were people who could not afford to buy the equipment and software for video gaming but would like to have the first-person shooter experience in a representational setting. So he hired some actors, gave them protective costumes, and invited customers to shoot at them with paint bullets. He counted on his takers to understand the various codes being evoked by the real life imagery he was constructing.

Notice that all these images are taken from a paper of record that is archived on the legal databases, Lexis-Nexis and Westlaw, but that the pictures are not part of the database. Setting aside questions of copyright, how can the full story be researched and understood without the pictures? 'Step Right Up, Live Human Target' gets our attention, but its full cultural meaning is opaque without the accompanying picture.

56 *The New York Times*, front page, 23 January 2004.

57 *The New York Times*, front page, 29 January 2004.

58 Dean had been reported as losing control at a large campaign rally when he came in third. He was calling out to his supporters that they were going to go forward, but using a sound-cancelling microphone (intended to clarify) to a large crowd made it seem that he was yelling inappropriately. The press seized on this as an example of why he would be an unreliable leader and reported repeatedly that Dean had lost control of himself in the heat of primary passions.

59 Photo: Ting-Li Wang; article: Saturday 23 August 2003, by Marek Fuchs (NYT) Metropolitan Desk Late Edition – Final, Section B, Page 1.

I have been describing elements of culture that are broadly comprehensible because of their mainstream settings. The visual materials that come the way of legal professionals may or may not be drawn from these sources, but what they will all have in common is the fact that they are not anointed masterpieces for which there are scholarly pedigrees. They are by and large ephemera, visuals made to document or analyze scientific data, photographic documents pertaining to matters at bar – the list is long. There is little time for the lawyer to investigate them, little scholarly literature about them and, like mastering the art of reading the law, lawyers need to practice connoisseurship so that they yield their range of meanings quickly. We are far from there as yet.

On 14 June 2002 Judge Stephen N. Limbaugh decided the *Interactive Digital Software* case. At issue was a county ordinance restricting the sale of violent video games. The manufacturers sought a summary judgment declaring the ordinance to be unconstitutional on grounds that video games are protected speech. The judge wrote in his opinion denying summary judgment:

> If an entirely new 'medium' is being given First Amendment protection, there does need to be at least some type of communication of ideas in that medium. It has to be designed to express or inform, and there has to be the likelihood that others will understand that there has been some type of expression. … Although some of the games 'talk' to the participant, play music, or have written instructions, that alone does not provide the missing element of 'information.[60]

In defense of the ordinance, the county's lawyers showed the court game play videos of selected published games which the ordinance's proponents had earlier prepared in their efforts to obtain its passage. One of the games was a popular game called *Resident Evil* that concerns 'bad science' in the form of a genetically altered virus that makes monsters of the people it infects. In the portion of the play tape that I was able to view,[61] the heroine, Jill, whose pixel features look vaguely like the actress Sandra Bullock, moves through an underground landscape, then above ground through architecture of increasing splendor; she selects various tools, weapons reloads, and so on, and has to confront scary creatures; presumably the result of genetic engineering gone bad. Our heroine encounters a typewriter, an old diary, snapshots.

The homey spaces emphasize different materials, tactile and visual comforts; the institutional spaces are cold, hard spaces, often with puddles of water like the tunnels

---

60 Judge Stephen N. Limbaugh decided the case, *Interactive Digital Software Association, et. al., Plaintiffs, v. St Louis County, Missouri, et. al. Defendants*, 14 June 2002.

61 I would like to thank Michael Shuman, Associate County Counselor, St. Louis (MO) County, for responding to Neal Feigenson's request to see the materials referenced in the case. He generously provided us with a chance to view this tape in his case files. The first instance of the *Resident Evil* series was released in a PlayStation version on 30 March 1996. 'The brainchild of Capcom director Shinji Mikami, RE [*Resident Evil*](as we'll refer to the series) was the first in a line of survival horror games.' IGN Staff at 2 February 2005. It continues to come out in new versions.

under ground, a clear metaphorical alignment of the two worlds. The point of view keeps shifting. The 180° rule[62] and its relatives are repeatedly broken; in this way it is unlike film. The game has both cuts and fades, just like a video, but gives us a different immersion as our point of view moves from inside the character to outside; each change of scene is marked by a doorway, a passage from one module to another. Once we are outside, we can see her from myriad angles with little conventional plot- related motivations for the change in viewing point. The game environment is not a film environment. *Resident Evil* calls on all the deep symbolism of space so sympathetically enumerated by Gaston Bachelard.[63] It is not hard to make a claim that this is a literate game. It has also been a hugely popular game, going through four versions and two full length feature films. The meaning of the video game emerges for the player as a consequence of playing, not just watching, and it requires metaphorical thinking.[64] Clearly, for Judge Limbaugh, video games lack the metonymic connection to what he considers to be 'true' expression and 'information.' [65] We must ask how much the sociology of the law[66] is an influence on how images are understood when they enter legal discourses and how much difficulty will arise when the demand is made for metaphor and not metonymy.

Seemingly on the other side of the world is an essay by Paul Carrington, 'On Virtual Civil Litigation, A Visit to John Bunyan's Celestial City',[67] published some four years before Judge Limbaugh's decision (in 1998) in which Carrington posits a future on-line court for civil litigation. He sees a time when 'trial advocacy will more closely resemble the work of a Hollywood film producer rather than that of a Hollywood actor.'[68] His is a quite detailed projection of how the process might work and what the changes from (and some continuity with) current practice might

---

62 This is a cinematic convention concerning permissible camera movement in relation to a subject – in its simplest form, the camera should not starting shooting a subject in front and then suddenly, without motivating changes, be coming from behind.

63 Gaston Bachelard, *The Poetics of Space* (Boston: Beacon Press, 1969).

64 In her important new book, Ann Kibbey explores the role of Calvinist thinking in the emergence of modern capitalist culture, where metonymy substitutes for representational meaning and 'living images of the Protestant sacrament articulated a corporate theory of the image, not just inadvertently, but consciously and crucially.' Metonymy involves simple substitution, not metaphorical understanding. Ann Kibbey, *Theory of the Image, Capitalism, Contemporary Film, and Women* (Bloomington: Indiana University Press, 2005) p. 15.

65 Readers are urged to read Neal Feigenson's contribution to this volume in its entirety, 'Digital Visual and Multimedia Software and the Reshaping of Legal Knowledge'. Of particular relevance here is his observation that: 'The implicit model of *knowledge as interaction* which computer gaming visualizes has been propounded often in the last 20 years in cognitive linguistics, cognitive neuroscience, and philosophy, but the virtual reality view evokes the *experience* (and not just the declarative knowledge) of this notion.' pp. 97-98).

66 Lawyers came overwhelmingly from Protestant backgrounds in the early twentieth century. See Abel,1989.

67 Paul Carrington, 'Virtual Civil Litigation: A Visit to John Bunyon's Celestial City', *Columbia Law Review*, October 1998.

68 Carrington, p. 10.

be. I cannot describe his whole vision here, but the most striking feature of it, from my point of view, is the utter lack of any suggestions about how the legal meaning itself will shift when it is framed on screen. Were Carrington more sensitive to these issues, would he ask for a regulatory regime about what can be shown, what must not be shown, what camera angles need to be used, and so on? Everything on the screen will carry legal meaning as will all the aspects of realization of the pictured space containing legal elements. Here is an example from his thinking: 'The interrogation of witnesses for a virtual trial could be managed with incomparably greater efficiency. They would be interrogated under oath by video conference, at a time and place convenient to the witness, generally at the witness' home or workplace. The interrogator could be thousands of miles away…'[69] But what about the impression which the views of the personal environment of the witness, whether home or work, will have on the reliability and credibility of that witness? What about the effects of camera angle and lighting? Much more real information will be included but not consciously dealt with in the proceeding itself in contrast to real world arrangements. Traditional courtrooms provide a 'neutral' space into which the various legal actors come. Depositions are typically taken in studios or offices, not homes and workspaces. In real life, participants enter carefully controlled ceremonial spaces and participate in ritually organized behaviors. Natural environments are not neutral and they are not subsumed under a common set of values. What will become of the notion of a common ground represented by the courtroom? How will the public view the roles of judge and attorneys and jurors? Presumably officers of the court would not want their offices to be viewed and so they will need the equivalent of a public space. Perhaps Carrington's vision will be transformed into game play in an old fashioned court where all participants are represented by avatars of pixels made from code in an on-line environment like *Second Life* or other multi-user games. Who will design these?

If the law is going to move into virtual space, then one of its most important features will become a dominant issue. 'We are embracing aggregate space, discontinuous, made up of aggregations of spatial containers, as a new norm, both metaphorically and literally. The space of the Web, in principle, cannot be thought of as a coherent totality: it is, rather, a collection of numerous files, hyperlinked but without any overall perspective to unite them.'[70] While Lev Manovitch sees computerization as 'an opportunity to see the world and the human being anew,'[71] the grand narratives that have given the law the force of people's belief are going to have to adjust to life in an aggregate space, more like the game space realized by the designers of *Resident Evil*, less like film. That said, the act of reading and making pictures can build the 'melody of thought' into the flux of phenomena. The

69 Carrington, p. 17.

70 Lev Manovitch, *The Language of New Media* (Cambridge, Massachusetts: MIT Press, 2001, p. 254.

71 Manovitch, p. 333.

visual semiotic task can renew the law by putting its disparate elements not into a hierarchy, but into a frame.

Epilogue

Returning to my first epigraph, it seems that Marshall Blonsky was worried that semiotics had become too preoccupied with verbal arrangements and that it was irrelevant to the world because actors in the world had to reject its claims or they would not be able to act: they would have entered a hall mirrors – unstable meaning in a world of flux – that would make it hard to be decisive about anything. I hope I have demonstrated that, far from being irrelevant, semiotics is now at the center, not of academia, but of what is happening in the world.

Law, because it is always embodied in real human conflict, real human problems, and it has outcomes that can absolutely influence people's lives, is a semiotic enterprise that remains grounded. It is crucial that lawyers understand the complexity of their communicative task in this new world ecology of writing with pictures. Whether lawyers like it or not, they are thrust back into the realm of rhetoric where they must think of crafting their messages to a new audience that expects to be shown as well as told; that expects to participate in the creation of textual meaning and which, in all likelihood, arrives with a complex compendium of interrelated 'texts' across media, experienced as casually morphing into one another.

The lawyer-painter will have to understand the catalog of ways of seeing and the non-linear ways in which the elements will speak to each other and to their audiences. This is not a matter of 'manipulation' in any nefarious sense, of concocting relationships among images and words that mislead juries, judges, and publics. Rather, it is a matter of identifying and articulating multiple meanings in a world in which meanings are multiplying and overlapping as never before, and in which what happens in court and what happens in mass media and popular culture are intersecting as never before. And then finally, the lawyer must deploy meanings in ways that educate juries, judges, and publics to reach, insofar as possible, reasoned decisions.

Reasoned decisions are usually thought of as propositional, as logically flowing from the facts and legal rules. It is always nice, from a rhetorical perspective, to believe that facts and rules are in some sense inevitable and immutable; it is comforting. But the opposite does not have to be either chaos or a hall of mirrors. Pictures can make many elements sit together simultaneously within their frame. Some things can be more important than others but everything has a place. We can and must say both/and rather than either/or with pictures. This then becomes the way we think about the law itself.[72]

---

72 See Pierre Schlag, 'The Aesthetics of American Law', *Harvard Law Review*, February 2002, for a rather different analysis.

PART 2
Legal Language in Action

Chapter 8

Legal Language in Action: Raising Basic Awareness about and Understanding of Competing Legal Systems in the Legal Classroom

Nicola M. Langton

Introduction

In most legal jurisdictions, there is a common legal system that operates in such a way that questions of interpretation and application are decided in a 'tried and tested' way. For example, in common law jurisdictions, the approach to interpreting and applying the law is determined by the doctrine of precedent. This doctrine forms the basis for establishing, developing, interpreting, applying, refining and amending the law. It governs the way cases are to be read or decided in the context of other decided cases and manifests itself through legal reasoning patterns and how judges discuss legal authorities. This approach involves a combination of a consideration of legislative intent as well as the body of elaborating case law that establishes legal rules that generally must be followed. In contrast to the common law, civil law legal systems place much more importance on codes of law and academic commentary rather than case law. However, in more recent times, considerations of other jurisdictional approaches to interpretation and application of cross-jurisdictional bodies and systems of law have become more important, as has the increasing need to understand and apply competing legal systems, laws and practices. One example of this is the increasing role and influence of European law in domestic jurisdictions within the EU zone; another example is the adoption of 'one country two systems' in Hong Kong in 1997. In both examples, we have the situation where the common law system of the UK or Hong Kong occasionally has to consider and incorporate the rather different civil law systems and practices of Europe or the People's Republic of China (PRC) respectively into their considerations. Some may argue that the potential conflicts that arise between common law and civil law jurisdictions are not as significant as those that potentially arise in the UK or Hong Kong because of the lesser role case law plays in civil code jurisdictions and because of the greater parity in conceptual aspects of the law itself. Whatever the viewpoint, cross-jurisdictional issues of interpretation and application involve an understanding of not only the legal systems themselves but also the way in which the different systems, cultures and ideologies are expressed in the legal texts themselves, and how conflicts can arise.

On 1 July 1997, the Basic Law of Hong Kong came into effect with the result that not only was the concept of 'one country, two systems' adopted but also a dual common law and civil law legal system. This has meant in practical terms that law students and law practitioners in Hong Kong need to master three languages and two writing systems as well as a dual legal system. This outcome is reflected in a study by CELECR (1998)[1] at City University of Hong Kong on the strategies and competencies in legal communication in Hong Kong. This study identified an increase in the perceived need to be fluent in written and spoken Putonghua (Mandarin), to be able to effectively use bilingual skills in preparing and conducting court hearings (in Cantonese and English), to be able to translate documents (into or from Putonghua, Cantonese and English), and to be generally proficient in both English and Putonghua. The idea of 'one country, two systems' is not one to be dismissed easily since it forms the basis for the Basic Law which represents the 'mini-constitution' for Hong Kong and part of the constitution of the PRC. The Basic Law therefore also represents an attempted marriage of competing legal systems, discourses and ideologies which in turn has meant that law practitioners, law students, translators and so on have to address various issues on how to interpret and communicate legal matters in ways that best reflect the two sides of the union. While these challenges can be met to a certain extent through an understanding of the legal systems as explained by books and theory, greater insights as to what the potential or actual problems are and how to deal with them can be gained from a consideration of and understanding of the linguistic evidence that can reveal more about the competing legal systems and their underlying cultural or ideological identities.

The purpose of this chapter is therefore to illustrate some of the problems law students in Hong Kong may have in dealing with a dual legal system. In particular, this chapter will focus on examples used in a classroom context to raise awareness about what the legal system differences are and how to consider and use linguistic and cultural differences evident in the competing legal texts and discourses as tools for developing strategies for reading, interpreting or otherwise accessing the different types of legal text or discourse.

Revealing the Potential Nature of a Common Law/Civil Law Union

In considering how to raise awareness about the potential conflicts that exist in the dual legal system of Hong Kong, it is perhaps useful to consider first the legal traditions of the common law system, as well as the lexical and grammatical features

1 CELECR. 'The Law Society of Hong Kong Project: Strategies and Competencies in Legal Communication. A study to investigate the communicative needs of legal Professionals' (Hong Kong: Department of English & Communication, City University of Hong Kong, 1998).

used in common law texts and which form part of the legal culture students are to study and eventually practise in. This initial focus is important, for while law students in Hong Kong do study aspects of the Chinese legal system, the essential focus of their study is on the common law system. Also, at the heart of any legal system is a legal tradition which is reflected to some degree in the language used in and the legal culture that underpins a set of rules of law, and the way in which the system manifests itself in the society within which it operates. As Merryman (1985: 2)[2] points out, a legal tradition is

> … a set of deeply rooted, historically conditioned attitudes about the nature of law, about the role of law in the society and the polity, about the proper organization and operation of a legal system and about the way law is or should be made, applied, studied, perfected, and taught. The legal tradition relates the legal system to the culture of which it is a partial expression. It puts the legal system into cultural perspective.

The idea of a time-honoured legal culture and tradition can be seen, for example, in the way that 'frozen' (legislation) and 'formal' (contracts, insurance policies and so on) legal texts are drafted.[3] Various studies of these texts have revealed that they share a number of lexical and grammatical features due to an initially historical and later traditional approach to organising the legal content. For example, Mellinkoff (1963)[4] found these texts tend to rely on the use of common words with uncommon meaning (for example, *consideration*), technical words and legal slang (for example, *lessor*, *without prejudice*), old-fashioned formal phrasings (for example, *pursuant to*, *in witnesseth hereof*) law latin (*ex parte*, *per sterpes*) and so on. Also, while this use of lexicon represents attempts to be flexible (for example, *forthwith, reasonable force*) as well as precise (for example, *change, alter or modify*), the overall effect is one of pomposity and inaccessibility. This critique of the language of the common law is helpful in terms of identifying the type of lexicon one can expect to find in such legal texts; however, it is also necessary to consider how the texts are constructed grammatically. For example, Danet (1980)[5] found in her study that common law texts generally also featured extensive use of modals/modality (for example, *shall/shall not*, *is bound by*), passives and nominalisations (for example, *payment shall be made*), subjunctives (for example, *It is ordered that payment be made*), conditionals/conditionality (for example, *in the event that*, *provided that sth be x*, *whether … depends on*), unusual multiple negatives (for example, *no person shall do x without*), complex adverbial clauses (for example, *Tenant may, with the prior consent of …, …, assign the Lease*), provisos (for example, *provided that*), unusual prepositional

---

2 Merryman, John Henry, *The Civil Law Tradition: An Introduction to the Legal Systems of Western Europe and Latin America* (2nd ed. Stanford: Stanford University Press, 1985).

3 Danet, Brenda, 'Language in the Legal Process', *Law and Society Review* 14, no. 3 (1980): 445–564.

4 Mellinkoff, David, *The Language of the Law* (Boston: Little Brown, 1963).

5 Danet, 'Language in the Legal Process'.

phrases (for example, *to the order of, in respect of*), impersonality (for example, *no person shall, a lessor may*), unique determiners/back referents (for example, *Such conditions, aforesaid, hereinafter referred to as*), and whiz (*wh*-words) deletion (*a person being a civil servant*). Like Mellinkoff, Danet also considered the historical and social reasons for the way legal English came about and concluded that some of the main reasons why legal English is generally considered incomprehensible included not only very long sentences and producing information in lists, but also extensive use of unknown/uncommon words, complex sentence structures, passives, and negative sentences.

An initial awareness-raising exercise on the general linguistic characteristics of legal English would be to give students a selection of sample legislative texts and ask them to try and identify: a) the text, the author, and the intended reader; b) what features make the text easy or difficult to read and why; and c) whether those features are necessary. In eliciting the answers, the students would be likely to come up with a list of features similar to those described by Mellinkoff and Danet. They would also be likely to state that the features are necessary because such law texts are like that.

Adherents of these legal traditions would agree that the use of such lexical and grammatical features is vital since it has always been used this way and must remain so if the law is to be 'precise, clear, unambiguous and all inclusive'. Bhatia (1982, 1983a, 1993)[6] has shown, through his use of cognitive structuring to reveal how a legislative text is constructed, why this argument may hold true for some legal texts and that the way the text is constructed is intrinsically linked to and dependent on the lexico-grammatical structures typically used in some classes of text. By way of example, consider the following extract from Part IV Miscellaneous provisions of the Hong Kong Import and Export (Registration) Regulations Cap 60e:

> Regulation 13: Information and documents obtained under these regulations not admissible in proceedings under other enactments.
>
> No person who is or has been employed in carrying out or in assisting any other person to carry out the provisions of these regulations shall be required in any civil or criminal proceedings to divulge or produce to any court any information or document relating to the affairs of any person which has been obtained by him or come to his knowledge or into his possession in the course of or in connection with his employment as aforesaid, but this regulation shall not apply in respect of criminal proceedings instituted for any offence against these regulations or civil proceedings instituted for the recovery of any sum under these regulations.[7]

---

6 Bhatia, V.K., 'An Investigation into Formal and Functional Characteristics of Qualifications into Legislative Writing and Its Application to English for Academic Legal Purposes' (British Library, 1982); Bhatia, V.K., 'An Applied Discourse Analysis of English Legislative Writing' (Birmingham: University of Aston, 1983); Bhatia, V.K., *Analysing Genre: Language Use in Professional Settings, Applied Linguistics and Language Study* (London: Longman, 1993).

7 Import and Export (Registration) Regulations Cap 60e.

We can see that many of the lexical and grammatical features identified by Mellinkoff[8] and Danet[9] and discussed above are present. In this particular text, the striking features are the typical use of unusual negation and impersonality in the opening phrase (*no person who*), complex prepositional phrases (*in carrying out, in the course of, in connection with, in respect of, for any offence against, for the recovery of*), attempts at flexibility and precision (*is or has been employed, in carrying out or in assisting, any civil or criminal proceedings, divulge or produce, any information or document* and so on), multiple use of '*or*' and the creation of a 110-word sentence due to the use of passive voice, subjunctive mood and multiple clause insertions. Some would argue that at the very least, this provision could just as easily be set out in two sentences by replacing the only comma (between 'aforesaid' and 'but') with a full stop and replacing 'but' with 'however'. Others would argue that limited use of punctuation is also a feature of legal English, and that in this case the clause elaborations are clear as they list the items to be considered in deciding what the rule encompasses and how it applies. This argument becomes clearer if, as Bhatia (1993)[10] suggests, the text of Hong Kong Import and Export (Registration) Regulations Cap 60e is set out according to its cognitive structure as follows:

Main Provision	*Subsidiary Provisions/Qualifications*
No person who is employed	or has been
in carrying out	or in assisting any other person to carry out
the provisions of these regulations	
shall be required	in any civil or criminal proceedings
to divulge	or produce
to any court	
any information	or document relating to the affairs of any person
which has been obtained by him	or come to his knowledge or into his possession
in the course of	or in connection with
his employment	as aforesaid,
but this regulation	
shall not apply [to]	in respect of
criminal proceedings instituted for any offence against these regulations or civil proceedings instituted for the recovery of any sum under these regulations.	

This cognitive structure reveals that by effectively 'removing' the various clause insertions, the basic provision or essential rule(s) can be identified. While it is also clear that it is the use of and position of these various elaborations and insertions that make the text harder to read and the sentence very long, there is still coherence in the text in that each elaboration or insertion in the right-hand column clearly

8 Mellinkoff, *The Language of the Law.*

9 Danet, 'Language in the Legal Process'.

10 Bhatia, *Analysing Genre: Language Use in Professional Settings.*

refers back to what it elaborates or adds to. The placement of these qualifications essentially make it possible to effectively answer the 'who, what, when, where, how' type questions about the context and how the rule or provision applies in a number of possible scenarios. As Bhatia (1993)[11] points out, it is in fact the interactive role of these elaborations and qualifications which make the provision precise, clear, unambiguous and all inclusive. While this particular provision is coherent because of the particular placement of the elaborations and qualifications, it is still possible to tidy it up using some Plain English conventions, formatting techniques and removing some of the unusual grammatical features present in the text (unusual negation, use of shall) as follows:

(1) A person who is (or has been) employed in carrying out (or assisting any other person to carry out) the provisions of these regulations will not be required in any civil or criminal proceedings to divulge or produce to any court any information or document relating to the affairs of any person which has been
a) obtained by him, or
b) come to his knowledge, or
c) come into his possession
in the course of (or in connection with) this employment.

(2) This regulation shall not apply to
a) criminal proceedings instituted for any offence against these regulations, or
b) civil proceedings instituted for the recovery of any sum under these regulations.

If the original were rewritten completely in Plain English to avoid particular legal English features, the result would probably be a less coherent and much longer text. Also, there would be a risk of serious changes in scope and intention. There are of course the occasional cases where the cognitive structure of the original legislative text will reveal poor rhetorical structure and hint at ways in which principles of Plain English will render the text more coherent and readable. This may well result in a substantial reordering of content, removal of redundancy and rephrasing of legal content. However, whatever Plain English principles are adopted in the reformulation of the original legislative text, it is essential not to change the intended scope or purpose of the text in any way (Bhatia, 1983b).[12] This is why the cognitive structure of the text must form the basis of the final structure as it reveals how to regroup ideas that should go together. For example, the cognitive structure of s10 (2) of the Hong Kong Prevention of Bribery Ordinance Cap 201 set out below reveals that some insertions and qualifications are not as well placed as they could be (as shown in italics) and that there is possible unnecessary repetition of key terms.

11 Bhatia, *Analysing Genre: Language Use in Professional Settings*.

12 Bhatia, V.K., 'Simplification V Easification: The Case of Legal Texts', *Applied Linguistics* 4, no. 1 (1983b): 42-45.

Main Provision	*Subsidiary Provisions/Qualifications*
Where a court is satisfied	in proceedings for an offence under subsection (1(*b*))
that,	*having regard to the closeness of the relationship to the accused and to other circumstances,*
there is reason to believe that any person was holding	
pecuniary resources	or property
in trust for	or otherwise on behalf of
the accused	or acquired such resources
or property as a gift from the accused,	
such resources	or property
shall,	*until the contrary is proved,*
be presumed to have been in the control of the accused[13]	

The particular problematic parts are the opening 'Where' clause and the elaborations in italics (my emphasis). While the 'where' describes the situation or conditions in which the following rule is to apply and the italicised sections are grammatically next to what they qualify and reflect legal customs and traditions of legal drafting, the position of the italicised sections do make the flow of information disjointed. The focus of the rule is when the presumption will arise. Therefore, by applying certain Plain English writing principles to this section without altering intended scope and intention and maintaining legal drafting traditions, the following possible rewrite shows how greater clarity can be achieved:

(2) In proceedings under (1)(b), the court will presume that resources or property have been under the control of the accused **if**,
after reviewing the relationship with the accused and other circumstances, it is satisfied that a person:
a) was holding pecuniary resources or property in trust for or on behalf of the accused; or
b) acquired such resources or property as a gift from the accused.
However, this presumption will not arise if the contrary is proved.

When first presenting students with texts such as this, they will effectively be trying to identify the rhetorical structure of the text. This is because people draw on their previous knowledge and experience to make sense of things – a schema(ta) or generally accepted way of organising ideas – which provides a basis for readers' expectations of how a text will develop.[14] This interaction is essential in understanding the rhetorical organisation of texts and why considering the cognitive structure is a

13 S 10 (2) Prevention of Bribery Ordinance cap 201.

14 Widdowson, H.G., *Learning Purpose and Language Use* (Oxford: Oxford University Press, 1983).

useful tool. A more effective way to identify the traditional rhetorical structure and language of different legal texts is to also conduct a genre analysis of the types of texts in question.

There are a number of views as to what genre is. At a basic level, it is a way to identify and explain the structure, meaning and functional variations that appear in a text (spoken or written) or particular discourse as well as the contextual motivations for those differences. For some, genre is 'a staged, goal-oriented social process'[15] and so the way in which a genre realises its social purpose in a number of steps is an important aspect to consider. These steps have been identified as 'moves' for some genres (see Swales, 1990; Bhatia, 1993)[16] and it is these 'moves' which give the genre its general standard, conventional shape and dictate to a certain extent the lexico-grammatical realisations within and across each move. For example, judgments in a common law jurisdiction generally comprise of a number of common, repeating 'moves' which help to structure the text itself and dictate the type of language used within each move (see Maley, 1985; Bhatia, 1993; Fredrickson, 1996).[17] There are a number of closely related pedagogical legal genres including answers to legal problem questions (see Beasley, 1994; Howe, 1990; Langton, 2001)[18] and legal case notes (Iedema, 1993)[19] which, while having their own particular moves and lexico-grammatical realisations, contain sufficient overall similarity to the legal judgments genre. A common feature of the related genres is their use of and reference to legislative texts, which, as is shown in the discussion on cognitive structuring, form a genre set of their own.

A further awareness-raising exercise about the particular features of the legislative genre would be to give students more samples of a range of legislative texts (or have them collect their own) and ask them to analyse the texts to identify: a) what typical textual characteristics (special words, grammar and cognitive structures) are used in

15 Martin, J.R., *A Contextual Theory of Language in the Powers of Literacy: A Genre Approach to Teaching Writing* (Pittsburgh: University of Pittsburgh Press, 1993).

16 Swales, John M., *Genre Analysis: English in Academic and Research Settings* (Cambridge: Cambridge University Press, 1990); Bhatia, *Analysing Genre: Language Use in Professional Settings*.

17 Maley, Yon, 'Judicial Discourse: The Case of the Legal Judgment', in *The Cultivated Australian: Festschrift for Arthur Delbridge*, edited by J.E. Clark, 159-73 (Hamburg: Helmut Buske Verlag, 1985); Bhatia, *Analysing Genre: Language Use in Professional Settings*; Fredrickson, Kirstin M., 'Genre and Local Discourse Community: Cultural Variation in Legal Opinions', in *AAAL*, Orlando, Florida (1997).

18 Beasley, Colin J., 'Picking up the Problems: An Applied Linguistic Analysis of the Legal Problem Genre' (MA, Edith Cowan University, 1994); Howe, P.M., 'The Problem of the Problem Question in English for Academic Legal Purposes', *English for Specific Purposes* 9 (1990): 215-36; Langton, Nicola M., 'To Hedge or Not to Hedge: Certainty and Doubt in Answers to Legal Problem Questions' (MA, City University, 2001).

19 Iedema, R.A.M., 'Legal English: Subject Specific Literacy and Genre Theory', *Australian Review of Applied Linguistics* 16, no. 2 (1993): 86-122.

this kind of legal writing; b) why these features are used in this type of writing; and c) what problems these features can create in the understanding of legislative rules.

Considering the features of a genre such as legislative texts in this way provides a way to raise awareness about the potential conflicts that exist in the dual legal system of Hong Kong. Using lexico-grammatical and genre analysis can also provide a simple way into comparing the two legal systems and help students to identify and appreciate the different structural, linguistic and cultural frameworks that may be present. For example, when considering criminal law provisions from the PRC, students will be able to draw on their insights about the legal customs and traditions of common law system criminal law provisions in terms of how they are constructed and interpreted to better identify the different legal customs and traditions of the PRC legal system. For example, s10(1) of the Hong Kong Prevention of Bribery Ordinance Cap 201 set out below illustrates the common law custom of setting out the legal requirements that the prosecution must establish to prove guilt. Consequently, the section specifies who the law may apply to, what specific actions or omissions they need to have undertaken, what the consequences may be, whether there is a rebuttable presumption and who has the burden of rebutting that presumption.

> 10. (1) Any person who, being or having been a Crown servant
> (*a*) maintains a standard of living above that which is commensurate with his present or past official emoluments; or
> (*b*) is in control of pecuniary resources or property disproportionate to his present or past official emoluments,
> shall, unless he gives a satisfactory explanation to the court as to how he was able to maintain such a standard of living or how such pecuniary resources or property came came under his control, be guilty of an offence.[20]

Subject to the presumption arising in the way described in subsection 10(2) (see earlier discussion), the section is clear in how it operates. Students will know that any questions as to application will be resolved by considering case law decisions in similar circumstances and that the doctrine of precedent is to be followed. They may well use this knowledge and expectation when they first encounter an equivalent provision from the PRC criminal law. However, they will immediately see that the whole approach to structure, content, linguistic choices and interpretation are very different as Article 155 of the Criminal Law of the PRC (1980) on the next page illustrates.

> State personnel who take advantage of their office to engage in corruption involving articles of public property are to be sentenced to not more than five years of fixed-term imprisonment or criminal intention; if the amount involved is huge and the circumstances are serious, the sentence is to be not less than five years of fixed-term imprisonment; if the circumstances are especially serious, the sentence is to be life imprisonment or death.

20 S 10 (1) Prevention of Bribery Ordinance cap 201.

> A person who commits the crime in the preceding paragraph is to be sentenced in addition to confiscation of property or ordered to make restitution or pay compensation.
>
> Personnel entrusted by state organs, enterprises, institutions or people's organisations to engage in public service who commit the crime in the first paragraph are to be punished in accordance with the stipulations of the two preceding paragraphs.[21]

This English version of the law reveals certain similarities with the common law traditions, namely: a long opening noun clause, use of passive voice structures (*are/is to be*), some nominalisation (*confiscation of property, make restitution, pay compensation*), some complex prepositional phrases (*in addition to, in accordance with*), and attempts to be precise (*not more than ..., not less than ...*), or flexible (*huge, serious, especially serious*). It also reveals the use of *are/is to be* instead of *shall be*, and use of ordinary vocabulary (*huge, serious, especially serious*). The overall effect is a text that is easy to read due to simple vocabulary and grammar and a clear cognitive structure, although the last paragraph could be incorporated into the first to reduce redundancy, greater use of parallel structures could be made and a few sentence structures changed as follows:

> Any state personnel or personnel entrusted by state organs, enterprises, institutions or people's organisations to engage in public service who take advantage of their office to engage in corruption involving public property are to be sentenced
> (a) to a maximum of five years fixed-term imprisonment or criminal detention; or
> (b) to a minimum of five years fixed-term imprisonment if the amount involved is huge and the circumstances are serious; or
> (c) to life imprisonment or death if the circumstances are especially serious.
> In addition, the court is to order
> i) confiscation of property; or
> ii) restitution or payment of compensation by the offender.

On the face of it, this text shares rather similar properties to that of s10 (1) Prevention of Bribery Ordinance Cap 201. However, what is very different is how to apply the law as set out in the text itself. There is no indication of what must be established to prove guilt, indeed the focus is entirely on punishment. This leads to the question of how to interpret the rather vague but important terms *if the amount involved is huge and the circumstances are serious/especially serious*? These words are clearly important as they directly relate to the type of punishment finally awarded. As in reading common law legislative texts, students would look for clues in the legislative document itself. Article 155 appears in the section entitled 'Chapter V: Crimes of Property Violation'. This heading is not helpful. Nor would the students find a definition section at the beginning of the document as they would expect in a common law piece of legislation. Instead, they will find that interpretation is to be based on applying the principles set out in the first two articles of Chapter 1: Guiding Ideology, Tasks and the Scope of Application of the Criminal Law.

---

21 Article 155, Criminal Law (1980) of the PRC.

Article 1: The Criminal Law of the People's Republic of China, which takes Marxism-Leninism-Mao Zedong Thought as its guide and the Constitution as its basis, is formulated in accordance with the policy of combining punishment with leniency and in the light of actual circumstances and the concrete experiences of all our country's ethnic groups in carrying out the people's democratic dictatorship led by the proletariat and based on the worker-peasant alliance, that is the dictatorship of the proletariat, and in conducting socialist revolution and socialist construction.

Article 2: The tasks of the Criminal Law of the People's Republic of China are to use criminal punishments to struggle against all counterrevolutionary and other criminal acts in order to defend the system of the dictatorship of the proletariat, to protect socialist property owned by the whole people and property collectively owned by the labouring masses, to protect citizens' lawfully privately-owned property, to protect citizens' rights of the person, democratic rights and other rights, to maintain social order, order in production, order in work, order in education and scientific research and order in the lives of the masses of people, and to safeguard the smooth progress of the cause of socialist revolution and socialist construction.[22]

For the students, these two articles do not really help in deciding what *huge, serious* and *especially serious* mean other than to indicate that interpretation is based on an ideology they are unlikely to understand or appreciate from personal experience or knowledge without actually studying the constitution and legal system of the PRC first. These two articles indicate a legal system, legal tradition and culture very different to that of Hong Kong. The collocation of words such as *combining punishment with leniency, the people's democratic dictatorship, dictatorship of the proletariat, struggle against all counterrevolutionary ... acts* seem discordant and political, even subjective, instead of apolitical and objective. The students should also quickly appreciate that the whole basis of the PRC legal system will require them to consider cultural aspects of the legal traditions in a much wider way. For example, the two articles from the Criminal Law of the PRC 1980 set out below illustrate not only the culture of 'criminal punishment through leniency', but also that the criminal law impacts on the traditional superstitions of the country too.

Article 165: Sorcerers or witches who use superstitions to engage in the activities of rumour-mongering or swindling articles of property are to be sentenced to not more than two years of fixed-term imprisonment, criminal detention or control; when the circumstances are serious, the sentence is to be not less than two years and not more than seven years of fixed-term imprisonment.

Article 166: Whoever poses as state personnel to cheat and bluff is to be sentenced to not more than three years of fixed-term imprisonment, criminal detention, control or deprivation of political rights; when the circumstances are serious, the sentence is to be not less than three years and not more than ten years of fixed-term imprisonment.[23]

22 Chapter 1, Criminal Law (1980) of the PRC.
23 Criminal Law (1980) of the PRC.

While it may be surprising to find a legal system that specifically legislates against superstitions, these two examples also illustrate the fact that the language of the Chinese law is not as formal as that of the language of the common law (for example, *rumour-mongering, swindling, cheat and bluff*). On the one hand it seems more descriptive and illustrative of the ideology that underpins the system, yet on the other hand it seems subjective and limited in scope. The lexico-grammatical realisations help the Chinese legislative genre achieve its legal and social purposes in similar ways to common law legislation, but what happens when the legal traditions and culture of the PRC legal system merge or mix with those of the Hong Kong common law system?

Potential Conflicts in a Common Law/Civil Law Union

As has been illustrated so far, by considering the lexico-grammatical features and structural aspects of a genre, students can gain insights into the traditions, nature, structure, features and function of a particular legal system's legislative texts. This knowledge will then help them decide whether the appropriation and/or mixing of different systems in one text or genre can be complementary and supportive, or whether there are in fact underlying problems or tensions which need to be borne in mind when interpreting the laws. Good examples of this mixing or appropriation from two different legal systems into a common genre and what can happen can be found in both the Joint Declaration 1984 and the Basic Law 1997. The principal concerns of the UK and PRC that provide the framework for these two documents involved issues of rights and obligations, law, the constitution, ideology and nationality. These concerns are reflected in the content of both the Joint Declaration and Basic Law, which in turn reflect clearly the different legal traditions, genres, purposes and ideologies of the two sides.

The Joint Declaration was issued as a memorandum of understanding on issues of concern to the UK and PRC and to state the common purpose of not affecting the future stability of Hong Kong. Not all issues were easy to identify or resolve at the time of its publication, so it was agreed these would be left to a later date when the Basic Law was being drafted (Ghai, 1997, 1999).[24] What is interesting about the Joint Declaration is how it reveals an attempt to blend the different styles of drafting from the two legal systems to create an impression of unity and agreement, as the following opening paragraph from the Joint Declaration illustrates:

> The Government of the United Kingdom and Northern Ireland and the Government of the People's Republic of China have reviewed with satisfaction the friendly relations existing between the two Governments and peoples in recent years and agreed that a

---

24 Ghai, Yash P., *Hong Kong's New Constitutional Order: The Resumption of Chinese Sovereignty and the Basic Law* (Hong Kong: Hong Kong University Press, 1997); Ghai, Yash P., *The Nature of Constitutional Transition in Hong Kong* (Hong Kong: Faculty of Law, University of Hong Kong, 1997).

> proper negotiated settlement of the question of Hong Kong, which is left over from the past, is conducive to the maintenance of the prosperity and stability of Hong Kong and to the further strengthening and development of the relations between the two countries on a new basis.[25]

Bearing in mind that the Joint Declaration was not an agreement but a memorandum of understanding, the potential conflicts within it do not arise from these reassurances about the common goal of stability for Hong Kong but from the different attitudes towards how the transfer of power was to be achieved through the Basic Law, and why. This conflict is clearly revealed in Articles 1 and 2 of the Joint Declaration as set out below, where China's reasons for wanting to 'recover' Hong Kong are given but the UK's are not, and where the UK simply states that Hong Kong will be 'restored' to China.

> Article 1. The Government of the People's Republic of China declares that to recover the Hong Kong area … is the common aspiration of the entire Chinese people, and that it has decided to resume the exercise of sovereignty over Hong Kong with effect from 1 July 1997.

> Article 2. The Government of the United Kingdom declares that it will restore Hong Kong to the People's Republic of China with effect from 1 July 1997.[26]

Article 3 of the Joint Declaration sets out what the PRC will do upon resumption of sovereignty including creating a Special Administrative Zone, and stating what this new Special Administrative Region (SAR) will be allowed to do. What is interesting about Article 3 is that while most statements of intention employ the use of 'will', as in ensuring social and economic systems 'will remain unchanged' (Article 3(5)), there are occasional statements where China's right to restrict or possibly restrict the SAR's autonomy are clearly stated as in :

> Article 3 (3): … The laws currently in force in Hong Kong will remain basically unchanged.

> Article 3 (9): The Hong Kong Special Administrative Region may establish mutually beneficial economic relations with the United Kingdom and other countries, whose economic interests in Hong Kong will be given due regard.[27]

The intention that the laws in Hong Kong will not change much does not seem a problem, nor does the use of '*may*' if taken to mean 'allowed to'. The problem arises in the final clause '*whose economic interests in Hong Kong will be given due regard*'. What is unclear is, who gives 'due regard' and whether in establishing relations, the SAR must simply consider what the other countries will get out of the arrangement;

---

25 Preamble, Joint Declaration 1984.

26 Joint Declaration 1984.

27 Joint Declaration 1984.

or that the SAR must first consider China's view of the other countries and whether they are permitted trading partners (for example, Taiwan). While Article 3(9) of the Joint Declaration successfully adopts the drafting style of the common law system, it is the embedded content and lexicon of Chinese legal system values that create the potential conflict in meaning. However, adopting the common law approach to drafting may not be the best way to reflect the Chinese legal system and can result in something quite unintended as illustrated by Article 3(12) of the Joint Declaration which infers that it is the members of the National People's Congress who '*remain unchanged for 50 years*'!

> Article 3(12): The above-stated policies of the People's Republic of China regarding Hong Kong and the elaboration of them in Annex 1 to this Joint Declaration will be stipulated, in a Basic Law of the Hong Kong Special Administrative Region of the People's Republic of China, by the National People's Congress of the People's Republic of China, and they will remain unchanged for 50 years.[28]

While the Joint Declaration is a good document to use with students to show some of the problems that can arise when attempting to blend two different legal systems and their drafting practices, the Basic Law itself is also a good source of material to illustrate how two different legal systems and their traditions can also be represented in the same genre. Students will already be aware that any specific definitions of terms employed in a particular piece of legislation will generally be stated in section 2 of the relevant ordinance, otherwise they will look at the intention behind the legislation as well as case law and the doctrine of precedent to guide their interpretation. They will also be aware that the laws of the PRC will contain an opening chapter, similar to Articles 1 and 2 of PRC Criminal Law 1980 discussed earlier, that will set out the guiding ideology on how to interpret the law. They will have learnt from lectures and their reading that Chinese constitutional documents all commence with a preamble. Consequently, when presented with the preamble of the Basic Law (see below), they will recognise it as being very representative of the PRC legal system and its traditions. They will also appreciate from their reading of the Joint Declaration that, since it is the PRC that has created the Basic Law, the Basic Law forms part of both the Chinese and Hong Kong legal systems. They may also be aware that the UK has no written constitution and that therefore the Basic Law is a rather unique document.

> Preamble:
>
> Hong Kong has been part of the territory of China since ancient times; it was occupied by Britain after the Opium War in 1840. On 19 December 1984, the Chinese and British Governments signed the Joint Declaration on the Question of Hong Kong, affirming that the Government of the People's Republic of China will resume the exercise of sovereignty over Hong Kong with effect from 1 July 1997, thus fulfilling the long-cherished common aspiration of the Chinese people for the recovery of Hong Kong.

---

28 Joint Declaration 1984.

> Upholding national unity and territorial integrity, maintaining the prosperity and stability of Hong Kong, and taking account of its histories and realities, the People's Republic of China has decided that upon China's resumption of the exercise of sovereignty over Hong Kong, …
>
> In accordance with the Constitution of the People's Republic of China, the National People's Congress hereby enacts the Basic Law of the Hong Kong Special Administrative Region of the People's Republic of China, prescribing the systems to be practised in the Hong Kong Special Administrative Region, in order to ensure the implementation of the basic policies of the People's Republic of China regarding Hong Kong.[29]

This extract is rather similar in tone and style to the PRC laws, especially the first two paragraphs. These reflect the ideology and fundamental traditions of the Chinese legal system with the focus on historical events and the common aspirations of the people. Unlike in the Joint Declaration where it was important to appear to agree on what happened historically, this account of why the Basic Law has come into existence reflects the true Chinese view that Hong Kong was and always has been theirs. It also sets the framework for interpreting the Basic Law, and makes it very clear that the Chinese constitution is the highest authority on this question. The frequent repetition of key phrases, although rather typical of common law drafting techniques, reinforces the message portrayed that the Chinese legal system is of particular importance. By having students consider different parts of the Basic Law, they will soon discover that it reflects the Chinese legal system approach and philosophy more in that it is structured the same way as the Chinese constitution with chapters and articles, as opposed to Parts and sections. So, while elements of the common law system approach to drafting and phrasing are adopted, in particular certain formal phrasings and use of 'shall/shall be', the Basic Law is essentially a legal Chinese document.

This conclusion reflects the fact that the constitution of the PRC and the Basic Law of Hong Kong both represent one genre, a constitution. However, there are two very different legal systems and two very different systems of interpretation in force and represented in the same genre. This means that, unlike the Joint Declaration where it is the different purposes underlying the two legal systems which give rise to the possible conflicts, it is the context of use and interpretation of the Basic Law that will and has given rise to conflict.

Conclusion

In jurisdictions where there are two competing legal systems in force, it is important to understand how these two systems interact and why potential conflict can arise, either from competing purposes in a common text, or from competing approaches to practice and interpretation in particular contexts of use. This chapter has suggested that the legal traditions that dictate how each legal system operates and is expressed

29 Basic Law of Hong Kong SAR.

can form the basis for gaining insights into the two different cultures and ideologies, as well as the linguistic practices used to express such cultures and ideologies. Awareness-raising activities using legislative texts have been suggested, whereby students consider the lexico-grammatical features and cognitive structures of one or related types of text from one system before comparing with similar types of text from the other system. In this way, they build a framework or schemata of expectation to gain access to unfamiliar texts or ideas. This approach can be adapted to fit particular needs, promote understanding, and develop strategies for identifying possible conflicts that can actually or potentially arise.

Chapter 9

Discourses of the Ideal and the Actual in the Courtroom: The Conflict for Jurors in 'Making Sense' of General Instructions

Philip Gaines

Introduction: General Jury Instructions as the Discourse of the Ideal

Scholarly studies of trial judges' instructions to juries have generally focused on issues of comprehensibility and communication (for example, see Buchanan et al., 1978; Charrow and Charrow, 1979; Severance and Loftus, 1982, 1984; Elwork et al., 1982, 1987; Stygall, 1991; and Dumas, 2000).[1] These analyses, often coupled with recommendations for improvement, address the difficulties that jurors have in understanding judges' explanations of the applicability of evidence, burden of proof, application of the law, the concept of reasonable doubt, and so on, and the instructions for using these explanations in deliberation. Such instructions can often be quite challenging for jurors: 'Comprehension of the law, as communicated to the

1 Buchanan, Raymond W., Bert Pryor, Phillip N. Taylor, and David U. Strawn, 'Legal Communication: An Investigation of Juror Comprehension of Pattern Instructions', *Communication Quarterly* 26 (1978): 31-36; Charrow, R. and V. Charrow, 'Making Legal Language Understandable: A Psycholinguistic Study of Jury Instructions', *Columbia Law Review* 79 (1979): 1306-74; Severance, L. J. and Elizabeth F. Loftus, 'Improving Jurors' Abilities to Comprehend and Apply Criminal Jury Instructions', *Law and Society Review* 17 (1982): 153-197; Severance, L. J. and Elizabeth F. Loftus, 'Improving Criminal Justice: Making Jury Instructions Understandable for American Jurors', *International Review of Applied Psychology* 33 (1984): 97-119; Elwork, Amiram, Bruce D. Sales and James J. Alfini, *Making Jury Instructions Understandable* (Charlottesville, VA: Michie, 1982); Elwork, Amiram, James J. Alfini and Bruce D. Sales, 'Towards Increasing the Comprehensibility of Jury Instructions', in *In the Jury Box: Controversies in the Courtroom*, edited by L. Wrightsman, S. Kassin and C. Willis (Beverly Hills, CA: Sage, 1987); Stygall, G., 'Texts in Oral Context: The "Transmission" of Jury Instructions in an Indiana Trial', in *Textual Dynamics of the Professions: Historical and Contemporary Studies Of Writing in Professional Communities,* edited by C. Bazerman and J. Paradis (Madison, WI: University of Wisconsin Press, 1991); Dumas, Bethany K., 'US Pattern Jury Instructions: Problems and Proposals', *Forensic Linguistics* 7, no. 1 (2000), 49-71.

jury, is more problematic than the profession generally realises …' (Jackson, 1995).[2] The communication of some concepts may, in fact, never be successful:

> …[T]he communication of a precise, unambiguous meaning of the standard of proof to jurors is a notoriously impossible task (Hastie, 1993).[3]

In contrast to the myriad communication and comprehensibility issues associated with case-specific instructions is the almost total transparency and ease of interpretation of the general pattern instructions given by the judge at the beginning (and often the end) of a trial. These instructions, the purposes of which are to: 1) mandate a schema through which jurors are to approach, understand, and interpret what they are about to hear in the presentation of cases; and 2) specify the juridical responsibilities of the jurors with respect to that discourse, are usually quite brief and tend to be given orally without an accompanying text being made available to jurors (Charrow and Charrow, 1979).[4] Although slight variations in general jury instructions appear in individual situations at the discretion of the judge, the following extracts of federal court pattern instructions apply broadly to criminal cases:

Pattern instructions suggested at the beginning of proceedings are:

> It will be your duty to decide from the evidence what the facts are ... You will hear the evidence [and] decide what the facts are ... The evidence will consist of the testimony of witnesses[5] ... and any facts on which the lawyers agree ... (Ninth Circuit Criminal Jury Instruction 1.01 1995).[6]

The following things are *not* evidence, and you must not consider them as evidence in deciding the facts of this case:

> 1. Statements and arguments of the attorneys.
> 2. Questions and objections of the attorneys ... (Ninth Circuit Criminal Jury Instruction 1.03 1995).[7]

---

2 Jackson, Bernard, *Making Sense in Law: Linguistic, Psychological, and Semiotic Perspectives* (Liverpool: Deborah Charles Publications, 1995), p. 442.

3 Hastie, Reid, 'Algebraic Models of Jury Decision Processes', in *Inside the Juror: The Psychology of Juror Decision Making*, edited by Reid Hastie (Cambridge: Cambridge University Press, 1993), p. 101.

4 Charrow and Charrow, p. 1310.

5 Types of evidence other than that delivered by witnesses under examination include writings, material objects, or anything presented for the purpose of proving the existence or nonexistence of a fact.

6 *Ninth Circuit Manual of Model Jury Instructions: Criminal* (St. Paul, MN: West Publishing Company, 1995).

7 Ibid.

Suggested pattern instructions – similar but slightly more extensive – to be used following the presentation of the cases are:

> The evidence from which you are to decide what the facts are consists [in part] of (1) the sworn testimony of witnesses, both on direct and cross-examination ... (3) any facts to which all the lawyers have agreed or stipulated (Ninth Circuit Criminal Jury Instruction 3.04 1995).[8]
>
> In reaching your verdict you may consider only the testimony and exhibits received into evidence. Certain things are not evidence and you may not consider them in deciding what the facts are. I will list them for you:
>
> 1. Arguments and statements by lawyers are not evidence. The lawyers are not witnesses. What they have said in their opening statements, closing arguments and at other times is intended to help you interpret the evidence, but it is not evidence. If the facts as you remember them differ from the way the lawyers have stated them, your memory of them controls.
> 2. Questions and objections by lawyers are not evidence ... (Ninth Circuit Criminal Jury Instruction 3.05 1995).[9]

These general instructions, the only official guidelines given by the court with respect to the jury's responsibilities in evaluating evidence, suggest that the jurors' task is a clear and uncomplicated one: make a decision, based on the evidence, as to what the facts are and then decide whether or not the facts show, beyond a reasonable doubt, that the defendant is guilty. (Instructions regarding the understanding and application of the law with regard to specific offenses are of considerably greater complexity and difficulty. For a treatment of issues regarding the transmission of law-specific instructions, see Charrow and Charrow, 1979[10] and Stygall, 1991.[11]) Verbal *evidence* is simply and unproblematically defined for the jury as the *testimony of witnesses* (as well as stipulations agreed to by the attorneys). This narrow definition of evidence mandates – in view of the obviously extensive verbal role of attorneys in a trial – instructions regarding specifically what is *not* evidence: statements, arguments, questions, and objections made by the attorneys in the course of the trial. This clear demarcation is based on the legal fact that, in the Anglo-American adversarial tradition, attorneys are not witnesses and hence cannot offer testimony/evidence.

The specific charges to the jury contained in general instructions presuppose the following principles:

1. *Facts exist as objective truth*: For the court to require jurors to decide on the facts of a case, it is presupposed that there exist facts to be decided upon.

8 Ibid.

9 Ibid.

10 Charrow and Charrow.

11 Stygall.

Since no uncommon definition of facts is offered, the default denotation applies: a fact is something that is true, that has objective reality or 'material truth' (Landsman, 1988).[12]

2. *Facts are accessible to determination*: In order for facts to be decided upon by jurors, it is presupposed that they are not elusive but accessible and determinable.
3. *Evidence, that is, testimony of witnesses, is an adequate source of data from which to extract data*: Since jurors are required to determine facts from court-sanctioned evidence, it is presupposed that evidence alone is sufficient as a database from which facts can be extracted.
4. *Jurors have the capacity to adequately analyze and interpret evidence in* order *to extract facts*: Since jurors are charged to determine facts from evidence, it is presupposed that they possess the requisite capacity to sift through the mass of evidential data, establish the relative quality and value of its elements, and extract facts.
5. *Jurors have the capacity to clearly distinguish, in the stream of interactive speech, that which is evidence from that which is not evidence*: Since jurors are required to identify what constitutes evidence in a discourse that involves a multiplicity of speakers, it is presupposed that they possess the capacity to identify and isolate evidential utterances and maintain a clear distinction, throughout the course of the trial, between those utterances which constitute evidence and those which do not.
6. *Failure to extract from evidence sufficient facts upon which to base a verdict constitutes failure of duty*: Since jurors are assigned the duty of determining facts based on evidence and of reaching a verdict and since no indication is given that adequate resources for fulfillment of that duty may not be available, it is presupposed that a failure to reach a verdict based on facts is a failure not of the system or its procedures but of the duty of the jurors.

These presuppositions suggest that evidence, facts, and truth are all co-implicated in one another's meaning: facts are a construction built upon evidence, and evidence is to be 'the truth, the whole truth, and nothing but the truth'. Note the linear dependency: (A subset of) *truth* constitutes→ *evidence* which generates→ *facts*.

Both the general jury instructions themselves and the presuppositions underlying them constitute a highly idealized discourse, involving uncomplicated and unproblematized notions of facts, truth, and evidence. This discourse assumes a traditional quasi-scientific standard of proof, where facts can be extracted and determinations based on those facts can be right or wrong, versus the more relative concept of proof usually involved in human affairs (Perelman, 1963).[13] The

12 Landsman, S., *Readings on Adversarial Justice: The American Approach to Adjudication* (St. Paul, MN: West Publishing Company, 1988), p. 2.

13 Perelman, C., *The Idea of Justice and The Problem of Argument* (London: Routledge & Kegan Paul, 1963).

positivistic notion of *facts* forms the foundation of evidence law, since 'without facts there is no proof, no evidence, no legal process at all' (den Boer, 1990).[14] Den Boer sees this assumption as grounded in an essential positivism: 'Law describes its own reality. At this point the ideal positivistic idea comes in, which is that language depicts reality ("facts") as purely as possible.' Philips sees the underlying positivism of the law as broadly informed by Western traditions:

> *Factuality*, a concept heavily influenced by scientific ideology, and *truth*, a concept heavily influenced by Christian notions of moral worth, become inextricably linked in evidence law, so linked that it is difficult for Americans to disentangle them when thinking about legal cases (Philips, 1992).[15]

This positivistic approach to evidence embraces, of course, the actions and situations of individuals – realms of activity that supply the bulk of evidence in a criminal trial – and demands determinations by fact-finders with respect to not only what individuals said and did but also how those actions are evaluated with respect to the law. Scheff has called this 'absolute responsibility':

> The basic premise of the doctrine of absolute responsibility is that both actions and intentions on the one hand and the criteria of responsibility on the other are absolute, in that they can be assessed independently of social context (Scheff, 1968:3).[16]

The idea that jurors are called upon to make clear-cut determinations in such a decontexualized manner is, of course, completely unreasonable. Although, as Philips points out, 'it is quite taken for granted that deciding "what really happened" is the overriding task of the American trial' (Philips, 1992),[17] jurors are mandated to make specific determinations in the face of a bewildering swirl of information and argument, a situation which forces jurors into what Garfinkel calls a 'dialectic':

> [To express it] in something like the jurors' own terms, and trying to capture the jurors' dialectic: jurors decide between what is fact and what is fancy; between what actually happened and what 'merely appeared' to happen; between what is put on and what is truth, regardless of detracting appearances; between what is credible and ... the opposite of credible, what is calculated and said by design ... (Garfinkel, 1967).[18]

---

14 Den Boer, Monica, 'A Linguistic Analysis of Narrative Coherence in the Courtroom', in *Law, Interpretation, and Reality: Essays in Epistemology*, edited by P. Nerhof (Dordrecht: Kluwer Academic Publishers, 1990), p. 353.

15 Philips, S., 'Evidentiary Standards for American Trials: Just the Facts', in *Responsibility and Evidence in Oral Discourse*, edited by J. Hill and J. Irvine (Cambridge: Cambridge University Press, 1992), p. 249.

16 Scheff, T., 'Negotiating Reality: Notes on Power in the Assessment of Responsibility', *Social Problems* 16 (1968): 3-17.

17 Philips, p. 249.

18 Garfinkel, H., *Studies in Ethnomethodology* (Englewood Cliffs, NJ: Prentice Hall, 1967), p. 105.

Thus are the operating principles for the work of jurors established: a positivistic discourse concerning the nature of evidence, facts, and truth reveals certain presuppositions which drive juror expectation and sense of responsibility. These presuppositions provide a kind of 'deep-structure' discourse of the *ideal* which informs and justifies the specifics of jury instructions.

Adversarial Practice: The Discourse of the Actual

However, a second discourse[19] underlies and informs actual evidentiary processes in the courtroom. The responsibility for the presentation of evidence, based upon which jurors are to make their determinations, falls to attorneys. Within the adversarial tradition, however, the very nature of evidence is immediately complicated by the fact that evidence is the quintessential site of discursive struggle in the courtroom. Evidence is constantly subject to an evolving dialectical process of presentation→refutation, reformulation→re-refutation, and so on, with its many 'factual' details being now asserted/now denied, now proven/now debunked. The inevitable elusiveness of factual evidence resulting from the operation of partisan opposition in the courtroom clearly contradicts the discourse of the ideal, represented in institutional assumptions and realized in jury instructions, and dislocates it by means of a discourse of the *actual*, represented in party strategy and realized in courtroom processes.

> The central precept of the adversarial process is that out of the sharp clash of proofs presented by adversaries in a highly structured forensic setting is most likely to come the information upon which a neutral and passive decision maker can base the resolution of a litigated dispute acceptable to both the parties and society (Landsman, 1988).[20]

Although Landsman here is oriented toward civil trial practice, the principles underlying his discussion are equally applicable to criminal cases. The 'dispute' in the criminal system is between the state and the defendant, and the 'neutral and passive decision maker' is the jury panel, charged to make its determination irrespective of bias of any kind. This representative statement of the discourse of the actual constitutes a sweeping displacement/reformulation of the idealized presuppositions and practices of jury instructions:

1. *Presentation of evidence* becomes *clash of proofs*: In the ideal, attorneys present witness testimony. Individual witnesses and their utterances are foregrounded, and that which emerges from this display constitutes evidence. In the actual, attorneys and their proofs clash. Multiple attorneys and their contradictory utterances are foregrounded, and that which emerges from this

19 See Garfinkel, 1967 for a discussion of other 'normative orders of interaction' (107) which contribute to jurors' decision-making rules.

20 Landsman, p. 2.

display is a contest of opposing arguments. [Note: The notion of clashing proofs is somewhat paradoxical, since proof suggests the end of argument – 'discursive techniques which make it possible to evoke or further people's assent to the theses presented for their acceptance' (Perelman, 1963).[21]]

2. *Facts* become *information*: In the ideal, facts exist as representations of objective reality which jurors are able to discover. In the actual, jurors work with information – arguably an explosion of information – consisting of an intermingling of facts, suggestions, possibilities, opinions, emotional appeals, ethical invocations, claims to authority, syllogisms, and so on.
3. *Reaching a verdict* becomes *acceptably resolving a dispute*: In the ideal, means and purposes of the process are presented as absolute: jurors determine what the right decision is with respect to the facts and the law. In the actual, means and purposes are relative, socially constructed, and negotiable: the goal is the resolution of a dispute, the crucial quality of which is its acceptability to both the disputants and society.

The actual is the discourse constructed by attorneys and that which dominates trial processes and to which jurors are ultimately subject – calling as it does on the communicative competence of jurors. According to Weinreb (1977),[22] the dominance of this discourse is a historical development:

> The criminal trial in this country ... has experienced a gradual, cumulative transformation of the roles of prosecutor and defense counsel from rather narrowly defined aides in a judicial process in which the main responsibilities were those of the judge and jury into the dominant actors in an adversary process which the judge referees and the jury observes.

In spite of such asymmetry in the salience of agency in the courtroom, however, the discourse of the ideal is far from excluded and, in fact, remains conspicuous and authoritative. It is conspicuous in that it is foregrounded directly to the jury both at the beginning and the end of the presentation of the cases and is reiterated in certain details as part of the process of dealing with objections; it is authoritative in that it is presented by the figure with the greatest administrative power in the proceedings, that is, the presiding judge, and is assigned the status of the governing discourse in the trial.

The public institution of the court enacts a normative (thus authoritative), idealized (thus making powerful, absolute claims), and positivistic (thus inflexible and not open to interpretation) discourse. The presumption is that there is compatibility between the expectations generated by this discourse and what the jurors will hear in the courtroom. The intra-professional discourse of attorneys, on the other hand, as described by Weinreb's discussion, explicitly dismisses much of the institutional discourse, including the notion of its relation to the talk in the courtroom. Attorney

21 Perelman, p. 155.

22 Weinreb, L., *Denial of Justice: Criminal Process in the United States* (New York: Free Press, 1977), pp. 103-4.

courtroom discourse thus becomes not an effort to instantiate the talk which is regarded by the institution as providing the raw material for realizing the elements of evidence, facts, and truth, but rather a strategy for presenting a partisan substitute for those elements – one which is, of course, allowable by virtue of the nature of the adversarial system. The courtroom – and, critically, the consciousness of the jurors – becomes the scene of a struggle of conflicting discourses, crucially not the one between opposing party advocates but between the legal institution on one side and both party advocates on the other. The institution claims the authority to make juridically normative its presuppositions, while the party advocates assume the right to ignore the imputed primacy of these presuppositions and to conduct a strategy of persuasion that is manifestly subversive – *on principle* – of the institution's ostensible aims.

At least two specific sites of this conflict of discourses and the resulting sense-making (see Jackson, 1995[23]) dilemma are identifiable: 1) the nature of truth and evidence, and 2) the role and function of the advocate and the advocate's speech.

Conflict Regarding the Nature of Truth and Evidence

Truth

The conflict of discourses is especially salient with respect to notions of truth. Jurors are told that they are responsible for establishing objective truth through the determination of facts and are further presented with witnesses who testify under a court-mandated oath to tell 'the truth, the whole truth, and nothing but the truth.' The truth is a knowledge-object, realized at the level of 1) separate facts testified to, 2) complete individual testimony, and, ultimately, 3) total state of affairs with respect to the entire case. The institutional discourse foregrounds for the jury the preeminent value of the truth, the possibility of discovery of the truth, and the responsibility for determination of the truth. It is the truth, realized as facts, that is to be the preoccupation of the jury – in a sense, its sole object of interest and inquiry. However, this idealized, positivistic notion of truth is, of course, untenable in view of the most socially-constructed nature of truth, as here summarized by Danet (1980):[24]

> In human affairs there is no direct and immediate means of attaining truth, the employment of which would be preliminary to any rhetoric. Truth is rather the outcome of dialogue, discussion, and the confrontation of opinions (p. 509).

In the realm of the legal, such dialogue, and so on, is realized as argument:

---

23 Jackson.

24 Danet, Brenda, 'Language in the Legal Process', *Law & Society Review* 14, no. 3 (1980): 445-564.

> No matter how precisely a norm is written nor how carefully a legal concept is defined, there is always a background of uncertainty and probability which cannot be removed by any deductive or apodictic method. The only solution is to employ the inventive art ... of finding points of view or 'common places' (*loci communes*, *topoi*) which, being widely accepted, will help to fill in the gaps, thus rendering the reasoning convincing and the conclusion acceptable ... These *topoi* ... are endowed with conviction power, not with truth power (Santos, 1977:14-15).[25]

Objective truth is thus constructed through a process of rhetorical (versus logical) argument and is ultimately replaced by the subjective facsimile of conviction. This relativistic conception of truth is both presupposed by and embedded in the discourse of the actual and thus dislocates and contradicts the status of the truth as constituted by the ideal:

1. *Value of and* preoccupation *with truth are contradicted*:

> [O]ur *system* of justice does not really involve a search for truth (Kestler, 1982).[26]

> *Truth* is not the end the courts seek. It is to the advantage of the adversary system that it does not define its objectives in such an absolute and unrealistic fashion ... Truth is nothing more than a means of achieving the end, justice. The disclosure of material facts is not the only means of achieving justice ... (Landsman, 1988).[27]

Here, the opposition of discourses is virtually polar. The statement (in both the conventional and the Foucauldian sense) of the actual directly and absolutely contradicts the statement of the ideal with respect to truth. There is no suggestion of cooperation by advocates in a realization of the institutional objective. For advocates, of course, there is no conflict with respect to courtroom processes, since the discourse of the ideal has not been directed to them and the discourse of the actual mandates their dismissal of notions of truth, albeit with an strategic eye toward the possibility of an inconvenient intrusion of institutional enforcement of rules – administrative details which micro-manage specific discourse constraints. Jurors, on the other hand, remain in the position of accountability to the institutional ideal of the value of and preoccupation with the truth while at the same time are confronted with the practice of its abrogation by the advocates.

---

25 Santos, B. de S., 'The Law of the Oppressed: The Construction and Reproduction of Legality in Pasargada', *Law & Society Review* 12 (1977): 5-26.

26 Kestler, J., *Questioning Techniques and Tactics* (Colorado Springs, CO: Shepard's/McGraw Hill, 1982), p. 4.

27 Landsman, p. 27.

2. *Possibility of discovery is contradicted*:

> ... [P]ursuit of 'the truth' is not only naive, but ultimately impossible (Burnham, 1995).[28]

> The weakness of human perception, memory, and expression will often render the discovery of material truth impossible. To become preoccupied with truth may be both naive and futile (Landsman, 1988).[29]

Here, the discourse of the actual contradicts the assumption that discovery of the truth is possible. Condescension toward the ideal is implied by characterizing as 'naive' its expectation that the truth can be usefully pursued. The impossibility of the pursuit is explained by reference to complicating and obscuring aspects of human agency, providing a justification for a release of responsibility for undertaking the pursuit.

3. *Real knowledge-object status of truth is contradicted*:

> The idea is not to find '*the* truth' of an event, but to find *which communicated perception* of an event is the *most plausible account* of that event. A system that gives full leeway to competing perceptions of an event throughout the trial and right up until the time for decision is one that accurately reflects reality ... Defenders of the adversary system would point out that the cause of truth is routinely *better* served in an adversary system since in every case at least two versions of the truth get presented – one more version than would routinely be unearthed in a less adversarial system (Burnham, 1995).[30]

> [Younger] stated that the trial lawyer is concerned with building a *model* of events that occurred outside the courtroom. Once that model is constructed, it supplants external reality, rendering the objective *truth* irrelevant (Kestler, 1982).[31]

The foundation for the first two contradictions is found here in assumptions about the nature of the truth. Truth is relativized, is made available in multiple versions, and is displaced and rendered irrelevant by models of reality. Once the notion of truth is dismissed as an item of importance, advocates are free – and obliged, by the exigencies of partisan opposition – to construct alternatives to fill the void left by the discarding of the truth so that jurors have material to work with.

Evidence

The conflict of discourses also complicates the notion of evidence.

---

28 Burnham, W., *Introduction to the Law and Legal System of the United States* (St. Paul, MN: West Publishing Company, 1995), p. 122.

29 Landsman, p. 27.

30 Burnham, p. 122.

31 Kestler, p. 4.

1. *The value of evidence is problematized.*

> ... [I]n *reaching* the final outcome of any legal dispute ... there is ... always much more involved than evidence, the facts, and the law (Crawford, 1989).[32]

The discourse of the actual extends the database from which jurors are to make their determinations: information and inputs beyond simply evidence are included. In view of the narrow definition of evidence given in jury instructions, this move suggests much more than simply an incremental shifting of the boundaries and concomitant enlargement of the domain of what constitutes evidence and rather provides for a broad array of non-evidential signs, the introduction of which is, again, circumscribed and delimited only by the adjusting force of sustained objections, that is, the interruption by an opposing attorney to an examination on the grounds of an alleged violation of a rule of the court.

2. *The identification of evidence is problematized.*

> ... [G]*iven* the nature of credibility and evidence, jurors are not able to distinguish between the advocate's argument and actual evidence ... At one level ... what a juror 'uses' to draw an inference or arrive at a conclusion *is* the real evidence in a trial (Crawford, 1989).[33]

In the discourse of the actual, evidence is rendered unidentifiable due to admixture with the arguments of the advocate. Ultimately, access to real evidence is lost, and resort to an alternative database, that is, material deemed usable by virtue of its acceptability as a source for drawing inferences, is necessary. The use here of the phrase 'real evidence' to identify this alternative database suggests, on one level, the functional component of evidence as that which provides appropriate information upon which to make determinations of fact (but see immediately below for another level of implication).

3. *The nature of evidence is problematized.*

> Evidence should not be regarded as an entity or as a substantive reality, but rather as a perceptual phenomenon. For some piece of testimony or fact or circumstance to become persuasive as evidence, it must first be granted that status in the mind of the juror. If that perception is not present, then neither – for all practical purposes – is the evidence (Crawford, 1989).[34]

Here, evidence is reinvented for the juror. No longer is it simply inaccessible, forcing resort to an alternative source of material consisting of a compound of evidence and other things, but real evidence actually ceases to exist. At the same time, the

32 Crawford, R., *The Persuasion Edge: Winning Psychological Strategies and Tactics for Lawyers* (Eau Claire, WI: Professional Education Systems, 1989), p. xxiii.

33 Ibid., p. 21.

34 Ibid., p. 20.

perception of the existence of real evidence continues in the consciousness of the juror; however, the object of that perception has been replaced by a construction generated by the advocate – a construction which may or may not include real, that is, institutionally defined, evidence.

Conflict Regarding the Role and Function of the Advocate and the Advocate's Discourse

During instructions, jurors are given clear guidelines as to the estimation they are to hold of both the role of attorneys and their utterances in the examination process. Attorneys are 'not witnesses' and their questions are 'not evidence'. Thus, the institutional discourse of the ideal entails the necessity of jurors monitoring their assessment of the evidential value of utterances they hear during examination in order to maintain a clear distinction between what is evidence and what is not. As noted above, the presupposition is that this is possible. However, as practitioners of the discourse of the actual have stated and shown, it is not. Jurors are unable to effectively or consistently make distinctions, during the interactive flow of examination speech, between bona fide evidence and advocate contributions. Although the actual role of attorneys can probably be successfully abstracted out by the juror, the same is not true for their utterances. This situation sets the stage for a crucial phenomenon to come into play:

> In a very real sense, advocates 'testify' during their opening and closing statements as well as during witness questioning and voir dire [jury selection] (Crawford, 1989).[35]

One aspect of what is 'very real' about the 'testifying' of the advocate is that it is perceived as such by jurors. The complex nature of what is conceptualized as evidence by jurors makes it impossible for them to not be susceptible to attributing evidential value to some utterances of attorneys. [Note: Some experimental research supports this observation: 'The responses of a witness on cross-examination often are nothing more than "Yes" or "No." The testimony of the witness is reduced to mere corroboration or denial of facts cited by the examining attorney. Since the witness testifies in such an indirect fashion in these circumstances, one might wonder how credible testimony of this sort appears to jurors, perhaps on the theory that unless the witness utters the crucial words personally, no juror will believe the facts asserted. The startling finding by psychological researchers is that the indirect assertion of facts provides a very potent means to create a picture or model of the events described in the minds of jurors – a model which may go far beyond the actual words spoken' (Goodman and Loftus, 1984: 55).[36] However, the 'very real'

35 Ibid., p. 21.

36 Goodman, J., and E. Loftus, 'Social Science Looks at Witness Examination', *Trial* 20 (1984): 52-7.

refers not only to this receptive process on the part of jurors but also to a highly productive process on the part of attorneys:

> In oral communication, one must speak to the other person or persons in order to persuade or project into their mind(s) a set of ideas or propositions ... One of the most difficult aspects of cross-examination is that the lawyer is trying to persuade the fact-finder without speaking directly to the jurors ... Counsel is asking the witness questions, but the message is directed to the jury ... (Aron et al., 1989).[37]

The discourse of the actual establishes a meta-testimonial trajectory of commentary (Gaines, 1996)[38] from attorney to juror which carries more than simply the information necessary for the juror to understand the answer the witness gives in response to the question; it carries testimony-like assertions and representations which are intended exactly as such by the attorney and which are intentionally directed to jurors. The institutional priority of the examination moment would seem to be in conflict with a policy that effectively permits a process of attorney testimony. However, this apparent conflict vanishes when it is seen that the phenomenon of the 'testifying' attorney is not a contradiction of the precise prescription for courtroom procedure but only of the apparent intent underlying that prescription and is a direct and inevitable outworking of the principle of adversarial trial practice.

It is at this point that the conflict of the discourses of the ideal and the actual are revealed in the public sphere in perhaps their sharpest form, for at this site is an apparent disruption of the institution's stated primary interest in the trial: the ability of the jurors to determine facts based on evidence presented by witnesses only. As was mentioned earlier, the situation with regard to the examination portion of the trial is fundamentally different, with respect to the responsibility of jurors to effectively and consistently categorize utterances as to their evidential value, than with regard to opening statements and closing arguments. Both of the latter are framed by the court and understood by the jurors to be devices to aid them in organizing and processing the evidence which they will hear and have heard, respectively. Jurors are in a mode of 'leaning back' to take in with a grain of salt, if they wish, the monologic, non-evidential discourse of attorneys before and after examination[39] but in a mode of 'leaning forward' to intently focus on the dialogic discourse of attorney and witness during examination, since it is there that their true object of interest – facts from evidence – lies.

---

37 Aron, R., K. Duffy and J. Rosner, *Cross-Examination of Witnesses: The Litigator's Puzzle* (Colorado Springs, CO: Shepard's/McGraw Hill, 1989), pp. 134-5.

38 Gaines, Philip, 'The Grammar of Credibility Assessment: A Functional Analysis of Two Legal Questioning Styles', *Social Semiotics* 6 (1996): 199-230.

39 Note this somewhat naive observation: 'Preliminary research into the operation of juries ... reveals that jurors profess to be not nearly so enamoured with the use of linguistic tricks as lawyers think they ought to be.' (Dunstan, R., 'Context for Coercion: Analysing Properties of Courtroom "Questions"', *British Journal of Law and Society* 7 (1980): 61-77.)

Conclusion

It should be obvious at this point that the notion of a conflict of discourses in the courtroom – and crucially not one between the conflicting versions of reality presented by opposing advocates – is of more than theoretical interest. The conflict becomes a real-life psychological one: the struggle of discourses is acted out in the field of jurors' consciousness of their responsibilities, since it is the perception of jurors that 'the good juror does not innovate upon the judge's instructions' (Garfinkel, 1967).[40] In an early study of the perceptions of jurors as to their process of deliberation and decision-making, Garfinkel conducted interviews following a criminal trial and determined that jurors are strongly committed to 'justifying a course of action'[41] in the face of the ambiguities presented in a trial. Garfinkel observed that jurors 'masked the actual extent to which ambiguities were part of the situation'.[42] Evidence for jurors' strong sense of accountability to the institutionalized discourse is suggested by observations that 'regardless of the procedures that were actually followed [in deliberations] ... jurors identified them with procedures depicted in the official line' and that 'in their ideal accounts of how [they] arrived at their decisions, jurors told how the *right* decision was arrived at'.[43] Garfinkel noted that when it was pointed out to jurors that their claimed adherence to the prescriptions of the court appeared to be compromised by the ways in which they deliberated in regard to the evidence, interviewees became noticeably anxious and 'looked to the interviewer for assurance that the verdict nevertheless had been correct in the judge's opinion'.[44]

It is not surprising that jurors would find themselves subject in this way to a 'will to truth' (Foucault, 1972),[45] since the courtroom presents itself, through its institutional discourse, as a bastion of truth. Foucault's claim that the will to truth 'relies on institutional support … [and is] both reinforced and accompanied by whole strata of practices'[46] is transparently exemplified in the institutional structure and practices of court systems, embedded as they are in a monolithic discourse of justice which finds expression of its expectations in instructions to the jury. The difficulty emerges from the fact that the will to truth 'tends to exercise a sort of pressure, a power of constraint upon other forms of discourse'.[47] This principle, actualized in jurors' consideration of evidence, suggests that jurors are constrained from fully participating in the relativistic discourse generated by attorneys and instead seek to base their deliberations 'upon sincerity and science'.[48] Such a wide discrepancy

40 Garfinkel, p. 109.

41 Ibid., p. 114.

42 Ibid., p. 112.

43 Ibid., p. 113.

44 Ibid.

45 Foucault, Michel, *The Archaeology of Knowledge and The Discourse on Language* (New York: Pantheon Books, 1972), p. 218.

46 Ibid., p. 219.

47 Ibid.

48 Ibid.

between discourses – particularly in view of the problems it creates for its neutral decision-makers – suggests reason for concern about adversarial practice as a system of justice.

Chapter 10

Jurors' Recorded Deliberations: An Analysis

Paul Robertshaw

Introduction

Jury research in the United Kingdom did not come to an end with the passage of section 8 of the Contempt of Court Act 1981, but it certainly became more difficult.[1] Little research has been published in the UK since 1981; this consists mainly of indirect research by experimental method, by questionnaires or opinion survey, by the use of comparative statistics, and by observation. Thus, in the field of experimental psychology the Law Commission returned to Sealy and Cornish's experiments at the London School of Economics of the early 1970s,[2] with many limitations in the scope of its inquiry;[3] similarly experimental method on the role of juries in complex fraud trials.[4] There has also been experimental work on the optimum size of the jury.[5]

Questionnaire research has been undertaken in Northern Ireland[6] on the treatment of jurors during trial, and on defendants' perceptions of fairness of treatment in jury trials,[7] and on a large scale for the Royal Commission on Criminal Justice[8] on such matters as comprehension of evidence and summing up. Public opinion research has continued, following research on attitudes to the 'Crown Court or Magistrates' in

1 P. Robertshaw, 'A Human Rights Conflict', 22 *Civil Justice Quarterly* (2003) 265-274.

2 A. Sealy and W. Cornish, 'Jurors and their Verdicts', 36 *Modern Law Review* (1973) 496.

3 Law Commission, *Previous Misconduct of a Defendant*, Consultation Paper 141 Appendix D (1996).

4 T. Honess, M. Levi and E. Charman, 'Juror Competence in Processing Complex Information from a Simulation of the Maxwell Trial', *Criminal Law Review* (1998) 63-73.

5 N. Fay, S. Garrod and J. Carletta, 'Group Discussion as Interactive Dialogue or as a Serial Monologue', 11 *Psychological Science* (2000) 481-486.

6 J. Jackson, R. Kilpatrick and C. Harvey, *Called to Court* (Belfast: SLS Legal Publications, 1991).

7 R. Hood, S. Shute and F. Seemungal, *Ethnic Minorities in the Criminal Courts*, Lord Chancellor's Department No 2/03 (3/2003).

8 M. Zander and P. Henderson, *The Crown Court Study*, Research Study No 19 ch.8 (1993).

1976.[9] These studies of opinion have been undertaken in the context of the political disputes over the scope of jury trial.[10]

Before 1981 there had been a number of statistical studies of aspects of the jury.[11] Some additions have been made: on the amount and effect of challenging of jurors,[12] on venue choice and jury acquittal rates for ethnic minority defendants,[13] on acquittal rates generally,[14] and variations in local acquittal and majority conviction rates.[15] There have been studies of jury selection and the excusing process.[16] There has been one observational study of the trial processes and verdicts of magistrates and juries.[17]

Direct research on juries, in particular their deliberations, raises issues as much of ethics as of method. The only work that can be considered within the concept of 'direct' jury research here is that by Purves and McCabe before 1981 using 'shadow juries' in real trials.[18] The major advantage of this method is that it confronts the myriad of contingencies that are present, unlike experimental method, which attempts to excise them. There is an important limitation in that the shadow jury's deliberations are not existentially valid, in that however genuine the role-play their 'verdict' is reached in the knowledge that it can have no impact on the defendant. This view is supported by the difference in verdict between jury and shadow jury in a quarter of trials. Counter to that are the studies of local variation; it may be that any expectation of consistency is mistaken and that it is decisions within parameters of '*Wednesbury* reasonableness' of outcome that is a more mature expectation. Another problem with the shadow jury method is the possibility of existential inauthenticity,

---

9 J. Gregory, Office of Population and Census Studies, London.

10 C. Hedderman and D. Moxon, *Magistrate Court or Crown Court?*, Home Office Research Study No 98, London (1992); *Views on Trial by Jury*, (London: SWR World-wide, 2002).

11 S. McCabe, *The Jury at Work* (Oxford: Blackwell, 1972); M. Zander, 'Are too many Professional Criminals avoiding Conviction?', 37 *Modern Law Review* (1974) 28; J. Baldwin and M. McConville, *Jury Trials* (Oxford: Clarendon, 1979).

12 J. Vennard and D. Riley, 'The Use of Peremptory Challenge and Stand-by of Jurors', *Criminal Law Review* (1988) 731-738.

13 M. Walker, 28 *British Journal of Criminology* (1988) 441-460 T5, 6; L. Bridges, S. Choongh and M. McConville, *Ethnic Minority Defendants and the Right to Elect Jury Trial*, Commission for Racial Equality, London (2000).

14 S. Butler, 'Acquittal Rates', ch.13 in D. Moxon (ed.), *Managing Criminal Justice*, Home Office Research Unit, London (1985).

15 P. Robertshaw, *Regional Jury Verdicts in Scotland*, Juridical Review (1991) 221; *Jury and Judge – the Crown Court in Action*, (Aldershot: Dartmouth, 1995).

16 P. Robertshaw, S. Cox and N. Van Hoen, 'Jury Populations and Jury Verdicts', 20 *International Journal of the Sociology of Law* (1992) 271; J. Airs and A. Shaw, *Jury Excusal and Deferral*, No 102 Home Office Development Directorate, London (1999).

17 J. Vennard, 'The Outcomes of Contested Trials', ch.12 in D. Moxon (ed.) (1985) op.cit.

18 S. McCabe and R. Purves, *The Shadow Jury at Work* (Oxford: Blackwell, 1974).

typically from the knowledge that it is being recorded. These issues were necessarily present in the otherwise excellent BBC TV series of 'mock jury' trials in 1997.

Another limited but legal method canvassed was the 'Sound-shape' jury, which would provide accurate indications of participation levels of all jurors, but nothing more.[19] This can be contrasted with the also lawful, but practically difficult proposal for a 'double shadow' jury, which would have constituted a double-blind experiment.[20]

The ability to publish accounts of one's own experiences as a juror has also succumbed to section 8. Such instances did occur before 1981.[21] Since 1981 we have the account of Trevor Grove in *The Juryman's Tale*,[22] which necessarily avoids all discussion of the deliberation. This can be contrasted with the American genre of juror accounts such as D. Graham Burnett's *A Trial by Jury*.[23] It was one such account which precipitated the overreaction of section 8 of the Contempt of Court Act 1981.[24] Fascinating though such accounts are, they cannot escape the limitations of editing, memory, and self-justification. The same criticism can be levelled at a study which exceeds anything produced in the UK: the work commissioned of academics[25] by New Zealand's Law Commisssion.[26] This study interviewed (pre- and post-trial in 48 jury trials) just over half the jurors in each jury.

Attempts to undertake direct research on jury deliberation were put back for many years by the court controlled 'bugging' of a number of (civil) juries in Kansas City in 1961, which was immediately prohibited. In that context it has been television which has taken forward access to the jury. The first video-recorded jury deliberation was made, with judicial supervision and with full consents, by the US Public Broadcasting Service in 1986 in the trial of *Leroy Read*. There has been academic work conducted from that recording, in the ethnomethodological school.[27] There is one limited analysis of the deliberation and its eventual unanimous 'jury equity' verdict.[28] There is also the interview research by the ethnomethodologist

---

19 P. Robertshaw and M. Greenhough, 'The Jury Sound-shape Project', 6 *International Journal for the Semiotics of Law* (1993) 305-314.

20 P. Robertshaw, 'Jury Trial or Magistrates' Justice', *The Times*, 17 January 1989.

21 Including E. Devons, 'Serving as a Juryman in Britain', 28 *Modern Law Review* (1965) 561-570.

22 London: Bloomsbury (1998).

23 London: Bloomsbury (2001).

24 'Inside the Jury's Mind', *New Statesman* 7 December 1979, 882-884; *Attorney General v New Statesman and Nation Co.*[1981] QB1.

25 N. Cameron, S. Potter and W. Young.

26 Law Commission, *Juries in Criminal Trials*, vols 1 and 2, Wellington (1999).

27 D. Maynard and J. Manzo, 'Theoretical Notes from an Actual Jury Deliberation', 11 *Sociological Theory* (1993) 171-193 – on the use of the word 'justice' by the jurors; and J. Manzo, 'You wouldn't Take a 7-Year-Old and Ask him all those Questions', 19 *Law and Social Inquiry* (1996) 639-663.

28 P. Robertshaw, 'Method and Ethics in Jury Research', 38 *Medicine Science and the Law* (1998) 328.

who conducted the prohibited Kansas City recordings.[29] A further opportunity for research on actually deliberating juries arose in the USA when the Supreme Court of Arizona agreed to recording of four trials, again with full consents and co-operation of the American Bar Association. This is where the current article commences.

Deliberating on Margherita Serrano

In 1995 a Mexican woman ('Margherita Serrano') was tried in Arizona for various offences relating to possession and transportation of marijuana and cocaine for sale. The first (eight person) jury 'hung', after a long deliberation. The retrial jury convicted (unanimously, as state law provides) after a much shorter deliberation. Both these trials, including their jury deliberations, were video-recorded by CBS Television. The ensuing TV programme showed excerpts from these and other trials, including their juries' deliberations, but audiences could gain little idea of the actual course of those deliberations. This author successfully tendered to the American Bar Foundation for copies of these unedited trials, from which I have transcribed their jury deliberations with speaker attribution.[30] The full deliberation of the jury that convicted Margherita follows.

This chapter will analyse it, with focus on its decision track; it will make some reference to the preceding jury, especially its two dissentients. The defendant and her colleagues, as well as the jurors and police witnesses, are anonymised here. The trial and offence narrative will not be entered into here since they will be referred to as is necessary when they arise from the jurors' discussions. The deliberations have been divided into 67 thematic segments – acts of categorisation – each of which is presented in sequence. There is some discussion which is technically post-verdict but it has not been omitted as it is germane to understanding the verdict, but its numbering is italicised. A small amount of purely technical and administrative talk, connected with the tape recordings and transcripts the jury use, is omitted. Two tape recordings are played; these are included but are not numbered. Period marks indicate silence.

---

29 H. Garfinkel, 'Some Rules of Correct Decision-making that Jurors Respect', ch. 4 in his *Studies in Ethnomethodology* (Englewood Cliffs, New Jersey: Prentice-Hall, 1964).

30 A grant was provided by the British Academy. The transcription was too demanding for professional transcribers so I learnt this skill. The grant went to my students, Jocelyn Jones LLB (Wales) and Helen Freemantle LLB (Criminology) (Wales). It was invaluable to have them go over my work and cope with overtalk, interpreting American English and Mexican accents, and in voice attribution. In one respect we too were defeated, by the two sets of tape recorded evidence on which the trial turned. There are a number of limitations in any transcription to text, for example, body language, and gesture are absent.

Transcript of the Jury Deliberation in *People of Arizona* v *'Margherita* Serrano'[31]

Jurors left to right: **Tom, Donald** (older than the other jurors; this jury does not include anyone under 25 years old) **June, Vanessa Puente: *VP* Foreperson, Alberta, Dick, Peter, Zoldan** (moustached; has a standard American accent, so presumably his forbears came from Eastern Europe)

Bailiff I'll come in and get your question – LEAVES 09. 03. 11
1 Tom okay who wants to do it [LAUGHTER]
Peter any volunteers first just a suggestion just in case because it's a lady defendant maybe we ought to have one of these young ladies volunteer
Alberta she'll do it Ness'll do it
VP I have no problem with…you know telling someone that this is this is what the decision was
Dick okay sounds good
Tom okay we'll go ahead and let you do that
2 Donald that's the stuff we wanted
June um don't we have the transcript somewhere in here already
VP yeh it's in evidence it's in evidence so we should have it wasn't it at number 37
Alberta yeah [**Dick** yeah it was limited] well it was limited to the effect to the effect of the tape
VP we should listen to the tape instead of reading it
Peter transcript number 37 a transcript was you know was a copy of the tape
Alberta it's just that because part of it is in Spanish we need the translation [**Dick** here it is] okay cool
Peter you want the tape [PAUSE searching for the tape]
3 *VP* does anybody need to **see** anything in particular or they want to listen to a particular **part** of the tape or one of the tapes or
Alberta no I wanna compare what she says in that to what…Detective Jode had told her was in the suitcases…whether she said that the key [PR: 'key' is argot for kilogram] was in
VP that should be the telephone from Madison [PR: Madison Street, Phoenix, Maricopa County holding jail; also 'The Horseshoe']
Alberta the black one or she said that there was cocaine there
Donald do you think it is. it doesn't say
VP I think so because the big one was uh [**Alberta** the big ones was yeh was yeh] those ones are the detective's tapes
Peter those are the Jode's ones yeh [PAUSE]
4 June what I'm just trying to remember [PAUSE reading papers] so we need to determine the facts
Peter I was going to say the same. . .[Right]
June we must decide the facts so maybe the first charge is figure out **facts** for the first charge...page 6...
Tom that's what you wanna do you want take the first charge here and you want to look at those er ...it's on page 6...n'what you want to do is find facts. that either confirm those elements like er number 1 2 3 and 4 if there's any facts in here that would confirm those

31 Copyright Paul Robertshaw 2002.

or dispute them then that's what we need to decide [**Peter** these four things] exactly that's what y're...what needs to be proved right here

Alberta four items [***VP*** the first count] 2 3 4

Tom then if there's anything is there anything that you heard or that any facts that you know that would actually confirm that...then that's what we wanna do

5 Peter well the most relevant one then would probably be the very first one as that's the custody

[**Alberta** did she know] yeah that's really the only question [yeah] these four things 2 3 and 4

June did she know

Alberta 2 is yes

Peter 2 is a fact 3 is a fact [**Tom** okay] so on the first Count one is a fact 2 is yes 3 is it a usable amount [**June** yes it certainly was] it was for sale

June too much for personal use so it's only number 1 that we...

6 Tom so was there anything in there throughout everything that we've heard that would substantiate number one [**June** showed she knew] she actually was aware

Peter probably her most incriminating evidence was the tape from [**Zoldan** number 37] call from the jail her own phone calls early. was it mentioned

7 June the other thing that we have to consider in figuring out if she knew ahead of time was the meeting that that Hermanno says they held the Sunday before...so then the question is how credible was Hermanno

Zoldan do you think that matters though I think with what she says in the tape. does it matter

June I think you're right

8 Dick I think what we have to find out specifically find out in the tape is not just the tapes in general. what did she say in the tape that makes this a fact

VP okay we can listen to the detective when they're in the interview where she says well what was in the suitcases. or do you know what was in the suitcases that...

Peter was she talking who was she talking with in that who was she talking with her sister

VP Esmerelda

Zoldan her friend not her sister

Peter why don't you read that to us

Tom um okay…let me see if I can find that [***VP*** it was like wasn't it call number 3] shall we use the tape or shall we read it

Peter we can do both but I think part of it was in Spanish [**Tom** yah]

June it's difficult to hear [***VP*** right]

9 Tom well. I can start right here. this is that on that page 9 and where that where the Esmerelda she said and where's homeboy and they laughed and she says he's about two things down and he's... (Chuckles) I don't even like reading this stuff. I don't talk like this [***VP*** it's pretty graphic][yeah] blankety blank blank...yeh there's a lot of blanks in there yeah um yeah he effing told them everything was mine that he didn't have any bags with him nothing they were all mine believe that and is that Esmerelda says is that what he said yeah that's exactly what he said. I told you full of...whatever two are mine and two are his...I'll take the blame for my stuff but I ain't taking the blame for his and then in Spanish and how much was it...and she says 128 and a kilo

10 Dick how would she have known the amounts

Alberta the only question would be as far as one of us concerned is is that Jode did tell her that there was drugs in there but she did not mention specifics as to how much weight [no] [**Tom** m'in that time]

VP well they wouldn't have known [**Dick** they wouldn't have known **Zoldan** they did not know]

Peter didn't didn't she also say that they didn't open it in front of her she didn't actually see it

June yes in these conversations [**Peter** the fact that they were witnesses] she says we didn't I didn't even get to see'em open it and so what kind of case do they have...they could say there's anything in there

Peter yeah cos I didn't see it and er she looked in there as if she knew what was there but since they didn't open it in front of her it doesn't matter

Zoldan I think if you keep readin they say they mess their own case up or something. . .

Donald didn't they say somewhere they're gonna weigh it [***VP*** right]

11 Tom okay and then she goes ahah and then ahah and a key girl and um MS laughs and EV who had the key yours or his [laughing] this is MS again no it was mine

Peter so she knew that the cocaine was in the black box

VP she says it was **in mine** so she claimed possession of it right there

12 Peter when was it actually weighed when did they actually come up with this

June wasn't that during the lab crime lab [***VP*** crime lab] the lab part when that one man testified that he knew what the substances were and how much they weighed

Peter right so no one from the police knew exactly right then what it weighed that was later

June this was

VP they could eyeball but they couldn't tell you exactly

Alberta but they knew that it was more than two pound or whatever that

Tom that's not their job to worry about it

Peter so the fact that she knew the weights relatively accurately had to come from some predetermined

13 Dick were they accurate I don't remember exactly what they said [***VP*** 125]

June well I wrote it down. I25. . .

Zoldan but bear in mind they didn't weigh the little package [**Several** right]...

June but they weighed the marijuana at 109 pounds but without the small package [**Zoldan** okay] and the kilo [***VP*** kilogram][**June** at 49]

Alberta I guess that's kilograms [***VP*** 49 pounds]

Alberta no 2.2 pounds per kilograms [**Peter** so 49..**Dick** so 49 what **June** I think it was]

VP cos I wrote down 125 pounds [**Dick** okay]

Alberta okay I've got 125 and then one kilogram...of the coke

Tom do we need do we need to find out exactly what it is [it's 4.9 pounds] or does that matter does that matter [**Peter** it doesn't matter]

June 2.2 pounds is a kilogram

VP anything over nine grams

Dick 4.9 times 2.2is...er

14 Tom but see the point is did she know did she know how much it was

Zoldan I think she admitted it right there

VP yes it was a key

Peter I was sure they didn't tell her that they told her what she was being booked for

Zoldan but even if they

15 June but they wouldn't have to tell her that fast this was in intake. . .[**Dick** right] that she is making these phone calls so what did they say about the times how long did she get for the calls
Alberta they got the time at the top of each call...it's got the date and time
Tom yes it does I'll have to go back...um. no it doesn't say [***VP*** it doesn't]
June somewhere in the
Tom no it's call number 3 ringing to n'whatever number it doesn't have. .
VP what are the calls to Esmerelda
Tom oh on July ten [**Several** right]. .before eleven o'clock
VP yeah she said I've been here 15 minutes but [**Tom** that's right.] I've been with the police since 9 am
Alberta she says I'm **going** to I'm **going** to see the judge at 11 am
June so she was just there at the jail less than a half-hour [***VP*** mm]
16 Peter another thing too that she didn't realise I think it mentions in there that exactly maybe what she was saying because 'member when she made the second or third phone call she mentioned the fact that did you hear them say they'd pay for this I didn't hear that when I called you before [**June** yes]
VP in the very beginning though it says this is she says they're recordin this so she knew
Alberta she knew so she knew
Peter she must have forgotten
Tom she had a conversation
Alberta she just got she just got too upset too...[**Peter** too carried away] too ticked off
17 Zoldan I think the other thing that has to be taken into consideration is when she gets on the call as she leads into the phone call the other person already knows what she's in trouble for there wasn't I mean if you were to make a phone call [**Alberta** I'm in jail **uh** huh why] yeah they go
Dick what do you think
June why are you in jail
Tom she says hey what happened and it says what do you think she says nahah call **him** and tell him where are you I don't know
Peter so she knew she knew ahead of time
18 June that takes care of number one
Dick well really that takes care of
Alberta that takes care of just about all of em [**Dick** one and also what um the other one] and also for count 3
Peter for number one the only question is did she know
Alberta yeah that was the big thing
Donald so are we ready to vote…Simpson jury...[LAUGHTER]
Dick I think that's the time we get off the door...
Tom proportion wise ratio [I mean]
Zoldan we can vote and if it comes out the way we think it's gonna to we're out of here
Tom I mean really what is the sense of er debating debating any issues if everyone feels the same
Donald we'll throw in any questions if anyone has questions let's discuss it if no questions let's go...
Tom right that's pretty much what it comes down to unless somebody. . .
19 Dick my only question is is there any...did someone tell her roughly how much there was during her booking process [**Tom** alright]

VP they wouldn't know
June let's think about this she's making phone calls in reference to weight within thirty minutes of her her arrival at Madison Street Jail the police themselves probably didn't weigh that stuff for
Dick they wouldn't have to weigh it they would
VP they knew it you can tell that a a zip locked bag holds like more than three pounds
Dick they would make an estimate even in their own mind
20 Peter and another thing that is a little irrelevant but it still may have something to do with the fact of her knowledge of this is the fact that she'd already made a previous trip and brought a relatively large sum of money back I mean what kind of explanation would you give for...[***VP*** for ten thousand dollars worth of cash] why would she be bringing some money back for someone if it has to have some relation to what she was doing
Donald so if you go back the second time for sight seeing
Alberta the only thing that clarifies is the tape
Tom when was the criminologist's report done [we could do]
Zoldan yeah we could do that if you're unemployed are you going to buy one-way tickets back to New York I'm sorry...[**Alberta** I'm employed I can't afford to buy a one-way ticket] yeah you got two kids you're gonna try plan ahead you're not gonna go one week and go right back the next [yeah] if mom's gonna buy you a ticket how come mom doesn't know she's in jail
Peter and another thing as far as taking this merchandise back. this is a little irrelevant too but how cost effective is it selling shirts buying six hundred dollar tickets to return them to New York you know that's one way this alibi thing it just doesn't add up that's just **one** trip [yeah]
June and that's just one trip and that's just **one way** one trip
21 Alberta and the fact that all **lie** consistently [***VP*** that was **both** of them]
Peter I mean with things like this going on him or herself
Alberta you can't... you can't... no matter how...the idiot question that I had asked that they wouldn't ask how was of the officer was how often is someone unknowingly used as a mule because it I mean no matter how gullible you are if someone asks you gee can you take this package for me to New York fine you want me to use an assumed name **why** yeah I got a warrant but the airport doesn't check for **warrants**
June but that was that was when when on the tape with Detective Jode when they're at Denny's and she gets the suitcases and later she's being interviewed and the detective says don't you think it was kind of weird that somebody drops off these two suitcases didn't you start to wonder and she said well yeah I kind of wondered you're travelling under an assumed name and you've got these suitcases yeah I kind of wondered but I wasn't sure...
22 *VP* I think it kind of goes back for me is you know she said she knew the guy for a year well I mean if I knew somebody for a year I'm gonna know what their **job** is their **family** um you know and even if I know what someone for three months I'm at least gonna know where they **live** what they do for a living I'm gonna know if they do **drugs** ...I mean you know you know if they're good friends right I mean you know…[**Zoldan** strange guy] do you pick up hitchhikers okay do you know what I mean
23 June well if we didn't have the tapes we'd have to evaluate all this more carefully [***VP*** right…] because wouldn't this be what they're calling circumstantial evidence but because we have a direct conversation spoken from her
Tom this is very **strong** here [**Peter** yeah very strong]

June I'm sure that is why they left it till last
Zoldan I think that right there basically everything else...just kinda [**Peter** falls into place...] is leading us up there
24 Tom but what the key issue is is did they ever tell her how much did at **any** point
Alberta because because you can sit there playing devil's advocate you can sit and say that Jode told her there was marijuana in there I can remember she told her there was coke in there so the question is did she tell her what the weights were did she guesstimate what the weights were
June I don't think it matters
25 *VP* you know what why don't we listen to the tape just to satisfy
Alberta no actually I'm fairly satisfied I'm just playing devil's advocate they could say well this information was given to her by the police
VP we'll see this is what we are supposed to do reasonable doubt so let's play the tape and hear what Jode told her...
26 June this way you know that way you know that way devil's yeah
Peter what question did you say you asked
Alberta I ask I asked it basically comes down how often can someone unknowingly unknowingly completely blindly innocently transport drugs for someone else [***VP*** see if…] and that is what the whole case is about basically
June well that's what the defence is saying that she was an innocent victim and going on vacation and we can't it it would be easy if it was allowed to go through and see if their if the testimony we've heard for her supports what they said in opening statements but we can't because they're the defence and we have to go with what the prosecution says but if you **could** the the points that they presented **don't** hold up
Dick what you got 28 and 29
27 Peter did you notice something else too the question I asked. some reasons for some of the other [**Dick** 28 and 29 **Tom** this is 28] one of the facts was that she used a false name and they had a reason for that quickly the fact that she had a [**June** warrant] warrant for arrest but you knows the question I asked when she went to New York the previous time...[**June** did she use...] what name did she use they said she used her own name why was it it important then because it was **after** the warrant was issued see it came up later it was **after** the warrant was issued that she travelled to New York the first time but she never used a false name **then** simply because she didn't have anything with her that would get her in trouble I mean ten thousand dollars cash may be hard to explain but it's not illegal
June no right
28 *VP* you know and a few other things that are like in the phone conversation and um well she has a warrant out for failing to pay traffic tickets or whatever it is so she's kinda... you know I mean maybe some of us in here may have done that
June but I could have. I could have done that
Zoldan we have a lot of our drivers who just forget okay fine
29 *VP* okay that's okay you know we can discount that **but** in her phone conversation she talks about her lawyer in Tucson [**June** yes]
Zoldan I've got his portable and his home number I'm sorry
June she made a reference to you know how they are down at that jail or that ...
Peter that was Green Valley wasn't it
June yes but you know how they **are** and they're always
VP so she **knows** the system cos she was talking how horrible Madison is compared to

30 Zoldan but how come she is in the situation she ended in whatshisface her had his bail made
VP right that is one of the questions I wanted to asks how did she get bail and when
June she did she went free they said
TAPE STARTS 09.21.35 Crackling background noise [Transcription's accuracy is not warranted]
You want me to be
Detective*...New York trip together on the flight that you travelled together and that you went there for a week for a week then you came back together. I mean I know it's hard for you to be frank because.... I mean I understand. Now I'm kinda positive there's something there... Did Hermanno pay you to go to with him, did he give you money to go with him. Take the suitcases or do anything that he did*
MS *No*
Det *There's always supposed to be*
MS *No obligation to go with him*
Det *Did you see anybody pay him*
MS *No I don't remember anything*
Det *Do you know where he got that money? Did you see if that guy at Denny's... pay him*
MS *I wasn't looking anyway I warned Hermanno that we weren't that we we're gonna miss the flight*
Det *Where did you get that fifty-dollar bill that you had?*
MS *The fifty dollars? Um . . . My Ma gave me 100 dollars so that I could come ...*
[**Peter** so that would explain why she has eighty four cos that shirt was probably sixteen… in New York City with 84 dollars for a week...should do this every week]
Det *When you told me before you think he's involved in drugs what kind of drugs do you think he's involved in?*
MS *I don't know... marijuana*
Det *why do you think that ...*
MS *well because you said about small dogs* [PR: trained to detect various drugs]
Det *a small bunch of different kinds of drugs. That is one of them.*
MS *He remarked that he would make all the money*
Det *Have you ever seen him with marijuana? Any. Even personal use amounts. Did he tell you that when you guys went to New York that he would make a lot of money?*
MS *No he said it was a vacation. He has family that's up there*
Det *Well how did he pay for the trips if he's not working. That's what I don't understand*
MS *that's the thing that's the reason I think that maybe he's involved in something I mean we don't money don't grow on trees*
Det *I wish it did [LAUGHTER]*
MS *So you know that's why I might you know yeah I kinda think he's involved in it but I wouldn't get involved you know what I'm saying*
Det *You know did he tell you that he would y' know take all the money..*
Det *May I ask you this. You said you'd known him for a* ***year*** *and in that year okay a couple of weeks ago you went to New York you said separately you were gonna meet him there. Has he gone on any other trips that you know of?*
MS *Well he leaves a lot I don't know exactly where he goes a hundred percent of the time he goes and visits me at my house or to my mother's house you know he does he tries to with the girls it's nothing like that*
Det *uh*

MS *and that don't bother me I'm not that vicious bitch looking for I don't look at him that way just as friend you know and uh*
Det *Okay if it makes you feel any better he went to the judge to get the warrant so you're updated.*
Okay (END OF TAPE) **9.26.00** PAUSE [Winding the tape]
31 June was it Detective Jode asked in the testimony if she ever said if she ever told Margherita the amounts
Dick I think that it's a question I'd like answered was she ever told the amounts either during the initial booking or even...rough amounts
Alberta I'm kinda more interested in like which bag if she told them which bag that coke was in because if she didn't...she was told coke was found... [**Dick** but she knew it was in her bag] but wasn't told which bag just found then if she says yeah it was in my stuff then that hangs her
Dick so two questions was she ever told what was found in what bag and was she ever told the weight
32 Dick we have to decide if we wanna send this or do we wanna wait for the answer
Alberta they'll have to track down Jode
June well and is it just Jode couldn't Blau or
Dick they wouldn't track I think they would it has to be the evidence that we heard [9.28.30]
June it has to be in the testimony [**Dick** or on booking papers] we can't just say does anybody know if any detective asked her or ever told her what the
33 Alberta the only person that she ever had much contact with [***VP*** was Judd] was Judd
VP n'see the people that book them they don't know what they're coming in for until they fill out that paper and it says possession of marijuana you know or whatever it is so the people in there over there bookin them they don't know they frisk em they finger print em you know give me your valuables you know they might ask them what are you here for you know something like that but they would have no_idea what the circumstances were...
34 Dick see if those are the best parts if it's the right questions
Peter well isn't this something we should be able to obtain from our own evidence [***VP*** yeah]
June so what you're saying that what we want is a transcript of Jode's testimony [***VP*** yeah]
Peter but we have it there on the tapes
June no her testimony in the courtroom [**Peter** oh that's um]
Tom no I don't think we'll have it [**Peter** no]
Alberta so we should be able to hear it the big thing is did she tell her anytime during the questioning
35 Dick did they ever admit in evidence the her her booking yerknow the papers they were filled out for her and um ... [**Tom** oh yes]
VP no that wouldn't be the ones they do over Madison Jail no that's just for their files over there
Tom the Jode's [PAUSE finding the place on the tape]
36 Peter well you know it's important it's important information but as far as the context of everything I dunno that it's [**Dick** I thought it should be] all that decisive one way or the other I mean even if she had been told she still might have known [yeh] that's the point

[**June** well that's true] and I'm sure she did know whether she was told or not [PAUSE looking for papers]
37 Dick it'd kinda somewhere she had to be told the charges...right
Peter they told her right then at the airport when they arrested her
VP when they handcuffed her possession and transportation of drugs
June but that part we just listened to Detective Jode said how how did she said you found marijuana Detective Jode said how did you know it was marijuana well your **dog** sniffed it well our dog sniffs lots of scents that's **one** of them but there are others too
VP yeah that's incriminating
Zoldan I think she knew
June I think...it's it's really clear
38 Tom yeah…I don't think this [PR: the tape] is going to help us…I don't recall anybody ever telling her how much [***VP*** how much] at any
June well I recall her question to Detective Jode did you tell her the weights and the answer was no [***VP*** yeah] that was in there the testimony [***VP*** yeah yeah]
Peter well I understand it was never weighed till it went to the crime lab
Dick that's right I agree with that
June but even a guesstimate that police officers can figure out cos they **see** it
Peter but it can't be used as any kind of evidence unless it's **accurately** done because they can't say
Dick but they weren't using it as evidence [yehyeh] [PAUSE, looking for papers from the crime lab]
39 June wasn't that the testimony [no] he did take the stand briefly just to [***VP*** *w*hat was there][yeh]
Peter they agreed upon that so there was no issue [***VP*** yeh]
Tom I think it was Mick Blau that gave the actual weights
Peter well they brought in that technician
Tom Mick Blau told you how much weights cos he broke it down as far as usage [right] he also broke it down how much each one was worth broken down to parts how much each was worth and much it could be broken down for street use
Peter that technician in the lab that did the actual measurement
Tom okay and they say they didn't measure the one
Alberta because they were busy and had measured all the rest
Peter there was so much already there [***VP*** well over the amount]
Alberta and it was all useable
Tom so it's not relevant the amount as long as it's over [right] [***VP*** okay]
40 Dick the only reason it would be relevant is that she **knew** almost **exactly** what...
June but in her other in her other conversations she knows I mean she she **talks** in other ways [mmm]
Zoldan I mean before the tape yeah there could have been some doubt but after that it's like ppsst
Tom I don't even know where it's at if it's at the beginning or the end
Dick just to me if we could answer if we knew the answer to those two questions she was never told and no one ever told her the cocaine was in the black bag then that to me there's absolutely no doubt that that she she knew exactly what she was doing ...probably don't need those pieces of information
Zoldan I don't think so
Peter no I don't think so either

VP well we've got reasonable doubt we don't have any
Donald that might be the frosting on the cake but we got the cake
[9.34.34 PAUSE Searching for tape]
41 Zoldan well the other thing I thought that is kind of ironic is if you're go go on vacation why would you have clothes and so on that are already soiled [**June** yeah that's what I was wondering when he said that] well how can you have different sized clothes that that did anyone else catch that [**Peter** the shorts and different waist sizes] she's got that's 38 size shorts [**Dick** well that was his] 28 size when you go on how can you [**Dick** that was his]
42 Alberta and the difference in her accent was very marked between when she was talking to the detective and when she was talking on the phone [**Zoldan** oh yeah]
June well she wasn't intimidated I'm I'm sure what the defence was going for there during all that it's a very scared place and are all kinds of criminals and insane people [**Alberta** it's very traumatic] was that she was gonna say anything or something else [Tape Rewound and at 9.36.34 Tape starts again]
Det *when I first asked you where why you were travelling under a false name you said and then in here you told me that he gave you those names*
43 Dick what are we trying to find
Alberta we're trying to find out if she was told the cocaine was not in which bag
VP see because they didn't know till after the warrant
Dick at this point they wouldn't know because at the end of the last tape he said
VP he just got the warrant so we'll find out what's in there [**Dick** right]
Peter she wasn't there when they opened it [***VP*** right] she never even witnessed it
Tom Jode wasn't there earlier [***VP*** Jode **nor** them]
Alberta well there we are then we don't have to worry about it
Peter then there's no question [**Alberta** then there's no question]
Tom they couldn't tell her if they wanted to [**Peter** right] they didn't know yeh you know even if they did know they wouldn't tell you but...
Alberta I just couldn't remember if she had said the coke had been found and if it had been found in the particular bag that's the only thing I wanted to clarify [**Donald** no Jode didn't ever say that] okay
Dick no I didn't I didn't think that we heard in there. I just wondered if she was ever told in between Terminal 3 and...[**Several** no **Alberta** okay]…and seeing the Jode next time [**Alberta** okay] okay she had been told at some point and just wanted to put her phone call
44 Alberta well then we know for sure that she knew about the coke she knew about the heroin everything was usable [**Peter** marijuana] I mean the marijuana...and the drugs
Dick you know **way** too much about this case [GENERAL LAUGHTER]
Alberta I got drugs on the mind now
45 so she knows about the marijuana she knows about the coke's definitely a usable amount and it's more than you are gonna use for personal use and she's obviously
June she's at the airport... [***VP*** yeah]...which looks like we're going somewhere they're in suitcases which further... looks like
Alberta she had possession she had possession she had a ticket and she had the stubs for the baggage
June it sounded like yesterday the transportation part could even be from Tucson Phoenix...[uh uh] . from the way the ...

46 Peter something else I thought was interesting too the defence tried to portray um a lot of things the fact that she was sort of given the er short end of the deal by Hermanno because he plea bargained and therefore that was part of his deal
June his testimony can't be as pure because he did it for reasons [**Dick** right]
Peter but common sense would tell you that she somehow came up with this money very easily and got bail and he had to sit there had things been reversed the the police might have very well have given her the same option to plea bargain but they didn't have access to her
June but you see that's exactly my thought my thought is it could be reversed there's no reason she couldn't have done the same thing
Peter but she'd have stayed in jail...that's the only way
47 Zoldan but well this is just a thing and I don't know how to say this I think she's the one that was higher up on the ladder than Hermanno [**VP** I do too]
Peter much more so [General agreement]
VP if anything was Hermanno was the **mule** he said three thousand dollars to me God I have a mortgage two vehicles three kids three thousand dollars a **heck** of a lot of money you know
Zoldan in some of that thingy there in the Exhibit 37 she's saying something like you know five six hundred dollars what the hell I mean it's no big deal five hundred six hundred bucks is a big deal
VP fifty bucks is a big deal to me
Peter and the fact that she found some she got that bail. which she didn't say you know
June didn't say how much it was either
Peter didn't say how much it who got it or who posted it or what the situation was
June didn't say how fast she was out
Dick that's not important . we're not supposed to that
48 Alberta most people can't take cash to buy a car...
June why not
VP why can't we know how soon she got out of jail and how much her bail was
Peter well that's a matter of record as far as who posted it to maybe that's not a matter of record
VP but how much her bail was and they would have they should have if she's had priors but we can tell that because she had warrant out on her
Tom but we can't do that
Alberta that has nothing to do with this case thing so you can't take that into consideration
Peter no it has nothing to do with it
Tom and the other issue is you have to block out everything about Hermanno... [right]... like the Assistant Attorney said she said this has nothing to do with
Peter I would try to dispute the point the fact that they made it sound as if this plea bargain thing gave her the short end thing well y'know she would have the same opportunity had someone not posted her bond if she'd been setting there too and the police have access but once you post the bond the police don't have access to you until you go back to court
49 Dick if the only thing we had was Hermanno's word I'd I'd have a lot of reason to
Zoldan there would be a lot of doubt [**Peter** sure]
Alberta yes definitely because you know they're each trying to say they're both
Dick it's those phone it's those phone conversations
June well you'd have to evaluate his believability [**Dick** yes I did]

50 Zoldan see up until that conversation there was doubt there [*VP* yeh]
Tom but like you said once you had the phone conversation everything else went into place
Donald it was not only the contents it was her attitude [**Zoldan** the attitude sure]
June well she certainly wasn't scared as they would you know...we're leading
Tom covered in smokescreen though
Alberta she was cocky not upset that she had been caught
June she was laughing and having a great time on the phone
Peter well she also has enough money to hire these lawyers so the fact that she still has a money source and the fact that she did get out on bond now she has to be tried because they won't plea bargain with her I mean what other alternatives does she have but to go this route with this defence there isn't much more defence that she has
51 June no and I also notice that the defence didn't have...er any way to did she have any way to…phone calls. they really attacked Hermanno and all that but they didn't say anything about the phone calls
Donald well they tried to add just the Horseshoe and the fact that she was put under stress
June I guess that was it ...but
Donald that's what they were trying to do
Peter it didn't work too well…
June I don't think she was stressed she didn't sound stressed [**Donald** no]
Alberta she didn't sound stressed as in an innocent person who's been ...put who's in a horrible position
VP I think I would probably be on the phone bawling my eyes out oh **my** God oh my **God** what am I gonna do
Zoldan if you were...if their defence was that she got sucked in an innocent little girl got sucked in. you know if you're an innocent little girl you know you're not gonna have that type of an attitude when you get on the phone [right]
Alberta that's true you're gonna be crying all over the place
Peter as far as character is concerned that incriminates her [mm]
VP okay… it says you know to look at the witnesses and stuff...[**Alberta** credibility...] just the way she was sitting there with that look you know just like...
Zoldan I don't think it matters
Peter she is her own witness as far as the credibility on those tapes [uh uh]
52 Dick I would think that the prosecutor would've put her up on stage if she was like the defence lawyer and have her explain why she said things the way she said them you know what I mean
June we could have had something_
Dick we can't have something to hang on to really the defence didn't give us anything to to try to explain that
June and they don't have to see that's the thing
Dick I understand at this stage the state needs to prove
Zoldan every witness or anything that was done they kept trying to catch em into saying something or doing something that would be a technicality that would kinda distract us from what the facts were
June we've seen those techniques before [yeh] and it works...[LAUGHTER]... for some

Dick every time the defence showed the all the other witnesses saying something in the wrong way the prosecutor put em up and made her you know made them explain it the way they really meant it
VP right
53 Dick and I expected the same thing from the defence attorney... [okay] ...why were you acting tough like that
Peter we can't consider that well we can't hold it against her but the thing that was interesting though is the fact that their defence lawyer she said that don't hold that against her. hold it against me and I just kinda said to myself you know well who's on trial here you know what I mean we're not gonna hold either against you you know what I mean it was sort of a naïve statement to make...I thought yeah who's gonna go to jail
Zoldan it was actually a play on our sympathy [**Peter** okay right]
54 *VP* the whole defence was well the Horseshoe in Sunday's paper Valiant State there was a little article went on about the Horseshoe and it says it's pretty nasty you know and but I mean every jail's nasty you know it's not a party it says in there how she was saying on the phone two pieces of bread and a piece of **ham** meat it says you get a meat sandwich and a piece of fruit in there
Alberta more than a lot of people have that out on the street so why you complaining
55 Peter well shall we vote somehow or other
Alberta shall we vote [***VP*** okay]
June how do we do that let's see what this says [***VP*** okay] oh wait there's
Peter there's forms we have to sign after we vote okay just the foreman has to sign...do we do it private
Tom sure you can just everybody take a piece of paper write it down
VP you can put down Count 1 Count 2 Count 3 Count 4 put guilty or not guilty
Peter put 1 through 4 and put either guilty or not [PAUSE]
56 *VP* are we all discussing this because we're on (looks at camera and giggles) [PAUSE]
57 June do we need to break it down into the . . . [***VP*** no [9.45.45 PAUSE]
Dick we can do what we did for the first one but it's the same for all of them 2 3 n'4 the knowledge was
Alberta okay forewoman [**Peter** or foreperson]
Tom does it actually say fore**person** on there [LAUGHTER]
VP yes it does foreperson yes [**Tom** politically correct] are you going to count [**Alberta** okay] that makes 2...3...4... 5... 6... 7...and mine that makes 8 [**June** it's unanimous]
58 Peter shall we press the button I think she will tell us how to fill out these forms
VP actually it says right here it says um **we** the jury duly empanelled and sworn in the above entitled action upon our oaths do find the defendant Margherita Vargas Serranno as to Count 1 possession of marijuana for sale guilty and further find the amount of marijuana to be. was it more than 4 pounds or less than 4 pounds [**All** more] **okay** so she's guilty 4 pounds or more okay [**Tom** sign and print]
Dick I think the purpose for that is we could have decided in here that she only knew about two of the bags and if two of the bags supposing we found that she knew what of the two blue bags there was no cocaine in there
Peter it would only be half the case
Dick yes but I think we're saying we knew she knew there was something in all four of them
VP the key girl [yeah] all the same stuff duly empanelled and sworn

Peter it was a key of the other stuff
Tom and it exceeded the amounts that are set by law yeah
VP this is Count 2 transportation of marijuana for sale guilty and further find the amount of marijuana to be two pounds or more less than two pounds [**Alberta** yeah more than 2 pounds]
Peter chairlady do you want me to press the button [**Alberta** nn we'll finish the]
Peter do we have to sign too [**Tom** no] she just gets to. .
Zoldan just let her get them filled out [**Alberta** did you have to print your name]
59 ***VP*** this is kinda like Article 15 so that's why that's a decision I have no problem telling someone
Peter big difference between these and Article 15
Tom Article 15's a slap on the **hand** there so don't do that [***VP*** well **not** necessarily]
60 ***VP*** Count 3 possession of narcotic drugs for sale...everybody says guilty nine grams or more less than nine grams [**Alberta** it was more]
Zoldan it was a key [LAUGHTER **June** girl girlfriend ...] I forgot that part sorry
Donald do we have to all go back out here now reassemble now
Alberta I wonder when the judge does er sentencing I guess [**Several** not now]
VP Count 4 transportation of narcotic drugs for sale it said guilty nine grams or more…
June push the button [**male** get the show on the road]
Alberta and then do we have to wait until they get everybody assembled [**Several** yeah]
VP so we can take a break I would think
June I just thought that was very interesting about that whole plea bargain thing… [KNOCKING 9.49.25] how the defence went about their... [**Bailiff** enters and says she will return]
61 **June** you know I got I I you you hear about those phone calls but they they weren't coming and I thought Hermanno would be the last witness and the phone calls and I thought oh my gosh maybe they're not going to do that after all this talk [**Tom** I was thinking that too...] **when** are these phone calls coming
Zoldan exactly that's one of my questions in here when are we going to listen to the tape
VP that's why she held it till last
Alberta I think the most incriminating bit that's going to be
June I thought the witnesses they are going to have on the stand that's going to be the one that's gonna be the one that can introduce these phone calls [disposing of waste paper]
62 **Alberta** you gotta give Hermanno credit that you know yes he said he plea bargained he actually was [**June** oh no it's probably still in here] yes he did have a motive and he was very upfront about the fact he had a motive you could literally just see in his body language and the way he was talking that he was extremely **upset** by all of this too
June I found him fairly believable [**Alberta** yeah] tell me about yourself
Peter he looks believable [**June** you didn't]
Dick thank you no I I if it was only his testimony I thought there were holes in it
Alberta there would have been
June if it were only his but then you would have to couple it with her interview with all the other things and with **that** [**Alberta** but his alone isn't]
Dick without those phone calls I'm not sure which way I would have
VP Count 4 transportation of narcotic drugs for sale it said guilty nine grams or more…
Zoldan were you guys shocked when you saw Hermanno is that what you were expected

VP no no I expected someone dressed a little nicer not um quite as dark skinned I figured he was Mexican not Puerto Rican or Cuban [**Zoldan** more of a more of a drug type]
Peter I thought he'd be a little cockier and kind of swaggering
63 **June** that's it it makes you wonder kind of supports the theory that she was the brains and he was the brawn
Peter he was very unprofessional I'm sure she's smarter than he was a great deal much smarter
Tom she was intelligent I think you could say that
Peter did you notice her in the trial I mean she was taking notes
Alberta she was taking notes she was laughing and what's when I got a shock was when they opened up the the suitcases to show the marijuana she jumped up like I've never seen this before [**Peter** good acting] very good acting [**June** there's an element of acting in that]
64 **Alberta** yeah she was very well coached
Tom I've never seen anything like that before [LAUGHTER]
June the prosecution wasn't quite as dramatic but the defence was very dramatic [***VP*** oh yeah]
Zoldan I could have slapped her that one time when she kept talking to that Zbigniewski [***VP*** uh uh]
June about The Horseshoe shape
Zoldan and she keeps going going she keeps going going about The Horseshoe
Peter isn't it a horseshoe isn't it
June no it's a square actually that goes like that [***VP*** three sides of a square...] what is that all that about
VP it's a U she was just trying to get us...
Peter focussed on something else on that image of horseshoe
Alberta it was emotional she was just trying to emotionally suck you in [**June** yeah]
VP and that's what their defence was...to just
65 **Peter** they made it sound so kind of premeditated like Hermanno was you know in there and looking for a way out but like I said before they the police will go after whoever they have got access to as far as plea bargaining is concerned if she had not been bailed out she would have had exactly the same she would probably have been better off if she had not been bailed off
VP that's right she could have said you know I plead guilty to doing this for
66 **Peter** did you also notice on her tapes how she tried to protect you know who call you know who for God's sake let him know right away what's happened have him get me out of here
67 ***VP*** that's whereas Hermanno had hey I'll tell it like it is
Peter he wasn't in the system deep enough
VP right he'll turn in someone else
Peter he's freaked though he will notice he's a little scared
June at one point the defence asked one of the detectives did he cry were you there when he cried
[9.53.53] **Bailiff** Do you not have an estimate of time...does anyone smoke or want to go out for a cigarette or anything

In the next section the Decision Track will be presented in thematic terms with an indication of the types of discourse use in each segment – a further act of categorisation. These are Forensic language (addressed to fact-finding through mainly 'when', 'where' and 'who' questions), Institutional language (legal, procedural and formality matters) and Interactional language (management of personal relations within the group) in various combinations.

The Jury's Decision Track:

The Bailiff's parting question *Institutional language* [9.03.11]

1 Appointing the foreperson – motivation *Institutional/Interactional language*

2 The tapes and transcripts necessary for deliberation as most direct evidence *Forensic language*

3 ... focus on specific content: MS' initiative to Detective re cocaine *Forensic*

4 Role of the jury: fact-finding in relation to the elements of the charges *Institutional*

5 ... focus on element of advance knowledge *Forensic*

6 … jail taped phone calls *Forensic*

7 J and Z exclude an irrelevance *Forensic/Interactional*

8 Focus on particular content of tapes; the poor quality of their recording *Forensic/ Institutional*

9 Quotations of MS from tape: weights of the drugs *Forensic*

10 Key issue for deliberation identified *Forensic/Institutional*

11 A conclusion on the cocaine *Forensic*

12 The drugs identification with weights and the weighing process *Forensic*

13 Calculating the exact weights of the drugs *Forensic*_

14 The key issue restated: the timing of MS' jail phone calls *Forensic*

15 The chronology of MS' phonecalls *Forensic*

16 The jail phone recording system and MS' knowledge of their systematic recording *Forensic*

17 Inference from phone call recipient's foreknowledge of its subject matter *Forensic*

18 Primary conclusion reached with opportunity to challenge *Institutional/Interactional*

19 Double-checking: the temporal relationship between the jail call and weighing the drugs *Forensic*

20 Circumstantial: MS' previous visit to New York and her finances *Forensic*

21 Credibility: picking up more bags on route, the traffic warrants excuse and false names *Forensic*

22 Circumstantial: MS-HH's relationship and lack of knowledge of each other's background *Forensic*

23 Value of the tape recordings in relation to the circumstantial evidence *Forensic/ Institutional*

24 Recapitulation of key issue re knowledge of weights and types of drugs *Institutional/ Forensic*

25 Tapes in the deliberation: Devil's Advocate role and reasonable doubt *Interactional/ Institutional*

26 Defence and prosecution cases re MS and jury's role *Institutional* [poorly articulated]

27 MS' previous trip to New York; did not use false name despite her traffic warrants *Forensic*

28 Comment on the relative triviality of traffic warrants *Forensic*

29 Circumstantial: MS had knowledge of lawyers, criminal process and prisons *Forensic*

30 MS was able to get bail *Institutional*

31 Recapitulation: the two key questions *Institutional/Forensic*

32 Whether a deliberating jury can ask a police witness for further evidence I *Institutional*

33 The irrelevance of the jail booking procedure; evidential exclusion *Forensic/ Institutional*

34 Repeats that the police witness' evidence must be in the jury room II *Institutional*

35 Further refining the key issue *Institutional*

36 The tapes compared with other evidence *Institutional*

37 MS anticipated marijuana at the freetalk and dog investigation; *Forensic*

38 and weights could not be established until later at the crime lab *Forensic*

39 Measurement and valuation of the drugs was not disputed by the defence *Forensic/ Institutional*

40 Crucial value of the jail phone tapes and conclusion on reasonable doubt *Forensic/ Institutional*

41 Circumstantial evidence re MS' vacation clothes *Forensic*

42 Circumstantial: MS' differential demeanour and language at the airport and in jail *Forensic*

43 Deixis: Neither MS nor Detective present at opening of the cases for identification *Forensic*

44 Bonding joke: A misidentifies marijuana as heroin *Interactional*

45 Possession for the purpose of transportation: the airport's function for MS *Forensic/ Institutional*

46 HH's plea-bargain and MS' bail as irrelevant considerations I *Institutional*

47 MS and HH's relative status in the drugs organisation; also irrelevant *Institutional*

48 MS' bail and HH's plea deal irrelevant to the decision II *Institutional*

49 HH's credibility problem obviated by the taped evidence *Forensic*

50 MS' demeanour in jail *Forensic*

51 Defence tactics re the jail tapes: impact of the conditions in the Horseshoe Jail *Institutional/Forensic*

52 Prosecution response to defence tactics *Institutional*

53 More on the defence tactics *Institutional*

54 Newspaper article on conditions at the Horseshoe *Forensic*

55 Decision to vote on the verdict *Institutional/Interactional*

56 *VP* on deliberation and the television recording *Interactional/Institutional*

57 The vote *Institutional*

58 Formalities with the Counts *Institutional*

59 *VP* on her professional analogy with the foreperson's role *Interactional/Institutional*

60 Formalities continue *Institutional* [The Bailiff]

61 Prosecution tactics re the taped jail phone calls *Institutional* [Shredding jury notes]

62 HH's character and the value of the tapes *Forensic*

63 MS' role and demeanour in court *Forensic*

64 More on defence tactics regarding the jail *Institutional*

65 More on bail and plea deals for MS and HH *Institutional*

66 Circumstantial: MS' call to warn 'you know who' *Forensic*

67 More on HH's situation and demeanour *Forensic* [The Bailiff re-enters [9.53.53]

Segments are characterised by slightly more than one type of discourse in each segment (1.2). Forensic language forms almost half of the discourse used in this deliberation (41: 83: 49%), followed by Institutional language (34: 83: 41%). In this jury where relations were patently good and dissent absent, Interactional language was marginal at 10% (8: 83), apart from the omitted discussion of tape management. The term 'forensic' requires amplification as it is mainly forensic language of a specific type, 'deixis', that is the specific location of phenomena in space and time, such as where bags were at a given time, when they were opened, by whom, and what each contained. One sees this first in Segment 3 immediately after the jury have given epistemological priority to technically recorded live evidence. Further examples are to be found in Segments 10, 11, 19, 24, 27 and 28.

Participation Analysis

The jury institution, based on a notion of consensual representativeness in the USA, assumes approximate equality of access to deliberation. At its highest that might mean something close to actual equality of participation; at its lowest it might mean that nobody is excluded, their contributions denigrated, or that they are 'shut up'. That in turn imposes an expectation on jurors and their chosen foreperson. This expectation does not chime well with reality as there are quite large differentials in participation. However, that should not lead to adverse conclusions. First, there are personal differences, including topic interest – unless they lead to 'overparticipation' (possibly Alfred, a dissenter in the preceding hung jury); second, there was no evidence that the lower expectation was breached in either deliberation by any form of exclusion.

As the counting shows, Donald contributed significantly less than his colleagues, as did the Afro-American Lemuel in the previous hung jury; however, it can be argued that both these jurors had a non-deliberative approach to the verdict process and which prioritised the individual's committed vote. In neither jury was there a 'straw poll' taken at the outset, so the risks of foreclosing discussion through the formation of factions was much reduced. That said, three jurors appear as 'leaders' here, including the foreperson.

Total Input (including single syllable insertions): *Significant contributions* (1/+ lines):

109 *VP*	in 47 segments	70%	18 June, Peter
109 June	in 46 segments	69%	16 *VP*
103 Peter	in 44 segments	66%	11 Dick
87 Alberta	in 40 segments	55%	10 Alberta
66 Dick	in 28 segments	42%	8 Zoldan
64 Tom	in 32 segments	48%	6 Tom
44 Zoldan	in 28 segments	42%	/ Donald
14 Donald	in 8 segments	12%	

Evaluating Evidence by Reference to Juror Experience

One of the supposed values of the jury process is that it allows for 'common sense' to operate through the variegated experiences of a wide range of people, who can apply their personal knowledge of the world through applying personal experience to the evidence they have heard in courtroom testimony. There were a number of such instances in this deliberation, set out here. They cover mundane but relevant issues: the value of money and its availability as cash; degrees of knowledge of an acquaintance over time; the triviality or seriousness of unpaid road traffic fines; and how one would react to sudden imprisonment. These evaluative comments are restricted to a minority of the jury:

> Zoldan and Alberta **[20]** on unemployment and the cost of air travel; Vanessa the forewoman **[20]** on acquaintance and knowledge of a person's job, family and habits, **[28]** on Margherita's overreaction to her unpaid traffic tickets, and **[47]** with Zoldan and Alberta on typical readily available capital; and Alberta and Zoldan **[51]** on the typical reaction of an innocent person to sudden imprisonment.

Circumstantial Evidence in Considering Margherita

There was a body of circumstantial evidence, entirely negative, relating to Margherita. This was all noted by the jury but does not seem to have played any active role in their eventual verdict, which turned entirely on the forensic issue of whether there could have been any external source for her knowledge of the types of drugs seized and their exact weights:

1) **17**: The recipient of MS' phone call from the jail was already alert to her problem.

2) **20**: Peter and Vanessa on the fact that she'd already made a previous trip and brought a relatively large sum of money back.

3) **20**: Zoldan and Alberta on the probability of an unemployed person affording to buy one-way tickets to New York on a weekly basis.

4) **20**: Peter and June on the cost effectiveness of buying 600 dollar tickets to return unsold shirts to New York.

5) **21**: Alberta and June on how often might someone unknowingly be used as a mule in the context of someone asking them to take a package for them to New York and with an assumed name when it is not the practice of airports to check for traffic warrants.

6) **27**: MS did not use a false name on her trip to New York the previous week despite having the traffic warrants already outstanding against her.

7) **29**: Vanessa, June, Peter, and Zoldan on MS' previous knowledge of her lawyer and of prisons.

8) **41**: Zoldan and June on taking soiled clothes on vacation.

9) **42**: Alberta and June on the very marked contrast between MS' deportment and language when she was talking to the detective and when she was talking on the jail phone. (Also Segments **50**, ***63, 67.***)

10) ***66***: Peter on MS' trying to protect 'you know who', 'call you know who for God's sake let him know right away what's happened have him get me out of here'.

It is clear that these points would have been relevant considerations against reasonable doubt in the absence of the forensic determination that occurred, or if the evidence of Hermanno against Margherita had had to be seriously evaluated. It is suggested that its cumulative and unidirectional nature would have been important, though not necessarily decisive.

With the convicting jury the body of circumstantial evidence had another value, as corroboration of their consensus that there was no reasonable doubt because of their forensic conclusion.

Lay People and Legal Considerations

After complying with its obligation to appoint a foreperson (Segment 1) this jury's starting point was evidential and technical, but its legal role as fact-finder was established early (Segment 4).

This jury also raised a legal issue on evidence at the outset through a question to the court, but they eventually decided, correctly, that the court could not provide help on this point (Segments 32, 34). The jury maintained a clear distinction between direct and circumstantial evidence (from Segment 23). The circumstantial evidence has already been considered above.

One juror did refer to the Burden of Proof (Segment 52). One juror ineffectively described its role between prosecution and defence (Segment 26), but the jury had no difficulty in practising the balance required – indeed it produced an original mode of decision process, the 'Devil's Advocate' (Segments 24, 25 and 26), which by confronting the preliminary decision to convict (Segment 18) by thus operationalising the reasonable doubt requirement, eventually produced more cogently developed and expressed reasons for such conviction, leading to a second conclusion (Segments 43-45) and a postponed vote (Segments 55, 57, 58, 60). The Standard of Proof was certainly considered relevant and was operated: (Segments 24, 40, and 44).

The jurors made a decision, correctly, that the defendant's bail status and status relative to a separately processed defendant were irrelevant considerations (Segments 47-48); the Standard of Proof was considered particularly relevant to this other person's credibility as witness against the defendant, without and with the tape recorded evidence (Segments 49, 50 and *62*).

The eventual verdict may appear a little rough-hewn (there was, for example, no consideration given to a secret ballot) but given the defence concessions in the case (on the weights and types of drugs; and the *res ipsa loquitur* of transportation for sale) and the jury's concentrated focus on the one overriding issue, the court's own process obviated any short-circuiting by its detailed verdict form which had to be agreed to and then formally signed by the foreperson; also by the use of in-court polling of the individual jurors.

'The Beauty Contest': Evaluating Advocacy

Professional lawyers are aware of the potential for comment on their efforts on behalf of their clients in the privacy of the jury room. It is difficult to disentangle the evaluation of evidence from those leading it as much as from those giving it. There is also the potential for jury comment on courtroom tactics and their effectiveness. Both of these types of comment occurred in considering Margherita. The defence team were rated most often and awarded least value, but it was conceded that they had a weak case to defend in the first place. The jurors did not know that the prosecution had, in the light of their experience of the earlier hung jury, changed their timing of presentation of the jail phone call tapes to the very end of their case, but the jurors did notice that timing. This aspect of deliberation was widespread, prominent and involved much participation:

> **23**: June, Tom and Peter; **26**: June; **46**: Peter; **48**: Tom, Peter; **50**: Peter; **51**: June, Donald, Peter, Zoldan and Dick; **53**: Dick, Peter and Zoldan; **54**: Vanessa; **60**: June; **61**: June, Tom, Zoldan, Vanessa and Alberta; ***63***: Peter, Alberta and Julie; ***64***: Alberta, Tom, June, Zoldan, Vanessa and Peter; ***65***: Peter; and ***67***: June.

Reactivity and the Structure of the Deliberation

The jury reached a preliminary conclusion quickly in Segment 18, but they did not vote until segments 57-60. This is partly because that preliminary conclusion itself invited further discussion, but also because of the resort to the mode of 'Devil's Advocacy' from Segment 25 as a means of operationalising an autosceptical and more rigorous use of the Standard of Proof as reasonable doubt.

This led to a series of conclusionary stages, each more supported by evidence than its predecessors: Segments 37, 40, 43 and 55. None of these contradict the original conclusion but they are cumulatively better crafted, in that the jurors are more convinced. There is also some additional deliberation after the vote. So this jury could in theory have called in the Bailiff at Segment 18, and nothing that occurred later would in fact have shifted that early verdict. There is a possible explanation for this. It lies in the foreperson's single line in Segment 56:

> [PAUSE] ***VP***: are we all discussing this because we're on. (looks at camera and giggles) [PAUSE].

It is arguable that this jury might, absent the camera and a potential television audience, have voted and packed its bags at Segment 18, not causing any substantive injustice, but leaving many 'I's undotted and 'T's uncrossed. Defendants have a right to due process and that includes due deliberation by juries; in this instance if anything the reactivity enhanced the quality of justice. Further instances could be given from Margherita's first hung jury, relating in particular to one dissenter who during deliberation stated that a point must be made 'just for the record' (Transcript page 33 line 16); in other words he was not just conscious of the camera, it affected his behaviour. His first contribution was (Tr.1.16):

> 'otherwise you have a hung jury'.

Coda: a Paranarrative on 'Margherita Serrano'.

The deliberation analysed here comprises an essential, but normally hidden, part of 'the story of the trial' in the case of *People of Arizona v 'Margherita Serranno'*, in which certain previous events comprise the 'story in the trial', which the jury have to construct and evaluate.[32] There has been previous work on narrative in the jury trial.[33] Here I focus on the 'layering' of narrative.[34]

---

32 B.S. Jackson, *Making Sense in Law: Linguistic, Psychological and Semiotic Perspectives* (Liverpool: Deborah Charles Publications, 1996) chs 11-12.

33 Notably by W.L. Bennett and M.S. Feldman, *Reconstructing Reality in the Courtroom* (London: Tavistock Publications, 1981).

34 To be found in P. Robertshaw, *Summary Justice – Judges Address Juries* (London: Cassell, 1998) pp. 8-10.

My own application of layering is to be found in the analysis of an English Court of Appeal case *Spencer (John)*.[35] In that case there were for this purpose four narrative elements (I-IV) which both favoured and threatened the defendant. The analysis considered the role of subtraction, for example of element II which would (given element I) increase the probabilty of conviction; and of addition, for example of a new (and real) item V, which would (given item IV) decrease that threat.

Re-sequencing could also have significant impacts on credibility; for example, in *Margherita Serranno* the prosecution in the retrial held back the playing of the recordings of Margherita's jail phone calls until the end of their presentation. In the case of *Margherita Serranno* the paranarrative to be made does not impact on the verdict, but goes beyond 'the story in the trial' whilst incorporating all its elements. It does however give focus to one specific element in that story. For this purpose the mythos[36] can be divided into four temporal segments:

> I Preparatory: events before arriving at Phoenix airport;
>
> II Dysfunction: at the airport before police contact;
>
> III Police contact: process, reasonable suspicion and arrest;
>
> IV Contrastive: MS' behaviour in the holding jail that day.

The focus in the paranarrative is on II and III. Here are brief versions of II and III:

> MS and HH arrived at Phoenix airport. They waited with their bags at the kerbside and missed several flights. Eventually HH went in to buy the tickets for New York, using false names. Their behaviour drew the attention of 'Skycaps', the airport porters, who are trained to watch for suspicious behaviour, and who reported the couple to the airport police unit. The couple were approached by police who asked for interviews. The form of the interview was the informal 'freetalk' without caution since it is not used for arrest purposes. This took place in the public waiting area. The bags were kept together with MS. When the policewoman had developed reasonable suspicion from MS' conversation with her, she called for a 'sniffer' dog. Such dogs are trained to respond to the presence of a variety of prohibited drugs. The dog reacted positively to the bags which were not opened. After this MS and HH were given *Miranda* cautions and arrested on drug trafficking charges...

The paranarrative coincides in time with the segments just described, but transects them:

> In the airport carpark an 'Enrico' waits. He cannot move until MS and HH have caught the attention of Skycaps. It is only when they have informed the police, who only react to such prompting or to advance intelligence. This reporting led to police intervention. With the taking of MS and HH into the interior space of the airport, Enrico considered

35 *The Times*, 13 July 1994.

36 P. Robertshaw, *Summary Justice*, op. cit., pp. 7-10, 55-59, 74-76.

himself activated. When he has ascertained that all the bags are positioned with MS and the Detective for the freetalk he can prepare to move. That move is again predicated on the known procedures for the policing of narcotics at this site. Eventually the woman Detective calls in the sniffer dog. When it arrives at the bags next to M, he passes through the entrance as far as possible from the dog. With a briefcase containing, say, eight kilograms of cocaine, he proceeds immediately to departure. Two assumptions are now added: first, that there were no other sniffer dogs available. Second, that in 1995 there were no X-ray machines to scan passengers' hand luggage.

In this paranarative the core element is the transformation of apparent dysfunctionality into planned rational action in which a criminal organisation used its knowledge of the pragmatics and imperatives of policing to achieve a larger goal at the cost of a 'loss-leader': the value of eight kilos of cocaine is massively more than 128 pounds of marijuana. It is also possible that the single kilo of cocaine in one of the bags was discountable as being the personal property of Margherita. Also, her information gathered during the freetalk would be valuable to the organisation: that the sniffer dogs were trained to detect an array of drugs.

In the paranarrative one can construct a complex metaphoric characterisation for Margherita, in contrast with Hermanno, whose role and status is confined to 'Mule' as he was merely the 'mark' of the organisation for this particular transaction. Margherita certainly shares that metaphor, but is an insider with contacts and information, so she is additionally a 'Moll'. This can be evidenced by the impact on her legal status within hours of her transfer to the Horseshoe holding jail: money was provided from her contacts for bail with the consequent nine months of pretrial liberty denied to Hermanno.

There is a further point of significance which can demonstrate an elision between Moll and an expendable 'Doll' metaphor. This relates to one of the points of difference between the majority and the dissentient Jim in the first hung jury. Jim had contended that there had been a breach of the constitutional equal treatment entitlement in that the police had negotiated at length to produce an eventual plea agreement with Hermanno, whilst his co-trafficker Margherita never had such an opportunity. The majority took the view that such matters were irrelevant to their task. In this paranarrative that differential in treatment has a different explanation, not rooted in police custom and practice, but in the trafficking organisation's imperatives. It is trite that felony process in the USA is awash with 'plea-bargaining' of various kinds; without it the court system would drown. So to *not* bargain requires explanation.

In Margherita's case her organisation would not have been willing to allow her to enter into such negotiations, which although primarily concerned with docket cleansing, also have an important function in extracting information and intelligence. It would have been risky to the organisation to allow Margherita to come forward, with or without legal representation, to engage in such trading. Police interrogation on the 'irrationality' of her and Hermanno's behaviour might have led the police to discover the possiblity of the paranarrative. That was a risk to be avoided completely as it might have prejudiced future use of such a stratagem as may have occurred in this paranarrative.

Chapter 11

'Let Me See Your Hands': The Grammar of Physical Control in Police Directives

Phillip C. H. Shon

Introduction

The police are the most visible and accessible gatekeepers of the justice system; as such, they largely determine the relative quantity and quality of law that is applied to the public.[1] To that end, they are conferred the awesome capacity to 'coerce others to refrain from using illegitimate coercion'.[2] It is this capacity to exercise brute force that fundamentally differentiates the police from the public;[3] and while the banal task of peacekeeping constitutes the warp and woof of modern policing, it is not immune from the uncertainty and violence that permeates the quotidian affairs of the police.[4]

If the relationship between the police and the public is inherently asymmetrical, then recent shifts in the philosophy of policing have diminished this theoretical obliquity between the police and the public by conceptualizing them as partners and collaborators in the fight against crime and disorder.[5] The community-oriented model of policing has embraced and presupposed the principle of egalitarianism in its mission and mandate, thus proactively attempting to lessen the schism between the police and the public through a recontextualization of their footing in the community.[6] Such a move has been hailed by researchers, practitioners, and citizens alike, with community policing being proclaimed as the embodiment of democratic policing in the midst of pluralism.[7]

The principle of equality assumed in recent shifts in the policing paradigm, however, encounters an inconsistency given the coercive capacity of the police; aside from soldiering during times of war, no occupation encodes the threat to life and

1 Black, forthcoming; Bankowski and Mungham, 1976.
2 Muir, 1977: 44.
3 Bittner, 1978.
4 Meehan, 1992.
5 Meares and Kahan, 1999.
6 Skogan, 2004.
7 Roth et al., 2004.

limb as a matter of ideology.[8] Thus, as much as the rhetoric of community policing tinctures the organizational mission and prevailing ideology of the police, the fundamentally paradoxical capacity of the police to 'hurt and kill' the purveyors of their authority and clients of their service gives flesh and bone to their occupational identities.[9]

Police officers, ideologically and practically, have a justifiable reason to be concerned about their safety: between 1976 and 1998, 1,820 officers were killed in the line of duty; conversely, 8,578 felons – persons at the time of the shooting who were, or thought to be, involved in a violent crime – were killed by the police in the same period.[10] Police shootings of felons comprise a small fraction of the overall homicides in the US, but when young African-American males are killed by the police in disproportionate rates, accusations of police misconduct and racial bias inevitably appear;[11] such conspiratorial sentiments of minority citizens are reinforced when suspected felons who are killed are later found not to be felons at all – and unarmed. These facts have recently been highlighted in the well-publicized shootings of unarmed citizens such as Latanya Haggerty, Timothy Thomas, and Amadou Diallo.

On 4 June 1999 two Chicago police officers initiated a traffic stop of an Oldsmobile driven by Raymond Smith, with Latanya Haggerty in the passenger side. When Smith finally pulled the car over, officers forcibly removed him from the car. Officer Daniels had her service weapon aimed at Haggerty, and ordered her to show her hands and step out of the car. Officers and witnesses stated that Officer Daniels and other officers made repeated commands for her to exit the vehicle and to show her hands. Haggerty continued to hold a cellular phone in her left hand; Officer Daniels, mistaking the cell phone for a weapon, shot and killed Latanya Haggerty.[12]

Timothy Thomas – wanted for outstanding traffic warrants – was spotted by an off-duty Cincinnati police officer who was working a security detail at a bar during the summer of 2001. He radioed for assistance as he began a foot pursuit. Officer Roach joined the foot pursuit and was the first to encounter Thomas. Witnesses state that they saw Thomas running with his hands in his pockets or as if he were pulling up his baggy pants. Officer Roach stated that he feared for his safety since he had no way of verifying what was in Thomas's hands.[13] Officer Roach fatally shot Thomas.

Amadou Diallo was standing in the vestibule of his apartment on the night of 4 February 1999 when four New York City police officers asked if they could talk to him. They were looking for a serial rapist who was believed to be carrying a gun. Officer Carroll stated that instead of stopping and obliging the officers' request to

8 See Walzer, 1988.

9 Terrill et al., 2003.

10 Brown and Langan, 2001.

11 Brown and Langan, 2001.

12 Lighty, 1999.

13 Larson, 2004.

speak with him, Diallo walked backward in the entry way of his apartment and reached into his back pocket. Officer McMellon observed Diallo's hands in his pocket and asked, 'What are you doing? What are you doing?' He ordered Diallo to show his hands: 'Police, show me your hands, show me your hands.'[14] Officer Carroll stated that he saw Diallo pull out a black object that he thought was a gun; he also believed that Diallo had pulled a gun on his partner, Officer McMellon. The four officers fired a total of 41 bullets at Amadou Diallo. The gun turned out to be a wallet.

These highly publicized cases have catapulted to the social forefront issues such as police brutality and misconduct, constitutionality and legality of intrusive policing tactics such as 'stop and frisks,' and racial profiling.[15] Shootings such as the aforementioned overburden an already strained relationship between the police and minority communities. Police shootings of (suspected) felons, however, are part of a much broader scope of police-citizen (henceforth, P-C) encounters. For instance in 1996, those who were 12 years and older had an estimated 45 million contacts with the police; in about a third, the encounters were initiated by the police.[16] Out of the millions of contacts between the police and the public, how do P-C encounters such as the Diallo, Haggerty, and Thomas cases culminate with the death of unarmed citizens? How are such encounters interactionally organized and unfold? How do the police manage to control citizens who might be threatening them? Do the police shoot citizens in a tyrannical, authoritative, and criminal manner as some allege or is there a distinct pattern and order in the way such encounters are sequentially and discursively organized?

In this chapter, I will use directives – speech act that is intended to influence the actions of another – such as requests, orders, and commands to see suspects' and citizens' hands that police officers routinely issue during their encounters as the main units of analysis. I will argue that the directionality of hands (vertical, inspectable, controllable) of suspects and citizens is a symbolic indicator of officers' perceptions of threat to their safety, and that they are grammatically, structurally, and prosodically encoded in the opening sequences of P-C encounters. Put another way, this chapter examines the contextual and sequential environment in which such directives of physical control are made. As I will show, even institutional talk can be further differentiated from ordinary talk and other bureaucratic communication, depending on the officers' perceptions of threat to safety. To lay the foundation for such a project, I will need to do three things: 1) show how language use during bureaucratic interactions is different from natural talk; 2) discuss the structural and conversational differences between talk in P-C encounters and other institutions; 3) demonstrate how language is used during P-C encounters.

14 Associated Press, 2000.

15 Spitzer, 1999.

16 Greenfeld et al., 1997.

The Institutionality of Talk

Institutional talk is the derivative of natural talk: deviation from the ordinary conversational format marks the character of institutional talk.[17] Consequently, turn taking, turn order, turn allocation, and topic selection are not 'locally' managed but already built into the conversational structure of the encounter itself.[18] Using the opening sequences of traffic stops, I want to note here some salient differences between talk in P-C encounters and ordinary conversations and calls to emergency services, since the way P-C encounters are opened is configured into the context in which utterances such as 'let me see your hands' are made.

The seminal work on opening sequences in ordinary conversations has been in the area of telephone calls. Openings are marked by five 'core' sequences: The ringing of the telephone constitutes 1) a summons, beckoning the called party to answer. 2) The identification/recognition sequence is concerned with establishing the identity of the called party; this is accomplished through 3) the greeting sequence where 'each party asserts or claims recognition of the other.'[19] And it is after 4) the 'how are yous' that the reason for the call is introduced. That burden – 5) introducing the first topic – 'canonically' belongs to the caller.[20]

A key point of difference between openings in ordinary telephone conversations and institutional interactions such as emergency calls for assistance is the reduction of opening sequences: 'reduction plays an important role in achieving an institutionally constrained focus to the talk, for it routinely locates the first topic slot to the callers in their first turn, which is the second turn of the call.'[21] In emergency calls to 911, the task of self-identification falls to the institution, and it is 'categorical.' Whereas in ordinary talk, the topic can be introduced by the caller or the called party through preemptive moves, Zimmerman finds that the caller's first turn is the environment where topics are initiated.[22] Having reviewed the ways ordinary conversations and an institution related to law enforcement are opened, how are P-C encounters similar and different?

The work that police do begins in two ways: citizens contact the police through 911 emergency centers, and the request for assistance is symbolically encoded into organizationally relevant codes and dispatched to the police.[23] In the prototypical P-C encounter, the traffic stop, the police initiate the encounter – 'summoning another to interact' – by activating their flashing lights, sirens, and horns. And just as callers to emergency centers initiate contact 'to get assistance for troubles they have witnessed or experienced'[24] the police, much like callers to emergency centers,

17 Drew and Heritage, 1992.
18 Psathas, 1995.
19 Schegloff, 1968: 129.
20 Schegloff, 1968.
21 Whalen and Zimmerman, 1987: 175.
22 Zimmerman, 1992.
23 Manning, 1988.
24 Zimmerman, 1992: 418.

initiate contact with motorists concerning a particular 'problematic' relevancy. Consider the following opening sequences from a traffic stop in which motorists have been pulled over for speeding:

Excerpt 1 (Midwestern City: Traffic Stop #2)

8	→	PO:	How you doin >see your driver's license
9			en proof of insurance?<
10			(.7)
11		D:	I got it in my jacket can I get it?

Excerpt 2 (Midwestern City: Traffic Stop #3)

12	→	PO:	How you doin >can I see your driver's license
13			And proof of insurance?<
14			(.5)
15		D:	Sure

Excerpt 3 (Midwestern City: Traffic Stop #6)

3	→	PO:	How you [doin may I see your driver's license and=
4		D:	[Hi
5		PO:	= proof of insurance?
6			Do you have your insurance card?
7		D:	( )

Excerpt 4 (Midwestern City: Traffic Stop #5)

3	→	PO:	How you doin may I see your driver's
4			license and proof of insurance?
5			(.7)
6		D:	Hi

If activation of sirens, flashing lights, and horns constitutes a 'summons,' then the answering of that summons is the act of pulling over. Thus, traffic stops begin with a 'pre-beginning' where the officer activates the squad's lights; but there is no categorical self-introduction. The 'request' to see a driver's license is the officer's first verbal utterance. That is because in traffic stops the summons/answer sequence and identification/recognition sequence are reduced to one. By virtue of their uniforms, patrol cars, and other 'occupational accouterments' the task of verbal self-introduction and categorical-identification are not necessary since they are conveyed through their institutional identity.[25]

There are two distinct types of utterances that are interwoven into the officer's first turn, greetings and requests. The latter speech act is procedurally related to the

---

25 Niederhoffer, 1967.

bureaucratic action at hand, and gives the talk between the police and the public one of its institutional characters.[26] The first turns in excerpt 1-4 are articulated with little pause between the two speech acts. How that compressed first turn is understood by the motorists varies, for some orient to the prior turn as a request, some as a greeting. Those who respond to the 'How you doing may I see your driver's license and proof of insurance' with a 'sure' – request granting – are treating the [greeting + request] as a request, the sequentially preferred next turn response.[27] That some citizens respond to the [greeting + request] with a 'hi' demonstrates the way motorists orient to the social aspects of the encounter, not its institutionality, thus revealing some motorists' preference organization toward a non-institutionalized format of talk.

Greetings, as an activity that mutually ratifies and lubricates the social engine, come to be through a particular manner of police articulation, and only through the motorists' understanding of the officer's intention in a particular way, and their display of that understanding in the turn after the initial request. Having stated the way ordinary traffic stops are conversationally opened, I will present the data used in this chapter, as well as its method of analysis; next, I will examine the sequential contexts in which utterances such as 'let me see your hands' are made and how they are interactionally different from openings in routine P-C encounters.

Data and Method

As data, I use 30 P-C encounters as they appeared on *COPS*. As the first of its kind to blend entertainment and reality, *COPS* purports to show what policing is really like; that realistic bite is achieved through the presence of a cameraperson who accompanies ordinary officers throughout their patrol shift and faithfully records their actions and words. However, a justifiable criticism that could be raised regarding the use of such data is that it is edited – not 'natural' data.

Using a tape-recorded, 'live' view of P-C encounters and using the verbal accounts that police officers and citizens give for data allows researchers to examine the mundane aspects of police work in situ, as it emerges and unfolds, on a moment to moment basis.[28] And by examining how police officers and citizens talk to one another, we can gain insight into how those encounters are socially (discursively) organized, interactionally emergent, and how the social order of P-C encounter is produced, made orderly and relevant by all of the participants.[29] In other words, using the actual words that participants utter allows researchers to examine the mutually and collaboratively accomplished nature of P-C encounters.

Researchers who have studied *COPS* assert that there is little that is 'real' about the reality-based TV program; that the show emphasizes the bizarre and sensational

26 See Schegloff, 1992.
27 Atkinson and Heritage, 1984.
28 Heath and Luff, 2000.
29 Maynard and Clayman, 1991.

over the typical and ordinary.[30] It has also been argued that reality-based TV programs about crime 'cultivate' or shape how the viewers see the real world portrayed in the program.[31] Oliver posits that the show presents a skewed view of police work, one that is biased toward order, crime, and justice, that the police on *COPS* are highly authoritarian.[32] The viewers who see reality shows like *COPS* and similar programs are likely to believe that crime is rampant, report higher levels of fear, and thus push for tougher crime policy legislation.[33]

There are other conversation analysts who study discourse as it appears on television: 'Their [reporters] work practices are commonly broadcast "live" without the benefit of editorial review, and are thus open to the immediate scrutiny of fellow journalists, government officials, social scientists, and a mass audience ... accordingly, news interviewers continually face the problem of sustaining the accountability of their conduct under widespread scrutiny.'[34] The problem of editing, as it relates to this study, is precisely that. *COPS* is editorially reviewed, cut, and sliced as the editor desires, and it is not open to immediate scrutiny. Hence, this study is similar to other works in that the source of the data originates from a common medium (television), but the editing process and the product's immediate unavailability differentiates this data from other television programs that are used for data.

The 30 P-C encounters that appeared on *COPS* were recorded on video and audiotapes. All of the recorded P-C encounters were transcribed. These are noted as '*COPS* data.' They are followed by a topical phrase that provides an identifiable reference to the encounter that is being analyzed and discussed (for example, *COPS* data: Jimmy Dean Sausage). The police verbally directed citizens to display their hands in 19 out of 30 encounters. In some of the episodes, only one officer made the request to see a citizen/suspect's hands once; in others, several officers made repeated commands. In all, there were 49 distinct independent clausal level utterances (for example, Hands! Let me see your hands). For this chapter, I have selected excerpts that best illustrate these types of directives. I will discuss one particular incident (*COPS* data: Am I resisting?) in depth to demonstrate how encounters like that might be used to learn about encounters like Diallo, Haggerty, and Thomas. In addition, I will also use ten actual P-C encounters, mainly traffic stops. These stops were recorded using an audio recorder, and made available to me for secondary analysis by Officer 'Harry' of Midwestern City Police; they are referred to as (City + traffic stop #). I will use this data to contrast 'routine' assignments from 'dangerous' ones – ones which the police are more likely to view as a threat to their safety.

30 Kooistra et al., 1998.

31 Oliver and Armstrong, 1995.

32 Oliver, 1996.

33 Dobash et al., 1998.

34 Clayman, 1992: 163-164.

Safe Hands

The Sequential Environment of 'Vertical' Hands

Some P-C encounters (for example, felony stops) are symbolically encoded with danger before the police actually make contact with the participants – because, as the name suggests, the citizens involved are thought to be armed and dangerous. Consequently, they are conducted differently from ordinary traffic stops (for example, traffic violations). In these encounters, officers direct the occupants out of the car by issuing directives in a 'command' voice.

Directives can generally be classified according to the degree of force that is embedded within them, and the amount of social control the speaker wishes to exert over another speaker.[35] Thus, need imperatives (for example, I need to see your hands) and imperatives (for example, let me see your hands) constitute one of the most forceful ways to get a citizen to act, while imbedded imperatives (for example, could I see your hands?) and permission directives (for example, would it possible to take a look at your hands?) constitute weaker ways to get citizens to comply with their directives. In a similar way, the most forceful directives the police issue are phonetically and syntactically authoritative. Thus, commands are greater in volume than a normal conversational tone, and usually don the cloak of an imperative.[36]

Once the occupants are removed from the vehicle during felony stops, officers instruct them to prostrate on the ground, thereby rendering them controllable and less of a threat. In cases where the motorist is uncooperative, the police approach the car with their guns drawn and pointed. All throughout these scenarios officers demand that hands be visible. Hand visibility is a particular concern for those suspects whose moral character, as evidenced by the seriousness of the alleged crime (felony), implies a potential threat to officers' safety.

Consider the following data from a traffic stop. In the following excerpt, officers run the license plate number of a 'suspicious looking car' and it comes back stolen. Consequently, officers initiate a felony traffic stop:

Excerpt 5 (*COPS* data: 'Driving a baby and drinking a beer')

001		PO1:	STEP OUT OF THE CAR (1.6)
002			GET OUT OF THE CAR=
003	→	PO2:	=FEMALE PUT YOUR HANDS UP (2.2)
004	→		FEMALE PUT YOUR HANDS IN THE [AIR
005		MD:	[I
006			got a baby in the [car please
007		PO1:	[WALK TOWARDS ME

---

35 Ervin-Tripp, 1976: 29.

36 Ervin-Tripp, 1976.

The differences in the social organization of talk between ordinary traffic stops (potential threat to safety) and felony traffic stops (symbolically encoded threat to safety) can be preliminarily observed in excerpt 5. In excerpt 5, the officers order the occupants out of the car in a louder than normal ('command') voice, even the female passenger who is holding a baby on her lap. After they are ordered to exit the vehicle, officer #2 commands the woman to raise her hands vertically.

There are three notable points about excerpt 5. First, the officer's first turn at talk is opened with an imperative (lines 1-2) rather than an interrogative (that is, request). That is, he does not request, thus withdrawing the sequential opportunity to shape the trajectory of the interaction from the motorist, but tells the motorist to do something (lines 1-4); he syntactically exerts control over the opening moment and the uncertainty of the encounter by encapsulating his directives in the most grammatically forceful way of verbally controlling another speaker.

Second, the officer's first turn is organized toward a preference for action rather than talk; that is, the officer's opening turn projects – demands – physical compliance rather than verbal action as the conditionally relevant next turn response. Third, the male disputant (MD), rather than conforming to the action projected in the preceding turn, attempts to provide an account (lines 5-6) – an activity that is dispreferred from the action projected in the preceding turn. As a result, PO#1 barks out another command (line 7). Thus, in addition to grammar, turn type organization, and the tone and volume of the speaker's voice, this encounter is sequentially organized in a way that is markedly different from a routine traffic stop.

In the next excerpt, officers again encounter a stolen car. The primary officer observes the occupants of the car eating inside a restaurant; in order to prevent the situation from escalating to something more serious (for example, hostage/barricade), he waits until all of the occupants walk out of the restaurant and walk toward the stolen car:

Excerpt 6 (*COPS* data: 'Garden district')

001	→	PO1:	HANDS IN THE AIR
002			GET DOWN ON THE GROUND
003			GET DOWN ON THE GROUND
004			GET DOWN ON THE GROUND
005			DOWN Spread your hands out
006			spread it out put your hands behind your back
007			Allright fellas

The officer's first turn at talk is again opened with an imperative to vertically raise the occupants' hands. Much like excerpt 5, such commands are articulated with louder than normal volume. Moreover, the imperative 'opens' the encounter with the public, thus marking its deviation from the natural conversation format of ordinary P-C encounters.

Not all P-C encounters are on the same order as 'emergencies.' Hence, in felony traffic stops, where the citizens/suspects are semiotically encoded as a threat to safety, no greeting should take place. In excerpts 5 and 6, officers do not greet the motorist then issue the directive to raise hands into the air; commanding them to raise their hands vertically is the utterance that initializes the interaction and mobilizes a sequence of related directives.

In the following excerpt, an officer is dispatched to assist other officers who are investigating a man in a garage who is under the influence of narcotics:

Excerpt 7 (*COPS* data: 'Am I resisting?')

12		PO1: what's goin on man? ((puts his hand on his service weapon))
13		(1.8)
14	→	put your hands up
15		(2.6)
16		MC: put my hands up?
17		(.4)
18	→	PO2: PUT THE KNIFE DOWN (.)
19		((both officers have their weapons drawn and pointed at the male citizen))
20	→	PO1: put the knife down man (.6) PUT THE KNIFE DOWN
21		(.7)
22		He's got a knife
23		(.8)
24	→	PO2: PUT IT DOWN
25		(.9)
26	→	PO1: PUT THE KNIFE DOWN (1.2) PUT THE KNIFE DOWN
27	→	((citizen drops the knife))
28		NOW GET DOWN ON YOUR KNEES
29		(1.0)
30		GET DOWN ON YOUR KNEES
31		(1.4)
32		PO2: GET DOWN ON YOUR KNEES
33		((MC reaches over and grabs his pants and puts them on))
34		PO1: GET DOWN ON YOUR KNEES watch it he's.
35		(3.7)
36		John, get down on your knees
37		(7.0)
38		He's got a crowbar right here too
39		(1.0)
40		get down on your knees
41		(.)
42		MC: yeah I'm fixing my grandmother's car right dere
43		((looks toward the camera))
44		sorry about that (.6) mess here guys
45		(.3)
46		PO2: John I want you to step back here away
47		from all that trash you're standing around
48		(.)
49		MC: Yessir

50 ((MC zips up his pants and puts his hands into his pocket))
51 → PO1: get your hands out of your pocket John
52 (.5)
53 MC: yes sir=
54 ((takes his hands out of his pocket))
55 PO2: =get on your knees (1.1) get on your knees
56 ((MC gets on his knees))
57 PO3: put your hands behind your head
58 (.5)
59 MC: yes sir
60 ((MC puts his hands behind his head))
61 PO1: (got him John?)
62 ((officer walks over and begins to cuff MC))
63 PO3: keep your hands apart
64 (.4)
65 MC: yes <u>sir</u>
66 (1.9)
67 PO2: put your fingers out
68 (4.0)
69 okay lean forward, lean forward forward lean forward get on your stomach
70 ((slight struggle ensues; PO1 comes and gets on top of MC))
71 MC: all yous gotta to do is say that
72 (2.1)
73 am I resisting arrest?=
74 PO2: =[no you're doing just fine so far
75 PO1: =[no no
76 ((officers handcuff the suspect))
77 PO2: okay (1.6) go ahead and turn over=
78 PO1: =(twelve thirty one code four one) in custody ((to dispatch))
79 PO2: (all right listen up now you ready?)
80 ((two officers lift MC from the ground))
81 PO2: Come on okay
82 (2.0)
83 PO1: (it's more open over here)
84 PO2: you can get through there
85 (.)
86 PO3: sure
87 → PO2: maybe you can tell me what's going on
88 (1.5)
89 → why are we here?

Officer #1 first opens the encounter in excerpt 7 with a 'greeting like' utterance in a normal tone of voice, much like the way ordinary traffic stops are opened; however, after he sees an unknown object in the citizen's (MC) hand (threat to safety), he immediately commands the subject to raise his hands vertically (line 14). In excerpt 7, the ordinariness of the call is transformed after one of the officers visually confirms a knife in the citizen's hand. The male lets 1.8 seconds (line 13) pass before verbally responding to the officer's opening WH interrogative in line 12, but that opportunity to respond in a pragmatically relevant way is lost after the officers observe a weapon in the subject's hands. As a result there is a switch in the utterance type, from an interrogative (line 12: 'what's going on?') to an imperative, and an audibly noticeable increase in volume (line 14: 'put your hands up'; lines 18, 20, 24, 26: 'PUT THE KNIFE DOWN'). In line 18, another officer enters the talk and issues an identical directive.

The subject (MC) has no sequential and temporal opportunity to respond to the initial interrogative (what's going on?) after the officers see the weapon (1.8 seconds), and start to issue safety related directives. Officer #2 asks a slightly different version of line 12 (what's goin on?) in line 89 ('why are we here?'), but it occurs after the suspect is finally cuffed, and in controllable custody – one minute and forty five seconds after the first interrogative (line 12). Officers take the next five turns to repeat the initial directive. Notice what happens when the subject attempts to 'repair' the mishearing/misunderstanding in the opening moments in line 16: he is authoritatively commanded to put the knife down (line 18).

Notice the progressive character of the safety related directives in excerpt 7. The officers tell the subject to: a) Put your hands up (line 14); b) Put the knife down (lines 18, 20, 24, 26); c) Get down on your knees (lines 28, 30, 32 35, 37, 41, 56); d) Step back away (line 47); e) Get your hands out of your pocket (line 52); f) Put your hands behind your head (line 58); g) Keep your hands apart (line 64); h) Put your fingers out (line 68); i) Lean forward (line 70); j) Get on your stomach (line 70); k) Turn over (line 78).

There are eleven distinct commands issued to the subject until he is handcuffed and in controllable custody. In all three excerpts 'put your hands up' is the first utterance in the sequence of such directives of physical control. When officers perceive the situation to be a potential threat to their safety 'put your hands up' is the first imperative that mobilizes a series of directives. In excerpt 7, two officers repeat the command to the subject to vertically raise his hands and to relinquish the weapon a total of seven times within the first five turns of the opening encounter. As excerpt 7 demonstrates, the encounter does not progress, that is move toward a natural conversational model, until directives such as 'let me see your hands,' or 'put your hands up' are obliged.

If officers prevent harm – or 'do' safety – by issuing such statements, notice how the citizen prevents harm to himself. Deputies order the subject to drop the knife, and when he hesitates and does not comply, that directive is repeated a total of six times by two different officers. The subject does not move forward toward the officers, nor does he raise the knife overhead, as if to attack; he merely holds it. There is a lapse of approximately eight seconds between the first command to drop the knife (line 18) and the last one (line 26), where the subject finally complies; the next directive (get down on your knees) is repeated a total of eight times before he finally complies. Then when the subject puts his hands into his pocket (line 50), he is swiftly told to remove his hands from his pockets (line 51), which he does (line 54).

When he is commanded to step back and put his hands behind his head, he replies with a crisp 'yes sir' – show deference by obeying the police.

The MC finally acquiesces to the directives of physical control (one minute forty five seconds later) despite their intrusive character – contorting and transforming his body into a pliable and manipulable object of corporeal and social control. Had the subject failed to relinquish the knife or had he moved forward with the weapon in hand, the encounter would have turned fatal. The subject in excerpt 7 does not die and lives another day because he obeys all of the eleven distinct directives the police issue.

Officers issue vertically directed commands to raise one's hands in the context of a P-C encounter to confirm that the subject is not a threat to their safety. When they verify that subjects no longer have weapons in their hands, officers do not issue such statements: there is a switch in turn type, from an imperative to an interrogative. Thus, the officer's turns in line 87 ('maybe you can tell me what's going on here?') and 89 ('why are we here?') resemble the initial opening moments of the call where the officer asks a WH interrogative (line 12: 'What'' going on man?'). The noteworthy point is that in between these two functionally identical utterances lie an army of commands and directives; only after the directives are obeyed, first to raise his hands and finally to turn over, does the communicatively oriented WH interrogative reemerge in the encounter.

Inspectable 'All Purpose' Hands

In domestic dispute calls, claims of injury are common. In such cases the police check both parties for signs of physical injury. On other occasions, police officers may run into persons holding something in their hands, and a request to see their hands could be 'for-all-practical-purposes.'[37] 'Inspectable' hands mean that the context in which a request to see one's hands is not yet determinative.

Consider the following data from an episode of *COPS*. Officers are dispatched to the scene of a domestic dispute. The host officer is told that the man involved in the dispute may be leaving the scene in a pickup truck. When the officer shows up, a woman runs up to him and tells him that the involved man is leaving the scene; the officer stops him and brings both parties together to find out what happened The following excerpt is the first context of rendering hand visibility relevant to the interaction. The officer has just separated both disputants, and he asks the man for a narrative.

Excerpt 8 (*COPS* data: 'Jimmy Dean Sausage')

60	MD	[bit me in the hand tore up my shoulders scratched me up
61	WD:	[I didn't scratch you up
62	PO:	[Okay maam I'll hear your side relax

37 Garfinkel, 1967.

63 →		Do you need rescue sir?
64	MD:	I don't know she [
65 →	PO:	[Let me see your hands
66	MD:	She's gonna bit me here put a hole in it
67		right theuh [( ) call yaw cuz nobody round
68	PO:	[three two four dispatch
69	MD:	here wanna let me use they phone right quick
70		I'm like 'this is crazy' you know how she just
71		jumped [on me got=
72	PO:	[ten four we've got a subject here with a
73		bite on his hands
74	MD:	I ain't gonna worry about it cuz I'm bleeding
75	PO:	Is there any weapons in your car sir?

The male disputant (MD) claims that his girlfriend bit him during the course of a physical confrontation; the female disputant (WD) states that he assaulted her – the paradigmatic he said/she said nature of a domestic argument.[38] It is after the MD informs the officer about a possible injury (line 60) that he asks if the man needs medical attention (line 63). The MD's claim about his injury has implications for what the officer does next. When the disputant gives an indefinite answer (line 64), the officer asks to see his hands.

In excerpt 8, the officer's 'let me see your hands' (line 65) is temporally and sequentially related to 'do you need rescue sir?'; that utterance (line 63) occurs before the request to see the hands (line 65), in a prior talk about needing medical attention. 'Let me see your hands' is used as a preliminary to a call for medical assistance.[39] And that the MD has understood 'let me see your hands' as a call for medical assistance is verifiable in his response: when the officer asks to see his hands, he does not put them up vertically, as if to show he is weapon-free, as in excerpts 5-7, but he holds it out in front of him – pronates – and shows the officer where the injury occurred. And after seeing the bite mark the officer radios for paramedics (line 72).

In excerpt 8, 'let me see your hands' is not used as a directive of physical control (that is, safety), for the way the participants have organized their turns around each other's shows no empirically verifiable way of substantiating the utterance as a concern for officer's safety. It is uttered for the purpose of verifying the man's side of the story, 'for all practical purposes'; and its usage is related to the context of medical assistance. The officer asks the MD to show his hands to assess the validity of his claim.

Now, consider the following data from a felony traffic stop in which that same utterance is used as a control directive. In this episode of *COPS*, detectives observe a woman who is speeding through red lights. The detectives request the presence of a squad car to initiate a traffic stop:

38 Goodwin, 1990.

39 Schegloff, 1980.

Excerpt 9 (*COPS* data: 'Mentally ill')

001	→	PO1:	LET ME SEE YOUR HANDS
002	→		LET ME SEE BOTH OF YOUR HANDS
003	→		STICK YOUR HANDS OUT THE WINDOW NOW
004	→		LET ME SEE YOUR HANDS
005			OUT THE VEHICLE OUT THE VEHICLE
006			GET OUT OF THE CAR
007			304 perps in custody
008		PO2:	Ma'am go head and put your hands behind your back

In this episode, after the reckless motorist finally pulls over, the uniformed officer walks up to the car with his weapon pointed at the motorist. And as he is walking up to the car, he screams 'let me see your hands'; that directive is the officer's first turn utterance. There is no prior context of talk, no prior talk about medical assistance or injuries. And 'stick your hands out the window' is physically similar to putting them in the air: in both utterances, the hands and its contents are observable to the officer. Visible hands give a peace of mind to officers because, during the time citizens' hands are in officers' plain view, citizens are not a threat;[40] furthermore, they serve other practical functions – medical assistance, checking the validity of a disputant's story – besides safety driven concerns.

Controllable Hands

Thus far, we have delineated the directionality of hands for two different purposes: as an exigent safety motivated utterance and as an all purposive one. In the following excerpts, notice how the directionality of hands and the sequential environment in which such statements are issued are interwoven into the temporal context of the encounter:

Excerpt 10 (*COPS* data: 'Garden district')

001		PO1:	HANDS IN THE AIR
002			GET DOWN ON THE GROUND
003			GET DOWN ON THE GROUND
004			GET DOWN ON THE GROUND
005			DOWN Spread your hands out
006	→		spread it out put your hands behind your back
007			Allright fellas

Excerpt 11 (*COPS* data: 'Mentally ill')

001		PO1:	LET ME SEE YOUR HANDS
002			LET ME SEE BOTH OF YOUR HANDS

40 Rubinstein, 1978.

003 STICK YOUR HANDS OUT THE WINDOW NOW
004 LET ME SEE YOUR HANDS
005 OUT THE VEHICLE OUT THE VEHICLE
006 GET OUT OF THE CAR
007 304 perps in custody
008 → PO2: Ma'am go head and put your hands behind your back

In excerpts 10 and 11 the officers command the citizens to put their hands behind their back. They do so because putting hands behind one's back is the first sequence in placing a citizen/suspect into handcuffs. It is the beginning of a detention/arrest sequence. Consider again the following verbal data from excerpt 8. In this excerpt, the officer has listened to both parties of the domestic dispute; the female disputant (WD) gives her account and she tells the officer that the man (MD) has illegal drugs in his truck. The officer searches the vehicle and finds marijuana and other drug-related paraphernalia. The officer finds enough drugs to arrest him not only for possession, but also with intent to distribute, and this information is articulated to the viewing audience. The MD is with the paramedics being treated for the injury to his hand:

Excerpt 8 (*COPS* Data: 'Jimmy Dean Sausage')

156 → PO: Let me see your hands did they bandage it up?
157 MD: Yeah they put up a band aid on it (it just)
158 it ain't real bad right now though
159 → PO: Okay do me a favor okay put your hands
160 behind your back
161 MD: Wooooooooo oh for what?
162 → PO: Put your hands behind your back sir
163 MD: Whaz happening?
164 PO: Placin you under arrest for assault okay?
165 MD: Wait a minute[I'm the one with the blood
166 PO: [turn okay turn arou[nd
167 MD: [ho ho
168 ho man hol=
169 PO: =don't resist=
170 MD: =I'm not resisting=
171 PO: Okay don't resist
172 MD: =but she's the one supposed to be getting arrested
173 PO: Okay I'll explain something here in a minute okay?
174 → ((PO puts one handcuff on the suspect))
175 MD: Man come on with this (shit)
176 → PO: Put your other hand behind your back
177 MD: I got my daughter over there
178 → ((PO puts the other hand in cuffs))
179 PO: Uh okay we're gonna make arrangements
180 MD: Ma::n this is some bull(shit)
181 PO: Right now you're being placed under arrest for assault
182 and for possession of marijuana with the intent to distribute

After the officer comes back and finds drugs in the MD's truck, 'Let me see your hands' is disguised as a medically related utterance; he does so by suffixing the directive with an utterance that has had prior usage as a medically related one (did they bandage it up?) After the officer asks that question, the MD puts his hand out horizontally, and shows the officer his bandages. And that is how the disputant has understood that utterance, as a medically related utterance, one that has a prior usage in the encounter (line 63: Do you need rescue sir?) The phrase 'let me see your hands' is used in two different temporal contexts in the encounter; one at the beginning when the man claims injury to his hand and the officer asks to see it (line 65); and second, when he asks to see the bandage (line 156). Although the utterance is designed as a medically related utterance in form, it functions as a way of physically controlling the disputant in the pursuit of safety.

This analytical point can be supported two ways. First, that's what the officer says he will do; he finds the drugs and tells the viewing audience that he will go and arrest the male disputant. Second, the officer tells the man to put his hands behind his back – arrest sequence – only after he has verified that nothing is in his hands (except bandages). Had the officer issued the utterance 'put your hands behind your back' in line 156, it would have been recognizable as a 'pre' arrest sequence. But more importantly, the officer would not have had the chance to actually verify the contents of his hand. The MD could have grabbed something while the officer was away searching the car. Thus, using 'let me see your hands' in a medical way allows the officer to approach the disputant without arousing suspicion, and allows him to inspect the disputant's hands to make sure that he is weapon free, all while leading the disputant to believe that the officer is concerned about his hand. And notice that the MD has oriented his turn to that uptake: in line 158 the MD fulfills the conditional relevance of the yes/no question projected in the prior turn (line 156: Let me see your hands did they bandage it up?) by grammatically and physically conforming (line 157: Yeah they put up a band aid on it) to the semantic requirements projected in the interrogative;[41] then in line 158, the MD expands his turn by downgrading (line 158: it ain't real bad right now though) and elaborating on his injuries concurrently within one turn. This brief two-turn exchange resembles more of a sympathetic show and tell sequence than official police business.

The officer's actions and words assume a more institutional character after he inspects the disputant's hands and visually confirms that there is nothing there. In line 159, the turn after the disputant's response (lines 157-158) the officer prefaces the directive to place his hands behind his back with a politeness marker. In other words, there is a distinct change in the directionality of the disputant's hands, from the pronating position of a sympathetic (commiserative exhibition/hand display) showing to the behind the back placement as a prelude to detention. When the MD recognizes the sequence as such, notice that he begins to challenge the officer's actions (line 161: Woooooooo oh for what?) Consequently, the directive is issued again. When the MD challenges the officer again, he accuses the MD of resisting

41 Raymond, 2000.

arrest, which the subject denies. By inserting an utterance that is embedded in one context (line 63, 65) into another (line 156: let me see your hands did they bandage it up?; lines 159-160: okay do me a favor okay put your hands behind your back) the officer is able to control one of the most dangerous situations for police in general, arrest. By manipulating the historical and temporal context of talk, the officer is able to minimize the anticipatable threat to his safety (resistance) by duping the suspect into showing his hands.

Discussion and Conclusion

Safety, for the police, is practical and never theoretical, and permeates throughout their lives and actions.[42] One safety-related communicative action that police officers routinely engage in is requesting and ordering citizens and felons to show their hands. Hand visibility is a practical concern for police officers because they believe that suspects and citizens might be concealing and carrying weapons. As Rubinstein notes, 'anyone whose hands are concealed, wittingly or not, risks serious injury or worse when he attracts the attention of a policeman.'[43]

The police have a good reason to make sure that there is nothing in the citizens' hands since ordinary objects – pens, boxcutters, pocketknives – have the obvious capacity to be used as weapons. Some weapons, however, have the potential to be disguised as ordinary – harmless – objects. For example, the Chicago Police Department (CPD) issued three separate bulletins warning officers about ordinary objects such as garden hoses, cellular phones, and pens that had been converted into firearms.[44] These weapons had been confiscated by various CPD units (for example, gang crimes, tactical patrol), and the intelligence division had disseminated the findings to patrol officers. During the Diallo trial, NYC patrol officers testified that they were beginning to see 'wallet guns,' regular wallets that had been converted into firearms.

If innocent motorists and citizens have a reason to be wary of P-C encounters for fears of getting shot, the police, by definition, have reason to be apprehensive about their encounters with the public. The deaths of officers in the line of duty are civic tragedies, but that is a risk that is intrinsic to the occupation. Ordinary – unarmed – citizens who are killed during their encounters with the police, by definition, moor no such ideological anchor. Shootings of unarmed citizens bring to the forefront a social problem that is particularly salient in the US.

Self-generated P-C encounters and aggressive policing tactics such as traffic stops and, especially, 'stop and frisks' usually involve the minority.[45] The aforementioned types of tactics are inextricably tied to claims of racial profiling, police brutality and abuse, and civil rights violations, which engender a hostile attitude toward the

---

42 Barker, 1999.

43 Rubinstein, 1978: 256.

44 CPD, 2000a, b, c.

45 Spitzer, 1999.

police and create further gaps between the minority and the police.[46] These types of policing tactics, along with a tragic shooting of an unarmed civilian, can strain already tense police-community relations, and serve as the impetus for a violent, large-scale social protest.[47]

Debating the legality, constitutionality, and morality of police-initiated stops and searches, however, is not a fruitful endeavor since the claims and counter-claims in alleged police misconduct cases rely on recollections and memories of events from witnesses, participants, and organizational documents, and often assume an argumentative posture.[48] Rather than assuming such an approach, this chapter has used excerpts from actual traffic stops and *COPS* to show the contextual and sequential environments in which directives to show one's hands are issued; furthermore, this chapter has demonstrated how such directives are grammatically encoded in the verbal details of social and physical control.

As the frontline emissaries of the criminal law, the attempts of police officers to verbally control the actions of citizens through directives represent the symbolic, ideological, and practical mandate of modern law enforcement embodied in the mundane details of discursive action.[49] To that end, researchers have shown that police officers advise, request, warn, threaten, command – use language – to persuade citizens and suspects to do or desist from doing something.[50] In prior police research, however, there has been an empirical gap in explaining how police officers go about doing such things.

My data reveal that directives to show one's hands can be classified into three broad categories: 1) vertical hands; 2) inspectable hands; 3) controllable hands. Inspectable hands are best described as indeterminative in function – because a directive to see one's hands could be all purposive: as a way of verifying a disputant's story; as a way of sympathizing with an injured person; as a preliminary to medical assistance; and as a way of verifying the emptiness of a citizen's hands. The list is exhaustive. The intent behind asking citizens to place their hands behind their backs, however, is not. It is uttered as a prelude to an arrest/detention sequence.

My data indicate that directives such as 'put your hands up' – vertical hands – are consistently uttered as a way of controlling the uncertain outcomes in dealing with citizens – because they pose a potential threat to their safety. And this ideological and practical concern with safety is formally embodied in the grammar of the opening moments of the interaction itself. As I have shown, 'routine' traffic stops open with 'requests,' oftentimes preceded by a fundamental and ritualistic utterance that lies at the heart of sociality. Traffic stops open with interrogatives that are socially organized with a preference for communicative action: officers initialize the encounter with a question that projects a verbal answer in the next turn. In this

46 Anderson, 1999.

47 Bimstein, 1973.

48 Walker, 2001.

49 Bankowski and Mungham, 1976.

50 Mastrofski et al., 2000.

respect, the talk between the police and motorists resembles an ordinary conversation since both participants use the machinery of talk and the burden of implicativeness to mutually and collaboratively reproduce the interactional order of P-C encounters, turn by turn.

In felony traffic stops and other 'dangerous' contacts, imperatives precede interrogatives: directives such as 'put your hands in the air' or 'let me see your hands' are officers' first utterances that open the encounter with the public. There is no sequential room for mutual ratification such as greetings and recognitionals because police imperatives constrain the next turn response with a preference for physical conformity. That is, there is a qualitative difference in the preference organization of communicatively oriented requests and directives of physical control in the constraints and actions that are projected and embedded in the turn after. And until that initial command to display one's hands is obeyed, the talk between the police and citizens does not resume a normal conversational format: imperatives pave the road for interrogatives to follow.

There are other conversational and suprasegmental features of talk that differentiate vertical hands from others. The obvious difference is in the volume and stress that accompany such directives. Police officers ask for driver's licenses and proofs of insurance in traffic stops in a normal conversational voice and tone; however, officers scream out the directives in felony traffic stops; and unlike normal requests, commands are repeated over and over again until they are obeyed, thus giving recalcitrant citizens numerous opportunities to comply with the officer's orders. Again, it is only after the rebellious citizen is physically secured that the suprasegmental and grammatical features of talk resume a more natural talk format.

The time it takes for the linguistic transformation to occur, from imperatives to interrogatives, may be minute, but its ramifications contradict the principle of democracy since an officer's actions hinder freedom of speech and movement. But that minute or two – the time it takes for officers to secure a citizen (one minute and forty five seconds in excerpt 7) – between imperatives and interrogatives is also the difference between life and death, for officers possess the right to justifiably kill citizens if they believe that serious bodily injury or imminent death may occur. It is thus irresponsible of civic leaders and politicians to suggest that young minority citizens 'fight the police' in any way. A more practical and policy-oriented advice may be to instruct young minority males to delay that desire to question, defy, and verbally fight and resist the police, until the exigent danger has grammatically passed. In other words, first submit to the imperative to raise one's hands, and then interrogate. But as I have shown here, a citizen's chance to interrogate the police (for example, Why did you stop me? Why did you tell me to put my hands up? What did I do?) does not occur until he/she has first submitted to the coercive authority of the police.

In light of the recent highly publicized police shootings of unarmed citizens, civic leaders, policymakers, and citizens have urged unilateral organizational changes in police departments to improve the way the police treat the public. The 'standard' solution to implementing such organizational changes has been: 1) selective recruitment, or rigorous psychological screening processes to preclude certain types of personalities who might be predisposed toward violence; 2) educating the police to be more courteous, civil, and 'sensitive' toward its citizens;[51] 3) tracking of 'problematic' officers through a mandatory collection of demographic data of citizens involved in P-C encounters. The goal of such policy changes has been to reduce the tension between the police and (minority) citizens, and improve their satisfaction with the police; but more importantly, such changes, experts argue, open channels of communication – fosters a 'dialogue' between the public and the police.

In these types of policy-oriented conclusions, the police always stand at attention on the center stage of reform. The exclusive focus on individual police officers as agents of change presupposes the possibility of organizational reform through changes in the street-level bureaucrats themselves.[52] This type of policy directive, however, neglects to address a contingent variable that is crucial in explaining police behavior – one that lies outside of organizational control. There is overwhelming empirical and anecdotal evidence that the way a police officer treats citizens is largely contingent upon their moral attitude and behavior toward the police.[53] Official and unofficial sanction is contingent upon how citizens verbally behave toward the officers' requests, orders, and 'attitude tests,' a perspectival display of attitude.[54] The noteworthy point is that the police conduct those types of attitude tests through seemingly simple questions in the opening sequences of the encounter.[55] Physical conformity is one way to show deference and cooperation, but another is far more primordial.

Talk is the primordial site of sociality, and in a way, the empirical manifestation of egalitarianism: conversations over coffee or cold beer are managed by the participants in a grassroots sort of way;[56] consequently the burden of deciding who gets to talk, what gets talked about, and how much one gets to talk is not imposed exogenously but shouldered by the encumbered actors themselves, in situ;[57] and it is in such banal moments that people's identities, realities, and the social structure of everyday life is produced and reified.[58] In that sense, talk is the micro-embodiment of democracy-in-action – talk that is not concocted as a result of metaphysical assumptions presupposed into the outline of a political theory[59] or talk that is idealized as a basis for democratic and ethical systems in unrealizable conversational settings.[60] Institutional interactions fundamentally differ from social ones in that regard – because bureaucratic institutions possess the capacity to wield power in the

51 Bimstein, 1973.
52 Lipsky, 1980.
53 Riksheim and Chermak, 1993.
54 Maynard, 1991.
55 Muir, 1977.
56 Schegloff, 1999.
57 Sacks et al., 1974.
58 Schegloff, 1991; Maynard, 2003.
59 Rawls, 1971.
60 Habermas, 1996.

grammatical, syntactical, and sequential aspects of talk;[61] aside from brute coercion, it is along such linguistic systems that the police also differ from the public.[62]

And it is precisely that rift between the police and the public that shifts in policing philosophies have attempted to mitigate by conceptualizing citizens as equal partners in the fight against and discourse about crime. Consequently, activists, researchers, and police executives have forged an artificial space to foster a 'dialogue' between the public and the police.[63] If, however, the authority and legitimacy of the police is politically derived and sociologically enacted, its sustenance during perceived threats to officers' safety is not: one either obeys the directives or flouts them. There is nothing abstract about being commanded to 'put your hands up.' The lesson is brutally simple – compliance. Such theological assertions, however, are inconsistent with the contemporary fads in community policing because they contradict the principles of equity, egalitarianism, free speech, and movement.

As I have shown here, as much as citizens are conceptualized as partners in the fight against crime and disorder, communication first has to come to a standstill for it to resume when the safety of the police is at stake. That is to say that in order to arrive at a democratic – natural – state of talk, one must conform to the institutional – coercive – authority of the police. That is because despite the persuasive function of language, words have limited rhetorical force: there is no polite and indirect way to persuade a citizen/felon who is holding a gun, and threatens to use it against his/her fellow citizens or the police, except to issue commands to drop it, or to forcefully compel the rebel to comply.[64]

Using P-C encounters as they appeared on *COPS*, it possible to speculate on what might have happened in encounters like Haggerty, Diallo, and Thomas. That is, the way the police open encounters, or suddenly shift their footing from interrogatives to imperatives, already signifies how they have perceived the nature of the encounter as a potential threat to their welfare. The analytical point worth reiterating is that the directives which police officers issue are not orphans; they exist in a family of related utterances, progressive and sequential in character. Furthermore, the police make repeated commands to citizens to show their hands.

Just as significantly, citizens also collaborate in the production of outcomes of their contacts with the police: citizens, sometimes, do not immediately obey directives to vertically raise their hands; they attempt to 'repair' mishearings rather than comply with police directives; they respond to commands as invitations to tell an account while treating interlocked bureaucratic openings as occasions for social discourse rather than an institutional one; some resist verbally and physically when told to put their hands behind their back. Thus, it is entirely possible that unarmed citizens who have been shot may have collaborated in the production of their fatal outcomes by interpreting directives to see vertical hands for inspectable/controllable

61 Molotch and Boden, 1985.
62 Milovanovic, 1994: 141-184.
63 Skogan, 2004.
64 Klinger, 2004.

hands, thereby deviating from the preferred format of institutional encounters, and otherwise treating 'transactional' directives as interactional ones.[65] Did the police in the publicized cases give citizens ample time and sequential space to react to the directives? Could the citizens have interpreted the commands to see 'vertical' hands for 'inspectable' hands, and as mere warnings rather than threats? Without a recording of those incidents, the answers to those types of questions remain educated guesses at best.

Recent work, however, suggests that police officers exercise tremendous caution and perspicuity when they exercise lethal force. They are astutely aware of the position and placement of suspects' fingers – whether the suspects' fingers are indexed, on the trigger guard, or on the actual trigger itself.[66] Furthermore, it appears that officers experience 'tunnel vision' during such moments, and do not see the race and color of suspects as much as they see guns, hands, and fingers. Thus, to claim that the police irresponsibly and flippantly shoot unarmed citizens would be inconsistent with the findings in current research. This is especially true since police officers undergo traumatic psychological, legal, and economic repercussions as a result of their involvement in shootings.[67]

Safety, of citizenry and the police alike, then, is a collaborative accomplishment in that it does not exist independently, apart from the situated practices of the police who issue directives such as 'let me see your hands,' and citizens who conform to the physical constraints embodied in them. For the police safety is grammatically embodied in the utterance itself: asking and commanding citizens to display their hands is inseparable from their attempts to control the behavior of citizens; it is safety being performed in the actual situated discursive practices of the police. As I have shown in this chapter, it is in such micro moments of talk that the interactional order of P-C encounters is mutually brought to order.

65 Storey, 1995.
66 Klinger, 2004.
67 Klinger, 2004.

Chapter 12

Images of the Irish Family: A 'Slightly' Constitutional Arrangement[1]

Sophie Cacciaguidi-Fahy

Introduction

To say that Ireland has undergone radical social and legal changes over the last 30 years is a significant understatement. These changes have manifested themselves most noticeably in the emergence of new social realities and civil ideas; and have had a profound impact on its laws and the institutions of the State, most principally the Family. At law, the Family is considered a 'vital social institution' and one of the foundational pillars of the Irish constitutional order. It is not possible to overstate its importance in Irish culture. Its origins go back far in legal history[2] and Irish law is often cited as providing the 'most detailed evidence we have of Family law in pre-Christian Europe'.[3] Ancient Irish laws which regulated marriages (*Cain Lanama*), fosterage (*Cain Iarrath*) and the kin group (*Corus Fine*) were subsequently influenced by Roman notions of patriarchy, transforming familial relationships into a 'more administered, and rigidly hierarchical relationship where the key order was the institution of paternal authority over the family, which included wife, children, servants and property'.[4] These notions left an indelible mark on the regulation of the Irish family system via religious codes of behaviours and legal norms.

The overall purpose of this chapter is to reflect upon the Irishness of what has been recognised in Irish law as the 'Constitutional Family'. A semiotic reading of Article 41, concerning *The Family*, allows us to gain valuable insights into Irish culture and its interaction with the law. In addition, it provides us with an appreciation of how judicial interpretation of the various signs it contains has gender-coded and culturally encoded the role and rights of the constituent members of the Irish Family.

1 The latter part of the title was suggested by my colleague Donncha O'Connell.

2 See Casey, James, *Constitutional Law in Ireland* (Dublin: Round Hall, Sweet & Maxwell, 2000) p. 612; Whyte, Gerry, 'The Family and the State – Irish Constitutional Law', 7 *St Louis University Public Law Review* 237 (1988): 252.

3 Goody, Jack, *The Development of Family and Marriage in Europe* (Cambridge: Cambridge University Press, 1983) p. 41.

4 Birdwell-Pheasant, Donna, 'Family Systems and The Foundations of Class in Ireland and England', 3 *The History of the Family* 1 (1998): 17-34.

The first part of this chapter concentrates on the text of Article 41 in *Bunreacht na hEireann* and its semantic value. The focus here is on a textual analysis, which aims to identify the sign system the text paved for the judiciary. The second part provides a brief overview of the Courts' interpretation about the various icons the text contains, examining in particular the meaning of the 'Constitutional Family', Marriage, and Woman-Mothers. To do this, I will focus on the type of language the Courts have chosen to use to legitimise the signs and transmit their representation and implementation in social narratives. The third part will address the reframing of the signs in a more contemporary setting, following the lifting of the constitutional ban on divorce; and how of late the Courts have redefined the 'Constitutional Family' and its members in a non-Irish context. The fourth part provides a semiotic reading of the icons identified in Article 41; a reading which suggests that the concept of the Family as intended by the original drafters is much wider than the nuclear Family. It is a reading that reveals how legal discourse has forcefully gender-coded and framed acceptable social behaviours to secure the cultural stability of the State. It is a reading that demonstrates how legal discourse has cogently reframed and subtlety facilitated the legislature and political discourse to delineate the cultural contours of the Irish Family.

The Text

The dominant view of the Irish Constitution drafted by de Valera is that it acts as a pluri-vocal text, which receives its meaning from a univocal group of interpreters.[5] Notwithstanding its nominal dedication to a theistic view of natural law,[6] it is still considered as a legal, political and social text embracing overriding principles, which performs the function of a social contract between the State and its people.

5 For an extensive analysis of the role played by de Valera in the drafting of the Constitution, see Murphy, John A., 'The 1937 Constitution: Some Historical Reflections', in *Ireland's Evolving Constitution, 1937-97: Collected Essays*, edited by Tim Murphy and Patrick Twomey (Oxford: Hart, 1998): 11-27; Fitzgerald, Garret, 'The Irish Constitution in its Historical context', ibid., pp. 29-40.

6 Doyle, Oran, 'Legal Validity: Reflections on the Irish Constitution', *Dublin University Law Journal* 25 (2003); Whyte, Gerry, 'Natural Law and The Constitution', *I.L.T.* 16 (1996); Kelly, John, *The Irish Constitution* (Dublin: Butterworths, 1994): 671-711; O'Hanlon, Rory, 'Natural Rights and the Constitution', *I.L.T.* (January 1993); Quinn, Gerard, 'The Nature and Significance of Critical Legal Studies', *I.L.T.* 282 (1989); Hogan, Gerard, 'Legal Aspects of Church/State Relations in Ireland', 7 *St Louis University Public Law Review* 275 (1988). For case law, where statements, acknowledging the existence of higher law, antecedent to the Constitution, were made directly from the bench, see *Ryan v Attorney General [1965] IR 264*; *McGee v Attorney General [1974] IR 284*; *Northants County Council v A.B.F. [1982] ILRM 164*; *Finn v Attorney General [1983] IR 154*. However, it must be noted that the use of natural law by the Irish judiciary has not necessarily resulted in the judicial endorsement of any specific Roman Catholic teaching; as an example see *McGee v Attorney General [1974] IR 284*.

From an historical perspective, the 1937 Constitution was seen as the opportunity to de-anglicise and nationalise the Irish legal system. In this context, *Bunreacht na hEireann* was written with Irish cultural traditions and customs in mind.

Article 41 dealing primarily with the concept of the Family was a novel provision in the 1937 Constitution.[7] It states:

> The Family
>
> Article 41
>
> 1. 1° The State recognises the Family as the natural primary and fundamental unit group of Society, and as a moral institution possessing inalienable and imprescriptible rights, antecedent and superior to all positive law.
>
> 2° The State, therefore, guarantees to protect the Family in its constitution and authority, as the necessary basis of social order and as indispensable to the welfare of the Nation and the State.
>
> 2. 1° In particular, the State recognises that by her life within the home, woman gives to the State a support without which the common good cannot be achieved.
>
> 2° The State shall, therefore, endeavour to ensure that mothers shall not be obliged by economic necessity to engage in labour to the neglect of their duties in the home.
>
> 3. 1° The State pledges itself to guard with special care the institution of Marriage, on which the Family is founded, and to protect it against attack.
>
> 2° No law shall be enacted providing for the grant of a dissolution of marriage.

The original provision above epitomises the univocal application of a subtext, where the subject (the Law) is part of a dominant circle, and the meaning of the subject of the text (the Family) is trapped within that circle. In other words, the substantive textualisation of the Family through the law implies that the function of the legal subtext is to inform the dominant culture about what is and what ought to be acceptable in the context of the family.

On 24 November 1995, the Fifteenth Amendment of the Constitution, lifting the constitutional ban on divorce, was carried by the narrowest margin of any national ballot in the history of the State.[8] Article 41.3.2 above was subsequently repealed and replaced with:

> 2° A Court designated by law may grant a dissolution of marriage where, but only where, it is satisfied that
>
> i. at the date of the institution of the proceedings, the spouses have lived apart from one another for a period of, or periods amounting to, at least four years during the five years,

---

7 The earlier version of the Constitution, drafted in 1922, contained no provision in relation to the Family and Marriage.

8 Yes vote: 818,837; No vote: 809,739 – a difference of 9,098 votes at national level.

ii. there is no reasonable prospect of a reconciliation between the spouses,

iii. such provision as the Court considers proper having regard to the circumstances exists or will be made for the spouses, any children of either or both of them and any other person prescribed by law, and

iv. any further conditions prescribed by law are complied with.

3°. No person whose marriage has been dissolved under the civil law of any States but is a subsisting valid marriage under the law for the time being in force within the jurisdiction of the Government and Parliament established by this Constitution shall be capable of contracting a valid marriage within that jurisdiction during the life time of the other party to the marriage so dissolved.[9]

From the original Article, it is clear that the text is teleological. Its primary objective is to delineate boundaries, setting out the desired qualities of the Irish Family using the yardstick of morality. Its secondary purpose is to encode the Family within a particular linear matrix, raising its status to that of an icon, an 'annunciation'[10] with all the iconographic meanings it carries. Finally, in internalising the Family in the parameters of a legal text, the law locks the collective memories which the Family represents past, present and future.

The elegant architecture of Article 41 is quite significant as the original meaning of the text derives from its structure. It is located in the overall constitutional text as a distinct sub-heading, *The Family*, under the key heading of *Fundamental Rights*.[11] It is made up of three separate provisions, each one divided in two subheadings. Its purpose is to anchor the preferred reading of a certain image of the Family. At first glance, it assumes all the promise of a typical liberal-democratic statement.[12]

---

9 This is known as the 'no quickie foreign divorce' clause.

10 See Goodrich, Peter, *Languages of Law: From Logics of Memory to Nomadic Masks* (London: Weidenfeld and Nicolson, 1990).

11 This allows reference to formal canons of Irish constitutional laws interpretation, such as an harmonious interpretation; see Casey, pp. 376-385.

FUNDAMENTAL RIGHTS

Personal Rights

Article 40

1. All citizens shall, as human persons, be held equal before the law.

This shall not be held to mean that the State shall not in its enactments have due regard to differences of capacity, physical and moral, and of social function.

[...]

3. 1° The State guarantees in its laws to respect, and, as far as practicable, by its laws to defend and vindicate the personal rights of the citizen.

The subtitles of the Key heading are: Fundamental Rights (Article 40), The Family (Article 41), Education (Article 42), Private Property (Article 43) and Religion (Article 44).

12 Keogh, Dermot, 'The Irish Constitutional Revolution: An Analysis of the Making of the Constitution', *The Constitution of Ireland: 1937-1987*, edited by Frank Litton (Dublin:

However, a quick historical examination reveals that the provisions it contains were drafted with one Family in mind and only assumed one paradigm of Family unit: the Family based on a religious marriage between two heterosexual individuals.[13] Until the referendum on divorce in November 1995, the rhythm and movement of the text was syllogistic, articulated in three identical tempos, reminiscent of the three hypostases of the Trinitarian structure,[14] laid down earlier in the Preamble.

The meaning and the intellectual integrity of the text evolves from its internal coherence, which implies that the drafters' original intentions were to lock the meaning of the Family within the text istelf. The cartography of Article 41 maps the text towards higher spheres, beyond the realm of positive law. Its objective was to define '*The Family*' as a pure sign, based in pure law, which no law could alter.

The Semantic Value of the Text

At a first glance, Article 41 makes sweeping statements using abstract and vague language, providing the reader with either an active reading or a benign reading.[15] The opening provision begins by using a powerful grandiose and moral terminology while the last provision ends with the use of strong military language, rendering the overall tone of the text paradoxically declaratory and aspirational yet defensive. On the whole, it uses strong and uncompromising language giving little power to the judiciary to limit the rights it contains as it is not subject to qualifications, and does not include adverbial grammatical features as 'such as' or 'as such' often found in prescriptive texts.[16] Nonetheless, what matters in this particular narrative is not so much the text itself but rather the iteration of the concept behind the text.

Institute of Public Administration, 1988), p. 5.

13 Until the introduction of divorce, the churches were responsible for both the civil and religious ceremonies as well as keeping records of the civil register of marriages.

14 Preamble

In the Name of the Most Holy Trinity, from Whom is all authority and to Whom, as our final end, all actions both of men and States must be referred,

We, the people of Éire,

Humbly acknowledging all our obligations to our Divine Lord, Jesus Christ, Who sustained our fathers through centuries of trial,

Gratefully remembering their heroic and unremitting struggle to regain the rightful independence of our Nation,

And seeking to promote the common good, with due observance of Prudence, Justice and Charity, so that the dignity and freedom of the individual may be assured, true social order attained, the unity of our country restored, and concord established with other nations,

Do hereby adopt, enact, and give to ourselves this Constitution.

15 Beytagh, Francis X., *Constitutionalism in Contemporary Ireland: An American Perspective* (Dublin: Round Hall, Sweet and Maxwell, 1997) p. 130.

16 Though they have now been limited in *Lobe & Osayande v Minister for Justice, Equality & Law Reform [2003] IESC 1.*

Academic commentators agree that the meta-narrative emerging out of Article 41.1.1 not only invokes notions of natural law but exposes the ultimate thomistic and theocratic vision of natural rights law.[17] Today it is customarily agreed that certain clauses of Article 41 'provide textual support of the existence of natural jurisprudence'[18] superior to any positive law. Others argue that the concept of natural law implicit in the provisions should be read as a complement rather than superior to the Constitution.[19] To a large extent, the Article was informed by Roman Catholic teaching[20] indicating a clear concession to the teaching of the social Papal encyclicals.[21] Its rhetoric is markedly based on moral and natural law argurments used to protect the rights of the Family and to inform a political credo that was essentially communitarian, expressed in the notion of 'common good'.[22] Ironically, it equally reflects the non-interventionist language which was part of the liberal agenda at the time of its drafting.[23]

The representation of a unit group underpinning plays an essential role in the philosophical conception of Article 41, connoting in effect the idea of support, base, and stability. This type of legal-political ideology leans towards the collective rights/power of the group as theocracy 'bestows group rights on the patriarchal Family whereas liberal-democratic theory exhausts the legal universe with individual and the State'.[24] At first sight, the repetitive use of semantically similar and definite descriptors ('natural, primary and fundamental'; 'inalienable and imprescriptible') to express the rights of the unit group is formulated in an absolutist language, leading the reader to a strict interpretation. This is further compounded by the additional use of sequential related descriptors ('antecedent and superior'; 'constitution and authority'; 'Nation and the State') emphasising the relationship of conceptual dependence between the various icons: the State, the Woman-Mother and Marriage.

However, by looking at the varying language of the subsequent clauses, one quickly realises that it is other rights, the unenumerated rights, tacitly expressed in higher qualified forms, which cause the Courts difficulty of interpretation.[25] Notwithstanding that Thomistic natural law theory carries out the implicit belief

---

17 Beytagh, p. 37.

18 Ibid.

19 Ibid.; Clarke, Desmond, 'The Role of Natural Law in Irish Constitutional Law', 17 *Irish Jurist* 187 (1982).

20 Quinn, pp. 282-284; Whyte (1988), p. 237. Today most legal historians acknowledge that McQuaid had been quite influential in the drafting and the actual formulation of some of the constitutional provision, including Article 41; see Keogh, pp. 19-20.

21 Dooley, Dolores, 'Gendered Citizenship in the Irish Constitution', edited by Murphy and Twomey, pp. 127-129.

22 According to Quinn, p. 283, this position is likely to remain unless positive law expurgates natural law from the Constitution and from the collective legal consciousness of bench and bar.

23 See Fitzgerald, Garret, p. 37.

24 Quinn, p. 284.

25 For the doctrine of unenumerated rights, see Casey, pp. 394-397.

that the judiciary is not the exclusive arbiters of its content,[26] the assessment and construction of Article 41 must be interpreted within the wider context of the Constitution itself as observed by Justice Costello in *Attorney General v Paperlink Ltd*:

> The Constitution is a political instrument as well as a legal document and in its interpretation the Courts should not place the same significance on differences of language used in two succeeding sub-paragraphs as would, for example, be placed on differently drafted sub-sections of a Finance act.[27]

In addition, the use of capital letters confirms that the intention of the drafters was to raise the Family to the status of an institution, establishing a vertical relationship between State and Society where it plays the central connection, thereby reinforcing the hierarchical concept of the Family as a unit group = moral institution = inalienable + imprescriptible rights = antecedent and superior to all positive law. The reader should also reflect on the use of 'unit group', as if one uses the concept of group as a noun as opposed to an adjective, a different reading emerges with a different icon: the group being a cultural representation of a nation. The adjective 'natural' is deemed moral, underscoring the strength of the State commitment towards the special protection it affords to the Family and family life. The use of the archaic adjectives 'inalienable' and 'imprescriptible' further solemnise the discursive effect of the text. The adjectives 'antecedent' and 'superior' capture the concept of natural law's intemporality and tradition. Here the language approaches liturgy, introducing principles of spirituality, creating a unique space in the law for the Family.

Article 41.1.2 and subsequent provisions further restrict the parameters of the Family, expressing political and sociological aspirations. Using social and political terminology such as 'social order', 'welfare', 'Nation', 'State', 'home', 'common good', 'economic necessity', 'engage in labour', 'duties in the home', they represent a more communitarian view of a Society of which the Family is the foundational pillar.[28] More pointedly, at the time of the drafting, the use of the word 'authority' explicitly relied on the wage earner, de facto implying patriarchal authority.[29] Since then, the Courts have interpreted it in a wider context but only referring to the authority of the unit as opposed to the authority of any single individual member within the unit. Another point to note is the use of pairs of principles between Articles 41.1.1

---

26 Duncan, William, 'Can Natural Law be Used in Constitutional Interpretation?' 45 *Doctrine of Life* (1995) as cited in Whyte, Gerry, '*Natural Law and the Constitution', I.L.T.* 8 (1996) p. 9.

27 *Attorney General v Paperlink Ltd [1984] ILRM 373.*

28 'The Common Good' has been identified by most legal commentators as one of the most reiterated and vague terms of the Constitution; see Casey, p. 384.

29 Dooley.

and 41.1.2. It not only embodies the Family as a 'natural, primary and fundamental unit group of Society' but intrinsically ties its concept to the State social policy.[30]

Articles 41.2.1 and 41.2.2 are a bold expression and definite construction of gender role/identity which purpose was to anchor domestic patriarchy both in the normative text and within the unit group. The linguistic categorisation of the role of women as mothers is embedded in patriarchal nationalist discourse heavily influenced by previous historical folklore and events.[31] It frames their function in a dual categorisation, relinquishing them to the private sphere, equating them to domesticity in the home, so as to secure and support the social and political fabric of Irish society through the 'common good';[32] declaring them politically irrelevant and reinforcing the classical view of patriarchy.[33] As pointed out in earlier studies,[34] the purpose of this provision is to reinforce the hegemony of the Catholic doctrine, which revolves around the translation of religious preoccupations into law via the concept of natural law.[35] Furthermore, by assuming the interchangeability of woman with mother and domesticity,[36] women are made explicitly responsible for both the reproduction of the population and the transmission of the national identity through the practice of motherhood/maternity.[37] Two subtexts are detectable: firstly, by

30 *Bunreacht na hÉireann* is often viewed as de Valera's own personal social manifesto and legacy to the Irish people. It reflects his perceptions of the pressures put on the national community values threatened from the outside world, in particular by the ills of modernism and American constitutionalism.

31 Inglis, Tom, *Moral Monopoly – The Rise and Fall of the Catholic Church in Modern Ireland* (Dublin: University College Dublin Press, 1998); Kiberd, Declan, *Inventing Ireland* (Cambridge, Mass.: Harvard University Press, 1996); Hynes, Eugene, 'The Great Hunger and Irish Catholicism', 8 *Societas* 2 (1978): 132-56;

32 Larkin, Emmet, *Historical Dimensions of Irish Catholicism* (New York: Arno Press, 1976).

A ban on women's employment in any designated occupation was coupled with the marriage bar, or legal permission for women to be fired from their job on marriage, until the late 1960s. See Conroy, Pauline, 'Managing the Mothers: The Case of Ireland', *Women and Social Policies in Europe, Work, Family and the State*, edited by Jane Lewis (Aldershot: Edward Elgar, 1993).

33 Dooley, p. 127.

34 Cacciaguidi-Fahy, Sophie, 'The Substantive Issue and the Rhetoric of the Abortion Debate in Ireland', in *Contemporary Issues of the Semiotics of Law*, edited by Anne Wagner, Tracy Summerfield and Farid S. Benavides Vanegas (Oxford: Hart Publishing, 2005) pp. 143-144.

35 Fulton, John, *The Tragedy of Belief: Division, Politics, and Religion in Ireland* (Oxford: Clarendon Press, 1991).

36 Mullin, Molly, 'Representations of Irish Feminism and the Politics of Difference', *Feminist Studies* 17 (1991): 29-50.

37 See what Pateman has called the 'sexual contract', which depends precisely on this sharp distinction between public and private spheres in Pateman, Carole, *The Sexual Contract* (Cambridge: Polity, 1998). The woman is explicitly responsible for both the social contract and the sexual contract subject to both the political power and the paternal power.

equating women to reproductive continuity and representing the concept of common good, they become mothers and are the basis of the Family unit, granting them an incomparable social value; secondly, they acquire a special legal space with an expressed constitutional protection for the rights of mothers, and natural mothers in particular.[38]

The striking use of two military metaphors in Article 41.3.1 ('guard with special care'; 'protect it [the institution of Marriage] against any attack') suggest that at the time, the drafters feared an onslaught of 'paganism' from foreign shores, reminiscent of the Brehon laws where women cohabited with more than one man.[39] The pledge of 'special care' carries into effect a special protection[40] afforded to the Family which purpose is to sustain the guarantees as set out in the Preamble: 'to promote the common good [...] so that the dignity and freedom of the individual may be assured, true social order attained'.[41]This pledge is further emphasised throughout the text by the use of the indicative present ('recognises', 'guarantees', 'pledges') and subsequently the mandatory 'shall' reflecting an obligational construction on the subject, imposing positive obligations on the State to recognise and guarantee rights to the Family as defined. In addition, this verbal construction is augmented through the use of several forceful infinitives ('to protect', 'to ensure', 'to guard') and predicatives which lead some interpreters to believe that the text provides the reader with a clear and unambiguous interpretation.

The original provision 41.3.2 bluntly barred legislation to confer a divorce jurisdiction on the Courts but also nullity legislation which at the time was so widely framed that it was characterised as 'back door divorce'.[42] Until 1995, the Constitution had a ban on divorce which originated in the social teaching of the Catholic Church and deprived any other religious minorities of availing of civil divorce.[43] The amendment has in some way added extra linguistic incongruities. Unlike the previous subparagraphs, which are regarded as fervent patriarchal statements holding outdated moral and social principles, they contain clear and highly specific language relating to the divorce legislation.[44]

While many legal scholars believe that the text is not a shining example of limpidity and precision,[45] one should keep in mind that a lot of its criticism is not

---

38 See *G. v An Bord Uchtala [1980] IR 32.*

39 Dooley, p. 129.

40 It is also coupled with a legal ultimatum, which until 1997 left very little discretion to the judiciary to alter the status of marriage.

41 Preamble.

42 Casey, p. 621.

43 For an historical background on the history of Article 41.3.2, see Casey, p.621; Fanning, Ronan, *Irish Independent Ireland* (Dublin: Helicon, 1983), pp. 54-57.

44 These linguistic incongruities were subsequently teased out by the Family Law (Divorce) Act 1996.

45 As an example, see Martin, Frank, 'The Family in the Constitution: Principle and Practice', edited by Murphy and Twomey, p. 85, who speaks of the 'excessive verbiage of the text'.

necessarily attached to the concept which it endeavours to express. What is clear, however, is that Article 41 provides a definition of what constitutes the Family in the context of religious and State patriarchies. To begin with, it is the textual legacy of Catholic patriarchal traditions, committed to the principles of justice and morality impregnated by natural law. Secondly, it is the recognition of State patriarchy by the national community, acknowledging the special importance of nationalism – the 'common interest' – protected by the rule of law.[46] Ultimately, as pointed out by Whyte, it is the only emphatic subordination of positive law to natural rights in the text of the Constitution.[47]

The Interpretation of the Text

In Ireland, the Constitution has assigned the task of its interpretation to the Courts.[48] This allows the Supreme Court to engage de facto in decision-making which is political in its effect but not necessarily politically motivated. The judiciary often engages in interstitial law-making to fill in the gaps or perceived gaps in the interpretation of the legislature's intention, which enable the Courts to frequently guide as well as govern certain forms of social conduct.

When it comes to interpreting Article 41, the Irish Courts have taken its content seriously and have not treated it as merely aspirational.[49] Oddly enough, the rights of the Family are not clearly defined or exhaustively specified in the text and much depends on judicial instinct in cases where Family rights have been invoked. By and large the construction of Article 41 has repeatedly led the judiciary to stage strained linguistic contortions to reconcile the aspirations of the constitutional article with impinging social realities and the impact of European and human rights legal standards. Yet the judiciary has had a tendency to practise safe interpretivism[50] and strictly interpreted the text.[51] They have applied a strict constructionist rule, focusing on the literal meaning of the text as well as the intentions of the original framers, unresponsive to social changes and other areas of law. This allowed them to recognise only those rights which are explicitly stated as well as adopting a protective approach arising out of their constitutional duty to protect the Family – to the extent of finding some proposed Family law statutes by the legislature unconstitutional.[52]

46 Irish nationalism still occupies contemporary social discourse, thus often influencing jurisprudential discourse. See *Lobe & Osayande* case at para 14.

47 Whyte, fn. 5.

48 Articles 34 to 37.

49 Casey, pp. 612-620.

50 Twomey, Adrian F., 'Borks Originalism: Reconciling Judicial Constitutional Interpretation with the Rule of Law, 14 *I.L.T.* 278 (1996).

51 Ibid. for further analysis on Irish interpretivism.

52 Martin, p.85; see *Re Article 26 and The Matrimonial Home Bill, 1993. 1 [1994] ILRM 241.*

Most constitutional lawyers agree that the judiciary has focused on the definition and scope of what constitutes a Constitutional Family, what type of Family is protected by the Constitution,[53] as opposed to determining whether the text is about the Family or applies to the Family. In fact, the constitutional definition has controlled judicial reasoning which has taken a very structuralist approach, often using binary oppositions (marital family versus unmarried partnership; married fathers versus unmarried fathers and so on) to structure their interpretation and the meaning given to the text. The approach taken centres on the text, extracting meaning from the text as opposed to developing a meaning about the text. The meaning of the Family is trapped by a univocal dominant group.

Judicial interpretation of Article 41 concerning the Family can be summarised as follows:

1. Recognition and protection of the Family based on marriage and the rights of such Family units;
2. Protection for certain rights of parents and children resulting from the Constitutional Family and for other relationships recognised by the natural law, that is, those of the natural mother and children;
3. Recognition and support for a particular role of women and mothers within the home.

An examination of judicial decisions provides an important context in which the icons of the text emerge and the manner in which they were constructed with a view to model social narratives.

The 'Constitutional Family'

The Irish judiciary has always been unambigous in its interpretation of 'The Family', attaching its meaning to the institution of marriage.[54] Justice Walsh, in *Nicolaou v An Bord Uchtala*, observed that it is:

> … quite clear … that the Family referred to in [Article 41] is the Family which is founded on the institution of marriage and, in the context of the Article, Marriage means valid marriage under the laws for the time being in force in the State.[55]

This was reinforced by the Supreme Court in *Murphy v Attorney General*, with Hench ruling that:

53 Martin, p. 86.

54 Curiously neither Family nor marriage are explicitly defined in the Constitution. It has fallen to the Courts to clarify their meaning; see Whyte (1988), fn 1, p. 239.

55 *The State (Nicolaou) v An Bord Uchtala [1966] IR 567.* This symbolic definition of the Family has since become a slogan and is often cited in Family law decisions.

> The pledge [of Article 4.3.1.] to guard with special care the institution of marriage is a guarantee that this institution in all its constitutional connotations (…) will be given special protection so that it will continue to fulfil its function as the basis of the Family and as a permanent indissoluble union of man and woman.[56]

And subsequently by Justice Kelly:

> … it would seem that, in order to fulfil its obligations to guard with special care the institution of marriage, the State must ensure at least parity of treatment as between marital and non-marital families and may, if it so wishes, discriminate positively in favour of the former.[57]

In *Murray v Ireland*, Costello subsequently defined the constitutional meaning of 'marriage' from the Christian notion of

> a partnership based on an irrevocable personal consent […] which establishes a unique and very special lifelong relationship.[58]

In engaging in an uncompromising linear interpretation of provision 3.1., Walsh's intention was to convey a clear message, using a principled model of communication loaded with value judgements and confirming the State's idea of the Family to the receiver. In adopting a definitional approach to the meaning of Family, based on its membership, in terms of classic heterosexual marital structures contracted by a legal marriage, it allowed subsequent justices to go through an easy process of logical deduction, defining the meaning of the Family in a way which is socially and morally acceptable and which does not break up the normative content of Article 41. It approved a definition of good social behaviour, linking the concept of marriage with the common good, respecting domestic patriarchy and leaving State patriarchy untouched. These concepts were reaffirmed in *T.F. v Ireland*[59] when the Supreme Court reiterated what Justice McCarthy said about marriage earlier in *N. v K. v Ireland*:[60]

> Marriage is a civil contract which creates reciprocating rights and duties between the parties but, further establishes a status which affects both the parties to the contract and the community as a whole.

And again in *T.F. v Ireland*, the Supreme Court per Hamilton commented:

> It is because of its close connection with the Family that the institution of marriage receives the pledge of the State to guard it with special care and protect it against attack. It is clear, accordingly, that this pledge is given in recognition of the contribution made by

56 *Murphy v Attorney General [1982] IR 241.*
57 Ibid.
58 *Murray v Ireland [1985] I.R. 532.*
59 *T.F. v Ireland [1995] 1 I.R. 321.*
60 *N. v K. v Ireland [1985] I.R. 733* at 754.

the institution of marriage to the welfare of the nation and the State and the pledge must be seen in this light. It is not concerned solely with marriage itself, or with the spouses in a marriage, but also with the common good.[61]

To support these statements and demonstrate the protection afforded by the State to the institution of marriage, the legislature enacted many statutes with specific protections for the Family based on marriage, such as the Succession Act 1965, the Family Protection Act 1976 and the Domestic Violence Act 1996, which provide few restrictions on access to protective measures for the Family based on marriage compared with other de facto families. The Courts, on the other hand, were exceptionally vigilant in deterring legislative attacks on the Family based on marriage, in particular in the area of tax laws[62] and social welfare laws.[63] In these cases, the judiciary often felt that it was not unreasonable, unjust or arbitrary to positively discriminate in favour of the marital family against de facto unions, as Kelly J. observed in *Ennis v Butterly*:[64]

> Given the special care of marriage and the Family under the Irish Constitution, it appears to me that the public policy of this State ordains that non-marital cohabitation does not and cannot have the same constitutional status as marriage (…) The Constitution requires marriage to be guarded with special care. In my view this reinforces the existing common law doctrines concerning the non-enforceability of cohabitation contracts.

Nevertheless the 'inalienable and imprescriptible rights' guaranteed to the Family are not absolute and can be restricted in certain circumstances. Justice Kenny first defined what is meant by 'inalienable and imprescriptible' in *Ryan v Attorney General* as 'which cannot be transferred or given away' and 'which cannot be lost by the passage of time or abandoned by non-exercise'. Twenty years later, in *G. v An Bord Uchtala*, the Supreme Court ruled that some of the rights ascribed to the Family were labelled as 'absolutely' inalienable while others were 'relatively so'.[65] Again in *Murray v Ireland*, Costello felt that 'the rights of the unit may be validly restricted by the State'. However, in *M. v An Bord Uchtala*, an earlier case involving natural parents seeking an order returning their infant into their care after giving it up for adoption highlighted the Courts unconformability in defining such abstract language. Here a majority of the Supreme Court disregarded the rights of the child involved and ruled to return it to their natural parents, who were now married. This

61 *T.F. v Ireland* at 732.

62 *Murphy v Attorney General [1982] IR 241*. The Supreme Court struck down a section of the Income Tax Act 1967 which disadvantaged married couples.

63 *Hyland v Minister for Social Welfare [1989] IR 624*. Here the protection of marriage applied to invalidate a provision in the social welfare law which had the effect of reducing the unemployment assistance payable to a married claimant whose spouse was in receipt of some other form of welfare. See also *Mac Mathuna v Ireland [1989] IR 504 / [1995] IR 484*; *People (D.P.P.) v T. [1988] 3 Frewen 141*.

64 *Ennis v Butterly [1996] 1 I.R. 426* at 438-439.

65 Dunne, Anne, 'The Constitutional Family', *Irish Journal of Family Law* 1 (1992).

absolute rigidity in interpreting the inalienable and imprescriptible, and constitutional rights of a married unit highlights the inflexibility which the judiciary is willing to exercise at times when tension between social and legal narratives, involving the rights of adoptive and natural parents, needed a more accommodating approach.[66] This decision and the ensuing ones confirmed that natural parents who subsequently marry enjoy the full protection granted to the constitutional Family.[67]

The substantive issue arising out of the decisions examined above is that neither non-marital families nor its individual members are entitled to the constitutional protection contained in Article 41. The judiciary confirmed the boundaries, which the text had set on itself and in which the law itself can operate.

Woman and Mothers

At common law, marriage resulted in the incorporation of the legal existence of the wife into that of the husband during the duration of the marriage. The Constitution oddly enough, despite its idealised social function of motherhood and domesticity envisaged for 'woman' in Article 42.1, did not have this expectation, and regards marriage as a union of equals. As early as 1951, in *Re Tilson Infant*,[68] Murnaghan struck down the old common law rule of paternal supremacy, emphasising the public policy aspect of marriage,[69] holding that the principle of equality between the rights of married parents was implicit in Article 42.1:

> the word parents is in the plural and naturally should include both father and mother.

Article 41.2 and its subsequent interpretation by the Courts defines in Deriddean terms the conceptual opposition between the position and role of women and that of men, between mothers and fathers and their rights arising therein. Because of their unique place and attributed role in the Constitution, mothers have implicit rights under Article 41. It is in that context that some of the strongest statements, evidencing an infiltration of moral and political judgement into the legal process, have been made. In the case of *The State (Nicolaou) v An Bord Uchtala*, a natural father seeking to have an adoption order quashed partly on grounds that the Adoption Act 1952 infringed on his rights as a natural father with no provision for his consent, was spoken of in the following terms:

> When it is considered that an illegitimate child may be begotten by an act of rape, by a callous seduction or by an act of casual commerce by a man with a woman, as well as by the association of a man with a woman in making a common home without marriage in circumstances approximating to married life [...] it is rare for a natural father to take any

66 See *M. v AnBord Uchtala (1977) IR 287.*

67 See Whyte (1988), fn 1, p. 244.

68 *Re Tilson Infant [1951] IR 1.*

69 See Whyte (1988), fn 1, p. 240. Granting custody and control of the children's upbringing to fathers was replaced by the constitutional policy of joint parental rights.

interest in his offspring, it is not difficult to appreciate the difference in moral capacity and social function between the natural father and the several persons described in the sub-sections in question.

The above comment is more morally explicit than is required in the adjudication process and such use of language became a recurring feature of decisions taken where natural fathers applied for custody of their child. The careful choice of words by Justice Walsh, resonating moral depravity and criminality, acquire a mimetic function where the interpreter's intent is to explicitly convey a moral judgement and set down a marker in legal culture.[70] The language he selected is highly emotive and sometimes distasteful, setting up analogies between Nicolaou's relationship with the mother of his child conceived outside marriage, and rapists. By invoking the theme of the bad father, the unworthy father, the rhetoric of the Court displaces the reality of Nicolaou's legal situation, squeezing him between the unreliable natural father and the natural mother who is always portrayed as the caring parent. But the message of the Courts is quite effective. It sets out the role of the irresponsible reproducer-father on a punitive model: men are either fathers and married or else they have no parental rights. They must conform to the model of parenting set out in the Constitution that is of a responsible reproducer, a meritorious father legally tied to the nuclear Family by marriage, who engages in responsible reproduction as approved by the State, and is legally responsible for his offspring. In other words, the Supreme Court held that:

1. a natural father is not a member of a Family within Article 41,
2. a natural father is not a 'parent' within Article 42,
3. a natural father has no personal rights in relation to his child which the State is bound to protect under Article 40.3.

In *K v W.*,[71], *J.K. v V. W.*[72] and *Keegan v Ireland*,[73] involving natural fathers seeking to be appointed guardian under section 6A, sub-section 1, of the Guardianship of Infants Act 1964, which would enable them to challenge the adoption of their

---

70 Quite often the judiciary have engaged in unnecessarily critical and insensitive analysis on the position of unmarried parents and in particular unmarried fathers. See O'Mahony, Conor, 'Extra-Marital Families and Education Rights under the Irish Constitution', *Irish Journal of Family Law* 2 (2003).

71 *K v W [1990] ILRM 121.*

72 *J.K. v V. W. [1990] 2 IR 437.*

73 *Keegan v Ireland [1994] 18 EHRR 342*. This case which came to the EHRR defined the Family as 'not confined solely to marriage-based relationships and may encompass other de facto "Family" ties where the parties are living together outside of marriage. A child born out of such a relationship is ipso iure part of that "Family" unit from the moment of his birth and by the very fact of it. There thus exists between the child and his parents a bond amounting to Family life even if at the time of his or her birth the parents are no longer co-habiting or if their relationship has then ended', p. 12, para. 44.

respective child by third parties without their prior consent, the Court upheld the earlier decision taken in the Nicolaou case, which concluded that unlike the unmarried mother, unmarried fathers have no constitutional or natural rights in relation to the guardianship of their child under Article 40.3; and section 6A merely acknowledges a right to apply for guardianship[74] as distinct from a defeasible right to be guardian.

Chief Justice Finlay, delivering a majority judgement, added *inter alia*:

> ... although there may be rights of interest or concern arising from the blood link between the father and the child, no constitutional right to guardianship in the father of the child exists. This conclusion does not, of course, in any way infringe on such considerations appropriate to the welfare of the child in different circumstances as may make it desirable for the child to enjoy the society, protection and guardianship of its father, even though its father and mother are not married.
>
> The extent and character of the rights which accrue arising from the relationship of a father to a child to whose mother he is not married must vary very greatly indeed, depending on the circumstances of each individual case.
>
> The range of variation would, I am satisfied, extend from the situation of the father of a child conceived as the result of a casual intercourse, where the rights might well be so minimal as practically to be non-existent, to the situation of a child born as the result of a stable and established relationship and nurtured at the commencement of his life by his father and mother in a situation bearing nearly all of the characteristics of a constitutionally protected Family, when the rights would be very extensive indeed ...

He concluded that:

> ... regard should not be had to the objective of satisfying the wishes and desires of the father to be involved in the guardianship of and to enjoy the society of his child unless the Court has first concluded that the quality of welfare which would probably be achieved for the infant by its present custody which is with the prospective adoptive parents, as compared with the quality of welfare which would probably be achieved by custody with the father is not to an important extent better.

On the other hand, for the purpose of recognising express rights to natural mothers, the Courts have willingly leapfrogged the provision of Article 41 and looked into Article 40.3[75] and the theory of enumerated rights. This 'slightly constitutional arrangement' was acknowledged first in *The State (Nicolaou) v An Bord Uchtala* and subsequently in a compassionate plea by O'Higgins C.J. in *G. v An Bord Uchtala*, a case involving a natural mother claiming the restoration to her of the custody of her child.[76]

---

74 The definition of 'father' under section 2 of the 1964 Act did not include the father of a child born out of wedlock.

75 Article 40.3.1: 'The State guarantees in its laws to respect, and, as far as practicable, by its laws to defend and vindicate the personal rights of the citizen.'

76 *G. v An Bord Uchtala.*

> In the first place it should be noted that the mother is not the mother of a Family, in the sense in which the term is used in the Constitution. Article 41 of the Constitution, which recognises the Family as the natural, primary and fundamental unit group of society and as a moral institution possessing inalienable and imprescriptible rights antecedent and superior to all positive law, refers exclusively to the Family founded and based on the institution of marriage. (…) But the plaintiff is a mother and, as such, she has rights which derive from the fact of motherhood and from nature itself. These rights are among her personal rights as a human being and they are rights which, under Article 40, s3, subs1, the State is bound to respect, defend and vindicate. As a mother, she has the right to protect and care for, and to have the custody of, her infant child. (…) This right is clearly based on the natural relationship which exists between a mother and child. In my view, it arises from the infant's total dependency and helplessness and from the mother's natural determination to protect and sustain her child. How far and to what extent it survives as the child grows up is not a matter of concern in the present case. Suffice to say that this plaintiff, as a mother, had a natural right to the custody of her child who was an infant, and that this natural right of hers is recognised and protected by Article 40, s3, subs1, of the Constitution. Section 6, subs4, and s10, subs2(a), of the Guardianship of Infants Act, 1964, constitute a compliance by the State with its obligation in relation to the mother of an illegitimate child, to defend and vindicate in its laws this right to custody.

From the above, it is clear that the Court once again exploited the language of the law of nature as a cloak for judicial-making, in an attempt to reinforce the hermeneutics of Article 41. The imagery is quite distinctive and carefully selected. In celebrating maternal instinct, it provides a unique moral path distinguishing between fathers and mothers.

The result is a two-part narrative, a double-voiced discourse, a simultaneous double partaking where unmarried parents, and in particular unmarried fathers, have become hostage to the vagaries of subjective judicial interpretation and discretion.[77] On the one hand, the Courts have adopted a 'natural law reasoning' by making specific references to natural law and its unique position in the Constitution to preclude; or alternatively, they have adopted a staunch emotional and moral discourse to condemn and preclude from the protection of Article 41 those who do not conform to its model. As a result, the Courts have created a hierarchical structure in Irish Family law, establishing 'types' of units and their constituent members, leaving them inside or outside of the pale of the law.

---

77 See Martin, Frank, 'Judicial Discretion in Family Law', *I.L.T.* 15 (1997): 226–229; Woulfe, Seamus, 'K. v W. The Unmarried Father and the Child's Welfare', 8 *I.L.T.* 39 (1990); Walshe, Daniel, 'The Legal Rights of Unmarried Biological Fathers in Ireland and England, 1997-2002: A Comparative Analysis', *Irish Journal of Family Law* 2 (2003).

Redefining the Text

Lifting the Constitutional Ban on Divorce

The prohibition against civil divorce was removed by the Fifteenth Amendment in 1996 by including legislative details providing for divorce within Article 41. The reasons behind this blunt intrusion in the text are (1) to guarantee that the State continues to uphold its pledge towards married couples; and (2) to ensure that the judiciary applies a cautious and rigorous approach in any divorce proceedings. This new provision, however, altered the legal definition of marriage, shifting the traditional concept of the primary unit away from the original model of social organisation intended in Article 41. Most importantly, it opened up the question as to which unit now forms the Constitutional Family, a question which at the time of the referendum, the legislature deliberately fudged. When a Court allows the primary unit group to split and subsequent units groups to recompose, who makes up the constitutional unit group, the primary or the subsequent unit(s) group(s)? The answer given by most legal academics is that the re-composed unit, as long as it is legally married, reforms a Constitutional Family. A slight compromise from the original intent of Article 41!

Since the incursion of divorce legislation in provision 41.3 the text lacks normative coherence and one must wonder if sub-provision 41.3.1 is now not simply redundant. This incoherence in the text was subsequently underscored by the ECHR judgment in Keegan against Ireland where the European Court affirmed that the notion of the Family, under Article 8 of the European Convention of Human Rights, is not confined to a Family based on marriage and includes other de facto Family ties where the parties have been living together outside the realm of marriage.

Redefining the Text in a Non-Irish Context

Given the natural law foundation of the rights declared in Article 41, it would seem that they inhere by virtue of humanity and are not conferred on the basis of a positivist concept, such as citizenship. At the outset, it was always recognised that Article 41 applies equally to non-citizens and citizens alike. The rights of non-citizens to avail of the provisions of the Irish Constitution were argued in a number of family law cases. Justice Hamilton in *Northants Co Council v A.B.F.*, where an English father removed his child from the Irish jurisdiction, established that:

> The natural law is of universal application and applied to all human persons, be they citizens of the State or not, and it would be inconceivable that the father of an infant child would not be entitled to rely on the recognition of the Family contained in Article 41 for the purpose of enforcing his rights as the lawful father of the infant … These rights are recognised by [the Constitution] and the Courts created under it as antecedent and

superior to all positive law; they are not so recognised by the law of the Courts of the jurisdiction to which it is sought to have the infant return.[78]

However, since 1986,[79] there has been a trend towards limiting the benefits of the Constitution and of Article 41 specifically to Irish citizens.[80] In *Fajujonu v Minister for Justice*,[81] parents residing illegally in the State with their children, all of whom were Irish citizens, opposed a deportation order under the Aliens Act 1935 and sought a declaration that entitled them to remain in the country. The Supreme Court held that when an alien had resided for an appreciable time in Ireland and had become a member of an Irish Family including children who are citizens, those children have a constitutional right to 'the company, care, and parentage of their parents' within a Family unit, subject to the proper consideration of the common good. This right could be put into effect within the State, with parents asserting the choice of a residence on behalf of their children. However, it was made clear that alien parents of Irish citizens cannot assert a constitutional right of their own to reside in Ireland as they do not have the constitutional protection of Article 41, whether married or not.

Following the *Fajujonu* judgment, non-Irish parents were given the right to remain in Ireland on the basis of the children's right to the 'company, care and parentage' of their parents. This practice changed in January 2003, when the Supreme Court ruled in *Lobe & Osayande v Minister for Justice, Equality & Law Reform*[82] that the automatic right of residence granted to the parents of Irish-born children, regardless of the legal status of the parents, could no longer be sustained. The Supreme Court upheld that the common good required that restrictions be imposed on citizen children's right to the 'company, care and parentage' of their foreign parents within the State:

> The State can force a Family constituted of alien parents and children who are Irish citizens to leave the State only if, after due and proper consideration, it is satisfied that the interests of the common good and the protection of the State and society are so predominant and overwhelming as to justify such an interference with the rights of such a Family under the constitution.

The paramount notion of common good was first prompted in the *Fajujonu* case by Barrington in the High Court, where he bluntly declared that:

> It is clear from this that the Constitution does not contemplate the Family as existing in isolation but regards it as living in a larger community or society in which the State has a role to play as the guardian of the common good. [...] Whatever the 'inalienable and imprescriptible rights' of the Family may be, they hardly comprise the right to dictate the foreign policy of a state. In the present case the parents never had a right to live or to work

78 *Northants County Council v A.B.F. [1982] ILRM 164.*

79 *Pok Sun SHum v Ireland [1986] I.L.M.R. 593*; *Osheku v Ireland [1987] ILRM 330.*

80 Dunne, pp. 6-7.

81 *Fajujonu v Minister for Justice [1990] 2 IR 151.*

82 *Lobe & Osayande v Minister for Justice, Equality & Law Reform [2003] IESC 1.*

in Ireland. The child clearly has a certain right to be in Ireland. She also has a right to the society of her parents. But it does not follow from this that she has a right to the society of her parents in Ireland. I do not think that the parents can be positing on their child a wish to remain in Ireland in their society confer upon themselves a right to remain in Ireland such as could be invoked to override legislation passed by the Irish parliament to achieve its concept of what the common good of Irish citizens generally requires. [83]

In support of this interpretation, the Supreme Court used forceful and decisive language regarding the rights attributed to the Family under the Constitution when faced with the preservation of the common good:

> The Family is the fundamental unit group of the State but the State governs, not the Family. [...] The rights of the Family are not absolute. The State by its laws, made for the common good, may so order society as to restrict Family life in Ireland. The Family is the primary unit group – but it is a unit of the State. The State may make appropriate laws which may impinge upon the Family for the common good.[84]

It went on further to re-assert that:

> The rights given to the Family are not absolute. There are restrictions permitted for the common good.

But defined the restrictions as:

> Other factors, such as the fact that the members of the Family are non-nationals, their history, social and economic factors, and their status in the immigration process, and foreign policy, are all relevant.[85]

In issuing such a strapping statement, the Courts allayed public fears of inward migration flows in the State. They reiterated their objective, in a rather unsubtle nationalist discourse: to protect the cultural function of the sign by implicitly upholding its social and political function, that is to protect the organisation of the State through the common good as well as protecting the Irish nation and nationhood from non-nationals. The Courts handling of non-citizen rights to the Family further emphasised the anomalous treatment of other types of units under the Constitution. More importantly, it highlights the inconsistency of the rights language used in Articles 40-44, and in particular Article 41, when speaking of the various rights of citizens and rights of man.

The *Lobe and Osayande* case prompted the Government to take further action in tackling non-Irish citizens claiming a right of residence using Article 41 and the rights it confers upon their children born as Irish citizens. In June 2004, a referendum was held to amend the Constitution to restrict the entitlement to citizenship for children born on Irish soil to non-national parents. By a majority of almost four to one, the

---

83 Ibid., per Denham J. citing Barrington at pp. 156-157.

84 Ibid., para 14.

85 Ibid.

electorate voted to amend the Constitution, removing the right to citizenship from future generations of Irish-born children who could not demonstrate generations of belonging to the State. This was the last stretch to the notion of citizenship, to the notion of belonging to a culture, a group. The referendum confirmed that the concept of the Family is a strong static cultural sign, preserving the notion of Irishness for future generations.

A Semiotic Reading of Article 41

The departure point for a semiotic analysis of the Family in the Irish constitutional order is to distinguish between Article 41 as a state (the signifier) and the legal concept or phenomenon it purports to represent or give expression to (the signified – the Family). Article 41 is textually strong. It provides us with four key signs, namely: the State, the Family, The Woman-Mother, and Marriage. These signs have an important syllogistic quality with State/Nation dependent on the fundamental Unit Group-Family, which sequentially is founded on Woman as home maker and Mother, which in turn requires the institution of Marriage.

The sign State and its subsidiary or associated concepts 'Society, Social Order, Nation and Common Good' occupy the primary position within the Article and continue the themes of 'the rightful independence of our Nation', 'seeking to promote the common good', '"so that true social order attained', 'the unity of country restored', as set out in the Preamble to the Constitution. This immediately raises the question of whether Article 41 is only referring and aiming to protect the fundamental rights of the Family and if so, which Family? As referred to earlier, commentators have suggested that the drafting of the overall text, and Article 41 in particular, was heavily influenced by the Catholic hierarchy and papal encyclicals, supposing that de Valera's aim was to promote and protect the nuclear Irish Catholic Family. On closer examination of the sign and its recent interpretation by the Courts, it can be argued that the drafters' primary concern was in fact another Family – The Irish Family – the nation-state which emerged from 'centuries of trial' and 'heroic and unremitting struggle to regain the rightful independence of our Nation'.[86] In a post partition Republic, the sign State had an important emotional and political resonance. The birth of the new Irish Republic was the result of an acrimonious and painful separation, with Mother Ireland leaving one of her four sons in the custody of a foreign government. In an almost Freudian denial, de Valera attempts through Article 41 to paper over the reality of the new Republic as the product of a broken home and a dysfunctional Family. At the time Article 2 of the Constitution

86 It is worth noting the similarities to the language of the 1916 Irish Proclamation of Independence: 'In the name of God and of the dead generations from which she receives her old tradition of nationhood, Ireland, through us, summons her children to her flag and strikes for her freedom (…) We hereby proclaim the Irish Republic as a Sovereign Independent State, and we pledge our lives and the lives of our comrades-in-arms to the cause of its freedom, of its welfare (…).'

reflected this accommodation of created reality.[87] It has since been replaced with the notion of Irishness, 'Irish ancestry', 'cultural identity and heritage' to include those living outside the jurisdiction.[88] Over time, the State/Nation sign would become more important than the signified and the notion of Irishness would lose its default association with the physical island and move fully to the more ephemeral notion of Irishness as defined by a tradition and a culture.

The sign Family and its associated concepts 'natural primary', 'fundamental unit group', 'moral institution' invoke images of a utopian society of happy united families living in harmony under God. When it comes to the Irish Family, in cultural and semiotic terms, the concept is much more than a theological-moral tradition. It reflects a certain side of Irish history, an unconscious reservoir of folk symbols and images, a system of memories where the iconic unity of the Family is tied to its history of colonial survival. Again de Valera seeks to include the wider Irish Family, 'people of Irish ancestry living abroad who share its cultural identity and heritage', forced over the centuries to leave the country. Individual families were not as such the focus of protection but rather the ideological Irish Family made up of a nation of sons and daughters whose forebears had made the sacrifices needed to bring the State to fruition, to whom a debt of gratitude was owed. The Family became culturally coded, culturally specific, echoing specific political and social ideals of Irishness. In an ever increasing multicultural world and faced by the outside influence of incoming migration, the Courts have engaged in a great deal of social and cultural negotiations to preserve the notion of the Irish Family by reinforcing the citizenship concept; conceding a broader significance of the ultimate Family: the Irish nation, the Irish culture which the State now protects with the Citizenship Act. The evolutionary dialogue between social and legal discourse has rendered the notion of the Family as an institution in transition, subject to ongoing political pressure.

The sign Mother and the connected notions of 'woman' with a 'life within the home', bound to her 'duties in the home' project an image of domestic asymmetry where 'economic necessity' and the engagement in 'paid labour' outside the home are viewed as threats, 'neglect of their duties in the home', thereby menacing the harmonious social order of the State, 'the common good'. Woman derives her value from domestic unpaid labour and procreation. In Irish folklore, the Mother is by default a symbol of sacrifice. In Article 41 she represents good social order, essential to the common good by virtue of her support for 'The Family'. Constituted in this manner, the discursive regulation of the Mother as set out by the text and

87 Article 2 - The national territory consists of the whole island of Ireland, its islands and the territorial seas.

88 Article 2 above was repealed by the Nineteenth Amendment in 1998 and replaced by: 'It is the entitlement and birthright of every person born in the island of Ireland, which includes its islands and seas, to be part of the Irish Nation. That is also the entitlement of all persons otherwise qualified in accordance with law to be citizens of Ireland. Furthermore, the Irish nation cherishes its special affinity with people of Irish ancestry living abroad who share its cultural identity and heritage.'

its subsequent interpretations serves to establish a discursive space within which a meaningful sense of her ontological identity is maintained. The conflicting identity of the Father is established through a series of binary oppositions to the Mother[89] and the recurrent use of moral language. Since attitudes affect linguistic choices and linguistic choices entrench attitudes, it can be argued that legal language is a powerful tool of integration and has been used to mould behavioural patterns, sending a sharp message to 'unworthy' natural fathers. This enables the Woman-Mother sign to establish an internal logic of identity within the text and its interpretation which secures the social and patriarchal stability of the State. Her unique legal position and social role are further emphasised in the Constitution because of the pre-determined iconicity of the Irish mother as a cultural symbol and signifier in the folklore of independence and nationalism.[90] As for the sign Marriage, as an institution, it is seen as underpinning the Family and in need of protection from those that would undermine it. As a permanent fixed sign which cannot be altered, it stands at the front line in the protection of Mothers in the home, the Family and ultimately the State. The Courts have clearly identified it as the skeleton of the text, the essential condition on which the 'Constitutional Family' rests.

A semiotic reading shows that Article 41 is a system of interrelated uni-dimensional signs. They articulate a dual path and express a dual function: the path of public space and the path of private sphere bound by an aspired spirituality. The discourse chosen is emblematic, drawing its strength from a language that is servant to natural law, a higher form of legal reference. The discursive effect is to establish the Family as a true, fixed, immutable sign whose function is to confine its subjects within the defined limits of the text, instituting an order of reference; and in so doing inscribe the concept of the Family itself as a principle of interpretation. That way, as pointed out by Goodrich, the law is able to provide limits in which other discourses will operate, partly because of the symbolic status we invest in it and the type of language we allow the law to use on our behalf. It is the language that carries out our traditions, our most valued timeless and unconscious collective memories.[91] In the case of Article 41, whatever about the perceived linguistic imperfections, it is clear that the dense prose chosen by the drafters has stood the test of time.[92] For the Irish Courts, Article 41 and the Family remains an institution, best carrying the secular version of Christian values and traditions, reflecting indeed the 'theological character of the legal tradition ... the moral nature of common law' using 'a veridical language that carries ideals of meaning'.[93]

---

89 The Father is the non-identifiable subject in the Constitution.

90 Cacciaguidi-Fahy, p. 164.

91 Goodrich, pp. 209-259.

92 In 1996, the *Report of the Constitution Review Group*, p. 336 suggested only amending Article 41.2. and replacing it with a more neutral gender language, or alternatively deleting Article 41.2.1; 41.2.2.

93 Goodrich, p. 4.

The use of linguistic theology in Article 41 supports the sort of moral traditions which the drafters had in mind and convincingly established the Family as a sacred icon. Article 41 was intended to become the frame of reference, establishing the legitimacy of the concept at law, encoding social realities to come. Through staunch repetitions and coded terminology, it maps a linear message. The rationale behind this use of language was to establish the successful transmission of the concept in post-modern legal terminology, anchoring its meaning first in legal discourse and subsequently in social narratives. The semantic meaning of the subtext is reasonably unambiguous: its intention is to draw a pervasive contract between the State and the Family, a contract that is pre-existing positive law, based on absolute law, using a language that still haunts the Courts, binds them affectively to the timeless memory of 'our fathers' that sought 'true social order attained, the unity of our country restored'; a language that goes beyond our past and our contemporaneity.

Conclusion

The Family is a conscious part of a hegemonic culture and contemporary Irish law. Article 41 clearly sets out the concept of the Family as a structure of material life, whose legitimacy and authority stems from a more immaterial, divine form of life. It establishes the meaning of the Family as an institution resting upon a variety of signs (The State, Woman-Mothers and Marriage) built on a system of images to which authority and legitimacy have been given by the judiciary.

In interpreting the provision, the Courts have placed the Family at the nexus of relations between culture, power, law and morality, confirming that the original intent of the provision was never innocent. The Family was viewed as a long-term collective investment and experience, governed by distinct ethical practices, defined by a common membership of a unit in a particular set cultural group. The goal of Article 41 was undoubtedly to mould behavioural social patterns rather than reflect them, pointing to the vested socio-political interests of the time. Today, the legal text still carries the political message and intentions of the State as the Courts continue to define the Family and its constituent members in a rather monolithic ideal terminology, which does not respond to current sociological trends of Family units and forms. Lately, the legislature and the judiciary have endorsed that, at law, the Family is not only a social construction but also a cultural institution, which needs to be protected. The images the judiciary points towards are the sites at which the Family is formed and shaped. In this sense, legal interpretation becomes a discourse which teaches us and trains us to be what we are. It becomes the expression of the social contract in which various identities are assumed and transmitted. It reflects nothing else than the system of a sculpted culture tied to a sense of moral values and national political identity based on the notion of collective identity, commonly known as Irishness.

Yet, it is clear that in today's Ireland, the Courts need to move towards a more pluralistic and functional approach of the Family as opposed to a definitional notion expressed by its membership based on marriage;[94] and more recently its membership based on citizenship. Although the plain meaning of the Article is no doubt apparent, the expansion of existing textual rights, the identification and crafting of 'new' rights to the present-day Family, created by economic restructuring and cultural renegotiations, should not be handed over to the Courts to define.[95] This no doubt impoverishes the political debate which is where such debates should take place as, after all, accepting diversity as a value is rather difficult; and the law has never been too good at embracing diversity.

The substantive meaning of the Family and the rights arising from it has now reached a post-legal phase. A less legalised moralistic discourse and a more transcendent view of rights would present political opportunities for a more pragmatic inclusion of all types of units groups. This is both realistic and desirable as there is too much of a conceptual separation between the legal text and its social application.

---

94 Summerfield, Tracy, 'Families of Meaning: Dismantling The Boundaries Between Law and Society', 16 *IJSL* 1 (2003): 155-175.

95 Recently a call has been made to give constitutional protection to all Family units including those not based on marriage. See *Irish Times* (26 April 2004) and the recent *Consultation Paper on Rights and Duties of Cohabitees* (April 2004).

Chapter 13

Images of Racial Discrimination in France

Anne Wagner

Introduction

Measuring racial discrimination is virtually impossible.[1] Yet, just speaking about it acknowledges its existence, such a discrimination may go against tolerance, equality, and respect for the rights of others without reference to their identity, origin or associations. These values constitute, among other things, the fundamental principles of a State of laws.

One would hope that the mere declaration of equal rights should allow the creation of a certain harmony within human society. But some people are not concerned with respect and daily commit racist acts. In this respect, according to race relation specialists, such behaviours originate from two different lines of logic, the resultant acts differing depending on which line they follow. First, racial discrimination, in all its forms, is a way of making the targeted group feel inferior and therefore unequal. Secondly, racial discrimination denies a place to the targeted group, valuing criteria of difference, wilful rejection, distancing and exclusion, and, in extreme situations, of expulsion or even destruction. As Wieviorka explains, of the second logic which might be called 'differentialist':

> generally the logic of inequality goes back almost directly to the natural attitudes of the victimised group, whether in organicist terms or in the most contemporary genetic categorisation; the differentialist logic passes currently by a cultural detour, accenting the specifics of culture of the group victimised, where they see a menace for their own group, or a stain, a defilement which puts the homogeneity of the social body in question. The differentialist logic tends to segregate, it interferes with social relations or accompanies them, even while differentialism signifies the absence of social interaction, or its desire, separation more than oppression.[2]

In a general way, racial discrimination constitutes a hierarchical theory of races and includes, in its current definition, anti-Semitism, that is to say the rejection of Jews, and xenophobia (that is, the rejection of strangers). In the latter case, the stranger may be someone from a country other than that of the person rejecting them

1 See Hannoun, Michel, 1987.

2 See Wieviorka, Michel, 1993.

or, if between nationals, those from other regions, counties, communities, and so on. In this sense:

> racial discrimination includes racist ideology, prejudices, a discriminatory behaviour, structural arrangements and institutional practices involving racial inequalities as well as the erroneous notion that discriminatory relations between groups are justifiable from a moral and scientific viewpoint.[3]

The greater number of knowledgeable definitions of racial discrimination comes in general from the British sociologist Michael Banton's characterisation of racial discrimination as:

> the doctrine under which the behaviour of an individual is determined by stable hereditary characteristics which derive from separate racial stock with different attributes and which are ordinarily considered to have relations of superiority and inferiority between them.[4]

The birth of racial discrimination has been situated in the eighteenth century:

> that is to say at the moment where the elaboration of a project of a modern science of nature and scientific reflection on the human species started, which developed into physical anthropology.[5]

The historical context of its formation explains why racial discrimination remains an ambiguous, loose and ill-defined concept, which throws light on the confusion or indeterminacy of its contemporary usage. As such, racial discrimination is not to be understood as 'racialism', which is, by contrast:

> [T]he explicit theory of human races defined and classified by the methods of natural science, and implying the theory of biological (or genetic) determinism of the inequality of the races.[6]

Taking account of the 'ideological metamorphosis of racial discrimination', we will examine in detail, from a legal standpoint, the contemporary re-translation of racist acts undertaken by the law in its attempts to define them, because, it seems, 'racial discrimination only starts with the interpretation of differences'.[7]

Contemporary legislative practice is to enlarge the range of legal categories, allowing for exceptions to the common norms and, in consequence, for different, and more or less favourable, treatment of various racial categories. These are not constituted by identical and abstract subjects, but of individuals placed in various situations, therefore calling for a variety of rules.

---

3 See *Declaration on Race and Racial Prejudice*, UNESCO, 27 November 1978.

4 See Taguieff, Pierre-André, p. 13.

5 See Wieviorka, Michel, 1993.

6 See Taguieff, Pierre-André, p. 22.

7 Cf. Albert Memmi, *Racism* (Paris: Gallimard, 1982); see also, *Racism: Description, Definition, Treatment* (Paris: Gallimard, 1994).

Nevertheless, it is for the judge to construe in each case the eventual arbitrary or discriminatory character of different treatment, the distinction between nationals and aliens, which leads to the idea that the benefits of certain rights are reserved only for citizens. This is not contrary to the provisions of the French Constitution.

At the international level, the International Convention on the Elimination of All Forms of Racial Discrimination Part I, Article 1 states that:

> In this Convention, the term 'racial discrimination' shall mean any distinction, exclusion, restriction or preference based on race, colour, descent, or national or ethnic origin which has the purpose or effect of nullifying or impairing the recognition, enjoyment or exercise, on an equal footing, of human rights and fundamental freedoms in the political, economic, social, cultural or any other field of public life.

It also accepts:

> the discriminations, exclusions, restrictions or preferences established by a State (…) when it is a question of nationals and aliens.[8]

Racial discrimination remains the expression of a psychological dimension situated in the depths of the human being: the desire to affirm oneself through the negation of the other. For the past several years, racial discrimination in France has been foregrounded, despite its strong tradition of tolerance.

Racial Discrimination: An Existing Fact

It is difficult to legally define and identify racial discrimination. It is known that the law is fixed, from the time that it sets limits or determines certain forbidden behaviours, while racial discrimination is perpetually evolving; the attitudes and related ideological arguments are constantly being retranslated. This led Memmi to suggest, as early as 1964, the replacement of the term 'racism' by a phrase, a word which expresses the variety and origin of the racist acts at the same time: racial discrimination.[9] In spite of its intangibility, the existence of racial discrimination has still been officially proved.

The Official Recognition of Racial Discrimination

The National Committee for the Consultation on Human Rights[10] points out that France, like other European States, is sometimes affected by feverish fits of new

8 Adopted by the Assembly General of the United Nations, 21 December 1965 (Article 1–2), and ratified by France, 28 July 1971.

9 Cf. Article: 'Essai de definition du racisme' (An attempt to define racism), *La Nef*, n°19-20, September – October 1964, cited by P.A. Taguieff, p. 40.

10 Instituted by the Act of 13 July 1990, Article 2, notably in its first report: 1990. *La lutte contre le racisme et la xénophobie (The Struggle Against Racism and Xenophobia)*, La

forms of racial discrimination as, according to the Committee, the virus of racial discrimination mutates when it enters the social corpus. Therefore, even if it is morally and legally forbidden, that is to say, if its free expression is curbed, racial discrimination in its new forms is based on the principle of radical incommensurability of different cultural forms.

Legislators have attempted to recognise the metamorphosing nature of racial discrimination by adopting a definition of racial discrimination as a general process. In the Act of 1 July 1972 and its successive amendments, racial discrimination is globally defined in effect as the practical means of achieving the belittling of the other. This constitutes the preferred approach to legislating against racial discrimination and all forms of exclusion. Thus under Article 225-1 of the New Criminal Code (Articles 416 and 416-1 of the Old Criminal Code):

> All distinctions operating between physical persons for the reasons of their origin, sex, family situation, state of health, handicaps, morals, political opinions, union activities membership or non-membership real or imagined to a certain ethnic group, race or religion constitutes a discrimination.

In light of Article 432-7 of the Old Criminal Code:

> All distinctions operating between moral persons by reason of their origin, sex, family situation, state of health, handicap, morals, political opinions, union activities, membership or non-membership real or imagined to a certain ethnic group, race or religion determined by members or certain members of these moral persons is also considered to be discrimination.

From the same point of view, the United Nations Convention on the Elimination of All Forms of Racial Discrimination stipulates in Article 1:

> In this convention, the term 'racial discrimination' shall mean any distinction, exclusion, restriction or preference based on race, colour, descent, or national or ethnic origin which has the purpose or effect of nullifying or impairing the recognition, enjoyment or exercise, on an equal footing, of human rights and fundamental freedoms in the political, economic, social, cultural or any other field of public life.

Article 4:

> States Parties condemn all propaganda and all organisations which are based on…
> Paragraph (a)
> Shall declare an offence punishable by law all dissemination of ideas based on racial superiority or hatred, incitement to racial discrimination, as well as all acts of violence or incitement to acts against any race or group of persons of another colour or ethnic origin, and also the provision of assistance to racist activities, including the financing thereof; …

Documentation française, 1991.

The determination by the legislator of racist behaviours supposes their possible expression in the different domains of daily life as shown in the following examples.

Illustrations of Discriminatory Acts

The legislator determines which behaviours are forbidden and considered as discriminatory offences to private individuals, to official representatives of public authority and to organs of the press.

First of all, when considering private individuals, Article 225-2 of the New Criminal Code forbids any refusal to provide goods or services, any restriction on the normal exercise of any kind of economic activity, all refusals to hire, sanctions or terminations of a person, any limitation in providing goods or services or an offer of employment, based on any element provided for in Article 225-1. But, for the offence to be committed it is necessary that the discrimination occurs in a concrete manner in one of the contexts listed in Article 225-2.

For example, the offence of refusing to provide goods or services could be committed by a hotel owner refusing to rent a room to a mixed couple, where the husband is of African origin.[11] Another would be for a café owner to refuse to serve a drink to an Arab client,[12] or a meal to a handicapped person because of their handicap.

The offence of discrimination for refusal to hire, for sanctioning or terminating has been committed (1) in the case of circulation of a memo relating to recruitment of home workers asking that the hiring of persons of colour be avoided,[13] (2) by the refusal to promote due to 'excessive union activity' by the candidate[14] or (3) by the termination of a worker on a trial contract while giving him a job attestation stating that his work was satisfactory but that because of his Moroccan nationality, he was not 'adopted' by the personnel.[15]

The offence of discrimination through limiting an employment offer conditional on the basis of one of the elements provided for in Article 225-1 is committed when hiring is limited to a man (without legitimate reason) or a legal resident of the EEC. On the other hand, an offer conditional on membership of a religion (Islam, for example) cannot be considered a discrimination having a racial character since followers of that religion come from many races.[16]

---

11 Douai, 25 June 1974: D. 1975, p. 492, 1ère espèce, note Foulon-Piganiol; see also, Tribunal correctionnel, Paris 25 March.

12 Tribunal correctionnel, Strasbourg, 21 November 1974, D. 1975, p. 492, note Foulon-Piganiol. See also TGI de Nantes, 1 March 1990, Dr. Pénal 1991.

13 Crim., 14 November 1989, Droit Pénal, 1990, n° 129.

14 Le Tribunal de Grande Instance of Bastia, 3 June 1997, Revue de Sciences Criminelles, 1998, p. 99.

15 Crim., 14 October 1986, JCP 1987, éd. G., IV-3.

16 TGI Paris, 19 December 1991, Gaz. Pal. 1996-1-Somm. 52.

The action of authorised public officials or those charged with a public service mission in the exercise or at the occasion of the exercise of their functions or of their mission, is captured by Article 432-7. These forbid, firstly, all refusal of benefits from rights granted by the Act (the right must exist to the benefit of the plaintiff, which avoids complaints based on the simple exercise of the agent's right to make decisions) and, secondly, any refusal of the normal exercise of an economic activity or of economic discrimination, such as access to a public marketplace.

In the first case, it may be a question of a refusal of nomination, of forbidding access, of the deliverance of a document or of enrolment in a school, based on one of the elements stipulated in Article 225-1.[17] The refusal of a right cannot constitute a discriminatory offence unless a material act listed in the provisions of the text can be personally and/or directly imputed to the person accused.[18]

The law on the freedom of the press forbids provocation of racial discrimination or any other crime or offence when the provocation is followed by effects, through public, written or printed speeches or cartoons. Legal offences thereby include incitement to discrimination, hate or violence regarding a specifically named person, a group of people (foreign workers, African merchants), by reason of their origin, their membership or non-membership of an ethnic group, nation, race or specific religion. The incitement to racial discrimination under Article 24 of the Act of 29 July 1881 involves incitement to acts which are determined by Articles 187-1 and 416 of the Criminal Code.[19] It is to be understood that racial defamation (Article 32-2) and provocation constitute two offences of different nature and gravity.[20]

According to the terms of Article 29 of the New Criminal Code defamation consists of an allegation or imputation which impugns the honour or reputation of a person or a group. It is in this way that the author of a piece of writing which systematically denigrates immigrant workers, Africans, Arabs, West Indian and Reunionese in order to incite hatred may commit the offence of provocation to racial hate.[21] The offence is also committed by the use of such terms as 'invaders', 'occupiers of our land' and 'disrespectful and annoying foreigners', which invite the reader to think that foreign communities represent a danger for the French community. Such statements immediately and directly incite sentiments of hate and may give rise to discriminatory behaviour.[22]

---

17 Tribunal Correctionnel Grenoble, 18 July 1991, *Le Monde*, 20 July 1991.

18 CA Paris, 11th Ch. B, 5 June 1998, Prefect of police of Paris, Droit Pénal January 1999, n° 1, comm., n° 2: Refusal to deliver a resident's permit, the victim having alleged racial discrimination not based in kind.

19 Article 225-1 and 432-7 of the New Criminal Code: Crim., 22 May 1989, JCP-IV6296.

20 Crim., 28 June 1983, Bulletin criminel, n° 202.

21 Crim., 22 April 1976, Bulletin Criminel n°112.

22 Versailles, 10 February 1995, Gazette du Palais, 10-12 March 1996, confirmed by Crim., 24 June 1997, Bulletin criminel, n°253 ; Revue de Sciences Criminelles 1998, 102, observations Mayaud; JCP 1997-IV-2161.

The determination of acts considered as discriminatory is part of a global struggle against racial discrimination and all kinds of discrimination and exclusion. To struggle against racial discrimination and exclusion is to manifest a constant will to go further.

Racial Discrimination: the Outcast Act

Racial discrimination, a harmful social phenomenon, involves a great deal of irrationality and fantasy. It is crucial to take accurate measure of it, while strengthening guarantees of objectivity, and without taking sides. This was the recommendation of members in the 1990 Report of the National Committee for the Consultation on Human Rights. Its impetus was from the 1980s, when, racial discrimination became one of the major issues of public debate, channelled into the political space by a nationalist-populist movement, the National Front, which lives and prospers by exploiting the dread, fears and resentments of the French. Specialised in the demonisation of foreigners, the ideology of this party naturally appears racist; the national preference it advocates constitutes the justification of all forms of discrimination which come from the ignoble. This explains why these ideas are often represented in the most marginalised levels of society, who clash directly with the immigrant populations. In this context, the legislator must take the measure of those behaviours and legally cast them out, with the help of anti-racist organisations.

Legal Reprobation of Racial Discrimination

As previously explained the manifestations of racial discrimination can be grouped as, firstly, writings and statements of a racist character and, secondly, in activities performed for racist reasons (acts of aggression, attacks or refusal to provide goods and services).

Faithful to its tradition of tolerance and as a receiving country of immigrants, France rejects discrimination as well as all forms of exclusion by its constitutional documents. According to the 1958 Constitution:

> The French people solemnly proclaim their attachment to human rights and to the principles of national sovereignty as they are defined in the declaration of 1789 (and) as confirmed and completed by the constitution of 1946.

Further:

> The French people proclaim that all human beings, without distinction of race, religion, or belief, possess inalienable and sacred rights.

In the same way, the Universal Declaration of the Rights of Man, adopted by the General Assembly of the United Nations on 10 December 1948, stipulates in Articles 2, 3 and 7 that:

> Everyone is entitled to all the rights and freedoms set forth in this Declaration, without distinction of any kind, such as race, colour, sex, language, religion, political or other opinion, national or social origin, property, birth or other status. Furthermore, no distinction shall be made on the basis of the political, jurisdictional or international status of the country or territory to which a person belongs, whether it be independent, trust, non-self-governing or under any other limitation of sovereignty. (Article 2)
>
> Everyone has the right to life, liberty and security of person. (Article 3)
>
> All are equal before the law and are entitled without any discrimination to equal protection of the law. All are entitled to equal protection against any discrimination in violation of this Declaration and against any incitement to such discrimination. (Article 7)

Conforming to these values, the national legislation in this area is part of an international banning movement, as Article 55 of the Constitution places international conventions above the law.

In the same way, the European Convention for the Protection of Human Rights and Fundamental Freedoms, which came into effect on 3 September 1953, provides in Article 14:

> The enjoyment of the rights and freedoms set forth in this Convention shall be secured without discrimination on any ground such as sex, race, colour, language, religion, political or other opinion, national or social origin, association with a national minority, property, birth or other status. (Article 14)

The International Convention on the Elimination of All Forms of Racial Discrimination, which has, without doubt, had the greatest influence on French national legislation, declares in Article 2-1-d that:

> Each State Party shall prohibit and bring to an end, by all appropriate means, including legislation as required by circumstances, racial discrimination by any persons, group or organisation.[23]

In respect of this, the Act of 1 July 1972, accepted unanimously by the Parliament, harmonised the legislation with the principles imposed by this Convention, reinforced by several Acts. The law is evidence of the legislature's will to fight against this social phenomenon.

To take into account new racist manifestations, the Act of 13 July 1990 (Official Journal of 14 July) reaffirms under Article 1 the ban on discrimination based on membership or non-membership of an ethnic group, nation, race or a given religion.

---

23 Article 4 enumerates a certain number of measures to take to eliminate any encouragement to discrimination or any discriminatory act.

This Act is aimed at racial discrimination in its daily accepted form, that is to say, discrimination against those that some people consider 'alien' in the pejorative sense.

The principal role of enforcement is incumbent on the State. Article 2 of the Act of 1972 declares that 'the State shall assure the respect of this principle in the frame of the laws enforced', by exercising a constant regulation of their enforcement. Article 2 of the Act of 1990 provides in this sense that:

> On March 21, the date chosen by the United Nations for the International Day for the Elimination of All Forms of Racial Discrimination, the National Commission for the Consultation on Human Rights will deliver a report on the fight against racial discrimination to the government. This report shall be immediately made public.

Aside from the establishment of a National Committee for the Consultation on Human Rights, the law continues the repression of discriminatory acts by strengthening the sentences for such acts. The reinforcement of penalties will eventually permit, in the most serious cases, recourse to custody even in absence of *flagrante delicto.*

Complying with Article 225-2 of the New Criminal Code, the acts of discrimination defined in Article 225-1 committed by individuals against physical or moral persons, would now be punishable by three years imprisonment and a fine of 45,000 Euros instead of the light sentence previously provided, that is to say two months to one year and/or fine of 30,000 Euros. Additional penalties are also possible, such as the posting or publishing of the sentence given (the agreement of the victim is required before his/her name can be mentioned according to Article 131-35 line 3), the closure of the offending establishment, and the suspension of civic and civil rights. The judge is given discretion to pronounce these penalties, within the limits of the law.[24]

Acts of discrimination committed by persons holding posts of public authority also attract increased penalties. According to Article 432-7, discrimination as defined in Article 225-1, when committed by public authorities, is punishable by three years imprisonment and a 30,000 Euro fine. Additional penalties (suspension of rights, interdiction to exercise a function or an activity, posting or publishing of the decision) are provided for in Article 432-17.

It should be noted that among officials, members of the police and the gendarmes are charged with playing an important role in combating racial discrimination, whether by spontaneous action or as a result of a judicial charge. Article 7 of the Code of Ethics of 18 March 1986 defines their obligations to citizens thus:

> The function of the national police is absolute in respect of persons, whatever maybe their nationality or origin, their social condition or political convictions.

---

24 Crim., 4 September 1990, Bull. crim., n° 308.

This suggests that the police officer or gendarme must not be racist. However, the application of directives, notably the reinforced repression measures[25] aimed at forcing out aliens in irregular situations, leads them to perform controls '*au faciès*' (based on physical appearance), which are strictly condemned by the Court of Cassation.

Publishers also attract censure for racist offences. The main penalty concerning incitement to discrimination or calling for racial violence in the press involves facing at least one year of prison with suspension of rights, with posting or publishing the decision constituting the additional penalties. The director of the concerned publication is considered to be fully responsible; however, the author can be tried as an accomplice.

The will of the public powers in the fight against discrimination seems obvious, and their action continues on the ground, along with other public associations and organisations which are involved in the same struggle.

The Reprobation by the Anti-racist Organisations

The 'association movement', comprised of anti-racist organisations, plays an important role in the fight against all kinds of discrimination and exclusion, including the participation of members in the drafting of anti-racist laws in France. Their participation in the drafting of the laws of 1972 and 1990, considered by others as the benchmark in the subject, falls naturally in the framework of the stated objectives of one another in their diversity. Among these organisations are:

- *La ligue des droits de l'homme* (Human Rights League) most probably constitutes the oldest of the associations specifically defending human rights, defending civil and political rights, individual and political liberties and social and economic rights. Its members obviously consider that the problem of racial discrimination in contemporary society cannot be separated from problems such as immigration, especially its essentially economic origins.
- *LICRA* (International League against Racism and Anti-semitism) whose objective for over 30 years has been to fight against all racial discrimination. Though its main struggle has been against anti-semitism, its fight includes racial discrimination in general.
- *MRAP* (Movement against Racial Discrimination, Anti-semitism and for Friendship between Peoples) for whom racial discrimination constitutes a globality. The group's focus takes different forms according to the period and the context, as well as a different intensity according to the group. It contributes nonetheless to a redefining of the mental and ideological constructions on which racial discrimination is based.
- *GISTI* (Group for Information and Aid for Immigrant Workers) made up of

25 Cf. The Pasqua Laws, of which the Act of 10 August 1993 relaxed the regulations concerning identity checks by enlarging police powers.

social workers and jurists who have decided to defend the rights of immigrants in France, and to furnish information and legal analysis to other organisations engaged on the ground.

- *SOS-RACIAL DISCRIMINATIONE*, born in reaction to the hegemony of the racist discourse of the mid-1980s, especially that of the National Front, it constitutes a means of expression for claims of immigrant youth being subjected to discrimination because of their parents' origins.

The Act of 5 January 1985 authorises the participation of these organisations in trials before the criminal court, when crimes involve racial discrimination as a motive.

Even if the value of the fight against racial discrimination at an organisational level seems irrefutable, its effectiveness is judicially limited to the repression of marginal and visible or even ostentatious manifestations of racial discrimination (discriminations, calls to hate or inciting violence, and so on).

Conclusion

Law, in spite of the notable efforts of legislators with their adoption of the Law of 1990, does not take into account the 'symbolic racial discrimination' carried on in publicly held political discourse which, integrated in nationalism, can also claim to be part of the republican tradition. As a result, as Taguieff suggests,[26] the strategies of reformulation, the constant recourse to innuendo – from which the advantage of power is born – and the unforeseeable symbolic detours of neo-racial discrimination, mean that the application of the legislative system comes up against obstacles which are difficult to surmount.

The repressive method, reflected in France's laws, seems completely maladapted to the fight against the mass movement which makes up the National Front. In effect, the criminal law plays a pedagogical and dissuasive role, in that it participates in the evolution of mental attitudes.

This criticism also extends to the action of organisations in the fight against racial discrimination. Having based their fight for the last decade on the illegitimacy of one political party, the French National Front, which is the supposed incarnation of 'racial discrimination', they ignore the mutating character of the phenomenon, and its new forms and new places of expression.

> Communities which are part of a society, clear political choices of conflicts of interest within the society, augmentation in political participation: It is in the combination of these

26 Cf. *'Les raisons d'un échec' (The Reasons for Failure)*, in *Le racisme dans tous ses débats (Racism in All Its Debates)*, co-ordinated by Lucien Bitterlin (Paris: Panoramiques-Corlet, 1996), pp. 13-24.

three objectives of collective action that the possibility to effectively fight against racial discrimination will be found.[27]

27 Cf. Alain Tourraine, *'Le racisme aujourd'hui' (Racism Today)*, in *Racisme et modernité (Racism and Modernity)* (Paris : La Découverte, 1993).

Chapter 14

Law's Trouble with Images: Fetishism and Seduction from Athens and Jerusalem to Madison Avenue

Robert A. Yelle

Introduction: Iconoclash and the Law

What is law's trouble with images? Why have they been the target of so much vilification, condemnation, and proscription from the Ten Commandments to the present? And given such traditional, historical concerns over the image, what does the present profusion and celebration, and even fetishization, of images in today's media culture say about the particular moment in history that we inhabit? What, finally, is and ought to be the role of the law in establishing a regime of images? These are some of the questions addressed, though doubtless not resolved, in the present chapter.

Bruno Latour posed the question of a modern 'iconoclash' in the following way:

> [T]he second commandment can no longer be obeyed: 'You shall not make for yourself an idol in the form of anything in heaven above or on earth beneath or in the waters below.' No need to try to fudge the intention and tension of this exhibition as we have imagined it for the last four years: it is about the second commandment. Are we sure we have understood it correctly? Have we not made a long and terrifying mistake about its meaning? How can we reconcile this request for a totally aniconic society, religion and science with the fabulous proliferation of images that characterizes our media-filled cultures? . . . If images are so dangerous, why do we have so many of them? If they are innocent, why do they trigger so many and such enduring passions? Such is the enigma, the hesitation, the visual puzzle, the iconoclash that we wish to deploy under the eyes of the visitor and reader. (2002: 8)

As Latour points out, new media technologies forcefully pose an ancient conundrum regarding the proper government of images. This ought to be of special concern for lawyers. Outside the courtroom, new technologies raise important questions concerning the proper limits placed on images in the public domain. Modern media increasingly exploit the seductive properties of the image, in a way that brings new meaning, or at least new context, to the traditional legal concept of 'false advertising.' In addition to the proliferation of visual images, numerous verbal images, including jingles or slogans, music and other forms of sound, contribute to advertising's commercial mission. In keeping with this reality of the 'Total Work of Commercial Art' (to pilfer Richard Wagner's concept), I will throughout this chapter use the word 'image' to refer to both visual and verbal images somewhat interchangeably, and will approach such images from the standpoint of an integrated theory of their rhetorical function.

Apart from law's interest in the regulation of commercial advertising – a topic addressed more extensively below – law has itself entered the electronic age. Older cinematic techniques of manipulating images, facilitated by electronic media and the internet, are being employed increasingly by lawyers in the courtroom. Recently in the *New York Times*, a story with the title, 'Is a Cinema Studies Degree the New M.B.A.?' (6 March 2005), asked whether literacy in film and related imagistic media will become an increasingly powerful tool for a range of different endeavors, including law. The lead example was a former cinema studies major now attending Yale Law School who planned to put his media literacy to good use: 'People endowed with social power and prestige are able to use film and media images to reinforce their power – we need to look to film to grant power to those who are marginalized or currently not represented.' One can only wish this intrepid brave-new-worlder 'Godspeed.' Yet his hasty embrace of the power of images disturbs me more than his benevolent personal motive has the power to soothe. What about others, whose motives may not be so benevolent? And what about those of us who may lose more agency than we gain in the new media 'reality,' which the news article refers to, without irony, as a state of 'post-literacy?' The response of the law to these new developments will bear careful watching, especially where the increasing introduction of images into the courtroom may render the justice system itself 'post-literate.'

Richard Sherwin (2002: 6) argues that 'as the dominant media or technology of communication change, so too do the means of legal persuasion.' He takes a cautious, and cautionary, approach to the challenges the new media pose for law. Sherwin recognizes the need for lawyers to acquire literacy in the new media and their distinctive techniques of persuasion. At the same time, he articulates forcefully the potential dangers raised by the replacement of a text-based discourse of legal rationality with an image-based discourse that too often short-circuits thought by exploiting narrative devices derived from popular culture. Images are used increasingly to make one's case not only in the courtroom, but also in the court of public opinion. Sherwin (2002: x) puts the key question as follows: 'What happens when the line between reality and fiction, reason and desire, fact and fantasy can no longer be drawn? What then becomes of life in the law?'

The present chapter adopts an historical approach to these questions, in keeping with Latour's choice of the Second Commandment, the traditional Judeo-Christian prohibition against idolatry, as the 'frame' in which to view the contemporary phenomenon of imagistic media, and their relation to the law. The premise of such an approach is that we can learn, from a study of past legal treatments of images, what is at stake in the use and regulation of images. This premise will be more than vindicated by the historical examples chosen. Indeed, it will emerge that many earlier theorists of the image – including both proponents and opponents of their use – have been more aware of the power and danger of images than their contemporary legal counterparts. The rhetorical potential of the image is too often simply ignored or neglected under current law. In some cases, earlier debates help to illuminate elements of the contemporary situation better than current legal models do. For example, the rhetorical power of verbal images in contemporary advertising was both theorized and exploited already by the fifth century BCE Greek rhetorician Gorgias, as was well understood by his opponent Plato, who proposed to outlaw poetic 'imitation' (*mimesis*). The ancient Judeo-Christian concept of idolatry also anticipated aspects of the current commercial domain, as reflected in Marx's appropriation of this concept to define the phenomenon of 'commodity fetishism' (1992: Ch. 1, Sec. 4) in what Horkheimer and Adorno later called 'the culture industry' (2002: 120-167; cf. Hawkes, 2001).

If commercial advertising is a modern analogue of the ancient crimes of idolatry and sophistry, it is most ironic that modern law, as Sherwin depicts it, is now beginning itself to be influenced by the imagistic techniques of the new media. For law in the Judeo-Christian tradition was centrally concerned with the regulation of images. Iconoclasm was foundational, not only to the Decalogue (Ten Commandments), but also to the Protestant Reformation, and indeed to the modern, ostensibly 'secular' common law tradition that followed in its wake. Peter Goodrich (1995) has argued that the English common law tradition established its authority through an act of textual iconoclasm that borrowed from religious developments. He also noted the role of writing, or rather of print culture, in motivating such iconoclasm. The technological innovation of the printed book facilitated a return to the old opposition between word and image. Similarly, Yelle (2005) has shown how the Reformation opposition of a scriptural canon to idolatrous custom influenced Jeremy Bentham's proposal for a written code of law that excluded custom and other idolatrous 'fictions.' Ironically, the very process of excluding rhetoric from the authorized pronouncements of law may have contributed to the law's inability to appreciate, on a theoretical level, the dangers posed by rhetoric, a development that has paved the way for law's present (partial) openness to images.

The iconoclasm of law was primarily internal: it affected, first and foremost, the text of law itself, which sought to establish itself as an image-less, completely rational language, and largely succeeded in doing so, at least to most observers. However, except during episodes of the most fervent iconoclasm, in which the Puritan 'plain style' was established over broader domains of culture, society outside of the ideal world of the legal text was relatively saturated with images. The inherent 'disconnect' between the ideal, textual world of law and the world outside has now been widened and hastened by the arrival of electronic media. To the extent that the new media intrude both on the areas regulated by law, but more especially on the law itself, they call into question law's pretense to a lofty rationality; challenge the ideal of a neutral, non-rhetorical medium in which justice may prevail over power; and threaten the very fabric of the law and the social ideals it embodies. Among the possible responses to these challenges, two are diametrically opposed: law could embrace the new media, and adopt their techniques, thereby declining further into sophistry; or law could mount a new iconoclastic reform, by re-establishing severe boundaries on the permissible uses of images. Before choosing either course, it would be well to consider what history tells us about the relationship between law and the image. This will contribute to the formation of a theory of the rhetoric of images that, although sorely lacking in contemporary legal theory, provides the only possible basis for a normative rule of images.

To pursue this objective, we will first explore two primary historical examples of the conflict over images: the ancient Jewish and Christian prohibition against idolatry, and the debate between Plato and the Sophists (represented by Gorgias) over the proper limits of rhetoric. The two traditions reflected in these examples have provided the conceptual basis for historical theories of the rhetoric of images. Together, they illustrate not only the dangers of images, but also, and more especially, that the concern with and proper regulation of images is central (indeed foundational) to law. As previously mentioned, these two examples also anticipate certain aspects of the modern scene. Therefore, following a discussion of these examples, the chapter will proceed to address the problem of images in contemporary advertising, placing them in relation to these historical examples. The inadequacy of the current legal treatment of images will emerge in contrast.

The War Against Idols in Ancient Judaism

The biblical prohibition against idolatry has already been reproduced in the quote from Latour above. Idolatry derives from a Greek word *eidololatria* meaning 'image worship.' The original prohibition, however, extended to a range of related offenses, including not only the making and worship of images, but also the worship of 'strange gods' and, by extension, polytheism, or the worship of multiple gods. The importance of this prohibition to the symbolic constitution of the Mosaic law is indicated in the first instance by its placement at the head of all the laws, at the beginning of the Ten Commandments, immediately following the command to worship the one God. This suggests the deep antagonism between monotheism and idolatry, which constitutes a derogation from the absolute sovereignty of the one God, on whose authority the validity of all the remaining laws is based. Hence, idolatry calls into question *all* of the laws – not merely the injunction against the worship of images. In keeping with this, the early Church father Tertullian (ca. 150 - ca. 240) argued that idolatry was the root of all sins – an argument that required a fair bit of ingenuity in its application (Tertullian, 1885). He also condemned, in part because of their association with idolatry, the spectacles of the theatre, circus, and stadium (Tertullian, 1885). A modern commentator adds: 'The question of the attendance by Christians at Sporting or Entertainment Events, or participation in [the same], is raised from time to time. The same question is also valid about the use of the printed page, radio and T.V. for learning of these events. It is sometimes worthwhile looking at how this issue was dealt with in the past.' (http://www.the-faith.org.uk/tertullian1.html)

The prohibition against idolatry records the conviction that the image lies. The image is seductive or misleading. The images of the many gods are hollow, empty. They can neither see, nor hear, nor speak, nor act. Although idols were always associated with the practice of magic, there was also already an ambivalence, from early Judaism until the Reformation, about whether that magic was potentially effective or merely 'vain,' a form of rhetoric and self-deception on the part of those who believed in it. The faithlessness of the image, within the Christian tradition, incorporated Platonic criticisms that had already worked to deprive the phenomenal world, and especially human artistry or *poiesis*, of its pretensions to capture and figure truth and beauty, and even to exert magical influence. However, these interpretations were consonant with the Jewish tradition, which emphasized both the powerlessness of idols and the foolishness of human beings worshiping what they had made with their own hands, as if through an act of forgetfulness. The only real creator was God. It was the height of presumption to put oneself in this role by making (human or humanoid) images, in a manner analogous to that in which God had made man 'after His image' (*Genesis* 1:26). To then turn and worship created matter was a further rejection of God's transcendence of His own creation.

These early prohibitions against idolatry and entertainment already stressed the seductive power of such images. As Moshe Halbertal and Avishai Margalit (1992) point out, in early Judaism, idolatry was associated with adultery, with the breaking of a covenant of faith with God that was analogous to marriage. In this case, seduction equaled sedition, a violation of God's sovereignty and patriarchal authority. Over the centuries pagan practices of image-worship were also associated in Christian polemics with fornication, fertility rites and temple prostitution. There is a curious parallel in all of this to the early modern English common law tradition which, as Goodrich (1995: 108-80) has shown, founded itself partly on polemics against both images in general and feminine images in particular, thereby identifying iconoclasm with patriarchy.

The idol could be horrible – indeed, some idols are described this way – yet a beautiful idol could be even more dangerous. This idea coordinated with a deep distrust of external appearances. There was a debate in the early Church concerning whether Christ was beautiful or ugly. The question turned on several points. The first was the claim that Christ was the perfect image or *icon* of God. The second was the nature of the Incarnation. Supposedly, Christ had undergone 'abasement' or *kenosis* in the process of becoming human. This arguably meant a loss or evacuation of the divine attributes, an emptying. But then, divine beauty may have been translated into human ugliness. The side of the debate that advocated beauty and icon-worship won out. However, this did not end permanently the war against images. Similarly, tradition records that Socrates was ugly. For Nietzsche, this was a source of the philosopher's *ressentiment*. If true, this may have served Socrates as a metaphor for the abjuration of success. As we know, he declined to use beautiful words in his defense, a failing for which he was put to death. The more basic point is that a philosopher cannot trust in appearances. How fortunate the person who is ugly, for she is predisposed to distrust images!

Even Moses stuttered. When called upon to be God's mouthpiece, he protested that he was not an eloquent man, even after conversing with God, an experience that might have been expected to produce inspired oratory. Various translations of the relevant Biblical verse, *Exodus* 4:10, claim that Moses was referring to a speech impediment. A modern translation by Ronald Knox (1949), however, presents a more intriguing possibility: 'Then Moses said, Lord, have patience with me; but all my life I have been a man of little eloquence, and now that thou, my Master, hast spoken to me, I am more faltering, more tongue-tied than ever.' Moses claims he has become *less* articulate after encountering the deity. Is it that this encounter defied powers of verbal, as well as visual description? In line with this suggestion is the prohibition directed against pronouncing the true name of God. In traditional, magical cultures, the ability to represent something, in either words or images, was also the ability to control that thing; and this possibility was not allowed within Judaism, due to the limits that it would place on God's absolute sovereignty.

Images may well be dangerous – let us accept, provisionally, that they are – yet what is the alternative? Aren't we forced to choose between one regime of images and another – between the worship of Jupiter or Mammon? The Bible answers, *not necessarily*. Behind the abhorrence of images lay the strange, haunting figure of an invisible or hidden God – a *deus absconditus* – who cannot be reduced to an image, not only because it is prohibited, but also because He cannot be seen. Although the Bible speaks of Moses talking to God 'face to face,' it also recounts that when Moses asked to see God, he was told that 'No man may see Me and live' (*Exodus* 33:20). God granted Moses a glimpse of the divine presence from behind, already in the act of disappearing from view. Christianity, although it accorded Christ a special status as the image of God made flesh, nevertheless continued to assert that 'No man has seen God at any time' (*John* 1:18). And following the Passion, God's perfect image once again withdrew from the world.

What is the meaning of a vanishing God, so strange a figure in the history of religions, which establishes, as a rule, the nearly universal belief that the gods may be established in images and encountered in person? Even the prohibition against idolatry appears to acknowledge this belief, in the course of outlawing it. Reading the narrative device of a vanishing God from a political or sociological standpoint, it might be suggested that this device establishes the universality of the deity as opposed to all of the particular gods of the tribes, who have only local significance. The gods may be confined, or localized, in images; but the one God may not be confined in this way. The prohibition against idolatry is also a prohibition against tribalism, and an aspiration to universalism, although it of course served the interest of a particular tribe. This interpretation deviates from the interpretation of the invisible God as a totem, *à la* Freud, or a collective representation, *à la* Durkheim, since the invisible God is rather the *absence* of any totem. God cannot be known through images, but only through his voice – which no longer speaks to us – and through the writings in which that voice is recorded. This further establishes an opposition between the

Word and the Image – between verbal and plastic images, or between writing and other modes of representation. This is the fundamental opposition between canon and idolatry, already present in the opposition of the 'graven' words of the Ten Commandments to all 'graven' images. The idea of an invisible or image-less God, then, facilitated universalism, absolute sovereignty, and the priority of the written tradition: all features that have been inherited by the legal tradition, long after any trace of the God underlying that tradition has vanished.

Gorgias on the Seductions of Poetry

A number of these themes appear also in Plato's attack on the Sophists. Gorgias of Leontini (ca. 480-375 BCE) is frequently regarded as the first systematic rhetorician. He authored an *Encomium of Helen* in which he defended Helen of Troy against the charge of abandoning her husband Menelaus and going to Troy with Paris (Gorgias, 1990). Gorgias argued that she was blameless because 'by Fate's will and gods' wishes and Necessity's decrees she did what she did, or by force reduced, or by words seduced, or by love induced.' The translation preserves Gorgias's pervasive use of rhyming endings. His defense proceeded by the exhaustive enumeration of alternatives: Helen was either compelled by the gods, forced by human violence, persuaded by words, or seduced by the power of erotic love. Gorgias addressed each of these alternatives, and concluded in each case that Helen was blameless. There being no other alternatives, one must admit her innocence.

At a literal level, the *Helen* is a simple courtroom argument, an example of the type of forensic oratory that was central to the practice of rhetoric in ancient Greece. Closer examination suggests, however, that Gorgias's real argument was in defense of rhetoric itself. One of the four alternatives addressed was that Helen was persuaded by speech. This afforded an occasion for describing the power of language, and especially of a certain kind of rhetoric:

> Speech is a powerful lord that with the smallest and most invisible body accomplishes most god-like works . . . I shall show how this is so . . . All poetry I regard and name as speech having metre . . . Thus by entering into the opinion of the soul the force of incantation is wont to beguile and persuade and alter it by witchcraft, and the two arts of witchcraft and magic are errors of the soul and deceivers of opinion . . . What is there to prevent the conclusion that Helen, too, when still young, was carried off by speech just as if constrained by force?

Gorgias's definition of poetry as 'speech having metre' was self-referential: it described his own rhetoric, which employed poetic devices such as rhyme. We may infer that Gorgias's real goal was not to defend Helen, a fictional defendant, but to defend the power of rhetoric and its status as an art or technique that may be taught. His speech was a show piece, a prepared example of oratory delivered with the purpose of convincing students to sign up with Gorgias for a course of training in rhetoric – for a suitable tuition. It was the fifth-century BCE equivalent of a commercial advertisement, complete with jingles. And what Gorgias was selling was the power of rhetoric itself, or more particularly of his own brand of rhetoric. Partly in response to Gorgias's arguments, Plato sought to exclude poetry, as a form of imitation, from the ideal Republic. He embraced Gorgias's analogy between poetry and magic, but found in this analogy another reason to suspect the deceptive power of poetry (de Romilly, 1975). Plato's Socrates was the anti-Gorgias, the lawyer-as-defendant who refused to use beautiful words to save himself from a death sentence.

In hindsight, Gorgias's provocative introduction of poetry into legal discourse may strike us as less dangerous than silly: an obvious, indeed shameless attempt at manipulation, of the sort that can still be heard today on occasion. Think of Johnnie Cochrane's line, 'If the glove don't fit, you must acquit!' Such arguments may influence jurors, but in general, we do not see their poetry as a serious threat to legal rationality. There is, however, another domain, outside of law, in which the operation of such rhetorical devices is pervasively evident, and coordinated with visual images: that of modern commercial advertising. It is here that we will find the clearest analogues to Gorgias's rhetoric. Sherwin calls Gorgias

> [T]he father of the mass advertising and public relations movements that exert such a powerful influence on our world today ... [A]s in Socrates' day, experts profess to have reduced the persuasive power of communication to a science. Like the ancient Greek Sophists Gorgias and Protagoras, jury consultants, public relations professionals, and the legal advocates they serve understand the power of words and images and sounds to enchant the mind and move the passions... Moreover, as in Socrates' day, these techniques of persuasion have spread from mainstream culture into all major areas of social practice. As a result, law, like politics, is now in danger of merging into the culture of spectacle and sensation, the realm of contrived media events and calculated appearances. And as adulterated desire cycles into law, for a growing number of people enchantment has become a form of perverse seduction. (Sherwin, 2002: 227, 232)

Modern Commodity Fetishism on Madison Avenue

By now the 'shock of recognition' has probably set in for the modern reader not previously aware of these ancient examples. The historical phenomena of Gorgianic sophistry, and of idolatry as described by Jewish and Christian polemics, assume a disturbingly familiar aspect. There is a more than passing 'family resemblance' to a number of features of our modern media culture, especially in its purest form, that of commercial advertising. There is a confluence of persuasion, enchantment, and seduction in all of these forms that is summed up in the figure of the idol or 'fetish.' It is no coincidence that a science of images incorporating both the rhetorical and the erotic emerged once again in the tradition of Renaissance magic. Ioan Couliano (1987) saw in this tradition the true precursor of modern media techniques of mass manipulation.

The tradition was interrupted, however, by the burgeoning Enlightenment, which, beginning with Frances Bacon's criticism of various types of mental 'idols,' sought to exclude fantasy in order to clear the way for a true science (Yelle 2005: 165-67). It was no accident that the British tradition inaugurated by Bacon and represented by Hobbes, Locke, and, in the legal domain, Jeremy Bentham, criticized especially the habit of 'taking words for things' or idolizing words, often in terms borrowed from theology. The Protestant Reformation had already applied its iconoclasm to language, as reflected in its literalist hermeneutics, 'plain style,' and criticisms of 'vain repetitions' in the liturgy. Verbal images, like the images of false gods, could be hollow, empty. They must be regulated so as to conform to both reality and our ideas. Otherwise, they could assume an independent, though unreal and phantasmic, existence in which, although created by man, they could come to dominate him. Words ought to be servants, but could become our masters.

Drawing on this tradition from a very different perspective, Marx (1992) labeled capitalistic production an irrational form of 'commodity fetishism' because capitalist exchange introduced a gap between the original, natural, human use of the product (its 'use value') and the product's ability to be exchanged for something else ('exchange value'). The latter value was substantially alienated from any context of human use, as well as from the labor that had originally produced it. Horkheimer and Adorno (2002) developed this concept further with their concept of the 'culture industry' under twentieth-century capitalism. Recently, David Hawkes (2001) has argued for the contemporary relevance of the religiously inspired criticisms of commodity worship as 'idolatry' that emerged at the very beginning of the capitalist era.

Let us, then, look more closely at our own moment in history. Latour points out the contradiction between the proliferation of images in our present media culture, and the traditional iconoclastic approach to images. In what sense can our culture still be called 'iconoclastic' if, in fact, images are everywhere, and are the focus of secular worship, or commodity fetishism? Modern media increasingly exploit the seductive properties of the image, with its attendant culture, or rather cult, of beauty, celebrity, and success. On the other hand, juxtaposed to, and in sharp contrast with, a world saturated by images that have grown increasingly unruly, there is an ostensibly image-less domain of legal discourse, symbolized by a blindfolded justice. This domain inherited its iconoclasm, and indeed its rationalism, from an earlier era. Now both of those attributes are being called into question. The gap between the 'reality' of the new media, and the legal discourse that ostensibly regulates it, is increasingly visible. On the one hand, we have a regimented metadiscourse called 'law' that purports to embody sovereignty and rationality, and on the other hand nearly a no-holds-barred, anything-goes competition in the marketplace of images. This gulf is underlined by the fact that, while the formal legal rationality of contract governs only a very small portion of marketplace transactions, the vast majority of contracts in the so-called 'real' world consist of a set of image- and jingle-laden commercial advertisements that in lawyers' terms constitute both a set of 'seller's representations' and an 'offer' that may then be 'accepted' through the 'performance' of purchase on the part of a substantially manipulated consumer.

Ironically, given the law's traditional concern with the dangers of images, the laws regulating advertising in the United States are largely unable and, one expects, unwilling to address this open scandal of commodity fetishism with a new iconoclastic Reformation. The main reason for this is of course the strong bias in favor of an unfettered marketplace. From this perspective, law is simply a facilitator of capitalism, and anything goes so long as it is seen to promote the exchange of goods and services. This law and economics presumption, which is rarely raised to the level of explicit argument, has some evident flaws. After all, it is not a question of simply selling, but also of what is sold. What if rhetoric is employed to sell a worse product, at the expense of the purchase and, therefore, production, of a different product of better quality? (As Gorgias and other Sophists argued, rhetoric can often make the better case appear worse, and the worse better.) Moreover, what is the value of a product that has no inherent function or 'use value'? The gap between use value and exchange value is what initially prompted Marx to label capitalistic production an irrational form of 'commodity fetishism.'

The techniques of modern advertising bear an uncanny resemblance to the rituals, magic, phantasies, and rhetorical devices of earlier eras. Like some of these earlier systems, modern advertising even presents itself, if only subliminally, as a form of religion. Its narratives replace those of traditional mythology; its concatenation of colors, sounds, and words resemble nothing so much as the rituals of pre-modern cultures. Of course, just as some anthropologists have opined that these rituals are designed to do, modern advertising aims at imprinting itself on the memory of the viewer. There is one simple reason why the arts of memory and of persuasion merged, both in classical rhetoric and the tradition of Renaissance magic: the same techniques that produce persuasion also tend to produce memorability. Modern electronic media employ bright colors, moving objects, and fast-motion camera shifts and film splicings in order to preclude the 'boredom' or fatigue of the viewer, and to produce the mental associations that promote recall. Among the most familiar advertising techniques are the use of jingles, *à la* Gorgias, and of erotic images, which tend to produce seduction toward the product with which they are (temporarily, fantastically) associated. One presumes that these techniques must have some efficacy. Otherwise, why would there be such agreement on them, across so many cultures and time periods? And why would companies expend so much money on advertising, when it is now possible to conduct empirical studies as to its profitability?

Whereas modern media have resuscitated ancient techniques of manipulation and combined them with new, unheard-of ways of enhancing these techniques, modern law appears blissfully unaware of, or at least unconcerned with, the dangers that they pose. Take as examples the modern laws against false advertising in the United States. 15 U.S.C. §52 prohibits the dissemination of false advertisements. §55(a)(1) defines a false advertisement:

> The term 'false advertisement' means an advertisement, other than labeling, which is misleading in a material respect; and in determining whether any advertisement is misleading, there shall be taken into account (among other things) not only representations made or suggested by statement, word, design, device, sound, or any combination thereof, but also the extent to which the advertisement fails to reveal facts material in the light of such representations or material with respect to consequences which may result from the

use of the commodity to which the advertisement relates under the conditions prescribed in said advertisement, or under such conditions as are customary or usual.

The recognition that a 'representation' may be made by means, not only of statements, but also sounds and 'designs,' as well as omissions, appears to take a broader perspective on the rhetorical possibilities of the advertisement, and thus to take into account the realities of commercial advertising. However, the crucial determination is whether such a 'representation,' however made, is false or 'misleading,' and this reveals the crucial flaw in the current legal approach. Truth or falsity is a property of statements or propositions. California state law similarly reflects this understanding of false advertising. Cal. Bus. & Prof. Code §17500 prohibits an advertiser making 'any statement ... which is untrue or misleading ...' Other signs or semiotic modes contained in an advertisement can be true or false only if they can be reduced to the form of a statement of proposition, or what the law calls a 'representation.' Indeed, a 'representation' in a contract of sale standardly means a verbal statement that the seller warrants to be true of the goods for sale. In many cases, a picture can be used to make such a 'representation'; and in such cases, the definition of 'false advertising' would extend to pictures as well.

The problem with such a definition of 'false advertising,' however, is that it fails even to acknowledge, much less to propose reasonable limitations on, the rhetorical techniques employed by advertisers to persuade the public. 'Truth or falsity' strictly speaking is a property of propositions, but not of rhymes or images. Anthropologists have recognized this in recent decades. Stanley Tambiah (1985), for example, in attempting to rehabilitate indigenous rituals from the charge of 'falsity' has argued that such rituals, including the 'magical power of words,' should instead be evaluated as 'performative' and 'persuasive.' His 'performative approach' to ritual reflects a longer-term shift in our understanding of language, away from semantics and toward pragmatics. 'Truth or falsity' is a property of semantics, of meaning; pragmatics is concerned instead with effect, including the way that words operate upon us to influence our behavior. This seems a more appropriate standard against which to measure advertising. Indeed, if we consider some of the common techniques of modern advertising, it is clearly absurd to ask whether they are true or false. What is the truth value of a LOUD message (many advertisements modulate sound level, and/or are louder than the programs they interrupt)? Where is the truth in a combination of sound, color, and motion – the effect of which in ritual Maurice Bloch (1989: 28) has described as a form of rhetoric? What, finally, is the truth or falsity of a jingle? If poetry is more than simply the semantic 'content' it incorporates, and we must accept that it is, that something more cannot be regarded as either 'true' or 'false.' I agree with Tambiah that the function of such forms is persuasion, rather than the expression of truth or propositional content. However, in my view this does not exonerate such forms, but rather requires that we develop a broader critique of their rhetorical function.

Yet the law is ill-prepared to do so. Consider the following description of techniques employed in children's advertising, produced by a law professor who opposed the use of such techniques:

> They [advertisers] intentionally acquire and use a psychological advantage over children by designing commercials that blur the line between fact and fantasy so that children will be persuaded that illusions appearing on commercials are real. For example, advertisers commonly use accelerated camera speeds, trick shots such as low camera angles that make the product look taller than it is, or extreme closeups of the product to make it look larger. (Wolinsky and Econome, 1977: 254)

Now, these complaints still consist mainly of reducing images (camera angles and so on) to positive claims, such as 'The product is THIS BIG!', the truth value of which may in theory be ascertained. However, a plethora of advertising techniques cannot be reduced to propositional form. For example, what do we make of the fact that so many children's cartoon characters are depicted in primary colors, and with gigantic eyes (and heads) relative to their bodies? As a semiotician who is also a father, I have spent some time watching these programs, and I can tell you that the wide eyes of, for example, Dora the Explorer (another jingle!) are perhaps best explained in terms of our evolutionary adaptation to read the emotion of surprise or excitement, which is accompanied by 'eye popping' behaviors in some species, including humans. Our eyes are naturally drawn to those of another, and are held more fastly when those eyes are large or dilated. This, by the way, appears to be the same principle underlying mascara. And the use of primary colors corresponds to eye shadow, or lipstick. Which is as much as to say that the business of selling to children is not reducible to truth or falsity – it may be false to depict oneself as excited when one simply is not, but is it false to dress in primary colors? – as much as it is about seduction. Concerning such techniques, and their effects, the ancient rhetorical theories were way ahead of the modern legal system.

Which brings me to another point. Dora appears in a television program, which is punctuated by commercials, in which Dora sometimes also appears, and so the line between 'program' and 'commercial' or 'content' and 'form' has completely evaporated (just as it did under Gorgias's verbal prestidigitation). The death of pure semantics is the birth of rhetoric. So, the entire program becomes a 'commercial,' and the line between reality and fantasy is further blurred. Advertisers and parents know this, but the law chooses not to see it. Otherwise, would it be permissible for the Federal Communications Commission to make precious broadcast space available for programs that contained, in effect, 100 per cent commercial content? This question may be raised once again, from a legal perspective, given the increasing use of so-called 'product placements' in prime time television, as described in a recent *New York Times* article, 'On Television, Brands Go From Props to Stars' (2 October 2005). Increasingly, advertisers and the producers of television programs are crafting story lines around particular products. Products, instead of simply appearing mutely in shows, as a can of Coke perched on a coffee table, are now the focus of attention and discussion. Commentators are divided over whether this approach can succeed, given its potential to alienate viewers, as well as over its ethicality. And the FCC's disclosure laws, which require deals with advertisers to be noted, may place some limits on what programs may do. What is striking to this viewer, however, is the extent to which such allegedly 'new' developments simply extend an old, and indeed ancient practice of subterfuge or sleight-of-hand involved in many forms of commercial sale.

Conclusion

A study of the historical criticisms of idolatry and sophistry that informed, at a deep level, Western legal traditions, suggests the dangerous potential of images, both plastic and verbal, to mislead and seduce. Although these earlier attacks on the rhetoric of images continued to exert a formative influence on the development of the law well into modernity, we have reached a point at which the concern over the dangers posed by images appears to have waned. Not only are images increasingly regnant and unregulated in the surrounding society, but they have begun to intrude into the courtroom itself. The vulnerability of law to the rhetoric of images is underscored by its inability to define 'false advertising' in a way that coincides with commercial realities. Going forward, it appears likely that the inherent conflict between law and the image will deepen and rise more fully to consciousness. As a first step toward the establishment of a more viable, and more ethical, legal regime of images, this chapter has attempted to recuperate the value and significance of some classical legal criticisms of the image.

Bibliography

'Inside the Jury's Mind', *New Statesman* 7 December 1979, pp. 882-884.

'Is a Cinema Studies Degree the New M.B.A.?', *New York Times* (6 March 2005).

'On Television, Brands Go From Props to Stars', *New York Times* (2 October 2005).

'Best Friends Forever', *South Park*, The Comedy Channel (28 March 2005).

'Measuring the Blogosphere', *The New York Times* (5 August 2005) Friday, Late Edition – Final, Section A; Column 1; Editorial Desk.

Abass, Ademola, 'The New Collective Security Mechanism of ECOWAS: Innovations and Problems', *Journal of Conflict and Security Law*, Vol. 5, No. 2 (2000), pp. 211-229.

Abel, Richard L., *American Lawyers* (Oxford: Oxford University Press, 1989).

Airs, J. and Shaw, A., *Jury Excusal and Deferral*, No 102 Home Office Development Directorate, London (1999).

Almog, Shulamit and Aharonson, Ely, 'Law as Film: Representing Justice in the Age of Moving Images', *Canadian Journal of Law and Technology* 3(1) (2004), pp. 1-18.

Alpers, Svetlana, 'Interpretation without Representation, or, The Viewing of *Las Meninas*', *Representations*, Vol. 1, Number 1 (February 1983).

Amsterdam, Anthony and Bruner, Jerome, *Minding the Law* (Cambridge, MA: Harvard University Press, 2000).

Anderson, Elijah, *Code of the Street: Decency, Violence, and the Moral Life of the Inner City* (New York: W.W. Norton, 1999).

Angle, Stephen, *Human Rights and Chinese Thought: A Cross-Cultural Inquiry*, (Oxford: Oxford University Press, 2002).

Arkfield, Michael, *The Digital Practice of Law* (Phoenix, AZ: Law Partner Publishers, 2001).

Aron, R., Duffy, K. and Rosner, J., *Cross-Examination of Witnesses: The Litigator's Puzzle* (Colorado Springs, CO: Shepard's/McGraw Hill, 1989).

Associated Press, 'Officers acquitted on all charges in Diallo shooting trial', *CNN News* (25 February 2000).

Atkinson, J. Maxwell and Heritage, John, 'Preference organization', in *Structures of Social Action: Studies in Conversation Analysis*, edited by J.M. Atkinson and J. Heritage (Cambridge: Cambridge University Press, 1984) pp 53-56.

Austin, J.L., *How To Do Things With Words* (Cambridge, MA: Harvard University Press, 1962).

Bachelard, Gaston, *The Poetics of Space*, translated from the French by Maria Jolas; foreword by Étienne Gilson (Boston: Beacon Press, 1969).

Bailey, Steve, '"Professional Television": Three (Super) Texts and a (Super) Genre', *The Velvet Light Trap* (2001), pp. 45-61.

Baldwin, J. and McConville, M., *Jury Trials* (Oxford: Clarendon, 1979).

Balibar, Etienne, *Les frontières de la démocratie* (Paris: La Découverte, 1992).

Bankowski, Zenon and Mungham, Geoff. *Images of Law* (London: Routledge, 1976).

Bann, Stephen, *Parallel Lines: Printmakers, Painters and Photographers in Nineteenth-Century France* (New Haven: Yale University Press, 2001).

Barker, Joan C., *Danger, Duty, and Disillusion: The Worldview of Los Angeles Police Officers* (Prospect Heights, IL: Waveland Press, 1999).

Barthes, Roland, 'Myth Today', in *Mythologies* (Annette Lavers, trans.) (New York: Hill and Wang, 1972).

Barthes, Roland, *Image Music Text* (Stephen Heath, trans.) (New York: Hill and Wang, 1977).

Bastide, Françoise, 'The Iconography of Scientific Texts: Principles of Analysis', in Michael Lynch and Steve Woolgar (eds), *Representation in Scientific Practice* (Cambridge, MA: MIT Press, 1988), pp. 187-229.

Baucom, Ian, *Out of Place* (London, Durham: Duke University Press, 1999).

Bauman, Zygmunt, *Modernity and the Holocaust* (Cambridge: Cambridge University Press, 1989).

Beasley, Colin J., 'Picking up the Problems: An Applied Linguistic Analysis of the Legal Problem Genre' (MA, Edith Cowan University, 1994).

Bell, Brad and Loftus, Elizabeth, 'Vivid Persuasion in the Courtroom', *Journal of Personality Assessment* 49 (1985), pp. 659-664.

Bennett, W.L. and Feldman, M.S., *Reconstructing Reality in the Courtroom* (London: Tavistock Publications, 1981).

Benson, Richard, *Notes on Pictures*, Devane Lecture, Yale University, 1 May 2001.

Bernstein, Richard, *Beyond Objectivism and Relativism* (Philadelphia: University of Pennsylvania Press, 1985).

Beytagh, Francis X., *Constitutionalism in Contemporary Ireland: An American Perspective* (Dublin: Round Hall, Sweet and Maxwell, 1997).

Bhatia, V.K., 'An Investigation into Formal and Functional Characteristics of Qualifications into Legislative Writing and Its Application to English for Academic Legal Purposes', British Library (1982).

Bhatia, V.K., 'An Applied Discourse Analysis of English Legislative Writing' (Birmingham: University of Aston, 1983a).

Bhatia, V.K., 'Simplification V Easification: The Case of Legal Texts', *Applied Linguistics* 4, no. 1 (1983b): 42-45.

Bhatia, V.K., *Analysing Genre: Language Use in Professional Settings, Applied Linguistics and Language Study* (London: Longman, 1993).

Bimstein, Donald, 'Sensitivity training and the police', in *Police-Community Relations*, edited by Paul F. Cromwell Jr. and George Keefer (St. Paul, MN: West Publishing Co., 1973) pp. 165-177.

Biocca, Frank, Kim, Taeyong and Levy, Mark, 'The Vision of Virtual Reality', in Frank Biocca and Mark Levy (eds), *Communication in the Age of Virtual Reality* (Hillsdale, NJ: Lawrence Erlbaum Associates, 1995), pp. 3-14.

Birdwell-Pheasant, Donna, 'Family Systems and The Foundations of Class in Ireland and England', 3 *The History of the Family* 1 (1998).

Birnbaum, Pierre, *La France aux français* (Paris: Editions du Seuil, 1993).

Bittner, Egon 'The Functions of the Police in Modern Society', in *Policing: A View from the Street*, edited by J. Van Maanen and P. Manning (Santa Monica, CA: Goodyear Publishing, 1978) pp. 32-50.

Bizzell, Patricia and Herzberg, Bruce (eds), *The Rhetorical tradition: readings from classical times to the present* (Boston: Bedford/St. Martin's, 2001).

Black, Donald, 'Legal Relativity', in *Encyclopedia of Law and Society: American and Global Perspectives*, edited by David S. Clark (Thousand Oaks, CA: Sage Publications, forthcoming).

Bloch, Maurice, *Ritual, History, and Power: Selected Papers in Anthropology* (London: Athlone Press, 1989).

Blonsky, Marshall, 'Introduction' to *On Signs* (Baltimore, Maryland: The Johns Hopkins University Press, 1985).

Bodde, Derk and Morris, Clarence, *Law in Imperial China, Exemplified by 190 Ch'ing Dynasty Cases with Historical, Social, and Judicial Commentaries* (Philadelphia: University of Pennsylvania Press, 1973).

Bodde, Derk, *Chinese Thought, Society, and Science: The Intellectual and Social Background of Science and Technology in Pre-modern China* (Honolulu: University of Hawaii Press, 1991).

Bolter, Jay David and Grusin, Richard, *Remediation* (Cambridge, MA: MIT Press, 1999).

Bouissac, Paul (ed.), *Encyclopedia of Semiotics* (Oxford: Oxford University Press, 1998).

Brain, Robert, 'Standards and Semiotics', in Timothy Lenoir (ed.), *Inscribing Science* (Stanford, CA: Stanford University Press, 1998), pp. 249-284.

Braxton, G., 'In Ally's romance, race a non-issue', *The Daily Hampshire Gazette*, 15 February 1999, p. 28.

Bridges, L., Choongh, S. and McConville, M., *Ethnic Minority Defendants and the Right to Elect Jury Trial*, Commission for Racial Equality, London (2000).

Brown, Jonathan, Images and Ideas in Seventeenth-Century Spanish Painting (Princeton, NJ: Princeton University Press, 1978).

Brown, J. and Langan, P. A., *Policing and Homicide, 1976-98: Justifiable Homicide by Police, Police Officers Murdered by Felons* (Washington D.C.: U.S. Department of Justice, Office of Justice Programs, 2001).

Brown, Julie, 'Ally McBeal's Postmodern Soundtrack', *Journal of the Royal Musical Association* 126 (2001), pp. 275-303.

Bruner, Jerome, *Acts of Meaning* (Cambridge, MA: Harvard University Press, 1990).

Buchanan, Raymond W., Pryor, Bert, Taylor, Phillip N. and Strawn, David U., 'Legal Communication: An Investigation of Juror Comprehension of Pattern Instructions', *Communication Quarterly* 26 (1978): 31-36.

Burnett, D. Graham, *A Trial by Jury* (London: Bloomsbury, 2001).

Burnham, W., *Introduction to the Law and Legal System of the United States* (St. Paul, MN: West Publishing Company, 1995).

Burns, Robert, *A Theory of the Trial* (Princeton, NJ: Princeton University Press, 1999).

Butler, S., 'Acquittal Rates', ch.13 in D. Moxon (ed.), *Managing Criminal Justice*, Home Office Research Unit, London (1985).

Cao, Deborah, *Chinese Law: A Language Perspective* (Aldershot: Ashgate, 2004).

Carney, Brian and Feigenson, Neal, 'Visual Persuasion in the Michael Skakel Trial: Enhancing Advocacy Through Interactive Media Presentations', *Criminal Justice* 19 (2004), pp. 22-35.

Carrington, Paul, 'Virtual Civil Litigation: A Visit to John Bunyon's Celestial City', *Columbia Law Review* (October 1998).

Casey, James, *Constitutional Law in Ireland* (Dublin: Round Hall, Sweet & Maxwell, 2000).

Cassese, A., 'The International Community's "Legal" Response to Terrorism', *International and Comparative Law Quarterly* 38, (1989), pp. 558-596.

Cavalli-Sforza, L.L. and Feldman, M.W., *Cultural Transmission and Evolution: A Quantitative Approach* (Princeton: Princeton University Press, 1981).

Caygill, Howard, *Art of Judgment* (Oxford: Oxford University Press, 1989).

CELECR, 'The Law Society of Hong Kong Project: Strategies and Competencies in Legal Communication. A study to investigate the communicative needs of legal Professionals' (Hong Kong: Department of English & Communication, City University of Hong Kong, 1998).

Chandler, Daniel, *Semiotics: The Basics* (London: Routledge, 2002).

Charlesworth, H., 'International Law: A Discipline of Crisis', *Modern Law Review* 65 (2002), pp. 450-462.

Charrow, R. and Charrow, V., 'Making Legal Language Understandable: A Psycholinguistic Study of Jury Instructions', *Columbia Law Review* 79 (1979): 1306-74.

Chesterman, S., *Just War or Just Peace, Humanitarian Intervention and International Law* (Oxford: Oxford University Press, 2001).

Chicago Police Department, 'Officer Safety Alert: AHGM Pen/Gun, Hercules Munitions Corp.', Bulletin Vol. XLI #74 (Tuesday, 14 March 2000).

Chicago Police Department, 'Officer Safety Alert: Deadly Cell Phones', Bulletin Vol. XLI # 90 (Thursday, 30 March 2000).

Chicago Police Department, 'Officer Safety Alert: Mobile Phone gun', Special Bulletin Vol. XLI #333 (Tuesday, 28 November 2000).

Churchland, Patricia Smith, *Brain-Wise, Studies in Neurophilosophy* (Cambridge, Massachusetts and London: Bradford Book, MIT Press, 2002).

Clarke, Desmond, 'The Role of Natural Law in Irish Constitutional Law', 17 *Irish Jurist* 187 (1982).

Clayman, Steve, 'Footing in the achievement of neutrality: the case of news-interview discourse', in *Talk at Work: Interaction in Institutional Settings*, edited by P. Drew and J. Heritage (Cambridge: Cambridge University Press, 1992) pp. 163-198.

CNBC photograph, *The New York Times*, front page (10 July 2002).

Cohen, Jonathan, 'Deconstructing Ally: Explaining Viewers' Interpretations of Popular Television', *Media Psychology* 4 (2002), pp. 253-77.

Cohen, Jonathan and Ribak, Rivka, 'Sex differences in pleasure from television texts: the case of Ally McBeal', *Women's Studies in Communication* 26(1) (2003), pp. 118-35, [accessed via infotrack].

Commission Nationale consultative des droits de l'homme, *La lutte contre le racial discrimination et la xénophobie: rapport présenté par le Premier* (Paris: La Documentation française, 1991).

Conroy, Pauline, 'Managing the Mothers: The Case of Ireland', *Women and Social Policies in Europe, Work, Family and the State*, edited by Jane Lewis (Aldershot: Edward Elgar, 1993).

Consultation Paper on Rights and Duties of Cohabitees (April 2004).

Cooper, Brenda and Pease, Edward C., '"Don't want no short people round here": Confronting heterosexism's intolerance through comic and disruptive narratives in Ally McBeal', *Western Journal of Communication* 66(3) (2002), pp. 300-19. [accessed via infotrack].

Couliano, Ioan P., *Eros and Magic in the Renaissance* (Margaret Cook trans) (Chicago: University of Chicago Press, 1987).

Cox, Michael, 'The Empire's Back in Town: On America's Imperial Temptation – Again', *Millennium: Journal of International Studies*, 32/1 (2003): 1-26.

Crane, Diana, *The Transformation of the Avant-Garde, The New York Art World, 1940-1985* (Chicago and London: The University of Chicago Press, 1985).

Crawford, R., *The Persuasion Edge: Winning Psychological Strategies and Tactics for Lawyers* (Eau Claire, WI: Professional Education Systems, 1989).

Crow, David, *Visible Signs* (Crans-prè-Céligny, Switzerland: AVA Publishing SA, 2003).

Damasio, Antonio, *Descartes' Error: Emotion, Reason, and the Human Brain* (New York: Avon Books, 1994).

Damaška, Mirjan, 'Epistemology and Legal Regulation of Proof', *Law, Probability & Risk* (2003), pp. 117-130.

Danet, Brenda, 'Language in the Legal Process', *Law and Society Review* 14, no. 3 (1980) pp. 445-564.

De Romilly, Jacqueline, *Magic and Rhetoric in Ancient Greece* (Harvard: Harvard University Press, 1975).

Den Boer, M., 'A Linguistic Analysis of Narrative Coherence in the Courtroom', in *Law, Interpretation, and Reality: Essays in Epistemology*, edited by P. Nerhof (Dordrecht: Kluwer Academic Publishers, 1990).

Devons, E., 'Serving as a Juryman in Britain', 28 *Modern Law Review* (1965) pp. 561-570.

Diogenes Laertius, *Lives of eminent philosophers*, (R.D. Hicks trans), (London: Heinemann, 1925).

Dobash, R. Emerson, Schlesinger, Philip, Dobash, Russell and Weaver, C. Kay, '"Crimewatch UK": Women's interpretations of televised violence', in *Entertaining Crime: Television Reality Programs*, edited by M. Fishman and G. Cavender (New York: Aldine de Gruyter, 1998) pp. 37-58.

Doty, Alexander, *Making Things Perfectly Queer: Interpreting mass culture* (Minneapolis and London: University of Minnesota Press, 1993).

Dow, Bonnie J., 'Ally McBeal, Lifestyle Feminism, and the Politics of Personal Happiness', *The Communication Review* 5 (2002), pp. 259-264.

Doyle, A. '"Cops": Television policing as policing reality', in *Entertaining Crime: Television Reality Programs*, edited by M. Fishman and G. Cavender (New York: Aldine de Gruyter, 1998) pp. 95-116.

Doyle, Oran, 'Legal Validity: Reflections on the Irish Constitution', *Dublin University Law Journal* 25 (2003).

Drew, Paul and Heritage, John, 'Introduction', in *Talk at Work: Interaction in Institutional Settings*, edited by P. Drew and J. Heritage (Cambridge: Cambridge University Press, 1992) pp. 3-65.

Dubrofsky, Rachel, 'Ally McBeal as Postfeminist Icon: The Aestheticizing and Fetishizing of the Independent Working Woman', *The Communication Review* 5 (2002), pp. 265-84.

Dumas, Bethany K., 'US Pattern Jury Instructions: Problems and Proposals', *Forensic Linguistics* 7, no. 1 (2000), 49-71.

Duncan, William, 'Can Natural Law be Used in Constitutional Interpretation?', 45 *Doctrine of Life* (1995).

Dunne, Anne, 'The Constitutional Family', *Irish Journal of Family Law* 1 (1992).

Dunstan, R., 'Context for Coercion: Analysing Properties of Courtroom "Questions"', *British Journal of Law and Society* 7 (1980): 61-77.

Dzouinas, Costas and Nead, Linda, *Law and the Image, The Authority of Art and the Aesthetics of Law*, (Chicago and London: University of Chicago Press, 1999).

Elwork, Amiram, Sales, Bruce D. and Alfini, James J., *Making Jury Instructions Understandable* (Charlottesville, VA: Michie, 1982).

Elwork, Amiram, Alfini James J. and Sales, Bruce D., 'Towards Increasing the Comprehensibility of Jury Instructions', in *In the Jury Box: Controversies in the Courtroom*, edited by L. Wrightsman, S. Kassin and C. Willis (Beverly Hills, CA: Sage, 1987).

Ervin-Trip, S., 'Is Sybil There?: The Structures of Some American English Directives', *Language in Society* (1976) 5: 25-67.

Fanning, Ronan, *Irish Independent Ireland* (Dublin : Helicon, 1983).

Fassin, Didier, *Lois de l'inhospitalité: les politiques de l'immigration à l'épreuve des sans-papiers* (Paris: La Découverte, 1997).

Fay, N., Garrod, S. and Carletta, J., 'Group Discussion as Interactive Dialogue or as a Serial Monologue', 11 *Psychological Science* (2000) pp. 481-486.

Federal Judicial Center/National Institute for Trial Advocacy, *Effective Use of Courtroom Technology* (Washington, DC: Author, 2001).

Federal Rules of Evidence (St. Paul, MN: West Publishing, 2005).

Feigenson, Neal, 'The Rhetoric of Torts: How Advocates Help Jurors Think About Causation, Reasonableness, and Responsibility', *Hastings Law Journal* 47 (1995), pp. 61-165.

Feigenson, Neal, *Legal Blame* (Washington, DC: American Psychological Association, 2000).

Feigenson, Neal, 'Visual Rhetorics of Science and Law', paper presented at Law and Society Association annual meeting (Budapest, 2001).

Feigenson, Neal, 'Too Real? The Future of Visual Reality Evidence', *Law and Policy* (forthcoming).

Feigenson, Neal and Dunn, Meghan, 'New Visual Technologies in Court: Directions for Research', *Law & Human Behavior* 27 (2003), pp. 109-126.

Fischhoff, Baruch, 'Hindsight ≠ Foresight: The Effect of Outcome Knowledge on Judgment Under Uncertainty', *Journal of Experimental Social Psychology: Human Perception & Performance* 1 (1975), pp. 288-299.

Fitzpatrick, P., *Modernism and the Grounds of Law* (Cambridge: Cambridge University Press, 2001).

Foucault, Michel, 'Las Meninas', in *The Order of Things, An Archeology of the Human Sciences* (New York: Pantheon Books, Random House, 1970).

Foucault, Michel, *The Archaeology of Knowledge and The Discourse on Language* (New York: Pantheon Books, 1972).

Franck, Thomas M., *Recourse to Force, State Action Against Threats and Armed Attacks* (Cambridge: Cambridge University Press, 2002).

Fredrickson, Kirstin M., 'Genre and Local Discourse Community: Cultural Variation in Legal Opinions', in *AAAL*., Orlando, Florida (1997).

Fukuyama, Francis, 'The End of History', *The National Interest* 16/Summer (1989): 3-16.

Fulton, John, *The Tragedy of Belief: Division, Politics, and Religion in Ireland* (Oxford: Clarendon Press, 1991).

Gadamer, Hans-Georg, *Truth and Method* (New York: The Seabury Press, 1975) translated and edited by Garrett Barden and John Cumming, originally published in 1960 as *Wahrheit und Methode*, Tübingen.

Gadamer, Hans-Georg, *Philosophical Hermeneutics*, translated and edited by David E. Linge (Berkeley: University of California Press, 1976).

Gage, John, *Color and Culture, Practice and Meaning from Antiquity to Abstraction*, (Boston: Bulfinch Press Book, Little, Brown and Company, 1993).

Gaines, Philip, 'The Grammar of Credibility Assessment: A Functional Analysis of Two Legal Questioning Styles', *Social Semiotics* 6 (1996): 199-230.

Galison, Peter, *Image and Logic* (Cambridge, MA: Harvard University Press, 1997).

Garapon, Antoine, *Bien Juger – Essai sur le rituel judiciaire* (Paris: Odile Jacob, 2001).

Garfinkel, H., *Studies in Ethnomethodology* (Englewood Cliffs, NJ: Prentice Hall, 1967).

Geertz, Clifford, *Local Knowledge* (New York: Basic Books, 1983).

Gettleman, Jeffrey, 'A Judge for Sale on EBay, Shipping Included, Isn't Laughing', *The New York Times (Monday 13 December 2004)* Section B; Column 2; Metropolitan Desk.

Ghai, Yash P., *Hong Kong's New Constitutional Order: The Resumption of Chinese Sovereignty and the Basic Law* (Hong Kong: Hong Kong University Press, 1997).

Ghai, Yash P., *The Nature of Constitutional Transition in Hong Kong* (Hong Kong: Faculty of Law, University of Hong Kong, 1999).

Gies, Lieve, 'Up, Close and Personal: the Discursive Transformation of Judicial Politics in Post-Dutroux Belgium', in *International Journal for the Semiotics of Law* (Netherlands: Kluwer Academic Publications, 2003) pp. 259-284.

Goffman, E., *Forms of Talk* (Oxford: Blackwell Publishers, 1981).

Goodman, J. and Loftus, E., 'Social Science Looks at Witness Examination', *Trial* 20 (1984) pp. 52-7.

Goodrich, Peter, *Languages of Law: From Logics of Memory to Nomadic Masks* (London: Weidenfeld and Nicolson, 1990).

Goodrich, Peter, *Oedipus Lex: Psychoanalysis, History, Law* (Berkeley: University of California Press, 1995).

Goodwin, C., 'Audience diversity, participation and interpretation', *Text* 6(3) (1986) pp. 283-316.

Goodwin, Charles, 'Professional Vision', *American Anthropologist* 96 (1994), pp. 606-633.

Goodwin, M.H., *He Said She Said: Talk as Social Organization Among Black Children* (Bloomington, IN: Indiana University Press, 1990).

Goody, Jack, *The Development of Family and Marriage in Europe* (Cambridge,: Cambridge University Press, 1983).

Gordon, Robert W., 'Legal Thought and Legal Practice', in *Professionals and Professional Ideologies in America*, edited by Gerald Geison (Chapel Hill and London: The University of North Carolina Press, 1983).

Gorgias, *Helen* (George A. Kennedy trans.) in *Readings from Classical Rhetoric*, edited by Patricia P. Matsen, Philip Rollinson and Marion Sousa (Carbondale: Southern Illinois University Press, 1990), pp. 34-36.

Greenfeld, Lawrence A., Langan, Patrick A. and Smith, Steven K., *Police Use of Force: Collection of National Data* (Washington D.C.: U.S. Department of Justice, Office of Justice Programs, 1997).

Gregory, J., Office of Population and Census Studies, London.

Griffin, Dale and Tversky, Amos, 'The Weighting of Evidence and the Determinants of Confidence', in Thomas Gilovich, Dale Griffin and Daniel Kahneman (eds),

Heuristics and Biases: The Psychology of Intuitive Judgment (Cambridge, UK: Cambridge University Press, 2002), pp. 230-249.

Grove, Trevor, *The Juryman's Tale* (London: Bloomsbury, 1998).

Habermas, Jürgen, *Moral Consciousness and Communicative Action* (Cambridge: Cambridge University Press, 1996).

Habermas, Jurgen, *Between Facts and Norms: Contributions to a Discourse Theory of Law and Democracy* (Cambridge: MIT Press, 1996).

Habermas, Jürgen, *On the Pragmatics of Communication*, edited by Maeve Cooke (Cambridge: The MIT Press, 1998).

Hacking, Ian, *Representing and Intervening* (Cambridge, UK: Cambridge University Press, 1983).

Halbertal, Moshe and Margalit, Avishai, *Idolatry* (Naomi Glodblum trans.) (Cambridge: Harvard University Press, 1992).

Hall, Stuart, 'Encoding/decoding' in *Culture, Media, Language: Working papers in Cultural Studies* (London: Hutchinson, 1980) pp. 128-138.

Hannoun, Michel, *L'Homme est l'espérance de l'homme : rapport sur les discriminations raciales et les discriminations en France* (Paris : La Documentation Française, 1987).

Hans, Valerie P., 'Law and The Media: An Overview and Introduction', *Law and Human Behaviour* 14 (5) (1990), pp. 399-407.

Hardt, Michael and Negri, Toni, *Empire* (Cambridge: Harvard University Press, 2000).

Hart, H. L. A., *The Concept of Law* (Oxford: Clarendon Press, 1963).

Hastie, Reid, 'Algebraic Models of Jury Decision Processes', in *Inside the Juror: The Psychology of Juror Decision Making*, edited by Reid Hastie (Cambridge: Cambridge University Press, 1993).

Hawkes, David, *Idols of the Marketplace: Idolatry and Commodity Fetishism in English Literature, 1580-1680* (New York: Palgrave, 2001).

Heath, Christian and Luff, Paul, *Technology in Action* (Cambridge: Cambridge University Press, 2000).

Hedderman, C. and Moxon, D., *Magistrate Court or Crown Court?*, Home Office Research Study No 98, London (1992).

Heere, W., *Terrorism and the Military, International Legal Implications* (The Hague: Asser Press, 2003).

High Impact Graphics, 'Digistrip' (Boulder, CO: Author, 2004).

Higonnet, Anne, *Pictures of Innocence, History and Crisis of Ideal Childhood* (London: Thames and Hudson, 1998).

Hogan, Gerard, 'Legal Aspects of Church/State Relations in Ireland', 7 *St Louis University Public Law Review* 275 (1988).

Holzgrefe, J.L. and Keohane, R.O., *Humanitarian Intervention, ethical, legal and political dilemmas* (Cambridge: Cambridge University Press, 2003).

Honess, T., Levi, M. and Charman, E., 'Juror Competence in Processing Complex Information from a Simulation of the Maxwell Trial', *Criminal Law Review* (1998) pp. 63-73.

Hood, R., Shute, S. and Seemungal, F., *Ethnic Minorities in the Criminal Courts*, Lord Chancellor's Department No 2/03 (3/2003).

Horkheimer, Max and Adorno, Theodor, 'The Culture Industry: Enlightenment as Mass Deception', in *Dialectic of Enlightenment: Philosophical Fragments*, trans. Edmund Jephcott (Stanford: Stanford University Press, 2002) pp. 94-136.

Howe, P.M., 'The Problem of the Problem Question in English for Academic Legal Purposes', *English for Specific Purposes* 9 (1990): 215-36.

Hynes, Eugene, 'The Great Hunger and Irish Catholicism', 8 *Societas* 2 (1978).

Iedema, R.A.M., 'Legal English: Subject Specific Literacy and Genre Theory', *Australian Review of Applied Linguistics* 16, no. 2 (1993) pp. 86-122.

Ignatieff, Michael, 'America's Empire is an Empire Lite', *New York Times* (10 January 2003).

Inglis, Tom, *Moral Monopoly – The Rise and Fall of the Catholic Church in Modern Ireland* (Dublin: University College Dublin Press, 1998).

Jackson, Bernard, *Semiotics and Legal Theory* (London: Routledge & Kegan Paul, 1985).

Jackson, Bernard S., 'Narrative Theories in Legal Discourse', in Christopher Nash, *Narrative in Culture: The use of storytelling in the Sciences, Philosophy and Literature*,(London: Routledge, 1990), pp. 23-50.

Jackson, Bernard, *Making Sense in Law: Linguistic, Psychological and Semiotic Perspectives* (Liverpool: Deborah Charles Publications, 1995).

Jackson, J., Kilpatrick, R. and Harvey, C., *Called to Court* (Belfast: SLS Legal Publications, 1991).

James, Caryn, 'Splitting. Screens. For Minds. Divided', *The New York Times* (9 January 2004), E1.

Jameson, Fredric, 'The Politics of Utopia', *New Left Review* 25, Jan Feb issue (2004) pp. 35-54.

Jay, Martin, *Downcast Eyes, The Denigration of Vision in Twentieth-Century French Thought* (Berkeley, Los Angeles, London: University of California Press, 1994).

Johansen, Jorgen Dines and Larsen, Svend Erik, *Signs In Use* (London: Routledge, 2002).

Johnson, Marcia and Raye, Carol, 'Reality Monitoring', *Psychological Review* 88 (1981), pp. 67-85.

Johnson, Wallace S. Jr., *The T'ang Code*, trans. (Princeton: Princeton University Press, 1979).

Kassin, Saul and Dunn, Meghan, 'Computer-Animated Displays and the Jury: Facilitative and Prejudicial Effects', *Law & Human Behavior* 21 (1997), pp. 269-281.

Kassin, Saul and Fong, Christina, '"I'm Innocent!": Effects of Training on Judgments of Truth and Deception in the Interrogation Room' *Law & Human Behavior*, 23 (1999), pp. 499-516.

Katsh, Ethan, 'Bringing Online Dispute Resolution to Virtual Worlds', *New York Law School Law Review* 49 (2004), pp. 271-291.

Kaupen, W., 'Public Attitudes to Law and Legal Institutions in West Germany', *Anwaltsblatt* no. 3 March (1971).

Keil, Frank, Rozenblit, Leonid and Mills, Candice, 'What Lies Beneath: Understanding the Limits of Understanding', in Daniel Levin (ed.), *Thinking and Seeing* (Cambridge, MA: MIT Press, 2004), pp. 227-249.

Kelly, John, *The Irish Constitution* (Dublin: Butterworths, 1994).

Kendrick, Walter, *The Secret Museum* (New York: Viking, 1987).

Kennedy, D., *The Dark Side of Virtue: Reassessing International Humanitarianism* (Princeton: Princeton University Press, 2004).

Kennedy, Duncan, *Legal Education and the Reproduction of Hierarchy, A Polemic Against the System* (New York and London: New York University Press, 2004).

Keogh, Dermot, 'The Irish Constitutional Revolution: An Analysis of the Making of the Constitution', *The Constitution of Ireland: 1937-1987*, edited by Frank Litton (Dublin: Institute of Public Administration, 1988).

Kestler, J., *Questioning Techniques and Tactics* (Colorado Springs, CO: Shepard's/McGraw Hill, 1982).

Kevelson, R., 'Peirce as Catalyst in Modern Legal Science', in Michael Herzfeld and Margot D. Lenhart (eds) *Semiotics 1980* (New York: Plenum, 1982), pp. 241-254.

Kevelson, Roberta, *The Law as a System of Signs* (New York and London: Plenum Press, 1988).

Kevelson, Roberta (ed.), *Spaces and Significations* (New York: Peter Lang, 1996).

Kibbey, Ann, *Theory of the Image, Capitalism, Contemporary Film, and Women* (Bloomington and Indianapolis: Indiana University Press, 2005).

Kiberd, Declan, *Inventing Ireland* (Cambridge, Mass.: Harvard University Press, 1996).

Kioko, Ben, 'The Right of Intervention under the African Union's Constitutive Act: From non-interference to non-intervention', *RCIR* (2003) 85, pp. 807-825.

Klinger, David, *Into the Kill Zone: A Cop's Eye View of Deadly Force* (San Francisco, CA: Jossey-Bass, 2004).

Knox, Ronald, *The Old Testament, Newly Translated from the Latin Vulgate* (London: Burns, Oates and Washbourne, 1949).

Kooistra, P. G., Mahoney, J.S. and Westervelt, S.D., 'The world of crime according to "Cops"', in *Entertaining Crime: Television Reality Programs*, edited by M. Fishman and G. Cavender (New York: Aldine de Gruyter, 1998) pp. 141-158.

Kronman, Anthony, 'Rhetoric', 67 *University of Cincinnati Law Review* (1999).

Lacan, J., *The Four Fundamentals of Psycho-Analysis*, Jacques-Alain Miller (ed.), Alan Sheridan (trans.), (London: Penguin, 1977).

Lackner, Michael, Amelung, Iwo and Kurtz, Joachim (eds), *New Terms for New Ideas: Western Knowledge and Lexical Change in Late Imperial China*, (Leiden/Boston/Koln: Brill, 2001).

Lakoff, George and Johnson, Mark, *Metaphors We Live By* (Chicago: University of Chicago Press, 1980).

Lakoff, George and Johnson, Mark, *Philosophy in the Flesh* (New York: Basic Books, 1999).

Landsman, S., *Readings on Adversarial Justice: The American Approach to Adjudication* (St. Paul, MN: West Publishing Company, 1988).

Langton, Nicola M., 'To Hedge or Not to Hedge: Certainty and Doubt in Answers to Legal Problem Questions' (MA, City University, 2001).

Larkin, Emmet, *Historical Dimensions of Irish Catholicism* (New York: Arno Press, 1976).

Larson, John, 'Behind the death of Timothy Thomas', *MSNBC News* (10 April 2004).

Latour, Bruno, 'Drawing Things Together', in Michael Lynch and Steve Woolgar (eds), *Representation in Scientific Practice* (Cambridge, MA: MIT Press, 1988), pp. 19-68.

Latour, Bruno, *Pandora's Hope* (Cambridge, MA: Harvard University Press, 1999).

Latour, Bruno and Weibel, Peter (eds), *Iconoclash: Beyond the Image Wars in Science, Religion and Art* (Cambridge, Mass.: MIT Press, 2002).

Law Commission, *Previous Misconduct of a Defendant*, Consultation Paper 141 Appendix D (1996).

Law Commission, *Juries in Criminal Trials*, vols 1 and 2, Wellington (1999).

Legge, James, *The Chinese Classics: With a Translation, Critical and Exegetical Notes, Prolegomena, and Copious Indexes*, five volumes: 1. *The Confucian Analects, The Great Learning, The Doctrine of the Mean*; 2. *The Works of Mencius*; 3. *The Shoo-king*; 4. *The She-king*; 5. *The Ch'un Ts'ew with the Tso Chuen*, reprinted from the 1893-1895 Hong Kong Edition of Oxford University Press Hong Kong: Hong Kong University Press, 1970).

Lerner, Jennifer and Tetlock, Philip, 'Accounting for the Effects of Accountability', *Psychological Bulletin* 125 (1999), pp. 255-275.

Lessig, Lawrence, *Free Culture, How Big Media Uses Technology and the Law to Lock Down Culture and Control Creativity* (New York: The Penguin Press, 2004).

Lewis, Michael, *Next, The Future Just Happened* (New York: W.W. Norton, 2002).

Liang Zhiping, *Fayi yu renqing* (*Meaning of Law and Sentiment of People*) (Beijing: Zhongguo fazhi chubanshe, 2004).

Liang, Zhiping, 'Explicating "Law", A Comparative Perspective of Chinese and Western Legal Culture', *Journal of Chinese Law* 3 (1989), pp. 55-92.

Lighty, Todd, 'Untold story of Haggerty shooting: In OPS report, witnesses don't back cop's account', *Chicago Tribune* (12 September 1999).

Limbaugh, Judge Stephen N., *Interactive Digital Software Association, et. al., Plaintiffs, v. St Louis County, Missouri, et. al. Defendants* (14 June 2002).

Lippens, Ronnie, 'Imachinations of Peace', *Utopian Studies* 13/1 (2002), pp. 135-47.

Lippens, Ronnie, 'Viral Contagion and Anti-Terrorism. Notes on Medical Emergency, Legality, and Diplomacy', *International Journal for the Semiotics of Law* 17/3 (2004), pp. 125-39.

Lipsky, Michael, *Street-Level Bureaucracy: Dilemmas of the Individual in Public Services* (New York: Russell Sage Foundation, 1980).

Liu, Lydia H. (ed.), *Tokens of Exchange: the Problem of Translation in Global Circulations* (Durham and London: Duke University Press, 1999).

Llewellyn, Karl, *The Common Law Tradition* (Boston: Little, Brown, 1960).

Lowe, Richard, 'Extracting Information from an Animation During Complex Visual Learning', 14 *European Journal of Psychology of Education* 14 (1999), pp. 225-244.

Lurie, Alison, *The Language of Clothes* (USA: Random House, 1981).

MacCallum, Victoria, 'Switching on to Law', in *Law Society Gazette* 99(25) (2002) [accessed at www.lawgazette.co.uk].

Machura, Stefan and Ulbrich, Stefan, 'Law in Film: Globalizing the Hollywood Courtroom Drama', *Journal of Law and Society* 28(1) (2001), pp. 117-32.

Malcolm, Noel, 'The Titlepage of Leviathan, Seen in a Curious Perspective', *Seventeenth Century* 2 (1998), pp. 120-55.

Maley, Yon, 'Judicial Discourse: The Case of the Legal Judgment', in *The Cultivated Australian: Festschrift for Arthur Delbridge*, edited by J.E. Clark, 159-73 (Hamburg: Helmut Buske Verlag, 1985).

Manning, Peter K., *Symbolic Communication: Signifying Calls and the Police Response* (Cambridge, MA: MIT Press, 1988).

Manovich, Lev, *The Language of New Media* (Cambridge, MA: MIT Press, 2001).

Manzo, J., 'You wouldn't Take a 7-Year-Old and Ask him all those Questions', 19 *Law and Social Inquiry* (1996) pp. 639-663.

Marder, Nancy, 'Cyberjuries: A Model of Deliberative Democracy?', in Peter Shane (ed.), *Democracy Online* (New York: Routledge, 2004), pp. 35-46.

Marek, J., '*The Practice* and *Ally McBeal*: A New Image for Women Lawyers on Television?', *Journal of American Culture* 22(1) (1999), pp. 77-84.

Martin, Frank, 'Judicial Discretion in Family Law', *I.L.T.* 15 (1997).

Martin, J.R., *A Contextual Theory of Language in the Powers of Literacy: A Genre Approach to Teaching Writing* (Pittsburgh: University of Pittsburgh Press, 1993).

Martin, W.A.P., *Wanguo gongfa* (*Elements of International Law*), trans., (Beijing: Chongshiguan, 1864).

Marx, Karl, *Capital: Volume 1: A Critique of Political Economy*, trans. Ben Fowkes (London: Penguin, 1992).

Mastrofski, S. D., Snipes, J.B., Parks, R.B. and Maxwell, C. D., 'The Helping Hand of the Law: Police Control of Citizens on Request', *Criminology* 38(2) (2000) pp. 307-342.

Mayer, Richard and Anderson, Richard, 'The Instructive Animation: Helping Students Build Connections Between Words and Pictures in Multimedia Learning', *Journal of Educational Psychology* 84 (1992), pp. 444-452.

Mayer, Richard and Sims, Valerie, 'For Whom Is a Picture Worth a Thousand Words? Extensions of a Dual-Coding Theory of Multimedia Learning', *Journal of Educational Psychology* 86 (1994), pp. 389-401.

Maynard, Douglas W., 'Interaction and Asymmetry in Clinical Discourse', *American Journal of Sociology* 97 (1991), pp. 448-495.

Maynard, Douglas, *Bad News, Good News: Conversational Order in Everyday Talk and Clinical Settings* (Chicago: University of Chicago Press, 2003).

Maynard, Douglas W. and Clayman, Stephen E., 'The Diversity of Ethnomethodology', *Annual Review of Sociology* (1991), pp. 385-418.

Maynard, D. and Manzo, J., 'Theoretical Notes from an Actual Jury Deliberation', 11 *Sociological Theory* (1993) pp. 171-193.

McCabe, S., *The Jury at Work* (Oxford: Blackwell, 1972).

McCabe, S. and Purves, R., *The Shadow Jury at Work* (Oxford: Blackwell, 1974).

McKee, Alan, 'Views of Happiness in the Television Series Ally McBeal: The Philosophy of David E Kelley', *Journal of Happiness Studies* 5 (2004), pp. 385-411.

McKenna, Susan E., 'The Queer Insistence of *Ally McBeal*: Lesbian Chic, Postfeminism and Lesbian Reception', *The Communication Review* 5 (2002), pp. 285-314.

Meadows, Mark Stephen, *Pause and Effect, The Art of Interactive Narrative* (Indianapolis: New Riders, 2003).

Meares, Tracey L. and Kahan, Dan M., *Urgent Times: Policing and Rights in Inner-City Communities* (Boston, MA: Beacon Press, 1999).

Meehan, Albert J., 'I Don't Prevent Crime, I Prevent Calls": Policing as a Negotiated Order', *Symbolic Interaction* 15(4) (1992), pp. 455-480.

Megret, F., 'War? Legal Semantics and the Move to Violence', *European Journal of International Law* 13 (2002), pp. 361-401.

Mellinkoff, David, *The Language of the Law* (Boston: Little Brown, 1963).

Memmi, Albert, *Le racial discrimination: description, définitions, traitement* (Paris: Gaillimard, 1994).

Merryman, John Henry, *The Civil Law Tradition: An Introduction to the Legal Systems of Western Europe and Latin America* (2nd ed. Stanford: Stanford University Press, 1985).

Miller, Jonathan, *On Reflection*, National Gallery (London: Yale University Press, 1998).

Milovanovic, Dragan, *A Primer in the Sociology of Law* (Albany, NY: Harrow and Heston, 1994).

Mitchell, W.J.T., 'The Pictorial Turn', in *Picture Theory* (Chicago: University of Chicago Press, 1994).

Mnookin, Jennifer, 'The Image of Truth: Photographic Evidence and the Power of Analogy', *Yale Journal of Law & the Humanities* 10 (1998), pp. 1-74.

Molotch, Harvey L. and Boden, Deirdre, 'Talking Social Structure: Discourse, Domination and the Watergate Hearings', *American Sociological Review* 50 (1985), pp. 273-288.

Mortimer, John, *Rumpole and the Penge Bungalow Murders* (London: Viking, 2004).

Moseley, Rachel and Read, Jacinda, '"Having it Ally": Popular Television (Post-) Feminism', *Feminist Media Studies* 2(2) (2002), pp. 231-49.
Muir, William K., *Police: Street Corner Politicians* (Chicago: University of Chicago Press, 1977).
Mullin, Molly, 'Representations of Irish Feminism and the Politics of Difference', *Feminist Studies* 17 (1991), pp. 29-50.
Munstermann, G. Thomas, Hannaford, Paula and Whitehead, G. Mark (eds), *Jury Trial Innovation* (Williamsburg, VA: National Center for State Courts, 1997).
Murphy, Tim and Twomey, Patrick (eds), *Ireland's Evolving Constitution, 1937-97: Collected Essays* (Oxford: Hart, 1998).
Mutua, M., 'Savages, Victims and Saviors: The Metaphor of Human Rights', *Harvard International Law Journal*, (42), Winter, 2001 (accessible at: http://web.pdx.edu/~kinsella/ps448/mutua.html).
Nesson, Charles, 'The Evidence or the Event? On Judicial Proof and the Acceptability of Verdicts', *Harvard Law Review* 98 (1985), pp. 1357-1392.
Newhall, Beaumont, *The History of Photography* (New York: The Museum of Modern Art, 1982).
Newman, Kathleen, 'The Problem that has a name: *Ally McBeal* and the future of feminism', *Colby Quarterly* 36(4) (2000), pp. 319-24.
Nichols, Bill, *Representing Reality* (Bloomington, IN: University of Indiana Press, 1991).
Niederhoffer, Arthur, *Behind the Shield: The Police in Urban Society* (Garden City, NY: Anchor Books, 1967).
Ninth Circuit Manual of Model Jury Instructions: Criminal (St. Paul, MN: West Publishing Company, 1995).
Noë, Alva, *Action in Perception* (Cambridge, MA: MIT Press, 2004).
Noveck, Beth, 'Introduction: The State of Play', *New York Law School Law Review* 49 (2004), pp. 1-18.
Nussbaum, Martha, *Love's Knowledge* (New York: Oxford University Press, 1990).
Nussbaum, Martha, *Poetic Justice* (Boston: Beacon Press, 1995).
O'Hanlon, Rory, 'Natural Rights and the Constitution', *I.L.T.* (January 1993).
O'Mahony, Conor, 'Extra-Marital Families and Education Rights under the Irish Constitution', *Irish Journal of Family Law* 2 (2003).
O'Neill, Stephen C., 'Why are Judges' Robes Black?', in *The Court Legacy*, Vol. XI, No 1 (2003).
Oliver, Mary B., 'Influences of Authoritarianism and Portrayals of Race on Caucasian Viewers' Responses to Reality Based Crime Dramas', *Communication Reports* 9 (1996), pp. 141-150.
Oliver, Mary B. and Armstrong, G.B., 'Predictors of Viewing and Enjoyment of Reality Based and Fictional Crime Shows', *Journalism and Mass Communication Quarterly* 72 (1995), pp. 559-570.
Ondrejka, Cory, 'Escaping the Gilded Cage: User Created Content and Building the Metaverse', *New York Law School Law Review* 49 (2004), pp. 81-101.

Orford, A., 'Muscular Humanitarianism: Reading the Narratives of the New Interventionism', *European Journal of International Law* 10 (1999), pp. 679-711.

Orford, A., *Reading Humanitarian Intervention: Human Rights and the Use of Force in International Law* (Cambridge: Cambridge University Press, 2003).

Osborn, Guy, 'Borders and Boundaries: Locating the Law in Film', *Journal of Law and Society* 28(1) (2001), pp. 164-75.

Osborne, Robin, 'Law in Action in Classical Athens', *The Journal of Hellenic Studies* 105 (1985), pp. 40-58.

Ouellette, Laurie, 'Victims no More: Postfeminism, Television and *Ally McBeal*', *The Communication Review* 5 (2002), pp. 315-37.

Pastoureau, Michel, *Une histoire symbolique de Moyen Age occidental* (Paris : La librairie du XX1e siècle, Seuil, 2004).

Pateman, Carole, *The Sexual Contract* (Cambridge: Polity, 1998).

Pennington, Nancy and Hastie, Reid, 'The Story Model for Juror Decision Making', in Reid Hastie (ed.), *Inside the Juror* (Cambridge, UK: Cambridge University Press, 1993), pp. 192-221.

Perelman, C., *The Idea of Justice and The Problem of Argument* (London: Routledge & Kegan Paul, 1963).

Petty, Richard and Cacioppo, John, 'The Elaboration Likelihood Model of Persuasion', in Leonard Berkowitz (ed.), *Advances in Experimental Social Psychology* 19 (Orlando, FL: Academic Press, 1986), pp. 123-205.

Philips, S., 'Evidentiary Standards for American Trials: Just the Facts', in *Responsibility and Evidence in Oral Discourse*, edited by J. Hill and J. Irvine (Cambridge: Cambridge University Press, 1992).

Prentice, Deborah and Gerrig, Richard, 'Exploring the Boundary Between Fiction and Reality', in Shelley Chaiken and Yaacov Trope (eds), *Dual-Process Theories in Social Psychology* (New York: Guilford Press, 1999), pp. 529-546.

Psathas, George, *Conversation Analysis: The Study of Talk-in-Interaction* (Thousand Oaks, CA: Sage Publications, 1995).

Quinn, Gerard, 'The Nature and Significance of Critical Legal Studies', *I.L.T.* 282 (1989).

Rafter, Nicole, 'American Criminal Trial Films: An Overview of Their Development, 1930-2000', *Journal of Law and Society* 28(1) (2001), pp. 9-24.

Rankin, Ian, *A Question of Blood*, (London: Orion House, 2003).

Rawls, John, *A Theory of Justice* (Cambridge, MA: Harvard University Press, 1971).

Raymond, G., 'The Structure of Responding: Type-conforming and Nonconforming Responses to Yes/No Type Interrogatives', PhD dissertation (2000) UCLA (Sociology).

Reeves, Byron and Nass, Clifford, *The Media Equation: how people treat computers, televisions, and new media like real people and place* (Stanford, California: Center for the Study of Language and Information; New York: Cambridge University Press, 1996).

Reisman, W.M., 'Unilateral Action and the Transformations of the World Constitutive Process: The Special Problem of Humanitarian Intervention', *European Journal of International Law* 11 (2000), pp. 3-18.

Riksheim, E. and Chermak, S., 'Causes of Police Behavior Revisited', *Journal of Criminal Justice* 21 (1993), pp. 353-382.

Robbennolt, Jennifer K. and Studebaker, Christina A., 'News Media Reporting on Civil Litigation and Its Influence on Civil Justice Decision Making', *Law and Human Behaviour* 27 (1) (2003), pp. 5-27.

Robertshaw, P., 'Jury Trial or Magistrates' Justice', *The Times*, 17 January 1989.

Robertshaw, P., *Regional Jury Verdicts in Scotland*, Juridical Review (1991) p. 221.

Robertshaw, P., *Jury and Judge – the Crown Court in Action*, (Aldershot: Dartmouth, 1995).

Robertshaw, P., 'Method and Ethics in Jury Research', 38 *Medicine Science and the Law* (1998) p. 328.

Robertshaw, P., *Summary Justice – Judges Address Juries* (London: Cassell, 1998) pp. 8-10.

Robertshaw, P., 'A Human Rights Conflict', 22 *Civil Justice Quarterly* (2003) pp. 265-274.

Robertshaw, P., Cox, S. and Van Hoen, N., 'Jury Populations and Jury Verdicts', 20 *International Journal of the Sociology of Law* (1992) p. 271.

Robertshaw, P. and Greenhough, M., 'The Jury Sound-shape Project', 6 *International Journal for the Semiotics of Law* (1993) pp. 305-314.

Rose, Nikolas, 'The Biology of Culpability: Pathological Identity and Crime Control in a Biological Culture', *Theoretical Criminology* 4/1 (2000), pp. 5-34.

Roth, Jeffrey A., Roehl, J. and Johnson, Calvin C., 'Trends in the adoption of community policing', in *Community Policing: Can It Work?*, edited by Wesley G. Skogan (Belmont, CA: Wadsworth Publishing, 2004) pp. 3-29.

Rubinstein, Jonathan, 'Controlling people', in *Policing: A View From the Street*, edited by J.V. Maanen and P. K. Manning (Santa Monica, CA: Goodyear Publishing, 1978) pp. 255-265.

Runciman, David, 'What Kind of Person is Hobbes's State? A Reply to Skinner', *The Journal of Political Philosophy* 8/2 (2000), pp. 268-78.

Ruskola, Teemu, 'Legal Orientalism', *Michigan Law Review* 101(1) (2002) , pp. 179-234.

Sacks, Harvey, Schegloff, Emanuel A. and Jefferson, Gail, 'A Simplest Systematics for the Organization of Turn Taking for Conversation', *Language* 50(4) (1974), pp. 696-735.

Sandstrom, Stanley and Bloomberg, Adam, 'An Ancient Art Jazzed by High Tech', *The National Law Journal* (5 November 2001), B14-15.

Santos, B. de S., 'The Law of the Oppressed: The Construction and Reproduction of Legality in Pasargada', *Law & Society Review* 12 (1977), pp. 5-26.

Schauer, Federick (ed.), *Law and Language*, (Aldershot: Dartmouth, 1993).

Scheck, Barry, Neufeld, Peter and Dwyer, Jim, *Actual Innocence* (New York: Doubleday, 2000).

Scheff, T., 'Negotiating Reality: Notes on Power in the Assessment of Responsibility', *Social Problems* 16 (1968), pp. 3-17.

Schegloff, Emanuel A., 'Sequencing in Conversational Openings', *American Anthropologist* 70 (1968), pp. 1075-1095.

Schegloff, Emanuel A., 'Preliminaries to Preliminaries: "Can I Ask You a Question?"', *Sociological Inquiry* 50(3/4) (1980), pp. 104-152.

Schegloff, Emanuel A., 'Reflections on talk and social structure', in *Talk and Social Structure*, edited by D. Boden and D. Zimmerman (Cambridge: Polity Press, 1991) pp. 44-70.

Schegloff, Emanuel A., 'On Talk and its Institutional Occasions', in *Talk at Work*, edited by P. Drew and J. Heritage (New York: Cambridge University Press, 1992b) pp. 101-134.

Schegloff, Emanuel A., 'What next? Language and social interaction study at the century's turn', *Research on Language and Social Interaction* 32 (1&2) (1999), pp. 141-148.

Schlag, Pierre, 'The Aesthetics of American Law', *Harvard Law Review* (February, 2002).

Scholl, Brian, Simons, Daniel and Levin, Daniel, '"Change Blindness" Blindness: An Implicit Measure of a Metacognitive Error', in Daniel Levin (ed.), *Thinking and Seeing* (Cambridge, MA: MIT Press, 2004), pp. 145-163.

Schwartz, Benjamin I., *The World of Thought in Ancient China* (Cambridge/London: The Belknap Press of Harvard University Press, 1985).

Sealy, A. and Cornish, W., 'Jurors and their Verdicts', 36 *Modern Law Review* (1973) p. 496.

Searle, John R., '*Las Meninas* and the Paradoxes of Pictorial Representation', *Critical Inquiry*, Spring 1980, Vol. 6, Number 3.

Sebeok, Thomas, *Signs* (Toronto: University of Toronto Press, 1994).Severance, L. J. and Loftus, Elizabeth F., 'Improving Jurors' Abilities to Comprehend and Apply Criminal Jury Instructions', *Law and Society Review* 17 (1982), pp. 153-197.

Severance, L. J. and Loftus, Elizabeth F., 'Improving Criminal Justice: Making Jury Instructions Understandable for American Jurors', *International Review of Applied Psychology* 33 (1984), pp. 97-119.

Shapiro, Michael and Chock, T. Makana, 'Psychological Processes in Perceiving Reality', paper presented to the Association for Education in Journalism and Mass Communication (Baltimore, MD, 1998).

Sharp, Cassandra, 'Lawyers with Heart: An Oxymoron or Unrecognised Legal Identity? A Focus on the Representation of Lawyers in Ally McBeal', presented at the 19th Annual Law and Society Conference, Melbourne (10-12 December 2001).

Sharp, Cassandra, 'Scarlet Letter or Chastity Belt? What Legal Dramas of the Twenty-first Century are "Telling" Law Students About a Career in Law', *Legal Ethics* 5(1-2) (2002), pp. 90-102.

Sherwin, Richard, 'Dialects and Dominance: A Study of Rhetorical Fields in the Law of Confessions', *University of Pennsylvania Law Review* 136 (1988), pp. 729-849.

Sherwin, Richard, 'Law Frames: Historical Truth and Narrative Necessity in a Criminal Case', *Stanford Law Review* 47 (1994), pp. 39-83.

Sherwin, Richard, *When Law Goes Pop: The Vanishing Line Between Law and Popular Culture* (Chicago: University of Chicago Press, 2002).

Sherwin, Richard, 'Law in Popular Culture', in Austin Sarat (ed.), *The Blackwell Companion to Law and Society* (London: Blackwell, 2004), pp. 95-112.

Sherwin, Richard, Feigenson, Neal and Spiesel, Christina, 'Law in the Digital Age: How Visual Technologies are Transforming the Practice, Theory, and Teaching of Law', unpublished manuscript.

Shweder, Richard, *Thinking Through Cultures* (Chicago: University of Chicago Press, 1991).

Siemer, Deanne and Rothschild, Frank, *PowerPoint for Litigators* (Notre Dame, IN: National Institute for Trial Advocacy, 2002).

Skinner, Quentin, 'Hobbes and the Purely Artificial Person of the State', *The Journal of Political Philosophy* 7/1 (1999), pp. 1-29.

Skogan, Wesley G., 'Representing the community in community policing', in *Community Policing: Can It Work?*, edited by Wesley G. Skogan (Belmont, CA: Wadsworth Publishing, 2004), pp. 57-75.

Skogan, Wesley G. and Roth, Jeffrey A., 'Introduction', in *Community Policing: Can It Work?*, edited by Wesley G. Skogan (Belmont, CA: Wadsworth Publishing, 2004), pp. xvii-xxxiv.

Spiesel, Christina, Sherwin, Richard and Feigenson, Neal 'Law in the Age of Images: The Challenge of Visual Literacy', in Anne Wagner, Tracy Summerfield and Farid Benavides (eds), *Contemporary Issues of the Semiotics of Law* (Oxford: Hart Publishing, 2005), pp. 231-255.

Spitzer, Eliot, *The New York City Police Department's 'Stop & Frisk' Practices: A Report to the People of the State of New York from the Office of the Attorney General* (New York: New York State Attorney General, 1999).

Stafford, Barbara, *Good Looking, Essays on the Virtue of Images* (Cambridge, Massachusetts, and London: MIT Press, 1996).

Stark, Steven D., 'Lady's Night: Ally McBeal's quirky appeal', *The New Republic* (29 December 1997), pp. 13-14.

Steiner, George, *After Babel: Aspects of Language and Translation* (3rd edition, Oxford: Oxford University Press, 1998).

Steuer, Jonathan, 'Defining Virtual Reality: Dimensions Determining Telepresence', in Frank Biocca and Mark Levy (eds), *Communication in the Age of Virtual Reality* (Hillsdale, NJ: Lawrence Erlbaum Associates, 1995), pp. 33-56.

Storey, Karen, 'The language of threats', *Forensic Linguistics* 2(1) (1995), pp. 74-80.

Stygall, G., 'Texts in Oral Context: The "Transmission" of Jury Instructions in an Indiana Trial', in *Textual Dynamics of the Professions: Historical and*

Contemporary Studies Of Writing in Professional Communities, edited by C. Bazerman and J. Paradis (Madison, WI: University of Wisconsin Press, 1991).

Summerfield, Tracy, 'Families of Meaning: Dismantling The Boundaries Between Law and Society', 16 *IJSL* 1 (2003).

Swales, John M., *Genre Analysis: English in Academic and Research Settings* (Cambridge: Cambridge University Press, 1990).

Sweetser, Eve, *From Etymology to Pragmatics* (Cambridge, UK: Cambridge University Press, 1990).

Szasz, P.C., 'The Security Council Start Legislating', *American Journal of International Law* 96, 4 (2002), pp. 901-905.

Taguieff, Pierre-André, *La face du préjugé: essai sur la discrimination raciale et ses doubles*, 2 Tomes (Paris: La Découverte, 1990).

Talbot, Henry Fox, *The Pencil of Nature* (London: Longmans, England, 1844-45).

Tambiah, Stanley, *Culture, Thought, and Social Action* (Cambridge: Harvard University Press, 1985).

Te Heesen, Anke, 'News, Paper, Scissors: Clippings in the Sciences and Arts around 1920', in Lorraine Daston (ed.), *Things That Talk* (New York: Zone Books, 2004), pp. 297-327.

Teitz, Louise, 'Providing Legal Services for the Middle Class in Cyberspace: The Promise and Challenge of On-Line Dispute Resolution', *Fordham Law Review* 70 (2001), pp. 985-1016.

Terrill, William, Paoline III, Eugene A. and Manning, Peter K., 'Police Culture and Coercion', *Criminology* 41(4)(2003): 1003-1034.

Tertullian, 'On Idolatry' and 'On Spectacles' (trans. S. Thelwall), in *The Ante-Nicene Fathers*, edited by Alexander Roberts and James Donaldson, vol. 3 (Edinburgh, 1885).

Tesón, F.R., 'The Kantian Theory of International Law', *Colombia Law Review* (1991), pp. 53-102.

Tesón, F.R., *Humanitarian Intervention, An inquiry into law and morality* (New York: Transnational Publishers, 1997).

Twomey, Adrian F., 'Borks Originalism: Reconciling Judicial Constitutional Interpretation with the Rule of Law, 14 *I.L.T.* 278 (1996).

United States Government, *Occupations*, Vol. 13, United States Census.

Van Leeuwen, Theo and Jewitt, Carey, *Handbook of Visual Analysis*, (London, Thousand Oaks, New Delhi: Sage Publications, 2001).

Vennard, J., 'The Outcomes of Contested Trials', ch.12 in D. Moxon (ed.) *Managing Criminal Justice*, Home Office Research Unit, London (1985).

Vennard, J. and Riley, D., 'The Use of Peremptory Challenge and Stand-by of Jurors', *Criminal Law Review* (1988) pp. 731-738.

Verdict Systems LLC, 'Sanction II' (Tempe, AZ: Author, 2002).

Views on Trial by Jury, (London: SWR World-wide, 2002).

Vitae Publications (Brookfield, CT: Author, 2003).

Wagner, Anne and Cacciaguidi-Fahy, Sophie (eds), 'Law as Signs of Cultural Diversity', *International Journal for the Semiotics of Law* Vol.18, n°2 (2005).

Wagner, Anne, Summerfield, Tracey, and Benavides Vanegas, Farid, S., *Contemporary Issues on the Semiotics of Law* (Oxford: Hart Publishing, 2005).
Walker, M., 28 *British Journal of Criminology* (1988) pp. 441-460 T5, 6.
Walker, Samuel, *Police Accountability: The Role of Citizen Oversight* (Belmont, CA: Wadsworth Publishing, 2001).
Walshe, Daniel, 'The Legal Rights of Unmarried Biological Fathers in Ireland and England, 1997-2002: A Comparative Analysis', *Irish Journal of Family Law* 2 (2003).
Walzer, Michael, *Spheres of Justice: A Defense of Pluralism and Equality* (New York: Basic Books, 1988).
Wang, Gungwu, *The Chineseness of China: Selected Essays* (Hong Kong: Oxford University Press, 1991).
Watson, Burton, *Early Chinese Literature* (New York and London: Columbia University Press, 1962/1971).
Watson, Burton, *Han Feizi: Basic Writings*, trans. (New York and London: Columbia University Press, 2003).
Watts, Shelley, 'Technology Creates Winning Visual Evidence', *Trial* (September 2000), pp. 68-70.
Weinreb, L., *Denial of Justice: Criminal Process in the United States* (New York: Free Press, 1977).
Wellmer, A., *Revolution und Interpretation, Demokratie ohne Letztbegründung*, (Assen: Van Gorcum, 1998).
Werner, W.G., 'From Justus Hostis to Rogue State', *International Journal for the Semiotics of Law* 17 (2) (2004), pp. 155-168.
Whalen, Marilyn R. and Zimmerman, Don H., 'Sequential and Institutional Contexts in Calls for Help', *Social Psychology Quarterly* 50 (1987), pp. 172-185.
Wheaton, Henry, edited by A.C. Boyd, *Elements of International Law* (London: Stevens and Sons, 1836/1878).
Whyte, Gerry, 'The Family and the State – Irish Constitutional Law', 7 *St Louis University Public Law Review* 237 (1988).
Whyte, Gerry, 'Natural Law and The Constitution', *I.L.T.* 16 (1996).
Widdowson, H.G., *Learning Purpose and Language Use* (Oxford: Oxford University Press, 1983).
Wieviorka, Michel, *Discrimination raciale et modernité* (Paris : La Découverte, 1993).
WIN Interactive (Boston: Author, 2003).
Wittgenstein, Ludwig, *Philosophical Investigations* (G.E.M. Anscombe, trans.) (New York: Macmillan, 3rd edn. 1958).
Wolinsky, Sidney M. and Econome, Janet, 'Seduction in Wonderland: The Need for a Seller's Fiduciary Duty toward Children', *Hastings Constitutional Law Quarterly* 4 (1977), pp. 249-78.
Woulfe, Seamus, 'K. v W. The Unmarried Father and the Child's Welfare', 8 *I.L.T.* 39 (1990).

Yelle, Robert, 'Bentham's Fictions: Canon and Idolatry in the Genealogy of Law', in *Yale Journal of Law & the Humanities* (2005), pp. 151-179.

Zaltman, Gerald, *How Customers Think* (Boston, MA: Harvard Business School Press, 2003).

Zander, M., 'Are too many Professional Criminals avoiding Conviction?', 37 *Modern Law Review* (1974) p. 28.

Zander, M. and Henderson, P., *The Crown Court Study*, Research Study No 19 ch.8 (1993).

Zimmerman, Don H., 'The Interactional Organization of Calls for Emergency Assistance', in *Talk at Work: Interaction in Institutional Settings*, edited by P. Drew and J. Heritage (Cambridge, UK: Cambridge University Press, 1992) pp. 418-469.

Legislation

Archbold's Criminal Pleading, Evidence and Practice (London: Sweet and Maxwell, 2005)

Criminal Law of the PRC 1980 (China)

Halsbury's Laws of England (with cumulative supplements), (London: Butterworths, 4th edition, 1979)

Import and Export (Registration) Regulations Cap 60e (Hong Kong)

Joint Declaration 1984 (Hong Kong)

Prevention of Bribery Ordinance Cap 201 (Hong Kong)

The Basic Law 1997 (Hong Kong)

Case Law

Attorney General v New Statesman and Nation Co.[1981] QB1

Attorney General v Paperlink Ltd [1984] ILRM 373

Connecticut v. Swinton, 268 Conn. 781 (2004)

Ennis v Butterly [1996] 1 I.R. 426

Fajujonu v Minister for Justice [1990] 2 IR 151

Finn v Attorney General [1983] IR 154

G. v An Bord Uchtala [1980] IR 32

Hyland v Minister for Social Welfare [1989] IR 624

J.K. v V. W. [1990] 2 IR 437

K v W [1990] ILRM 121

Keegan v. Ireland [1994] 18 EHRR 342

Lobe & Osayande v Minister for Justice, Equality & Law Reform [2003] IESC 1

M. v An Bord Uchtala (1977) IR 287

Mac Mathuna v Ireland [1989] IR 504 / [1995] IR 484

McGee v Attorney General [1974] IR 284

Murphy v Attorney General [1982] IR 241

Murray v Ireland [1985] I.R. 532
N. v K. v Ireland [1985] I.R. 733 at 754
Northants County Council v. A.B.F. [1982] ILRM 164
Osheku v Ireland [1987] ILRM 330
People (D.P.P.) v T. [1988] 3 Frewen 141
Pok Sun SHum v Ireland [1986] I.L.M.R. 593
Re Article 26 and The Matrimonial Home Bill, 1993. 1 [1994] ILRM 241
Re Tilson Infant [1951] IR 1
Ryan v Attorney General [1965] IR 264
T.F. v Ireland [1995] 1 I.R. 321
The State (Nicolaou) v An Bord Uchtala [1966] IR 567
Universal v Ramierdes, 2001

Online Sources

'Advocates keen to keep wigs': http://news.bbc.co.uk/1/hi/scotland/232694.stem
'Barristers & Solicitors Wigs': http://www.sixthform.info.law/01_modules/mod2/11_3_legal_ profession/4_barristers_wigs.htm
'Brief Encounters', *Daily Telegraph*, 13 May 2004: http://www.telegraph.co.uk/news2004/05/13/nlaw113.xml
'Habit of a lifetime': http://www.lexonthenet/com/news.php
'Legal bigwigs in line for a modern makeover', *The Times*, 9 May 2003: http://www.peterjepson.com/law.htm
'Solicitor wants right to wear wig and gown in court': http://www.telegraph.co.uk/news/main.html
'Dr. Orvan Hess, Who Helped Develop Fetal Heart Monitor, Dies at 96', *Yale Bulletin and Calendar* 31(12) (22 November 2002), http://www.yale.edu/ opa/v31.n12/story13.html
A Lord Chancellor's Department Consultation Paper: Court Working Dress in England & Wales (May 2003): http://www.dca.gov.uk/consult/courtdress/html
Ashworth, Susan, 'TV Facts Then & Now', in *Digital World*, February 2005, at http://www.pcworld.com/news/article/0,aid,118945,00.asp, accessed on-line 26 March 2005.
Atlee, Michael, 'LAS MENINAS: The World's Best Painting', 2003, accessed 23 March 2005: http://www.artchive.com/ftp_site.htm
Baum, Kathleen Kelly, 'Courting Desire and the (Al)lure of David E. Kelley's Ally McBeal', *CLCWEB: Comparative Literature and Culture 4.1* (2002), www.clcwebjournal.lb.purdue.edu
Beer, Francis A. and Balleck, Barry J. 'Body, Mind, and Soul in the Gulf War Debate', 1993, at www.sobek.colorado.edu/~beer/PAPERS
Benjamin, Walter, *The Work of Art in the Age of Mechanical Reproduction*, 1936 at: http://www.marxists.org/reference/subject/philosophy/works/ge/benjamin.htm

Boehlert, Eric, 'Citizen journalists?' http://www.salon.com/news/feature/2005/04/08/schiavo_memo/index.html, accessed 8 April 2005.

Cargill, John, 'Writings of Tertullian: The Arena, Circus, and Theatre', http://www.the-faith.org.uk/tertullian1.html, accessed 31 October 2005.

Dagnan-Bouveret, Pascal-Adolphe-Jean, *Wedding at the Photographer's*, 1872-1875, in the collection of Musée des Beaux-Arts, Lyon, France. Colour reproduction at: http://www.atelier-rc.com/Atelier.RC/b-dayCalendar/01.07-PAJDagBouvt-NtAtPhotg.jpg

Denvir, John, 'Girl Lawyers and Boy Lawyers' (1997), http://www.usfca.edu/pj/articles

Denvir, John, 'Legal Tender: Reconsidering Ally McBeal' (1997) www.usfca.edu/pj

Denvir, John, 'What Ails Ally?' (1997) http://www.usfca.edu/pj/articles

Friedman, Elisabeth J., 'Is Ally our ally?', http://www.usfca.edu/pj/ally-no-ally.htm

Friedman, Lisa, 'Don't Call Me "Ally"' www.usfca.edu/pj/articles (Freidman, L)

http://terranova.blogs.com/terra_nova/2004/04/ebay_sales_rise.html

Jackson, Chris, 'The Music of Inner Justice in *Ally McBeal*', www.usfca.edu/pj/ally-music.htm

Kelvin, Lord, *Popular Lectures and Addresses* (1891-94), http://zapatopi.net/kelvin/quotes.html

Law Institute of Victoria: http://www.liv.asn.au/news/media/20031105_wnwpcv.html

Law Society Archives of Ontario: http://www.ontariocourts.on.ca/ojen/court&class/resources/articles/keepingtabs.htm

Legal history: http://campus.northpark.edu/history/WebChron/USA/WomanLawyer.CP.html

New South Wales Law Reform Commission (1982) Report 31 (1982) – The First Report on the Legal Profession: General Regulation and Structure (NSW, Australia): http://www.lawlink.nsw.gov.au/lrc.nsf

Peirce, Charles S., 'How to Make Our Ideas Clear', *Popular Science Monthly* 12, January 1878, at http://peirce.org/writings/pll9.html, accessed 24 March 2005.

Peirce, C.S.: http://www.helsinki.fi/science/commens/terms/firstness.html

Rangappa, Asha, 2002, Legal affairs – the magazine at the intersection of law and life. http://www.legalaffairs.org/issues/May-June-2002/scene_rangappa_mayjune2.html

Reeves, Peter, 1998, 'Silk Cut' ASI (Research), UK: http://www.adamsmith.org/policy/publications/pdf-files/silk-cut.pdf

Ross, Ysaiah, 'Legal Ethics on TV Through Australian Eyes', http://www.usfca.edu/pj/articles

The Bloody Sunday Inquiry, 'The Bloody Sunday Inquiry', http://www.bloody-sunday-inquiry.org.uk/

The Daily Show with Jon Stewart (Comedy Channel, 2005) can be seen at: http://newclips.crooksandliars.com/The_Daily_Show_Frist_Wingers.mov

The Digital Millenium Copyright Act of 1998, http://www.copyright.gov/ legislation/dmca.pdf

Willing, Richard, '"CSI Effect" Has Juries Wanting the Evidence', *USA Today* (5 August 2004), http://www.usatoday.com/news/nation/2004-08-05/csi-effect_x.htm

Zakon, Robert H., 'Hobbes' Internet Timeline', 2005 'Hosts', http://www.zakon.org/Robert/internet/timeline, accessed 26 March 2005.

Index

For Product Safety Concerns and Information please contact our EU representative GPSR@taylorandfrancis.com
Taylor & Francis Verlag GmbH, Kaufingerstraße 24, 80331 München, Germany

www.ingramcontent.com/pod-product-compliance
Ingram Content Group UK Ltd.
Pitfield, Milton Keynes, MK11 3LW, UK
UKHW020018200926
475702UK00014B/1958

* 9 7 8 1 1 3 8 2 6 4 4 9 6 *